Collins

D1758915

# Cambridge IGCSE™

# Physics

## STUDENT'S BOOK

Gurinder Chadha, Susan Gardner,
Malcolm Bradley, Chris Sunley

Published by Collins
An imprint of HarperCollins*Publishers*
The News Building,
1 London Bridge Street,
London, SE1 9GF

1st Floor, Watermarque Building,
Ringsend Road, Dublin 4, Ireland

Browse the complete Collins catalogue at
**www.collins.co.uk**

© HarperCollins*Publishers* Limited 2021

10 9 8 7 6 5 4 3 2

ISBN 978-0-00-843090-0

British Library Cataloguing-in-Publication Data
A catalogue record for this publication is available from the British Library.

Author of this update: **Gurinder Chadha**
Authors contibuting to previous editions: **Susan Gardner, Malcolm Bradley, Chris Sunley**
Publisher: **Elaine Higgleton**
In-house editor: **Letitia Luff**
Project manager: **Nivedhitha Harris**
Copyeditor: **Naomi MacKay**
Proofreader: **Jan Schubert**
Cover designer: **Gordon MacGilp**
Cover illustration: **Maria Herbert-Liew**
Internal designer, typesetter and illustrator: **Jouve India Private Limited**
Image permissions researcher: **Alison Prior**
Production controller: **Lyndsey Rogers**
Printed and bound by **Grafica Veneta S. P. A.**

Cambridge International copyright material in this publication is reproduced under licence and remains the intellectual property of Cambridge Assessment International Education.

Exam-style questions and sample answers have been written by the authors. In examinations, the way marks are awarded may be different. References to assessment and/or assessment preparation are the publisher's interpretation of the syllabus requirements and may not fully reflect the approach of Cambridge Assessment International Education.

## Acknowledgements

The publishers wish to thank the following for permission to reproduce photographs. Every effort has been made to trace copyright holders and to obtain their permission for the use of copyright materials. The publishers will gladly receive any information enabling them to rectify any error or omission at the first opportunity.

P 4 Getty Images/KateLeigh; p 5 Shutterstock/yarbeer; p 6(t) Shutterstock/Nasky; p 6(b) Shutterstock/I Love Photo; p 7 Shutterstock/Jim Lopes; pp 8–9 Shutterstock/WR Chen; p 10 Shutterstock/ Pretty Vectors; p 11 Shutterstock/Hung Chung Chih; p 18 Shutterstock/ wavebreakmedia; p 27 Shutterstock/ muroPhotographer; p 33 Dorling Kindersley ltd/Alamy Stock Photo; p 39 Shutterstock/CRStocker; p 39 Shutterstock/Michal Vitek; p 43 Shutterstock/Alones; p 44 Getty Images; p 45 Shutterstock/Pat Hastings; p 48 Shutterstock/George Marcel; p 51 Shutterstock/Kirk Geisler; p 67 Shutterstock/Andrew Barker; p 72 Shutterstock/I Love Photo; p 80 Shutterstock/ clearlens; p 82 Shutterstock/Sizov; p 83 Shutterstock/Chatchai Somwat; p 86 Shutterstock/Fabio tomat; p 89 Shutterstock/ Zoia Kostina; p 91(b) Shutterstock/Rido; p 91(t) Science Photo Library/Ocean Power Delivery/Look at Sciences; p 93 Shutterstock/Peteri; p 94 Shutterstock/Efman; p 106 Shutterstock/DenisNata; p 106 Shutterstock/ muroPhotographer; p 109 Shutterstock/John Milnes; p 110 Shutterstock/Mike H; pp 124–125 Shutterstock/Katrina Leigh; p 126 Shutterstock/jele; p 127 Shutterstock/Oleg_Yakovlev; p 128 Shutterstock/Geoffrey Kuchera; p 130 Shutterstock/ Mike Blanchard; p 133 Shutterstock/red mango; p 139 Shutterstock/Natursports; p 140 Shutterstock/jan kranendonk; p 150 Shutterstock/Alexandra Lande; p 154 Shutterstock/ Ulrich Mueller; p 157 Shutterstock/johimberbin; p 160 Shutterstock/ipongteerachai; p 164 Shutterstock/Jim Lopes; pp 168–169 Shutterstock/Willyam Bradberry; p 170 Shutterstock/Yuri Arcurs; p 178 Shutterstock; p 179 Shutterstock/fontoknak; p 181 Shutterstock/Paylee Images; p 183 Shutterstock/Kuki Ladron de Guevara; p 186 Alamy Stock Photo/sciencephotos; p 188 Shutterstock/Uew Bergwitz; p 190 Shutterstock/Nasky; p 201 Shutterstock/Lightfield Studios; p 203 Science Photo Library; p 205(l) Shutterstock/ Marko Aliaksandr; p 205(r) Shutterstock/Albert Lozano; p 206(b) Shutterstock/Anton Gvodzikov; p 206(t) Shutterstock/ courage007; p 213 Shutterstock/AnnGaysorn; p 214 Shutterstock/the goatman; p 219 Shutterstock/ GagliardPhotography; pp 226–227 Shutterstock/littlesam; p 228 Shutterstock/yarbeer; p 230 Shutterstock/New Africa; p 232 Getty Images/colematt; p 234 Shutterstock/Dario Lo Presti; p 237 Shutterstock/ToskanaINC; p 243 Shutterstock/Nir Levy; p 245 Shutterstock; p 245 Shutterstock/tdee photo cm; p 246 Andrew Lambert Photography/SPL; p 246 Shutterstock/ Mihancea Petru; p 257 Shutterstock/michaelmond; p 265 Bart Coenders/iStockphoto; p 271 Shutterstock/Joshua Havlv; p 284 Shutterstock/oilchai; p 285 Shutterstock/Photoseeker; p 288 Shutterstock/Cennet Karaca; p 291 Shutterstock/ oksana2010; p 293 Shutterstock/M.Niebuhr; p 298 Science Photo Library/TREVOR CLIFFORD PHOTOGRAPHY; p 303 Getty Images; p 308 Alamy/Paul Andrew Lawrence; p 309 Shutterstock/SuriyaPhoto; p 315 Shutterstock/BortN66; pp 318–319 Shutterstock/InnaFelker; p 320 Shutterstock/ Urbanbuzz; p 329 Toxicotravail/WikiMedia Commons; p 331t Shutterstock/Bergamont; p 331b Maurice Savage/Alamy Stock Photo; p 338 Alamy/Robin Weaver; p 341 Shutterstock/ pang_oasis; pp 352–353 NASA/CXC/HGST/SPL; p 354 NASA; p 357 Mark Garlick/SPL; p 358 DETLEV VAN RAVENSWAAY/ SPL; p 358 EUROPEAN SPACE AGENCY/ROSETTA/ORIRIS TEAM/SPL; p 359 NASA; p 361 CLAUS LUNAU / SCIENCE PHOTO LIBRARY; p 370 EESA; p 371 Shutterstock/ MartinMaritz; p 373 JUAN CARLOS CASADO(STARRYEARTH. COM)/SPL; p 373 NASA; p 375 NASA; p 375 ROBERT GENDLER/SPL; p 376 Getty/William Franklin Mahon; p 378 NASA/SPL; p 386 Shutterstock/Antares_StarExplorer; p 388 Shutterstock/Ed Phillips

# Contents

# Getting the best from the book

Welcome to Collins *Cambridge IGCSE™ Physics*.

This textbook has been designed to help you progress in your physics learning and understand all of the requirements needed to succeed in your Cambridge IGCSE Physics course.

Just as there are six sections in the syllabus, there are six sections in the textbook. Each section in the textbook covers the essential knowledge and skills you need. The textbook also has useful features which have been designed to help you understand all the aspects of physics you will need to know for this syllabus.

## SAFETY IN THE SCIENCE LESSON

This book is a textbook, not a laboratory or practical manual. As such, you should not interpret any information in this book that relates to practical work as including comprehensive safety instructions. Your teachers will provide full guidance for practical work and cover rules that are specific to your school.

A brief introduction gives context to the science covered in the section.

Starting points will help you to revise previous learning and see what you already know about the ideas in the section.

Section contents shows the syllabus topics covered in the section

Knowledge check reminds you of the ideas you should have already encountered in previous work before starting the topic.

Learning objectives show you what the syllabus requires in the topic.

Clearly differentiated Supplement material is only relevant for students studying the Extended syllabus content and so helps you focus your learning.

Examples of investigations are included with questions matched to the practical skills you will need to learn. It is not expected you will need to perform or learn all the methods of the example investigations.

---

## Simple phenomena of magnetism

△ Fig. 4.1 A compass.

### INTRODUCTION

The property of magnetism has been known for many centuries. Ancient travellers used naturally magnetic rocks such as lodestone to guide their journeys. Lodestone, which is magnetic, points towards the north when suspended. The development of the compass made it possible to make long sea voyages of discovery, whereas previously ships had stayed within sight of land. There is evidence that some animals, such as birds, can sense the **magnetic field** of the Earth and that they have their own 'in-built compass', which may help navigation during long migrations.

The magnetic field of the Earth has a wider importance. It acts as a shield, protecting the surface of the Earth from many charged particles emitted from the Sun. The Earth would have been a much hotter and inhabitable place without this protection from the Earth's magnetic fields. A study of magnetism helps us to understand our Earth better and will be crucial when we start to learn about electromagnetism later in this section.

### KNOWLEDGE CHECK

✓ The ends of a bar magnet are called poles and that is where the magnetic field is strongest.
✓ Not all materials are magnetic.
✓ The Earth has a magnetic field, which is how compasses are able to point to the north.

### LEARNING OBJECTIVES

✓ Describe the forces between magnetic poles and between magnets and magnetic materials, including the use of the terms north pole (N pole), south pole (S pole), attraction and repulsion, magnetised and unmagnetised.
✓ Describe induced magnetism.
✓ State the differences between the properties of temporary magnets (made of soft iron) and the properties of permanent magnets (made of steel).
✓ State the difference between magnetic and non-magnetic materials.
✓ Describe a magnetic field as a region in which a magnetic pole experiences a force.
✓ Draw the pattern and direction of magnetic field lines around a bar magnet.
✓ State that the direction of a magnetic field at a point is the direction of the force on the N pole of a magnet at that point.
✓ Describe the plotting of magnetic field lines with a compass or iron filings and the use of a compass to determine the direction of the magnetic field.
✓ Describe the uses of permanent magnets and electromagnets.
✓ **SUPPLEMENT** Explain that magnetic forces are due to interactions between magnetic fields.
✓ **SUPPLEMENT** Know that the relative strength of a magnetic field is represented by the spacing of the magnetic field lines.

### MAGNETS REPEL AND ATTRACT

When a permanent magnet is suspended and allowed to swing, it will line up approximately north–south. The two ends of a magnet, which are the most strongly magnetic parts, are called the north pole and the south pole, often labelled N and S. For the suspended magnet, the N pole points approximately towards the north, and the S pole points approximately towards the south.

△ Fig. 4.2 A bar magnet aligns itself with the Earth's magnetic field when it is suspended – it is being used as a compass.

There are forces between magnets, and between magnets and **magnetic materials**.

When two north poles from different magnets are brought together, there will be a repulsion between them. This also happens when two south poles are used. Two like poles (N–N or S–S) repel. However, when a north pole and a south pole are brought together, there will be an attraction. Two unlike poles (N–S or S–N) attract. Magnets will also attract magnetic materials that can be magnetised by the magnet such as iron, nickel and cobalt.

### QUESTIONS

1. You are provided with a bar magnet with its north pole marked. Describe how you can deduce the poles of another magnet.

2. The north pole of a compass points towards the Earth's north pole. Suggest the magnetic polarity of the Earth's north pole.

### Magnetically hard and soft materials

Several elements are magnetic, the most important of which are iron, cobalt and nickel. Scientists have developed alloys and ceramics made from combinations of elements to get the exact properties that they want. Some of these materials are magnetically hard (such as steel, which is an alloy of iron and other elements such as carbon or tungsten). This means that they stay magnetic once they have been magnetised. This is what you would want from a permanent magnet.

ELECTRICITY AND MAGNETISM

MAGNETS REPEL AND ATTRACT

---

### QUESTIONS

1. A man (70 kg) and a boy (35 kg) run up a set of stairs in the same time. Explain why the man is twice as powerful.

2. When a machine is called 'powerful', what does it mean?

3. State the unit of power.

4. Calculate the power of a motor that transfers 1200 J of energy every 5.0 s.

5. a) A crane lifts a mass of 60 kg to a height of 5.0 m. Calculate the work done by the crane.

   b) The crane takes 1.0 minute to do this. Calculate the output power of the crane.

### EFFICIENCY

Energy is always conserved – the total amount of energy after the transfer must be the same as the total amount of energy before the transfer. Unfortunately, in nearly all energy transfers some of the energy will end up as unusable internal (thermal) energy stored within objects or the surrounding air.

### SUPPLEMENT

In a power station only some of the energy originally produced from the fuel is transferred to useful electrical output. **Efficiency** can be calculated from the following equations:

$$\text{efficiency} = \frac{\text{useful energy output}}{\text{total energy input}} \times 100\%$$

or

$$\text{efficiency} = \frac{\text{useful power output}}{\text{total power input}} \times 100\%$$

For example, the electric motor that is used to power a train may take in 10 kW of electricity, and give out 9.5 kW of kinetic energy.

The useful power output is 9.5 kW and the power input is 10 kW.

$$\text{efficiency} = \frac{\text{useful power output}}{\text{total power input}} \times 100\%$$

$$\text{efficiency} = \frac{9.5}{10} \times 100\% = 95\%$$

The efficiency can also be expressed as 0.95, rather than 95%.

The other 5% of energy ends up increasing the temperature of the motor and passes to the surrounding air. This energy is wasted, and the motor may need cooling fans to prevent it from overheating.

A diesel engine is more efficient than a petrol engine, and can give out 200 kJ of kinetic energy from 500 kJ of stored chemical energy of diesel fuel. This equates to an efficiency of 40%. You will note that the engine will have dissipated 300 kJ to internal (thermal) energy – much of it down the exhaust pipe.

In a power station, as much as 70% of the energy transfers may not produce useful energy. This would mean that the power station was only 30% efficient.

Scientists are working hard to increase the efficiency of power stations. Many power stations are now trying to make use of the large amounts of internal (thermal) energy in the hot water produced by power stations. In some cities, the houses of whole regions of the city are heated by hot water from a nearby power station. Some of the most modern fossil-fuelled power stations have efficiencies nearer to 40%. This may not seem much, but if all power stations in the world could use 25% less fuel, it would save millions of tonnes of coal or gas per year.

#### Developing practical skills

A student investigates the efficiency of a small electric motor. She uses a motor to lift a mass through a constant distance of 1.0 m. She times how long it takes to lift the masses and makes a record of the potential difference and the current of the motor. The student's data is shown in the table.

△ Fig. 1.86 Apparatus for the investigation.

MOTION, FORCES AND ENERGY

EFFICIENCY

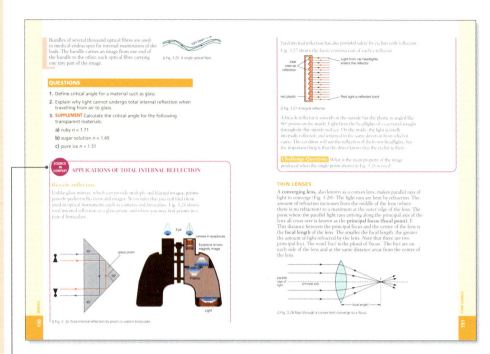

Science in context boxes put the ideas you are learning into real-life context. The content in these boxes is beyond the requirements of the syllabus. However, they do provide interesting examples of scientific application that are designed to enhance your understanding and a challenge question to encourage you to think more deeply beyond the syllabus content.

Remember boxes provide tips and guidance to help you during your course.

Questions regularly check your understanding.

Worked examples show you how to use formulas.

Key terms for the topic are defined in the glossary

A full checklist of all the content you need to cover the complete syllabus requirements covered in each topic.

End of topic questions allow you to apply the knowledge and understanding you have learned in the topic to answer the questions.

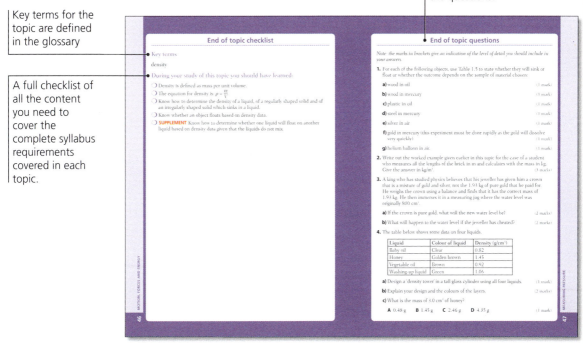

Regular exam-style questions provide a checkpoint for your learning and help you prepare for your exams.

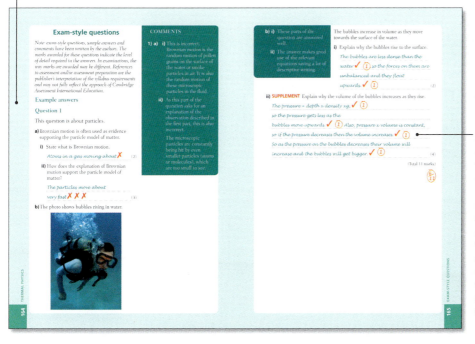

Sample answers and comments have been written by the authors to illustrate a possible response and show where it answers the question with the level of detail required or how it could be improved. Exam-style questions and sample answers have been written by the authors. In examinations, the way marks are awarded may be different.

This section covers concepts that will be important throughout your course. First, you will look at how to measure quantities such as length and time. Then you will look at speed, velocity and acceleration before considering mass, weight and density. You will then consider forces and their different effects, before looking at energy, work, power and pressure.

## STARTING POINTS

1. What would you use to measure: a) the width of this book; b) the length of the school playing field; c) the volume of milk needed to make a dessert?

2. How could you measure the time taken to: a) finish your physics homework; b) run 100 metres?

3. What do we mean when we say a car is travelling at 30 kilometres per hour?

4. An object is stationary. What must be true about the forces acting on this stationary object?

5. In physics, what do we mean when we say an object is accelerating?

6. How are mass and density related to each other?

7. List four different energy stores.

## SYLLABUS SECTIONS COVERED

1.1 Physical quantities and measurement techniques

1.2 Motion

1.3 Mass and weight

1.4 Density

1.5 Forces

1.6 Momentum

1.7 Energy, work and power

1.8 Pressure

# 1
# Motion, forces and energy

Δ In this topic you will learn about the forces at work on this parachutist.

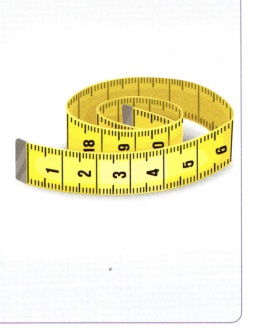

# Physical quantities and measurement techniques

## INTRODUCTION

Making measurements is very important in physics. Without numerical measurements, physicists would have to rely on descriptions, which could lead to inaccurate comparisons. Imagine trying to build a house if the only descriptions were 'big' and 'small'. Fig. 1.1 shows a tape measure for determining lengths. You can also use rulers to measure lengths.

You also need to make sure that you are consistent in your use of units.

△ Fig. 1.1 You can use this tape measure to find the circumference of a pillar or the length of a table.

## KNOWLEDGE CHECK

✓ Use a ruler to measure lengths to the nearest millimetre.
✓ Use a stopwatch to measure time to the nearest second.
✓ Use a measuring cylinder to measure volume.

## LEARNING OBJECTIVES

✓ Describe the use of rulers and measuring cylinders to find a length or a volume.
✓ Describe how to measure a variety of time intervals using clocks and digital timers.
✓ Determine an average value for a small distance and for a short interval of time by measuring multiples (including the period of oscillation of a pendulum).
✓ **SUPPLEMENT** Understand that a scalar quantity has magnitude (size) only and that a vector quantity has magnitude and direction.
✓ **SUPPLEMENT** Know that the following quantities are scalars: distance, speed, time, mass, energy and temperature.
✓ **SUPPLEMENT** Know that the following quantities are vectors: force, weight, velocity, acceleration, momentum, electric field strength and gravitational field strength.
✓ **SUPPLEMENT** Determine, by calculation or graphically, the resultant of two vectors at right angles, limited to forces or velocities only.

## MAKING MEASUREMENTS

When making measurements, physicists use different instruments, such as rulers to measure lengths, measuring cylinders to measure volume, and clocks and **digital** timers to measure time.

A physicist always takes care to make the measurements as accurate as possible. If she is using a ruler she will place the ruler along the object to be measured, and read off the scale the positions of the beginning and the end of the object. The length is the difference between these two readings. When the ruler is nearer to her eye than the object being measured, the reading will appear to change as she moves her eye. The correct reading is obtained when her eye is directly above the point being measured. To obtain an accurate value of the length, the line-of-sight must always be perpendicular to the ruler.

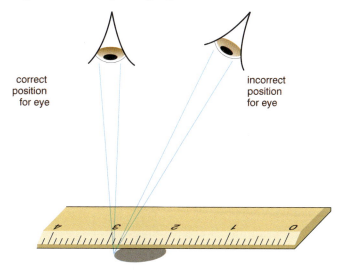

correct
position
for eye

incorrect
position
for eye

Δ Fig. 1.2 Making accurate measurements.

To improve accuracy further, she may take several readings and use the average of these readings as a better result. Fig. 1.3 shows an example, where for safety reasons, it is very important to have lengths measured precisely.

Δ Fig. 1.3 The Maglev train runs between Shanghai and Pudong Airport, reaching a top speed of 430 km/h. The train uses magnets to hover 10 mm above the track. The track must be placed within a few millimetres of the planned route, requiring great accuracy in all measurements.

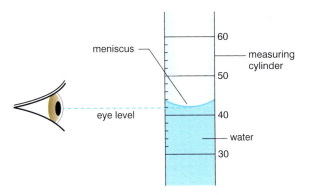

△ Fig. 1.4 The volume of water in the measuring cylinder must be read to the bottom of the meniscus.

To use a measuring cylinder, she will first make sure that the cylinder is standing on a level table. Then she will make sure that her eye is at the same level as the liquid inside the cylinder (Fig. 1.4). The surface of most liquids will bend up or down near the walls of the measuring cylinder. This bent shape is known as a meniscus. However, most of the surface is flat, and measurements are made to this flat surface.

### REMEMBER

Some measuring cylinders have unusual scales and one division may represent an unexpected quantity, perhaps 2 cm³ or 0.5 cm³. Check carefully.

In this book, volumes will be measured in cm³ or in m³. On some measuring cylinders, you will see the millilitre. A volume of 1 ml is the same as a volume of 1 cm³.

1000 cm³ = 1000 ml = 1 l (or 1 dm³ to avoid confusion between the number 1 and the letter l)

For measuring large volumes we also use the cubic metre.

1 m³ = 1000 dm³ = 1 000 000 cm³

Time intervals are measured using clocks. In the laboratory we would use a stopwatch or a stopclock.

Hand-operated stopwatches have an accuracy that is limited by the delay between your eye seeing the moment to start, your brain issuing the command to start the watch and your finger pressing the start button. The total delay is typically around 0.2 s. This delay is known as your 'reaction time', and it increases the danger of some tasks, such as driving a car.

When measuring time accurately is critical, such as in athletics, the clock has to be started and stopped automatically by the athlete breaking a light beam that shines across the track.

If you are determining the period of an oscillation, such as the swing of a pendulum, it is very easy to improve the accuracy of the measurement by timing a number of swings, perhaps 10 or 20. The period of a pendulum can be very short to measure using a single oscillation. This is why it would be sensible to determine the period using the time of several oscillations.

It is important to count correctly. Let the swing go, count zero and start the stopwatch as the pendulum crosses a mark at the bottom of the swing (we call this the fiducial mark). The next time the pendulum crosses the fiducial mark going in the same direction count one, and so on. In this way the count will be correct.

After measuring the time for 20 swings, say, divide the total time by 20 to give the period of oscillation of the pendulum.

## SUPPLEMENT

### SCALARS AND VECTORS

We make measurements and do calculations to understand the physical world. There are two types of physical quantities – **scalars** and **vectors**. Scalars and vectors are treated very differently in calculations.

### Scalar quantity

A scalar quantity only has magnitude (size).

Some scalar quantities, with examples, are shown in Table 1.1.

| Scalar quantity | Example |
|---|---|
| Distance | The distance between Nairobi and Mombasa in Kenya is 488 km. |
| Speed | The speed of Japan's bullet train is 320 km/h |
| Time | The Earth takes a time of 24 hours to spin on its axis. |
| Mass | The mass of a brick is 2.3 kg. |
| Energy | The energy of a moving car is 45 000 J |
| Temperature | Normal human body temperature is 37 °C. |
| Volume | The volume of a mug is 350 cm$^3$. |

Δ Table 1.1 Examples of scalar quantities.

### Adding scalar quantities

The sum of any two similar scalar quantities is very simple. We just add the values together.

Here are two examples:

- A bicycle of mass 80 kg with a rider of mass 60 kg.
  total mass = 80 + 60 = 140 kg
- A person travels 100 m, and then another 200 m.
  total distance = 100 + 200 = 300 m

### Vector quantity

A vector quantity has both magnitude and direction.

Some vector quantities, with examples, are shown in Table 1.2.

| Vector quantity | Example |
|---|---|
| Force | The force acting on a car is 500 N due east. |
| Weight | The weight of an apple is 1.0 N downwards. |
| Velocity | The velocity of an object is 3.0 m/s to the right. |
| Acceleration | The acceleration of a rocket is 50 m/s$^2$ upwards. |
| Momentum | An object has momentum of 20 kg m/s to the left. |
| **Electric field** strength | The electric field strength of a charged plate is 2000 N/C to the right. |
| Gravitational field strength | The **gravitational field strength** on the surface of the Earth is 9.8 N/kg towards the centre of the Earth. |

△ Table 1.2 Examples of vector quantities.

A vector quantity can be shown by an arrow. The length of the arrow, drawn to scale, represents the magnitude of the quantity and arrowhead on the arrow points in the direction of the vector. Fig. 1.5 shows three examples of vectors.

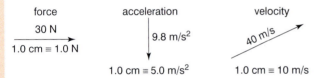

△ Fig. 1.5 Examples of vectors.

## Adding vectors quantities

When adding two (or more) vectors together, the total vector is referred to as the resultant vector. Consider two **forces** acting on an object. The resultant force is a single force that has the same effect on the object as the two forces acting together on the object.

It is relatively easy to determine the resultant vector (force, **velocity**, etc) when the vectors are in a straight line. The magnitudes of the vectors are either added or subtracted, as shown by the two examples below.

- 2.0 N and 3.0 N forces acting on an object, both towards the right.
  resultant force = 2.0 + 3.0 = 5.0 N to the right

△ Fig. 1.6 Forces in the same direction.

- A car travelling at 25 m/s to the right against a 10 m/s wind to the left.
  resultant velocity of car = 25 − 10 = 15 m/s to the right

△ Fig. 1.7 Velocities in opposite directions.

What are the rules when adding two vectors that happen to be at right angles to each other, and in the same plane? This is best illustrated by an example to determine the resultant of two forces acting on an object. You can apply the same procedure to determine the resultant of any two vectors (e.g. velocities, **momentum**, etc)

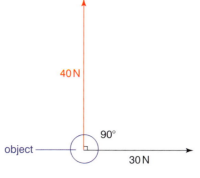

△ Fig. 1.8 Two forces acting on an object.

Fig. 1.8 shows two forces acting at right angles to each other. The resultant force $F$ can be determined either by doing a scale drawing, or by calculations using trigonometry.

## Rules for scale drawing (graphical technique)

1. Draw the first vector for the 30 N force using scale of 1.0 cm ≡ 10 N.

2. Draw the second vector for the 40 N force to the same scale at the end of the first vector.

3. Draw a straight line from the start of the first vector to the end of the last vector – this is the resultant force $F$. See Fig. 1.9.

4. The magnitude of the resultant force can be determined from the length of the 'hypotenuse' and the direction can be determined by the angle between the resultant force and the 30 N force using a protractor.

5. resultant force = 50 N at 53° to the 30 N force.

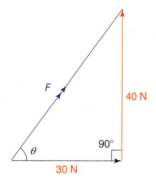

△ Fig. 1.9 A scale drawing to determine the resultant force $F$.

## Calculations

The magnitude of the resultant force $F$ can be determined using Pythagoras' rule.

$F^2 = 30^2 + 40^2$

$F = \sqrt{30^2 + 40^2} = \sqrt{2500}$

$F = 50$ N

The angle $\theta$ made by the resultant force with the 30 N force can be calculated as follows:

$\tan\theta = \dfrac{40}{30} = 1.333$

$\theta = \tan^{-1}(1.333) = 53°$

You will be using your knowledge of vectors, especially forces, in the section on Forces.

# End of topic checklist

### Key terms

period

**SUPPLEMENT** resultant, scalar, vector

## During your study of this topic you should have learned:

○ How to use rulers and measuring cylinders to find a length or a volume.

○ How to measure a variety of time intervals using clocks and digital timers.

○ Determine an average value for a small distance and for a short interval of time by measuring multiples (including the period of oscillation of a pendulum).

○ **SUPPLEMENT** Define a scalar quantity as having magnitude (size) only and a vector as having both magnitude and direction.

○ **SUPPLEMENT** Know that distance, speed, time, mass, energy and temperature are scalar quantities.

○ **SUPPLEMENT** Know that force, weight, velocity, acceleration, momentum, electric field strength and gravitational field strength are vector quantities.

○ **SUPPLEMENT** Determine, by calculation or graphically, the resultant of two vectors (e.g. force and velocity) at right angles to each other.

# End of topic questions

*Note: the marks in brackets give an indication of the level of detail you should include in your answers.*

1. Rulers that are 30 cm long are often made of wood or plastic that is thicker in the middle and thinner along the edges where the scale is printed. Explain why the user is less likely to make an error if the ruler is thinner at the edge, and suggest reasons why the ruler is thicker in the middle. (3 marks)

2. A plastic measuring cylinder is filled with water to the 100 cm³ mark. A student measures the column of water in the cylinder with a ruler and finds that it is 20 cm high.

   a) The student pours 10 cm³ of the water out of the cylinder. Determine how high the column of water will be now. (2 marks)

   b) The student then refills the cylinder back to the 100 cm³ mark by holding it under a dripping tap. She finds that it takes 180 drops of water to do this. Calculate the volume of one of these drops. (3 marks)

   c) What is the cross-sectional area of the cylinder? (Hint: The volume of a cylinder is given by the equation: volume = cross-sectional area × length.) (3 marks)

   d) From your answer to part c), calculate the internal diameter of the measuring cylinder. (3 marks)

3. A student tries to measure the period of a pendulum that is already swinging left and right. At the moment when the pendulum is fully to the left, she counts 'one' and starts a stopwatch. She counts successive swings each time the pendulum returns to the left. When she counts 'ten' she stops the stopwatch, and sees that it reads 12.0 s.

   a) What was her mistake? (2 marks)

   b) Calculate the period of oscillation of this pendulum. (3 marks)

   c) In this particular experiment, explain the likely effect of her reaction time on her answer. (3 marks)

4. **SUPPLEMENT** Which of the following quantities is **not** a scalar?
   A mass     B speed     C temperature     D weight     (1 mark)

5. **SUPPLEMENT** State one similarity, and one difference, between speed and velocity. (2 marks)

6. **SUPPLEMENT** Two forces are acting in a straight line on an object – a force of 10 N to the left and a 32 N force to the right. Calculate the resultant force acting on the object. (2 marks)

7. **SUPPLEMENT** A car is travelling at a velocity 10 m/s due north. The external wind velocity experienced by the car is 5.0 m/s due east. Calculate the magnitude of the resultant velocity. (3 marks)

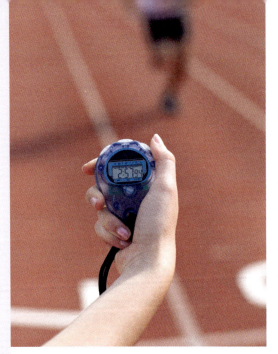

# Motion

## INTRODUCTION

To study almost anything about the world around us or out into space, we will need to describe where things are, where they were and where we expect them to go. It is even better if we are able to measure these things. Only when we have an organised system for doing this will we be able to look for the patterns in the way things move – the laws of motion – before going a step further and suggesting *why* things move as they do – using ideas about forces.

Δ Fig. 1.10 You can use a stopwatch to measure the time taken to run a certain distance.

Think about being a passenger in a car travelling at 90 kilometres per hour. This, of course, means that the car (if it kept travelling at this **speed** for 1 hour) would travel 90 km. During 1 second the same car travels 25 metres, so its speed can also be described as 25 metres per second. Scientists prefer to measure time in seconds and distance in metres. So they prefer to measure speed in metres per second, usually written as m/s.

### KNOWLEDGE CHECK

✓ Measure distances and times accurately.
✓ Calculate the area of a rectangle and a triangle.
✓ Plot a graph given particular points.
✓ Substitute values into a given equation.

### LEARNING OBJECTIVES

✓ Define speed as distance travelled per unit time; recall and use the equation $v = \dfrac{s}{t}$.
✓ Define velocity as speed in a given direction.
✓ Recall and use the equation average speed $= \dfrac{\text{total distance travelled}}{\text{total time taken}}$.
✓ Sketch, plot and interpret distance–time and speed–time graphs.
✓ Determine, qualitatively, from given data or the shape of a distance–time graph or speed–time graph when an object is: at rest, moving with constant speed, accelerating, and decelerating.
✓ Calculate speed from the gradient of a straight-line section of a distance–time graph.
✓ Calculate the area under a speed–time graph to determine the distance travelled for motion with constant speed or constant acceleration.
✓ State that the acceleration of free fall $g$ for an object near to the surface of the Earth is approximately constant and is approximately 9.8 m/s$^2$.

✓ **SUPPLEMENT** Define acceleration as change in velocity per unit time; recall and use the equation $a = \dfrac{\Delta v}{\Delta t}$.

✓ **SUPPLEMENT** Determine from given data or the shape of a speed–time graph when an object is moving with: constant acceleration or changing acceleration.

✓ **SUPPLEMENT** Calculate acceleration from the gradient of a speed–time graph.

✓ **SUPPLEMENT** Know that a deceleration is a negative acceleration and use this in calculations.

✓ **SUPPLEMENT** Describe the motion of objects falling in a uniform gravitational field with and without air/liquid resistance (including reference to terminal velocity).

## CALCULATING SPEED

The **speed** of an object is defined as the distance travelled per unit time and can be calculated using the following equation:

$$\text{speed} = \frac{\text{distance}}{\text{time}}$$

$$v = \frac{s}{t}$$

Where: $v$ = speed in m/s,

$s$ = distance in m, and

$t$ = time in s.

The equation above is ideal for an object travelling at a constant speed. However, in most situations, speed rarely stays the same. Consider a car journey between two places. The car will speed up, slow down and may even stop. In these situations, we can calculate the **average speed** using the equation:

$$\text{average speed} = \frac{\text{total distance travelled}}{\text{total time taken}}$$

You can still think of this as the equation $v = \dfrac{s}{t}$, but this time, $s$ = total distance and $t$ is the total time.

## WORKED EXAMPLES

**1.** Calculate the speed of a car that travels 500 m in 20 s.

Write down the equation: $\qquad\qquad\qquad\qquad v = \dfrac{s}{t}$

Substitute the values for $s$ and $t$: $\qquad\qquad v = \dfrac{500}{20}$

Work out the answer and write down the units: $\quad v = 25$ m/s

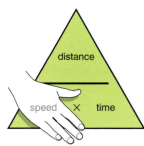

◁ Fig. 1.11 Cover speed to find that $\text{speed} = \dfrac{\text{distance}}{\text{time}}$

**2.** A cyclist has an average speed of 5.0 m/s for 2.0 minutes. Calculate the total distance travelled.

Write down the equation in terms of *s*:     $s = v \times t$

Substitute the values for *v* and *t*:     $s = 5.0 \times 2.0 \times 60$

Work out the answer and write down the units:     $s = 600$ m

◁ Fig. 1.12 Cover distance to find that distance = speed × time.

## ARE SPEED AND VELOCITY THE SAME?

We often want to know the direction in which an object is travelling. For example, when a space rocket is launched, it is likely to reach a speed of 280 m/s after about 30 seconds. However, it is extremely important to know whether this speed is upwards or downwards. You want to know the speed *and* the direction of the rocket. The **velocity** of an object is one piece of information, but it consists of two parts: the speed and the direction. In this case, the velocity of the rocket is 280 m/s (its speed) upwards (its direction). Velocity is defined as speed in a given direction.

A velocity can have a minus sign. This tells you that the object is travelling in the opposite direction. So a velocity of −280 m/s upwards is actually a velocity of 280 m/s downwards.

Fig. 1.13 shows two cars with the same speed but opposite velocities.

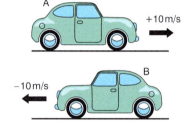

△ Fig. 1.13 Both cars have the same speed. Car A has a velocity of +10 m/s and car B has a velocity of −10 m/s. (The positive direction is to the right.)

## QUESTIONS

1. Imagine two cars travelling along a narrow road where it is not possible to pass each other. Describe what would happen when:

   **a)** both cars have a velocity of +15 m/s

   **b)** one car has a velocity of +15 m/s and the other −15 m/s

   **c)** both cars have a velocity of −15 m/s.

2. A journey to school is 10 km. It takes 15 minutes in a car. Calculate the average speed of the car.

3. How far does a bicycle travelling at 1.5 m/s travel in 15 s?

4. A person walks at an average speed of 0.5 m/s and travels a total distance of 1500 m. Calculate the time taken.

## USING GRAPHS TO STUDY MOTION

Journeys can be summarised using graphs. The simplest type is a **distance–time graph** where the distance travelled is plotted against the time of the journey.

At the beginning of any measurement of motion, time is usually given as 0 s and the position of the object 0 m. If the object is not moving, then time increases but distance does not. This gives a horizontal line. If the object is travelling at a steady speed, then both time and distance increase steadily, which gives a straight line of constant **gradient**.

You can calculate the speed of the object by finding the gradient of the line on a distance–time graph. If the speed is varying, then the line will not be straight. In Fig. 1.14, which shows a bicycle journey, the graph slopes when the bicycle is moving. The slope gets steeper when the bicycle goes faster. The slope is straight (has a constant gradient) when the bicycle's speed is constant. The cyclist falls off at about 150 m from the start. After this, the graph is horizontal because the bicycle is not moving.

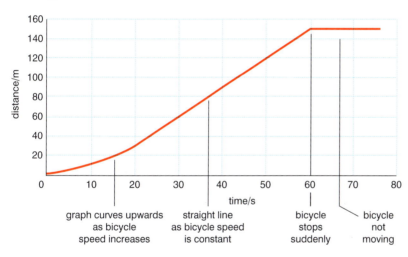

△ Fig. 1.14 A distance–time graph for a bicycle journey.

Table 1.3 summarises how the motion of an object can be deduced from the shape of the distance–time graph.

| State of object | Shape of distance–time graph |
|---|---|
| At rest | Horizontal line. |
| Moving at constant speed | Straight line of positive gradient. |
| Acceleration (speeding up) | Curve with increasing gradient as time increases. |
| Decelerating (slowing down) | Curve with decreasing gradient as time increases. |

△ Table 1.3 Deducing the motion of an object from a distance–time graph.

## Calculating speed from the gradient of a distance–time graph

Since $\text{speed} = \dfrac{\text{distance}}{\text{time}}$, you can calculate the constant speed from the gradient of a distance–time graph

In Fig. 1.13, the graph is a straight line between about 20 s and 60 s. In this time the distance increases from about 30 m to 150 m. So the speed between these points is

$$\text{speed} = \frac{120}{40} = 3.0 \text{ m/s}$$

## QUESTIONS

1. State the shape of the distance–time graph for an object travelling at a constant speed.

2. The distance–time graph for a car is shown below.

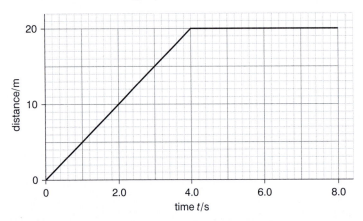

a) Describe the motion of the car from time $t = 0$ to time $t = 8.0$ s.

b) Calculate the constant speed of the car at time $t = 2.0$ s.

c) Calculate the average speed of the car during the 8.0 s.

## SPEED–TIME GRAPH

There is another way to represent the motion of an object travelling in a straight line, and that is to draw a **speed–time graph**.

Fig. 1.15 shows the speed–time graph for an object.

The speed $v$ is on the vertical axis, and the time $t$ is on the horizontal axis. The object has constant speed between $t = 0$ and $t = 2.0$ s of 1.0 m/s. After $t = 2.0$ s, the speed of the object increases at a steady rate of 0.5 m/s per second. It has a constant **acceleration**.

The area under the speed–time graph is equal to the distance travelled by the object. This is easier to see for the constant speed section of the graph. The distance $s$ travelled in the time of 2.0 s can be calculated using the equation:

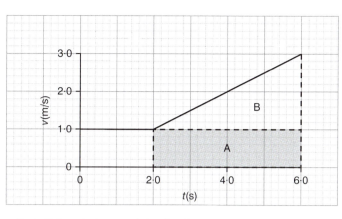

△ Fig.1.15 Speed–time graph for the object.

$s = v \times t$

$s = 1.0 \times 2.0$

$s = 2.0$ m

This value of 2.0 m is the same as the area under the graph. In fact, the area under the graph between any two times, is always equal to the distance travelled. See the worked example below.

## WORKED EXAMPLES

Use Fig. 1.14 to calculate the distance travelled by the object between $t = 2.0$ s and $t = 6.0$ s.

Write down the physics:

> distance travelled = area under the graph

> distance = area of rectangle A + area of triangle B

Substitute values to determine the areas of A and B:

> distance = $(1.0 \times 4.0) + (\frac{1}{2} \times 4.0 \times 2.0)$

Calculate the distance:

> distance = 8.0 m

## SUPPLEMENT

## ACCELERATION

An object is accelerating if its speed increases with time. A racing car will accelerate from rest to reach its top speed. When running, you may speed up for a short period of time, and hence accelerate. The opposite of acceleration is deceleration. This is a term used when the speed of an object decreases with time. A car decelerates when the brakes are applied. A ball hitting a wall will slow down, and hence decelerate.

Acceleration is defined as the change in velocity per unit time. We can use the following equation to calculate acceleration $a$:

$a = \dfrac{\Delta v}{\Delta t}$

Where $\Delta v$ is the change in velocity (or speed if the motion is in a straight line) and $\Delta t$ is the change in time. The Greek delta $\Delta$ symbol is used in mathematics to mean 'change in …'. The units for acceleration are $m/s^2$.

For an object accelerating, the value of $a$ is positive and for an object decelerating, the value of $a$ is negative. For example, a car with $a = +2.0$ $m/s^2$ must be accelerating with speed increasing by 2.0 m/s per second and a car with $a = -2.0$ $m/s^2$ must be decelerating with speed decreasing by 2.0 m/s per second.

### WORKED EXAMPLE

A car is travelling in a straight line. The speed of the car changes from 25 m/s to 15 m/s in a time of 2.0 s. Calculate the acceleration of the car.

Write the equation: $a = \dfrac{\Delta v}{\Delta t}$

Determine $\Delta v$: $\Delta v$ = final speed – initial speed = $15 - 25 = -10$ m/s
The minus sign is important. It shows that the speed is decreasing.

Substitute values into the equation: $a = \dfrac{-10}{2.0}$

Calculate $a$: $a = -5.0$ $m/s^2$
The minus sign shows deceleration. The magnitude of the deceleration is 5.0 $m/s^2$.

### Speed–time graph revisited

Table 1.4 summarises how the motion of an object can be deduced from the shape of the speed–time graph.

| State of object | Shape of distance–time graph |
|---|---|
| At rest | Horizontal line along the time axis. |
| Moving at constant speed | A non-zero horizontal line. |
| Constant acceleration | Straight line of positive gradient. |
| Changing acceleration | A curved graph. |
| Constant deceleration | Straight line of negative gradient. |

$\Delta$ Table 1.4 Deducing the motion of an object from a speed–time graph.

### SUPPLEMENT

In Fig. 1.15, the object has constant speed between $t = 0$ and $t = 2.0$ s and has constant acceleration between $t = 2.0$ s and $t = 6.0$ s. The acceleration of the object can be calculated as before using the equation $a = \dfrac{\Delta v}{\Delta t}$. This is the same as the gradient of the straight line.

Therefore, the acceleration a between $t = 2.0$ s and $t = 6.0$ s can be calculated as follows:

$a$ = gradient of speed–time graph

$a = \dfrac{3.0 - 1.0}{6.0 - 2.0}$

$a = 0.50$ $m/s^2$

1. State what can be calculated from the area under a speed–time graph.

2. The motion of an object is represented by the speed–time graph below.

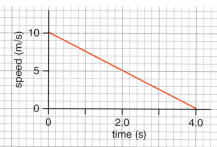

a) Describe the motion of the object.

b) Determine the total distance travelled by the object.

c) Determine the average speed of the object.

d) **SUPPLEMENT** Determine the deceleration of the object.

3. **SUPPLEMENT** A stone falls from rest. It reaches a speed of 19.6 m/s after a time of 2.0 s. Calculate the acceleration of the stone.

4. **SUPPLEMENT** A racing car slows down from a speed of 45 m/s to 0 m/s in 3.0 s. Calculate its acceleration. Comment on your answer.

5. **SUPPLEMENT** A runner has an initial speed of 2.0 m/s. She then accelerates at 0.5 m/s² for a time of 4.0 s. Calculate the final speed of the runner.

## Developing practical skills

△ Fig. 1.16 Apparatus needed for the investigation.

A student investigated the motion of a trolley rolling down a ramp. To measure the distance travelled by the trolley at different times, she used a ticker timer and ticker tape. A ticker timer has a moving arm that bounces up and down 50 times each second. When the arm moves down and hits the tape it makes a small dot on the tape.

The student attached the tape to the trolley and released the trolley to roll down the ramp.

After that she divided the tape into strips with five dots in each strip – at 50 dots per second this meant that a five-dot strip had taken 0.1 s.

She measured the length of each five-dot strip with a ruler. Her results are shown in the table.

| Time/s | Distance from start/cm | Distance covered in the last 0.1 s/cm | Average speed for last 0.1 s/cm/s |
|---|---|---|---|
| 0.0 | | 0.0 | |
| 0.1 | | 1.8 | |
| 0.2 | | 3.4 | |
| 0.3 | | 5.2 | |
| 0.4 | | 6.0 | |
| 0.5 | | 7.7 | |
| 0.6 | | 11.1 | |
| 0.7 | | 9.9 | |
| 0.8 | | 11.9 | |
| 0.9 | | 12.5 | |
| 1.0 | | 14.0 | |

## Planning experiments and investigations

1 Suggest how using this method might change the motion of the trolley as it rolls down the ramp.

2 How else could the student measure the position of the trolley every 0.1 s?

## Observing, measuring and recording data

3 Copy the table and complete the second column, showing the total distance travelled up to that time.

4 Draw a distance–time graph using the data in the first two columns. Use your graph to describe the motion of the trolley.

5 Use the equation speed = distance/time to complete the final column.

6 Draw a speed–time graph using the data in the first and fourth columns. Does this graph support the description of the motion you gave in question 4? Explain your answer.

## Interpreting and evaluating data

7 The student thought she had made a mistake in measuring the strips. Is there any evidence for this on either of the graphs?

## Evaluating methods

8 Would repeating the experiment make the data more reliable? Justify your answer.

## FALLING OBJECTS

When you drop an object it falls towards the ground. The force of **gravity** acts on the object and causes it to accelerate.

The acceleration due to gravity, also known as the **acceleration of free fall** $g$, acts downwards and has an approximate value of 9.8 m/s$^2$. This is assuming that there are either no **frictional forces**, or the frictional forces are negligible. All objects near the surface of the Earth have this acceleration. In a vacuum, all objects have a free fall acceleration of exactly 9.8 m/s$^2$.

△ Fig. 1.17 The forces on the skydiver are balanced at the terminal velocity.

SUPPLEMENT

### Falling objects and terminal velocity

As a skydiver jumps from a plane, the **weight** will be much greater than the opposing force caused by **air resistance**. Air resistance is a form of friction (see the topic on Forces). Initially she will accelerate downwards at 9.8 m/s$^2$.

The skydiver's speed will increase rapidly – and the force caused by the air resistance $F$ increases as the skydiver's speed increases. Eventually the resistive force will exactly match the weight $W$, the forces will be balanced and the velocity of the skydiver will remain constant. This downward velocity is known as the **terminal velocity**, typically 50 m/s.

△ Fig. 1.18 The terminal velocity of this parachutist is quite low so he will be able to land safely.

In Fig. 1.17, the skydiver has her arms outstretched so the air resistance force is fairly high. If the skydiver makes herself streamlined by going head first, with her arms by her side, then the air resistance force will be reduced and she will cut through the air more easily. She will then accelerate again, until the force of air resistance increases again to equal her weight. She will now be travelling at almost 80 m/s.

A parachute has a very large surface area and produces a very large resistive force, so the terminal velocity of a parachutist is quite low. This means that he or she can land relatively safely.

### REMEMBER

Make sure you think carefully about the *two* opposing forces that lead to terminal velocity. The force causing the motion (such as gravity or the force from a car engine) usually remains constant. It is the drag force (such as air or water resistance) that increases as the velocity increases, until the two are balanced and the velocity stays constant.

## Developing practical skills

Two students are investigating terminal velocity. They use a tall tube filled with wallpaper paste and drop a steel ball into it. The weight of the ball pulls it down through the paste. As it gets faster, the drag from the paste increases until the two forces are balanced.

The students mark every 10 cm along the tube using tape.

One of the students releases the ball carefully at the surface of the paste.

At the same time, the other student starts a stopclock.

As the ball passes each mark, the first student calls out and the second student makes a note of the time.

Since the marks on the tube are 10 cm apart, the students can calculate the speed of the ball in each section of the tube. Their results are shown in the table.

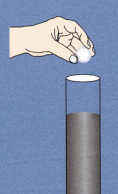

△ Fig. 1.19 Dropping the ball into the tall tube filled with wallpaper paste.

| Distance fallen through paste/cm | Time/s | Speed/cm/s |
|---|---|---|
| 0 | 0 | 0.0 |
| 10 | 4 | 2.5 |
| 20 | 4.5 | 4.4 |
| 30 | 5.3 | 5.7 |
| 40 | 6.6 | 6.1 |
| 50 | 7.8 | 6.4 |
| 60 | 9.4 | 6.4 |

## Planning experiments and investigations

1 What advantage is there for the students to work together on this investigation?

2 What factors should the students keep constant during this investigation?

## Observing, measuring and recording data

3 Draw a graph of speed against time for this experiment. Describe the pattern (if any) in the results.

4 Add a second line to your graph to indicate the expected results for a slightly larger ball with a slightly higher mass.

## Evaluating methods

5 Suggest how the method could be improved to gain more accurate measurements.

## QUESTIONS

1. State the acceleration of free fall close to the Earth's surface.

2. **SUPPLEMENT** Estimate the speed of an object dropped from rest after a time of 2.0 s.

3. **SUPPLEMENT** Explain what is meant by terminal velocity of an object falling through the air on the Earth.

4. **SUPPLEMENT** A skydiver has a weight of 700 N and a terminal velocity of 50 m/s.

   a) What is the magnitude of the air resistance?
      **A** 0 N     **B** 9.8 N     **C** 50 N     **D** 700 N

   b) Calculate the distance travelled by the skydiver in 0.50 minute.

# End of topic checklist

## Key terms

acceleration of free fall, acceleration, speed

**SUPPLEMENT** deceleration, terminal velocity, velocity

## During your study of this topic you should have learned:

◯ Speed is defined as the distance travelled per unit time.

◯ Recall and use the equation $v = \dfrac{s}{t}$

◯ Velocity is defined as the speed in a given direction.

◯ Recall and use the equation average speed $= \dfrac{\text{total distance travelled}}{\text{total time taken}}$.

◯ Sketch, plot and interpret distance–time and speed–time graphs.

◯ How to determine from given data, or the shape of a distance–time graph or speed–time graph when an object is at rest, moving with constant speed, accelerating and decelerating.

◯ How to calculate speed from the gradient of a straight-line section of a distance–time graph.

◯ How to calculate the area under a speed–time graph to determine the distance travelled.

◯ State that the acceleration of free fall $g$ for an object near to the surface of the Earth is approximately constant and is approximately $9.8 \text{ m/s}^2$.

◯ **SUPPLEMENT** Acceleration is defined as the change in velocity per unit time.

◯ **SUPPLEMENT** Recall and use the equation $a = \dfrac{\Delta v}{\Delta t}$.

◯ **SUPPLEMENT** How to determine from given data or the shape of a speed–time graph when an object is moving with constant acceleration or changing acceleration.

◯ **SUPPLEMENT** How to calculate acceleration from the gradient of a speed–time graph.

◯ **SUPPLEMENT** Know that a deceleration is a negative acceleration.

◯ **SUPPLEMENT** Describe the motion of objects falling on the Earth with and without air/liquid resistance.

◯ **SUPPLEMENT** Know about terminal velocity.

# End of topic questions

*Note: the marks in brackets give an indication of the level of detail you should include in your answers.*

1. A student's journey to school takes 10 minutes and is 3.6 kilometres. Calculate his average speed in km/min. (1 mark)

2. a) A runner runs 400 metres in 1 minute 20 seconds. What is the speed of the runner in m/s?

   **A** 3.3 m/s    **B** 5.0 m/s    **C** 6.7 m/s    **D** 20 m/s     (1 mark)

   b) At one point she is running due west at 6.0 m/s. Later she is running due east at 4.0 m/s. How could we write her velocities to show that they are in opposite directions? (2 marks)

3. **SUPPLEMENT** A train moves away from a station along a straight track, increasing its speed from 0 to 20 m/s in 16 s. Calculate its acceleration in m/s$^2$. (1 mark)

4. **SUPPLEMENT** A rally car accelerates from 100 km/h to 150 km/h in 5.0 s. What is its acceleration in:

   a) km/h per second (1 mark)

   b) m/s$^2$? (1 mark)

5. a) On a distance-time graph, what does a horizontal line indicate? (2 marks)

   b) A car is travelling at constant speed. What shape would the corresponding distance–time graph have? (2 marks)

6. a) Describe the difference between speed and velocity. (2 marks)

   b) Explain the significance of a positive or negative sign for a velocity. (2 marks)

   c) **SUPPLEMENT** Define acceleration. (2 marks)

   d) **SUPPLEMENT** State an everyday name for negative acceleration. (1 mark)

   e) Explain how to calculate the distance travelled from a speed–time graph. (3 marks)

7. A student cycles to his friend's house. In the first part of his journey, he rides 200 m from his house to a road junction in 20 s. After waiting for 10 s to cross the road, he cycles for 20 s at 8.0 m/s to reach his friend's house.

   a) Calculate his average speed for the first part of the journey. (3 marks)

   b) How far is it from the road junction to his friend's house? (2 marks)

   c) Calculate his average speed for the whole journey. (2 marks)

**8.** The graph shows a distance–time graph for a car journey.

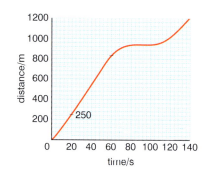

**a)** Describe the speed of the car between 20 s and 60 s. (2 marks)

**b)** How far did the car travel between 20 s and 60 s? (3 marks)

**c)** Calculate the speed of the car between 20 s and 60 s. (3 marks)

**d)** Describe what happened to the car between 80 s and 100 s. (2 marks)

**9. SUPPLEMENT** Look at the speed–time graph for a toy tractor.

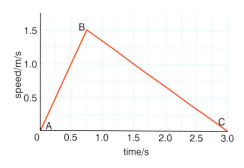

**a)** Calculate the total distance travelled by the tractor from A to C. (3 marks)

**b)** Calculate the acceleration of the tractor between A and B. (1 mark)

**c)** Calculate the deceleration of the tractor between B and C. (1 mark)

**10. SUPPLEMENT** The diagram shows the stages in the descent of a skydiver.

**a)** Describe and explain the motion of the skydiver at each stage. (10 marks)

**b)** In stage 5, suggest why the parachutist does not sink into the ground. (2 marks)

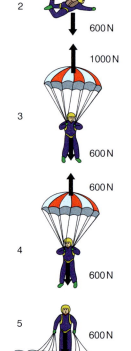

# Mass and weight

## INTRODUCTION

Scientists use the words 'mass' and 'weight' with special meanings. By the mass of an object we mean how much material is present in it when it is at rest relative to the observer. Weight is the force on the object due to gravity. It is measured in newtons (N). The weight of an object depends on its mass and gravitational field strength. The mass of a space probe will be the same on the surface of the Earth and on the Moon, but its weight will be greater on the Earth.

△ Fig. 1.20 An apple being weighed using a Newton meter.

## KNOWLEDGE CHECK

✓ Acceleration of free fall $g$ is approximately 9.8 m/s$^2$

## LEARNING OBJECTIVES

✓ State that mass is a measure of the quantity of matter in an object at rest relative to the observer.

✓ State that weight is a gravitational force on an object that has mass.

✓ Define gravitational field strength as force per unit mass; recall and use the equation
$$g = \frac{W}{m}$$
and know that this is equivalent to the acceleration of free fall.

✓ Know that weights (and masses) may be compared using a balance.

✓ **SUPPLEMENT** Describe, and use the concept of, weight as the effect of a gravitational field on a mass.

## MASS AND WEIGHT

**Mass** is a measure of the quantity, or amount, of matter in an object that is at rest relative to the observer (person) doing the measurement. Mass is measured in kilograms (kg). **Weight** is the gravitational force on an object that has mass. Weight is measured in newtons (N). For objects around you, the gravitational force is provided by the Earth. Objects on the Moon, such as rocks and the occasional space probe, experience a gravitational force due to the Moon itself. The weight of an object depends on its mass, and the **gravitational field strength**.

Gravitational field strength $g$ is defined as the gravitational force acting on an object per unit mass. It can be calculated using the equation

$$g = \frac{W}{m}$$

where $W$ is the weight of the object in N, and $m$ is the mass of the object in kg. This equation can be rearranged as below to determine the weight of the object:

$W = m \times g$

The gravitational field strength is equivalent to the acceleration of free fall. Therefore g on the Earth's surface is 9.8 m/s$^2$ or 9.8 N/kg. It is worth noticing that N/kg is equivalent to m/s$^2$.

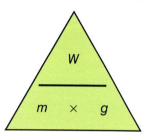

△ Fig. 1.21 The equation triangle for weight, mass and gravitational field strength.

## QUESTIONS

1. What is the difference between mass and weight?

2. Calculate the weight of someone whose mass is 60 kg.

3. Calculate the mass of someone whose weight is 500 N.

### THE EARTH'S GRAVITATIONAL FIELD

Scientists often use the word 'field'. We say that there is a 'gravitational field' around the Earth, and that any object with mass that enters this field will be attracted to the Earth.

The value of the gravitational field strength on Earth is 9.8 N/kg; a gravitational force of 9.8 N acts on an object of mass 1.0 kg on the Earth's surface.

Note that gravity does not stop suddenly as you leave the Earth. Satellites go around the Earth and do not escape, because the Earth is still pulling them, even if less strongly than before the satellites were launched. The Earth is even pulling the Moon, and this is why it orbits the Earth once every month. The Earth goes around the Sun because the Sun's gravity is pulling the Earth.

If you could stand on the Moon you would feel the gravity of the Moon pulling you down. Your mass would be the same as on Earth, but your weight would be less. This is because the gravitational field strength on the Moon is about one-sixth of that on the Earth, and so the force of attraction of an object to the Moon is about one-sixth of that on the Earth. The gravitational field strength on the Moon is 1.6 N/kg, so a force of 1.6 N is needed to support a 1.0 kg mass.

Weight is the effect of a gravitational field on a mass. This is illustrated in Fig. 1.22, where the gravitational field is provided by the Earth, and then by the Moon.

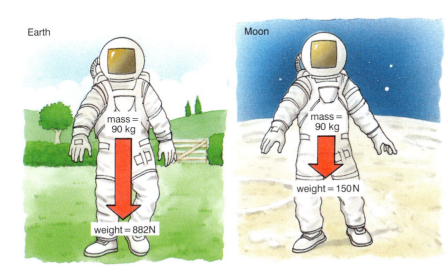

Δ Fig. 1.22 Though your mass remains the same, your weight is greater on Earth than it would be on the Moon.

If two astronauts played football on the Moon, it would be just as difficult to halt a tackle by one of them as it would be on the Earth, and any collision between them would hurt just as much. The reason for this is that the mass of an object resists any change in the motion of the object, and the mass of each astronaut is the same in both places.

## HOW DO YOU FIND THE MASS OF SOMETHING?

A balance is level when the forces pulling down on both sides are the same. In the balance shown in Fig. 1.23, the forces of 9.8 N and 19.6 N on one side balance the force of 29.4 N on the other side. If the balance is on the surface of the Earth, then the masses of these objects are 1.0 kg and 2.0 kg on one side, and 3.0 kg on the other. If the balance could be taken to the Moon, the forces on each side would become 4.8 N instead of 29.4 N, but they would still be balanced. So a balance allows you to compare masses no matter where you are.

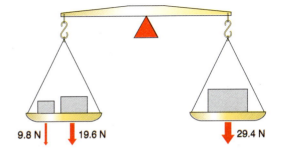

Δ Fig. 1.23 The total force is the same on each side of the balance.

In the laboratory, you may use a top-pan balance. This device is calibrated to compare masses just like the balance shown in Fig. 1.23.

## HOW DO YOU WEIGH SOMETHING?

A spring balance can also be used for weighing things, but works in a different way.

The top of the spring is hung from a hook, and the spring is stretched by the weight of the pan attached to its lower end. The scale can then be adjusted so that the pointer is aligned with the 'zero' mark.

When a known mass is placed in the pan, the spring stretches further due to the extra weight and the new pointer position can be marked. In the spring balance shown in Fig. 1.24, the pointer should be at the 29.4 N mark when the scale is set correctly. If this balance were moved to the Moon, the weight would be less and the spring would not stretch so far. In fact the pointer would indicate a weight of 4.8 N.

So the spring balance measures the weight of the object in newtons. For non-scientific use, these balances are often given a scale that indicates the mass of the object in kg, without the need for any calculations. This scale gives the correct mass on the surface of the Earth, but would definitely not give the correct mass if the spring balance were moved to the Moon.

See the topic on Forces for more about springs.

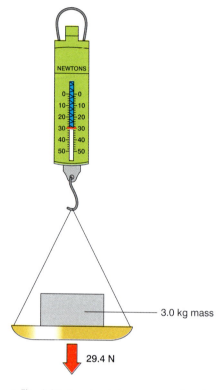

△ Fig. 1.24 A spring balance measuring the weight of a 3.0 kg mass.

# End of topic checklist

## Key terms

gravitational field, gravitational field strength, mass, weight

## During your study of this topic you should have learned:

- ◯ Mass is a measure of the quantity of matter in an object at rest relative to the observer.
- ◯ Weight is a gravitational force on an object that has mass.
- ◯ Gravitational field strength $g$ is defined as force per unit mass.
- ◯ The equation for gravitational field strength is $g = \dfrac{W}{m}$.
- ◯ Gravitational field strength is equivalent to the acceleration of free fall.
- ◯ Weights (and masses) may be compared using a balance.
- ◯ Weight of an object is the effect of a gravitational field on its mass.
- ◯ **SUPPLEMENT** How to describe, and use the concept of, weight as the effect of a gravitational field on a mass.

# End of topic questions

*Note: the marks in brackets give an indication of the level of detail you should include in your answers.*

**1. a)** Explain the difference between mass and weight. (2 marks)

   **b)** Explain why your weight would change if you stood on the surface of different planets. (3 marks)

**2.** A balance has 30 N on the left-hand side and 50 N on the right-hand side. What weight must be added so that the sides are balanced, and to which side? (3 marks)

**3. SUPPLEMENT** The height that you can jump has an inverse relationship to the gravitational field strength. When the field strength doubles, the height halves. The gravitational field strength on the surface of Mars is 3.8 N/kg. If the Olympic Games were held on Mars in a large dome to provide air to breathe, what would happen to the records for:

   **a)** weightlifting (weight in N) (2 marks)

   **b)** high jump (height) (2 marks)

   **c)** pole vault (height) (2 marks)

   **d)** throwing the javelin (distance) (2 marks)

   **e)** the 100 m race (time)? (2 marks)

In each case, explain if the record will increase, stay similar or decrease.

**4. SUPPLEMENT** What are the units for gravitational field strength?

   **A** N

   **B** kg

   **C** N kg

   **D** N/kg (1 mark)

# Density

## INTRODUCTION

**Density** is an important idea in physics and engineering. Not only is it tied to the mass and volume of an object, but density is also vital in determining whether something will float when placed on the surface of a liquid.

The Earth is not a uniform object – it has several layers of different densities. Its central core, made mainly of iron, is the densest. The mantle is mainly liquid. The **convection** currents in the mantle explains the movement of the continents. The thin crust is the least dense. You can think of the layers above the core as floated on top of each other.

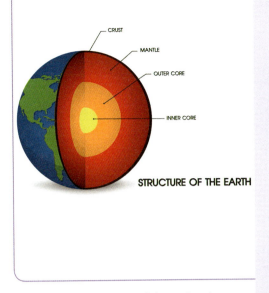

△ Fig.1.25 Different layers of the Earth – the densest structure is its inner core.

### KNOWLEDGE CHECK

✓ Calculate areas and volumes of regular shapes.

### LEARNING OBJECTIVES

✓ Define density as mass per unit volume; recall and use the equation:
$$\rho = \frac{m}{V}.$$
✓ Describe how to determine the density of a liquid, of a regularly shaped solid and of an irregularly shaped solid which sinks in a liquid (volume by displacement), including appropriate calculations.
✓ Determine whether an object floats based on density data.
✓ **SUPPLEMENT** Determine whether one liquid will float on another liquid based on density data given that the liquids do not mix.

## WHAT IS DENSITY?

You must have noticed that the weight of objects can vary greatly. A plastic teaspoon weighs less than a metal one, and a gold ring weighs twice as much as a silver one, even if the objects are exactly the same size.

The **density** of a substance describes how closely packed the particles (atoms or molecules) are in a solid, liquid or gas. A dense object contains more

△ Fig. 1.26 Gold is one of the densest metals. A block of gold the size of a one-litre carton of milk would have a mass of almost 20 kg.

mass than a light object of the same size. The density of a material is defined as the mass per unit volume.

The density of a material is calculated using this equation:

$$\rho = \frac{m}{V}$$

Where: $m$ = mass in g or kg

$V$ = volume in cm³ or m³

$\rho$ = density in g/cm³ or kg/m³

Note that in this equation you must use g and cm throughout, or you must use kg and m. Also note that if you measure the weight in N you must convert it into mass in g or kg. Table 1.1 shows some useful densities in both g/cm³ and kg/m³.

|  | Density in g/cm³ | Density in kg/m³ |
|---|---|---|
| Vacuum | 0 | 0 |
| Helium gas | 0.00017 | 0.17 |
| Air | 0.00124 | 1.24 |
| Oil (petroleum) | 0.88 | 880 |
| Water | 1.0 | 1000 |
| Sea water | 1.03 | 1030 |
| Plastic | 0.9–1.6 | 900–1600 |
| Wood | 0.5–1.3 | 500–1300 |
| Magnesium | 1.74 | 1740 |
| Aluminium | 2.7 | 2700 |
| Titanium | 4.5 | 4500 |
| Steel | 7.8 | 7800 |
| Mercury (liquid) | 13.6 | 13 600 |
| Silver | 10.5 | 10 500 |
| Gold | 19.3 | 19 300 |

Δ Table 1.5 Some useful densities.

## THE DENSITY OF A REGULARLY SHAPED OBJECT

The density of water is 1.0 g/cm³, and the rule is that an object of greater density will sink in a liquid of lower density. So, perhaps not surprisingly, a stone will sink in water. But will it sink in mercury? To decide whether it will sink in mercury, you need to compare the density of the stone (about 5.0 g/cm³) with the density of mercury using the same units. From Table 1.5, you can see that the density of

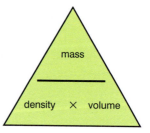

Δ Fig. 1.27 The equation triangle for mass, density and volume.

mercury is 13.6 g/cm³, which is very much greater than that of the stone, so the stone will float on liquid mercury.

The worked example below shows how the density of a rectangular-shaped brick can be determined.

## WORKED EXAMPLE

A brick has the dimensions 20.0 cm × 9.0 cm × 6.5 cm.

Weight of brick = 22.3 N

Calculate the density of the brick.

Mass of brick, $m$
$$= \frac{W}{g}$$
$$= \frac{22.3}{9.8}$$
$$= 2.276 \text{ kg}$$
$$= 2276 \text{ g}$$

(Remember that 1 kg = 1000 g)

Volume of brick, $V$
$$= 20.0 \times 9.0 \times 6.5$$
$$= 1170 \text{ cm}^3$$

Density of brick, $\rho$
$$= \frac{\text{mass}}{\text{volume}}$$
$$= \frac{2276}{1170}$$
$$= 1.945 \text{ g/cm}^3$$
$$= 1.9 \text{ g/cm}^3$$

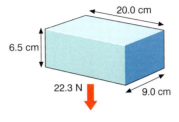

△ Fig. 1.28 Finding the density of a brick.

The final answer is given to 2 significant figures because the least significant figures in the data (dimensions) are given to 2 significant figures.

## Developing practical skills

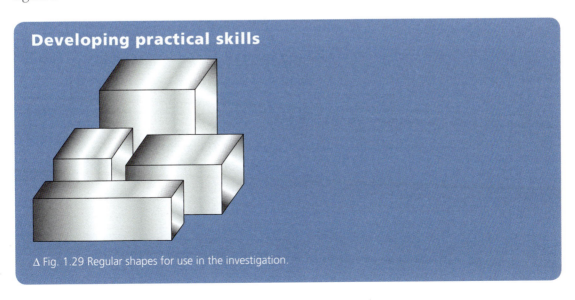

△ Fig. 1.29 Regular shapes for use in the investigation.

A student is finding the density of some different materials. The samples are all regular shapes.

The student has a ruler, marked in mm, and an electronic top-pan balance that measures to the nearest 0.1 g. The student finds the mass and the volume of each sample. The student's data is shown in the table.

| Sample | Mass/g | Volume/cm³ | Density/? |
|---|---|---|---|
| Aluminium | 97.2 | 36 | |
| Brass | 302.4 | 36 | |
| Copper | 321.5 | 36 | |
| Iron | 282.6 | 36 | |

## Planning experiments and investigations

**1.** Describe how the student should use the ruler to find the volume of each sample.

**2.** If the student checks that the balance reads zero before she puts the sample on, will this improve the accuracy or the precision of the experiment? Explain your answer.

## Observing, measuring and recording data

**3.** Copy the table and use the equation density $= \dfrac{\text{mass}}{\text{volume}}$ to complete it. Include the units at the top of the 'density' column.

**4.** How many significant figures should you give your values of density? Explain your answer.

## Evaluating methods

**5.** How could the method be changed to find the density of objects with an irregular shape?

## DETERMINING THE DENSITY OF A LIQUID

The density of a liquid can be determined using the procedure below.

**1.** Measure the mass $M_1$ of an empty measuring cylinder using a top-pan balance.

**2.** Pour the liquid into the measuring cylinder. Measure the volume $V$ of the liquid.

**3.** Measure the total mass $M_2$ of the liquid and measuring cylinder.

**4.** Calculate the mass $m$ of the liquid using: $m = M_2 - M_1$.

**5.** Finally, calculate the density of the liquid using the equation: $\rho = \dfrac{m}{V}$

## QUESTIONS

**1.** A small rectangular block of steel measures 2.0 cm by 4.0 cm by 5.0 cm and has a mass of 312 g. Calculate:

    **a)** its volume

    **b)** its density in g/cm³.

**2.** Suggest why bread is usually less dense than a root vegetable such as a potato or carrot.

**3.** A block of wood floats on sea water. What can you say about the density of the wood?

---

 **SCIENCE IN CONTEXT**    ## ICEBERGS

Icebergs are blocks of ice found in the Arctic, North Atlantic, and Southern Oceans. The size of icebergs varies – some can be tiny, but others can be as tall as a 50-story building from its bottom to its tip.

The icebergs float on sea-water because the density of ice (0.92 g/cm³) is less than the density of sea-water (1.0 g/cm³). The bulk of the iceberg is below the water. What is truly amazing is that a physicist can predict the volume of the iceberg below the water surface from these two density values. The fraction $f$ of the total volume of the iceberg below the water surface is given by the equation

$$f = \frac{\text{density of ice}}{\text{density of sea-water}}$$

You can substitute the data given to show that $f$ is about 0.9. This means that 90% of the iceberg is below the surface of the water. Only 10% is what we see floating above the water.

△ Fig. 1.30 Density plays an important role in how icebergs float on sea-water.

**Challenge Question:** For an ice cube floating in milk the fraction $f$ is slightly less than 0.9. What can you deduce about the density of milk compared with sea-water?

---

## DETERMINING THE DENSITY OF AN IRREGULAR OBJECT

This method involves submerging an object in a liquid and measuring the volume of the liquid that is displaced. It only works when the object is denser than the liquid used so that it sinks, although the method can be modified to measure a less dense object by attaching a 'sinker' to the object to hold it beneath the surface. It does not work when the object absorbs the liquid, or if it is damaged by the liquid.

1. A balance is used to weigh the object in question, as shown in Fig. 1.31, and find its mass, $m$.

2. A measuring cylinder is chosen that is wide and deep enough to hold the object. A narrower cylinder will give a more accurate answer than a wider one. Liquid is added to fill the cylinder to a deep enough level so that the object will be completely submerged. The volume of liquid, $V_1$, is then measured (see Fig. 1.32). The exact amount of liquid that you use is not at all critical. Water is the liquid normally used.

3. The object is lowered into the liquid (without splashing) and the new reading $V_2$ is measured (Fig. 1.32). This is the volume of the object and the liquid. The volume $V$ of the object is therefore $V_2 - V_1$.

4. The density of the object can now be calculated from its mass and volume using the equation for density: $\rho = \dfrac{m}{V}$.

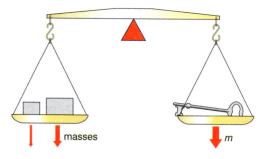

△ Fig. 1.31 Using a balance to find the mass of an object.

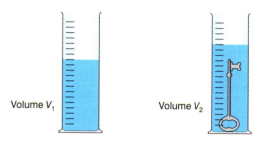

Volume $V_1$        Volume $V_2$

△ Fig. 1.32 Determining the volume of an object by the 'displacement' method.

## WORKED EXAMPLE

The mass of a small irregular metal object, like the one in Fig. 1.33, is found to be 90 g.

A measuring cylinder is filled with water to the 46 cm³ mark. The object is lowered into the measuring cylinder and the water rises to the 55 cm³ mark.

What metal is the object made of?

Volume of the object:       $V = 55 - 46$

                            $= 9 \text{ cm}^3$

Write down the equation: $\rho = \dfrac{m}{V}$

Substitute the values for $m$ and $V$:     $\rho = \dfrac{90}{9}$

Work out the answer and write down the units:       $\rho = 10 \text{ g/cm}^3$

So, from Table 1.1, what metal could the object be made of?

An experiment of this type is never perfectly accurate, so the density that you determine will never be exactly the same as the values given in tables.

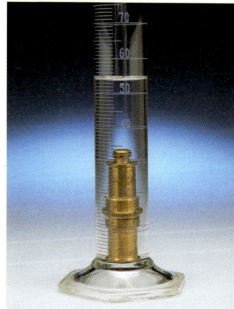

△ Fig. 1.33 Measuring the volume of an irregular metal object by displacing water.

## Making a column of different layers of liquid

The density of vegetable oil, which is yellowish in colour, is about 0.92 g/cm$^3$. When this vegetable oil is poured gently into water, two things will happen – the water and the oil will not mix, and in time, the oil will float on the surface of the water. This is because the density of the oil is less than the density 1.00 g/cm$^3$ of water. If you can find another liquid that has a density lower than that of the oil, then it too can be made to float on the surface of the oil.

You can extend the idea above to make your own layers, by using the information given in Table 1.6. Fig. 1.34 shows three layers formed using honey, milk and vegetable oil.

| Liquid | Density (g/cm$^3$) |
|---|---|
| Baby oil | 0.82 |
| Vegetable oil | 0.92 |
| Water | 1.00 |
| Milk | 1.03 |
| Washing-up liquid | 1.06 |
| Sugar syrup | 1.30 |
| Corn syrup | 1.40 |
| Honey | 1.45 |

Δ Table 1.6 Some density data of liquids at 20° C.

Δ Fig. 1.34 This three-layered 'density tower' is made from honey (bottom), milk (middle) and vegetable oil (top).

## QUESTIONS

Use Table 1.6 to answer the questions.

1. State a liquid that will float above washing-up liquid.

2. Liquid A floats on liquid B, and liquid C floats on liquid A. Explain the relative densities of these three liquids.

# End of topic checklist

## Key terms

density

## During your study of this topic you should have learned:

○ Density is defined as mass per unit volume.

○ The equation for density is: $\rho = \dfrac{m}{V}$.

○ Know how to determine the density of a liquid, of a regularly shaped solid and of an irregularly shaped solid which sinks in a liquid.

○ Know whether an object floats based on density data.

○ **SUPPLEMENT** Know how to determine whether one liquid will float on another liquid based on density data given that the liquids do not mix.

# End of topic questions

*Note: the marks in brackets give an indication of the level of detail you should include in your answers.*

1. For each of the following objects, use Table 1.5 to state whether they will sink or float or whether the outcome depends on the sample of material chosen:

   **a)** wood in oil (1 mark)

   **b)** wood in mercury (1 mark)

   **c)** plastic in oil (1 mark)

   **d)** steel in mercury (1 mark)

   **e)** silver in air (1 mark)

   **f)** gold in mercury (this experiment must be done rapidly as the gold will dissolve very quickly) (1 mark)

   **g)** helium balloon in air. (1 mark)

2. Write out the worked example given earlier in this topic for the case of a student who measures all the lengths of the brick in m and calculates with the mass in kg. Give the answer in $kg/m^3$. (3 marks)

3. A king who has studied physics believes that his jeweller has given him a crown that is a mixture of gold and silver, not the 1.93 kg of pure gold that he paid for. He weighs the crown using a balance and finds that it has the correct mass of 1.93 kg. He then immerses it in a measuring jug where the water level was originally 800 $cm^3$.

   **a)** If the crown is pure gold, what will the new water level be? (2 marks)

   **b)** What will happen to the water level if the jeweller has cheated? (2 marks)

4. The table below shows some data on four liquids.

| Liquid | Colour of liquid | Density $(g/cm^3)$ |
|---|---|---|
| Baby oil | Clear | 0.82 |
| Honey | Golden brown | 1.45 |
| Vegetable oil | Brown | 0.92 |
| Washing-up liquid | Green | 1.06 |

   **a)** Design a 'density tower' in a tall glass cylinder using all four liquids. (1 mark)

   **b)** Explain your design and the colours of the layers. (2 marks)

   **c)** What is the mass of 3.0 $cm^3$ of honey?

       **A** 0.48 g     **B** 1.45 g     **C** 2.46 g     **D** 4.35 g (1 mark)

△ Fig. 1.35 A crane lifting a concrete structure to place it on a pillar. There are immense forces at play here.

# Forces

## INTRODUCTION

We see the effect of forces all around us. The atoms within our bodies are all jiggling because there are electrical forces acting between them. A car moves faster because there is a resultant force acting on it. Planets move around the Sun because they experience the gravitational force of the Sun. Sometimes, forces acting on objects produce no motion at all. This is exactly what we would like from the concrete road being constructed in Fig. 1.35.

## KNOWLEDGE CHECK

✓ Mass is the amount of matter contained in a body.
✓ Weight is a gravitational force which acts on an object with mass.

## LEARNING OBJECTIVES

✓ Know that forces may produce changes in the size and shape of an object.
✓ Sketch, plot and interpret load–extension graphs for an elastic solid and describe the associated experimental procedures.
✓ Determine the resultant of two or more forces acting along the same straight line.
✓ Know that an object either remains at rest or continues in a straight line at constant speed unless acted on by a resultant force.
✓ State that a resultant force may change the velocity of an object by changing its direction of motion or its speed.
✓ Describe solid friction as the force between two surfaces that may impede motion and produce heating.
✓ Know that friction (drag) acts on an object moving through a liquid.
✓ Know that friction (drag) acts on an object moving through a gas (e.g. air resistance).
✓ **SUPPLEMENT** Define the spring constant as force per unit extension; recall and use the equation $k = \dfrac{F}{x}$
✓ **SUPPLEMENT** Define and use the term 'limit of proportionality' for a load–extension graph and identify this point on the graph (an understanding of the elastic limit is **not** required).
✓ **SUPPLEMENT** Recall and use the equation $F = ma$ and know that the force and the acceleration are in the same direction.
✓ **SUPPLEMENT** Describe, qualitatively, motion in a circular path due to a force perpendicular to the motion as:
(a) speed increases if force increases, with mass and radius constant

(b) radius decreases if force increases, with mass and speed constant

(c) an increased mass requires an increased force to keep speed and radius constant

(d) ($F = mv^2 / r$ is **not** required)

✓ Describe the moment of a force as a measure of its turning effect and give everyday examples.

✓ Define the moment of a force as moment = force × perpendicular distance from the pivot; recall and use this equation.

✓ Apply the principle of moments to situations with one force each side of the pivot, including balancing of a beam.

✓ State that, when there is no resultant force and no resultant moment, an object is in equilibrium.

✓ **SUPPLEMENT** Apply the principle of moments to other situations, including those with more than one force each side of the pivot.

✓ **SUPPLEMENT** Describe an experiment to demonstrate that there is no resultant moment on an object in equilibrium.

✓ State what is meant by centre of gravity.

✓ Describe an experiment to determine the position of the centre of gravity of an irregularly shaped plane lamina.

✓ Describe, qualitatively, the effect of the position of the centre of gravity on the stability of simple objects.

## WHAT ARE FORCES?

A **force** is a push or a pull. The way that an object behaves depends on all of the forces acting on it. A force may come from the pull of a chain or a rope, the push of a jet engine, the push of a pillar holding up a ceiling, or the pull of the gravitational field around the Earth.

### Effects of forces

It is unusual for a single force to be acting on an object. Usually there will be two or more. The sizes and directions of these forces determine whether the object will move and the direction it will move in.

Forces are measured in newtons (N). They take many forms and have many effects, including pushing, pulling, bending, stretching, squeezing and tearing. Forces can:

- change the speed of an object
- change the direction of movement of an object
- change the shape of an object.

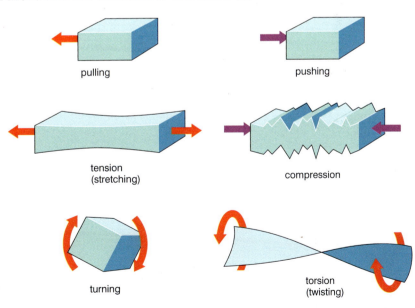

△ Fig. 1.36 Different types of force.

pulling

pushing

tension (stretching)

compression

turning

torsion (twisting)

**1.** Describe three effects of a force.

**2.** Give one example of each of the effects in Question 1.

## WHAT IS FRICTION?

A force that opposes motion may not be a bad thing. When you walk, your feet try to slide backwards on the ground. It is only because there is **friction** (working against this sliding) that you can move forwards. Where there is friction, heat is produced. Just think how much harder it is to walk on a slippery (that is, low friction) surface such as ice. A force which opposes motion is also very useful in applications such as between the brake pads and a bicycle wheel.

Force of pincers trying to remove the nail

Friction force preventing the nail from moving

Δ Fig. 1.37 Friction can stop any movement occurring at all, and it is friction that stops a nail coming out of a piece of wood.

There are two kinds of friction:

**Solid friction**: The force between two surfaces of solid objects that are sliding, or trying to slide, across each other. For example, pushing a crate along a floor is made harder because of friction. The floor and the crate would become slightly warmer because of the heating effect of friction.

**Friction (drag)**: This is the frictional force acting on an object moving through a **fluid** (liquid or gas). A submarine moving through sea-water will experience friction (drag) that impedes its motion. A skydiver falling through the air experiences friction (drag) we commonly refer to as air resistance. In both examples, the object and the fluid become warmer because of the heating effect of friction.

## QUESTIONS

**1.** Give an example of where friction may be useful.

**2.** Give an example of where friction may be a disadvantage.

## ADDING FORCES

When two or more forces are pulling or pushing an object in the same direction, then the effect of the forces will add up; when they are pulling it in opposite directions, then the backwards forces can be subtracted. The total of all the forces added-up is known as the **resultant force**.

△ Fig. 1.38 These husky dogs are able to pull the sledge due to the low level of friction between the sledge and the snow.

Eight husky dogs are pulling a sledge in Fig. 1.38. The sledge is travelling to the right and each dog is pulling with a force of 50 N. There is a friction force of 250 N that is trying to slow the sledge, and therefore must be pointing to the left.

The total force to the right is (8 × 50) N = 400 N.

The total force to the left is 250 N.

The resultant force (the total added-up force) = 400 − 250 N

= 150 N to the right.

Note that you must give the direction (to the right) of the resultant force as well as its magnitude (150 N).

What happens to an object that experiences no resultant force? If stationary, then it will remain stationary forever. A book resting on a table will remain there unless you pick it up. However, if the object is already travelling at constant speed, then it will carry on travelling in a straight line at that speed. A parachutist, falling through the air at 5.0 m/s, will keep moving at this speed until landing on the ground when there is a resultant force.

## BALANCED FORCES

Usually there are at least two forces acting on an object. When these two forces are **balanced** then the object will either be stationary or moving at a constant speed. If forces are balanced, there is no resultant force on the object. Two forces are balanced when their magnitude is the same but they act in opposite directions.

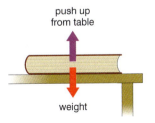

△ Fig. 1.39 The forces on this book are balanced.

The book in Fig. 1.39 is stationary because the push upwards from the table is equal to the weight downwards. If the table stopped pushing upwards, the book would fall.

The aircraft in Fig. 1.40 is flying 'straight and level' because the lift generated by the air flowing over the wings is equal and opposite to the weight of the aircraft. This diagram shows that the plane will neither climb nor dive, as it would if the forces were not equal.

△ Fig. 1.40 The balanced forces on this aircraft mean that its direction of motion will not change.

### UNBALANCED FORCES

For an object's speed or direction of movement to change, the forces acting on it must be **unbalanced** (there must be a resultant force). You can find the resultant of two unbalanced forces by adding them up, taking into account their direction. So, when the driving force on a car is 1000 N to the left but the total friction is 400 N to the right, the resultant force is 600 N to the left.

### WORKED EXAMPLES

**1.** Calculate the resultant force when a skydiver of mass 60 kg jumps from a plane and the air resistance is 188 N.

Force downwards $= m \times g$
$= 60 \times 9.8$
$= 588$ N

Force upwards $= -188$ N (downwards direction is taken as positive)

Resultant force $= 588 - 188$ N
$= 400$ N downwards

**2.** Calculate the resultant force on a car when the driving force is 1500 N to the left and the total friction is 100 N to the right.

Resultant force $= 1500 - 100$
$= 1400$ N to the left

As a gymnast gently steps on to a trampoline, his weight is much greater than the opposing supporting force from the trampoline, so he moves downwards, stretching the trampoline. As the trampoline stretches, its supporting force increases until the supporting force is equal to the gymnast's weight. When the two forces are balanced, the trampoline stops stretching.

You see the same effect when you stand on snow or soft ground. When you stand on quicksand, the supporting force will not equal your weight, and you will continue to sink.

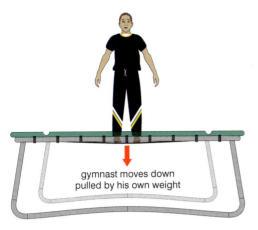
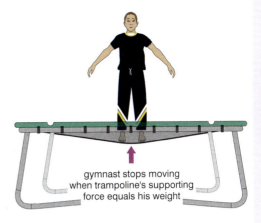

gymnast moves down
pulled by his own weight

gymnast stops moving
when trampoline's supporting
force equals his weight

Δ Fig. 1.41 A trampoline stretches until it supports the weight on it.

## QUESTIONS

1. Describe the motion of an object when the forces on it are balanced.

2. Describe the motion of an object when the forces on it are unbalanced.

3. In Fig. 1.40, if the gymnast is standing at rest on the trampoline, what must the supporting force from the trampoline be equal to?

### ANALYSING THE FORCES ON AN OBJECT

An excellent method of observing forces in action is to consider the forces acting on an aircraft from take-off to landing. The aircraft will have several different forces acting on it at any one time – some will balance one another but others will be unbalanced. In this example, all the forces considered act on the same object (the plane).

Your task is to produce a storyboard to illustrate these forces at certain parts of the aircraft's journey. For each section, you should draw force arrows on the aircraft to represent the direction and the size of the forces acting on it.

Your storyboard should include the following stages of the journey:

1. The aircraft is sitting on the runway, ready for take-off.

2. The aircraft is accelerating down the runway.

3. The aircraft has taken off and is rising through the air.

4. The aircraft has reached its maximum height and is travelling at a steady speed.

5. The pilot decides to decrease the altitude of the aircraft because of turbulence.

6. The aircraft is slowing down as it approaches the runway.

7. The aircraft has landed, and decelerates to try stop.

8. The aircraft has stopped on the runway.

For each section, you should write a line to describe what is happening.

## HOW ARE MATERIALS AFFECTED BY STRETCHING?

When weights are added to a length of wire, the wire will stretch. The graph in Fig. 1.42 shows how the amount that the wire stretches (the **extension**) varies with the load attached to it (the force). The extension of the wire is defined as the difference between the new length of the wire with the load, and its original length. The wire will stretch in proportion to the load up to a certain point, which depends on the material of the wire. Beyond this point, the extension is no longer directly proportional to the load, and so this point is called the limit of proportionality.

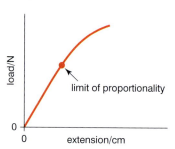

△ Fig. 1.42 Load–extension graph for a wire.

A string on a musical instrument, such as a guitar string, will behave as shown in the graph for wire, but will break shortly after the limit of proportionality is reached. This means that, when tuning a string on a musical instrument, we need to take care that we do not tighten the string too much or we risk it breaking.

### Loading a spring

For a wire, there is a section of the load–extension graph that is linear. Like a wire, when a spring stretches, the extension of the spring is directly proportional to the force stretching it, provided the limit of proportionality of the spring is not exceeded, see Fig. 1.43.

The gradient of the line is an indication of the stiffness of the spring.

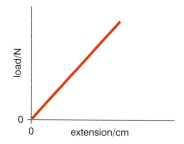

△ 1.43 The load–extension graph for a spring is a straight line through the origin.

### An experiment to show the linear behaviour of a spring

1. Secure the top end of the spring and let it hang vertically. Measure the starting position of the bottom end of the spring on the ruler.

2. Take the first mass, which consists of the hook and base plate, typically of mass 100 g (a weight of 0.98 N to 2 decimal places or 1.0 N to 1 decimal place.), and hang it on the spring (take care to

ensure that the mass does not fall on your feet). Measure the new position of the bottom end of the spring on the ruler. The difference in the readings is the extension of the spring.

**3.** Add masses one by one to the first one. Typically each mass is C-shaped, and adds an additional 100 g. Add the masses carefully so that the spring stretches slowly.

**4.** You should then reverse the experiment to see what happens as the masses are removed.

**5.** Calculate the extension (Table 1.7) and plot a graph of load against extension (Fig. 1.44).

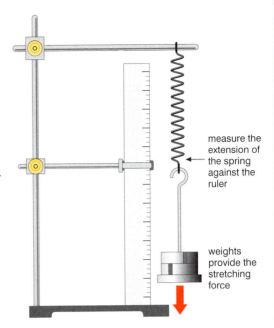

measure the extension of the spring against the ruler

weights provide the stretching force

△ Fig. 1.44 Apparatus to investigate the linear behaviour of a spring.

| Mass/g | Load/N | Reading/cm | Calculation of the extension/cm | Extension/cm |
|---|---|---|---|---|
| 0 | 0 | 15.2 | – | – |
| 100 | 0.98 | 16.8 | 16.8–15.2 | 1.6 |
| 200 | 1.96 | 18.5 | 18.5–15.2 | 3.3 |
| 300 | 2.94 | 19.9 | 19.9–15.2 | 4.7 |
| 400 | 3.92 | 21.6 | 21.6–15.2 | 6.4 |
| etc. | etc. | | | |

△ Table 1.7 Results of experiment.

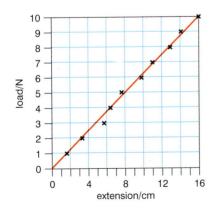

△ Fig. 1.45 Graph of results. The line of best-fit shows that the extension is directly proportional to the load.

## HOOKE'S LAW

Springs compress, and as long as the forces are not too large, they will return back to their original shapes. This elastic behaviour is used in pogo-sticks for jumping up and down, and in mattresses for giving us comfortable sleep.

The mathematical relationship, or law, that the extension of a spring is directly proportional to the load on a spring is credited to the scientist Robert Hooke (1635–1703). The law is often known as Hooke's law.

Hooke was an extraordinary person because he excelled in so many different fields of study. He was a rare polymath. He was the first person to use the term 'cell' to describe a basic unit of organisms. He was an astronomer who made his own telescope and suggested that the planet Jupiter spun around its own axis. He was also an architect. He designed many buildings and streets in London and was appointed Surveyor to the City of London after it was destroyed in a major fire in 1666. It is good to know that a large 36 km diameter crater on the Moon is named after him.

**Challenge Question:** A weight of 100 N hanging from a spring produces an extension of 12.0 cm. According to Hooke's law, what will be the extension caused by a weight of 125 N hanging from the same spring?

## Developing practical skills

A student assembled the apparatus as in Fig. 1.43, allowing the spring to hang vertically. Wearing safety glasses, the student measured the initial length of the spring and then measured it again after hanging an additional 100 g onto it. The student continued adding 100 g masses, measuring the length of the spring after each one. His measurements are shown in the table.

| Mass added/g | Load/N | Length of spring/cm | Extension of spring/cm |
|---|---|---|---|
| 0 | | 2.0 | |
| 100 | | 6.0 | |
| 200 | | 10.0 | |
| 300 | | 14.0 | |
| 400 | | 18.0 | |
| 500 | | 22.0 | |
| 600 | | 26.0 | |
| 700 | | 30.0 | |
| 800 | | 34.0 | |
| 900 | | 38.0 | |

| Mass added/g | Load/N | Length of spring/cm | Extension of spring/cm |
|---|---|---|---|
| 1 000 | | 42.0 | |
| 1 100 | | 46.0 | |
| 1 200 | | 52.0 | |
| 1 300 | | 59.0 | |
| 1 400 | | 77.0 | |

## Planning experiments and investigations

**1.** Why should the student wear eye protection during this experiment?

**2.** Describe how any other safety risks can be minimised.

**3.** The student carried out a preliminary experiment before deciding to use 100 g masses. Why is a preliminary experiment valuable?

## Observing, measuring and recording data

**4.** The force stretching the spring is equal to the weight of the 100 g masses that have been added. Use the equation: $W = mg$ to calculate the values for the 'load' column.

**5.** Use the equation: extension of spring = length – original length, to calculate the values for the 'extension' column.

**6.** Plot a graph of load (on the $y$-axis) against extension (on the $x$-axis).

## Interpreting and evaluating data

**7.** Use your graph to justify whether or not the extension is directly proportional to the load.

## Evaluating methods

**8.** The student could not repeat the experiment using this spring. Explain why not.

**9.** The student found it difficult to judge the 'end' of the spring. How could this be improved?

SUPPLEMENT

## SPRING CONSTANT

For a spring, the **spring constant** $k$ is defined as the force per unit extension. You can use the equation below to calculate the spring constant $k$:

$$k = \frac{F}{x}$$

where $F$ is the force or load and $x$ is the extension. The units for the force constant are N/m or N/cm or N/mm.

On a load–extension graph, you can determine the force constant from the gradient of the straight-line section of the graph shown in Fig. 1.42 or by simply dividing $F$ by $x$. The extension is directly proportional to the load up to the **limit of proportionality** of the spring. Beyond this point, you cannot use the equation $k = \dfrac{F}{x}$ and the spring will show permanent extension when the load is removed.

This equation above works for springs that are being stretched or compressed. The value of $k$ will be the same for both, but note that some springs cannot be compressed (if, for example, the turns of the spring are already in contact).

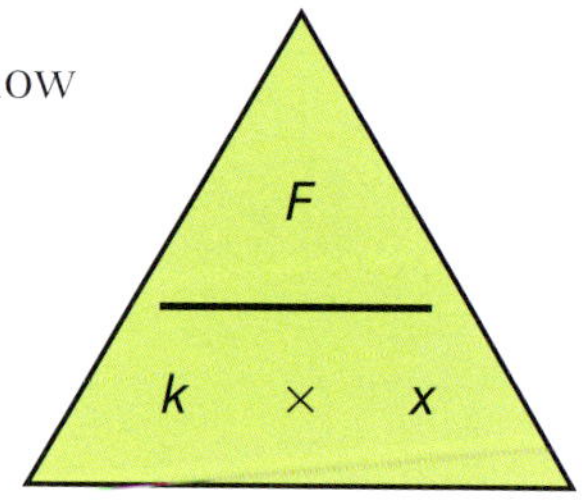

△ Fig. 1.46 The equation triangle for the equation $F = kx$

You can use the triangle in Fig. 1.46 to help you to rearrange the equation. Cover the quantity you want to find and the form of the other two will show you how to write the equation. For example, to find $x$, cover it and you will see that the equation should be written as $x = \dfrac{F}{k}$.

## WORKED EXAMPLE

One end of a spring is fixed and the other end supports a mass of 50 kg. The force constant of the spring is 60 N/cm. Calculate the extension of the spring.

| | |
|---|---|
| Write the equation for the weight: | $W = mg$ |
| Substitute the values for $m$ and $g$: | $W = 50 \times 9.8$ |
| Work out the answer and write down the units: | $W = 490$ N |
| Write down the equation for the extension of the spring: | $x = \dfrac{F}{k}$ |
| Substitute the values for $F$ and $k$: | $x = \dfrac{490}{60}$ |
| Work out the answer and write down the units: | $x = 8.2$ cm |

The spring extends by 8.2 cm. The extension is in cm because the force constant is given in N/cm.

## QUESTIONS

1. Calculate the force required to stretch a spring with spring constant 0.20 N/m a distance of 5.0 cm. (Note: 1 N/m = 100 N/cm)

2. A vertical spring stretches 5.0 cm under a load of 100 g. Calculate the spring constant.

3. A force of 600 N compresses a spring with spring constant 30 N/cm. Calculate the compression of the spring. (Note you can still use the equation $F = kx$, where $x$ is the compression.)

## HOW ARE MASS, FORCE AND ACCELERATION RELATED?

An object experiencing a resultant force will get faster. If stationary, it will start to move, and if already moving its speed will increase. A resultant force will produce an acceleration. The size of the acceleration depends on the mass of the object and the resultant force acting on it.

The relationship between mass, resultant force and acceleration is given by the equation:

force = mass × acceleration

$$F = ma$$

where:   $F$ = force in newtons (N)

$m$ = mass in kg

$a$ = acceleration in m/s$^2$

Both force and acceleration are vector quantities. This means that force and acceleration are in the same direction.

This equation helps to define the newton. 'One newton is the resultant force that will accelerate a mass of 1 kg at 1 m/s$^2$.'

The equation is perhaps easier to understand when we rearrange it into the form $a = \dfrac{F}{m}$. This shows us that when we use a big force we will get a larger acceleration, but when the object has more mass then we get a smaller acceleration.

The equation $F = ma$ shows that the acceleration of an object is directly proportional to the force acting (when its mass is constant) and is inversely proportional to its mass (when the force is constant). The gradient of a graph of force (on the $y$-axis) against acceleration (on the $x$-axis) is equal to the mass of the object.

### WORKED EXAMPLES

1. Calculate the force required to give a mass of 5.0 kg an acceleration of 10 m/s$^2$.

   Write down the equation:                                    $F = ma$
   Substitute the values for $m$ and $a$:                      $F = 5.0 \times 10$
   Work out the answer and write down the units:   $F = 50$ N

2. A car has a resultant force of 6000 N and a mass of 1200 kg. Calculate the car's initial acceleration.

   Write down the equation in terms of $a$:        $a = \dfrac{F}{m}$

   Substitute the values for $F$ and $m$:            $a = \dfrac{6000}{1200}$

   Work out the answer and write down the units:   $a = 5.0$ m/s$^2$

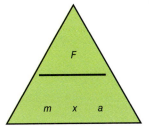

Δ Fig. 1.47 The equation triangle for force, mass and acceleration.

1. Write down the equation linking force, mass and acceleration.

2. Calculate the resultant force acting when a 60 kg object has an acceleration of 10 m/s².

3. The resultant force on an object of mass 3.2 kg is 2560 N. Calculate the acceleration of the object.

## RESULTANT FORCE AND MOTION

When a moving object has no resultant force acting on it, it will continue to move in a straight line at constant velocity (Fig. 1.48). What happens when the resultant force is not zero? The object will accelerate and its velocity will change. A change in velocity can either mean that its direction of travel will change, or its speed will change, or both direction and speed will change. For example, a resultant force acting on a car can make it go faster along a straight road or the car can go around a bend in the road.

no force

constant velocity in a straight line

Δ Fig. 1.48 This object is moving in a straight line at constant velocity and has no resultant acting on it.

SUPPLEMENT

## MOTION IN A CIRCULAR PATH DUE TO PERPENDICULAR RESULTANT FORCE

So, when an object is moving in a circle, or along the arc of a circle, there must be a resultant force acting on it to change its direction (Fig. 1.49). Moving in a circle means that the direction of motion is constantly changing, so this in turn means that the direction of the force is constantly changing.

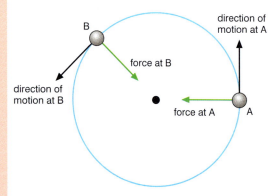

Δ Fig. 1.49 In order for an object to move on a circular path, the force must always be acting towards the centre of the circle.

This force, which always acts towards the centre of the circle, is given the name **centripetal force**. The force also acts perpendicularly to the direction of motion of the object at any instant. It changes the direction of motion of the object but does not change its speed.

The centripetal force is not a new and different force from any you have come across before, but is one or more of the forces already acting on the object that is moving in a circle. Table 1.8 gives some examples.

| Example | How is the centripetal force supplied? |
| --- | --- |
| A stone on the end of a string being whirled in a horizontal circle | By the tension in the string |
| The Moon orbiting the Earth | By the gravitational force of the Earth on the Moon |
| A car turning a corner | By the solid friction between the road and the tyres |
| A train going round a bend | By the sideways force of the rails on the wheels |
| A person standing on the Earth, which is spinning rapidly | By the gravitational force of the Earth on the person |

Δ Table 1.8 Some examples of centripetal force in action.

See if you can think of other examples of things moving around arcs of circles, and work out what force is providing the centripetal force. Remember that the centripetal force is always towards the centre of the arc and perpendicular to the direction in which the object is travelling at that instant.

Consider a stone being whirled in a horizontal circle on the end of a string (Fig. 1.50).

What happens if the string breaks?

In this case, the centripetal force is suddenly removed. There is now no force acting on the stone, so it continues to move in a straight line in whatever direction it had when the string broke (i.e. along the tangent to the circle at that point; Fig. 1.51), but falls vertically under gravity.

It is worth mentioning that the centripetal force acting on the object changes its velocity. The speed remains constant but the direction of travel changes.

The magnitude of the centripetal force depends on the mass of the object, its speed and the radius of the circle. Imagine whirling a stone in a horizontal circle. The tension in the string will be affected by the length of the string, the mass

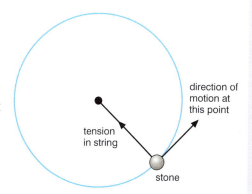

Δ Fig. 1.50 A stone being whirled in a horizontal circle on the end of a string, just before the string breaks.

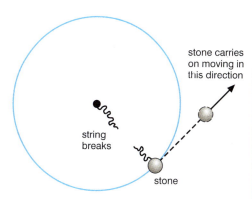

Δ Fig. 1.51 When the string breaks, the stone flies off along a tangent until the force of gravity takes over, and the stone falls to the ground.

of the stone and its speed. We can deduce the following about any object in circular motion:

The force increases

- when the speed increases (for a given mass and radius)
- when the radius decreases (for a given mass and speed)
- when the mass increases (for a given radius and speed).

## QUESTIONS

Suggest what would happen:

**1.** to the Moon if gravity suddenly ceased

**2.** to a car turning a corner when the road was very slippery

**3.** to a person on Earth if gravity suddenly ceased.

## TURNING EFFECT OF FORCES

If you have used a spanner to tighten a nut, or you have turned the handles of a bicycle, you have used a force to turn something. But turning applies to less obvious examples, such as when you push the door handle to close a door, or when a child sits on the end of a see-saw to push her end of it down.

The turning effect of a force is called the **moment** of the force. The moment of a force depends on two things:

- the *size* of the force
- the *perpendicular distance* between the line of the force and the turning point, which is called the **pivot**. So, if either the size of the force or the perpendicular distance from the pivot is increased, the moment of the force is increased.

### When moments balance

The **principle of moments** states that when a system of forces is not turning, then the sum of the clockwise moments equals the sum of the anticlockwise moments about any point.

The moment of a force is defined by the equation:

moment = force × perpendicular distance from pivot

moment = $Fd$

Moment is measured in newton metres (Nm) or newton centimetres (Ncm).

$F$ = force in newtons (N) and $d$ = distance in metres (m) or in centimetres (cm).

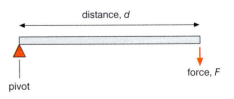

△ Fig. 1.52 The moment of the force $F$ about the pivot is given by $F \times d$

## WORKED EXAMPLE

Amy pushes open a door with a force of 20 N applied to the handle. The door handle is at a distance of 0.80 m from the hinges.

Write down the equation:          moment = force × distance from pivot
Substitute the values for $F$ and $d$:     moment = 20 × 0.80
Work out the answer and write down the units:   moment = 16 Nm

## WORKED EXAMPLE

Phil and Tom are sitting on a see-saw. The see-saw (a beam) is balanced on a pivot. Calculate Phil's weight.

Tom is causing the clockwise moment of 400 N × 3.0 m.

Phil is causing the anticlockwise moment of $W$ × 2.0 m.

The see-saw is balanced, so, taking moments about the pivot and applying the principle of moments, we have

sum of the clockwise moments = sum of the anticlockwise moments

$400 × 3.0 = W × 2.0$

$W = 600$ N

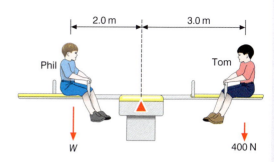

△ Fig. 1.53 Forces on the see-saw.

## Conditions for equilibrium

The word 'system' describes a collection of objects working together. So in the example of a see-saw, the two children and the see-saw form a system. We say that a system is in equilibrium when it is not moving in any direction and it is *not* rotating. You already know that for a system not to be moving, the forces on it must be equal and opposite. So:

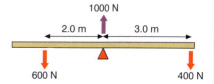

△ Fig. 1.54 This beam is balanced – the resultant moment and the resultant force on this beam are both zero.

For a system to be in equilibrium, there must be no resultant force and no resultant turning effect.

In the case of the balanced see-saw, there is no resultant turning effect on the see-saw because the clockwise and anticlockwise turning effects are equal and opposite. In addition, the downward weight of the two children on the see-saw is 1000 N, and the upward force on the see-saw from the pivot must also be 1000 N (Fig. 1.54).

What is the physics when a beam has more than one force on each side of the pivot? The principle of moments can still be applied. This is illustrated in the worked example below.

## WORKED EXAMPLE

Fig. 1.55 shows a metre rule balanced horizontally in an experiment done by a student.

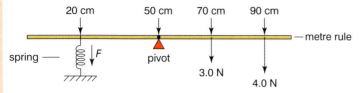

△ Fig. 1.55 The metre rule is balanced.

Use the principle of moments to calculate the tension $F$ in the spring.

Determine the distances of each force from the pivot:

The 3.0 N force is 20 cm from the pivot, the 4.0 N force is 40 cm from the pivot and the force $F$ is 30 cm from the pivot.

Apply the principle of moments:

sum of clockwise moments = sum of anticlockwise moments

$(3.0 \times 20) + (4.0 \times 40) = F \times 30$

Now solve, and determine $F$:

$220 = 30F$

$F = \dfrac{220}{30}$

$F = 7.3$ N

The tension in the spring is 7.3 N.

### An experiment to verify the principle of moments

**1.** Drill a hole at the 50 cm mark of a metre ruler.

**2.** Support the ruler on a pivot through the drilled hole.

**3.** Using two loops of thread and two mass hangers and some slotted masses, suspend different weights, $W_1$ and $W_2$, at different distances, $a$ and $b$, from the pivot. Carefully adjust the distances $a$ and $b$ until the ruler balances horizontally.

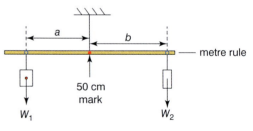

△ Fig. 1.56 An experiment to verify the principle of moments.

**4.** Record the values of $W_1$, $W_2$, $a$ and $b$.

**5.** Repeat stages 3 and 4 several times, with different values of $W_1$, $W_2$, $a$ and $b$.

**6.** For each set of results, calculate $(W_1 \times a)$ and $(W_2 \times b)$.

You will find that, within the limits of experimental accuracy, $(W_1 \times a)$ and $(W_2 \times b)$ will be equal for each set of readings.

| $W_1$/N | $W_2$/N | $a$/cm | $b$/cm | $(W_1 \times a)$/Ncm | $(W_2 \times b)$/Ncm |
|---|---|---|---|---|---|
| 0.5 | 1.0 | 41.6 | 20.4 | 20.8 | 20.4 |
| 1.5 | 1.0 | 25.7 | 38.8 | 38.6 | 38.8 |
| 1.5 | 0.5 | 15.8 | 47.8 | 23.7 | 23.9 |
| 2.0 | 2.5 | 44.4 | 35.4 | 88.8 | 88.5 |

You will see that for each set of readings, the last two columns are equal, within the limits of the accuracy of the experiment. So the results verify the principle of moments.

## QUESTIONS

1. State two things that moment of a force depends on.

2. Calculate the moment when a force of 4.0 N is 0.50 m from the pivot.

3. Calculate the moment when a force of 5.0 N is 0.25 m from a pivot.

4. A force of 4.0 N produces a moment of 1.6 N m about a pivot. Calculate how far is it from the pivot.

5. Two children are sitting on a see-saw. The child to the left of the pivot is sitting $x$ m from the pivot and has a weight of 400 N. The child on the right of the pivot is sitting 2.0 m from the pivot and has a weight of 300 N. Calculate the distance $x$.

### CENTRE OF GRAVITY AND STABILITY

When considering the motion of objects, it is useful to be able to make some assumptions. One assumption is that all the weight of the body appears to act at one point, which we call the **centre of gravity**. This is a useful simplification because we can assume that gravity only acts at a single point in the object, so a single arrow on a diagram can represent the weight of an object.

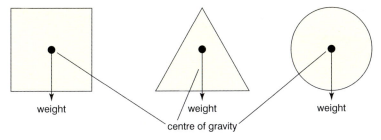

weight    weight    weight

centre of gravity

Δ Fig. 1.57 The centre of gravity for objects with a regular shape is in the centre.

To find the centre of gravity of simple objects, such as a piece of card (plane lamina), follow these steps:

**1.** Hang the object from a point close to its edge.

**2.** Suspend a mass attached to a thread (plumb-line) from the same point.

**3.** Mark the position of the thread on the card.

**4.** The centre of gravity is somewhere along the line of the thread.

**5.** Repeat steps 1 to 3 with the object suspended from different points.

**6.** The centre of gravity is where the two lines meet.

The idea of centre of gravity is useful when predicting whether or not an object will fall over – whether or not it is stable.

When displaced, the conical object shown in Fig. 1.59 will fall back onto its base because the weight is to the left of the pivoting edge of the cone. The moment of the force produced by its weight returns the object to its base. An object that is difficult to topple is said to be in stable equilibrium.

The object in Fig. 1.60 will topple over because of the clockwise moment created by the weight about the pivot. This object is not in stable equilibrium.

When the object in Fig. 1.61 is displaced it will move to a new, similar position. It is in neutral equilibrium.

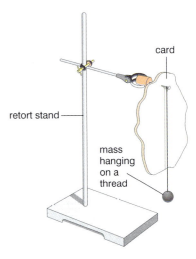

△ Fig. 1.58 Finding the centre of gravity of a plane object.

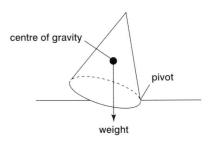

△ Fig. 1.59 This conical object will not topple when released from this position.

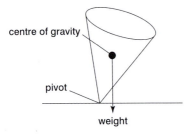

△ Fig. 1.60 This object is not stable.

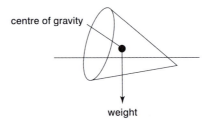

△ Fig. 1.61 This object is in neutral equilibrium.

**SCIENCE IN CONTEXT**

## CENTRE OF GRAVITY AND FLYING

The concept of centre of gravity is important in determining whether or not an aircraft is safe to fly. For an aircraft to be safe, its centre of gravity must fall within limits that are set by the manufacturer. The area between these limits is called the CG range for the aircraft. The centre of gravity needs to be calculated before each flight and, if it is not within the CG range, weight must be removed, added (which is rare) or redistributed until the centre of gravity falls within the range.

within the aircraft. The weights of fixed parts of the aircraft, such as engines and wings, do not change and are provided by the manufacturer. The manufacturer will also provide information about the effect of different fuel loads. The operator is responsible for allowing for removable weight such as passengers, crew and luggage, in the calculation.

Δ Fig. 1.62 An aeroplane taking off.

All aircraft have a maximum weight for flight. If this maximum is exceeded, then the aircraft may not be able to fly in a controlled, level flight. It may be impossible to take off with a given length of runway. Excess weight may make it impossible to climb beyond a particular altitude (so the aircraft may not be able to take its proper course determined by air traffic control).

**Challenge Question:** Why would it would not be sensible for all the passengers in a half-empty aeroplane to sit just at the back, or just at the front?

## QUESTIONS

1. What is the centre of gravity of an object?

2. Explain why a vase of flowers is less likely to fall over if it has a wide and heavy base.

# End of topic checklist

## Key terms

centre of gravity, elastic, extension, friction (drag), moment, principle of moments,

**SUPPLEMENT** acceleration, limit of proportionality, resultant force, spring constant

## During your study of this topic you should have learned:

○ Forces may produce changes in the size and shape of an object.

○ Know how to sketch, plot and interpret load–extension graphs for an elastic solid (e.g. metal wire) and be able to describe the any experimental procedures.

○ Know how to determine the resultant of two or more forces acting along the same straight line.

○ Know that an object either remains at rest (stationary) or continues in a straight line at constant speed unless acted on by a resultant force

○ A resultant force may change the velocity of an object by changing its direction of motion or its speed.

○ Solid friction is the force between two surfaces that may impede motion and produce heating.

○ Friction (drag) acts on an object moving through a liquid or a gas (air resistance).

○ Moment of a force as a measure of its turning effect.

○ Moment of a force is defined as: moment = force × perpendicular distance from the pivot.

○ Apply the principle of moments to situations with one force each side of the pivot, including balancing of a beam.

○ When there is no resultant force and no resultant moment, an object is in equilibrium.

○ The centre of gravity of an object is where its weight appears to act.

○ Describe an experiment to determine the position of the centre of gravity of an irregularly shaped plane lamina.

○ Know that the stability of an object depends on the position of the centre of gravity.

○ **SUPPLEMENT** Spring constant is defined as force per unit extension.

○ **SUPPLEMENT** Recall and use the equation $k = \dfrac{F}{x}$.

○ **SUPPLEMENT** The 'limit of proportionality' is a point on a load–extension graph beyond which the graph is no longer a straight line.

○ **SUPPLEMENT** Recall and use the equation $F = ma$ and know that the force and acceleration are in the same direction.

○ **SUPPLEMENT** Describe the motion in a circular path due to a force perpendicular to the motion.

○ **SUPPLEMENT** In circular motion, speed increases when the force increases (mass and radius are constants).

○ **SUPPLEMENT** In circular motion, radius decreases when the force increases (mass and speed are constants).

○ **SUPPLEMENT** In circular motion, an increased mass requires an increased force to keep speed and radius constant.

○ **SUPPLEMENT** Apply the principle of moments in situations with more than one force each side of the pivot.

○ **SUPPLEMENT** Describe an experiment to demonstrate that there is no resultant moment on an object in equilibrium.

# End of topic questions

*Note: the marks in brackets give an indication of the level of detail you should include in your answers.*

**1.** A student performed an experiment stretching a spring. She loaded masses onto the spring and measured its extension. Here are her results.

| Extension/cm | 0 | 4.0 | 8.9 | 12.0 | 16.0 | 20.0 | 24.0 |
|---|---|---|---|---|---|---|---|
| Load/N | 0 | 2.0 | 4.0 | 6.0 | 7.5 | 8.3 | 8.6 |

**a)** On graph paper, plot a graph of load (vertical axis) against extension (horizontal axis). Draw a suitable line through your points. *(3 marks)*

**b) SUPPLEMENT** Mark on the graph the limit of proportionality, and indicate the region where proportional behaviour occurs and the region where the behaviour is not elastic. *(3 marks)*

**c) SUPPLEMENT** How does she check whether the spring, after being loaded with 8.6 N, remains elastic? *(1 mark)*

**2. SUPPLEMENT** The manufacturer of a car gave the following information:

Mass of car: 1000 kg. The car will accelerate from 0 to 30 m/s in 12 s.

**a)** Calculate the acceleration of the car during the 12 s. *(2 marks)*

**b)** Calculate the force needed to produce this acceleration. *(2 marks)*

**3. a)** State two things that may change for an object experiencing a non-zero resultant force. *(2 marks)*

**b)** An object of weight 4.8 N is falling through sea-water. It experiences friction (drag) of 3.0 N. Calculate the resultant force on the object. *(2 marks)*

**c)** Which of the following statements about the effect of friction is always true?

    **A** It changes the shape of an object.

    **B** It generates an electrical current.

    **C** It produces heat.

    **D** It produces magnetism. *(1 mark)*

**d) SUPPLEMENT** The ship has a mass of 500 tonnes (1 tonne = 1000 kg).

    **i)** Calculate the acceleration of the ship. *(2 marks)*

    **ii)** Calculate the speed of the ship after 10 s. *(2 marks)*

**4.** Which of these containers is the most stable? Explain your answer. (2 marks)

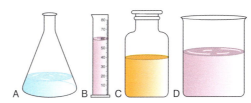

**5. SUPPLEMENT** A truck is going round a roundabout. The centripetal force is provided by the friction between the tyres and the road. State the effect on this centripetal force when

**a)** the speed of the truck increases (1 mark)

**b)** the mass of the truck decreases when the load it is carrying falls off. (1 mark)

**6.** For each figure shown below, the metre rule is balanced horizontally and pivoted at the 50.0 cm mark, calculate the force $F$.

**a)**

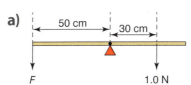

**b) SUPPLEMENT**

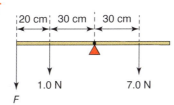

# Momentum

### INTRODUCTION

Momentum is a measure of how difficult it is to change the motion of an object. Momentum is useful in analysing the motion of objects. It is defined by the equation:

momentum = mass × velocity

$p = mv$

$m$ = mass in kg        $v$ = velocity in m/s

Momentum $p$ is usually measured in kg m/s.

Momentum is a vector quantity because velocity is a vector. The directions of momentum and velocity are the same.

### KNOWLEDGE CHECK

✓ Mass and velocity.
✓ Know the equation $F = ma$

### LEARNING OBJECTIVES

✓ **SUPPLEMENT** Define momentum as mass × velocity; recall and use the equation $p = mv$.
✓ **SUPPLEMENT** Define impulse as force × time for which force acts; recall and use the equation impulse = $F\Delta t = \Delta(mv)$.
✓ **SUPPLEMENT** Apply the principle of the conservation of momentum to solve simple problems in one dimension.
✓ **SUPPLEMENT** Define resultant force as the change in momentum per unit time; recall and use the equation
$F = \dfrac{\Delta p}{\Delta t}$ .

### UNDERSTANDING MOMENTUM

All moving objects will have momentum. The magnitude of this momentum will depend on the mass of the object and its velocity. A speck of dust hurtling through space at 1000 km/s can have the same momentum as a car moving at 10 m/s.

### WORKED EXAMPLE

Calculate the momentum of a racing car of mass 600 kg travelling at 75 m/s.

Write down the equation:                                   momentum = mass × velocity

Substitute the values for $m$ and $v$:                    $p = 600 \times 75$

Work out the answer and write down the units:            momentum = 45 000 kg m/s

## QUESTIONS

1. Calculate the momentum of a 58 g tennis ball travelling at 40 m/s.

2. Calculate the momentum of a 2000 kg car travelling at 25 m/s.

3. Calculate the mass of a car that is travelling at 20 m/s and has a momentum of 20 000 kg m/s.

4. Calculate the velocity of a car that has a mass of 1500 kg and a momentum of 37 500 kg m/s.

### CHANGING MOMENTUM

In practical applications, such as safety in cars, we are interested in the change in momentum. Since velocity is a vector quantity, momentum is also a vector quantity and has a direction. When working out problems, one direction is taken as the positive direction, for example, going to the right, with the opposite direction taken as the negative direction, for example, going to the left. The ball hitting a wall as shown in Figure 1.63 will have a positive momentum before it hits the wall and a negative momentum after it hits the wall.

The momentum of an object will change when its:

- mass changes
- velocity changes
- direction of travel changes.

The momentum of an object changes when a force acts on it. Fig. 1.63 shows an objects bouncing off a wall at the same speed. Its initial momentum is +$mv$ and its final momentum is −$mv$.

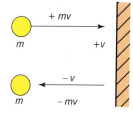

△ Fig. 1.63 Momentum before and after collision with a wall.

### Resultant force and momentum

The resultant force acting on an object is defined as the change in momentum per unit time. This definition is often known as Newton's second law of motion. You can use the following equation to calculate the resultant force $F$:

$$F = \frac{\Delta p}{\Delta t}$$

Where $\Delta p$ is the change in momentum and $\Delta t$ is the change in time. Remember the Greek delta $\Delta$ symbol is to show 'change in ...'. This equation can also be written as:

$$F = \frac{\Delta(mv)}{\Delta t}$$

Earlier, in section 1.5, we used the equation $F = ma$ to calculate the resultant force. We can show that these two equations are the same when the mass $m$ of the object remains the same. See the worked example below.

The change in momentum, $\Delta p$ or $\Delta(mv)$, can be calculated by rearranging the equation above:

$$\Delta(mv) = F\Delta t$$

The **impulse** of a force is defined as the product of the force $F$ and the change in time $\Delta t$. Therefore we have:

$$\text{impulse} = F\Delta t = \Delta(mv)$$

Impulse has the units N s, and change in momentum has units kg m/s. They are equivalent. For example, if the momentum of a car changes by 4000 kg m/s, then the impulse of the force acting on the car must be 4000 N s. If the force acts for a time of 2.0 s, then the force causing the change of momentum must be 2000 N.

## WORKED EXAMPLE

A 1000 kg car is initially at rest. The speed of the car is 6.0 m/s after 2.0 s.

Calculate the resultant force acting on the car.

**Method 1:** Using $F = \dfrac{\Delta p}{\Delta t}$

Determine the change in momentum:  $\Delta p = (1000 \times 6.0) - (1000 \times 0)$
$$= 6000 \text{ kg m/s}$$

Substitute the values into the equation:  $F = \dfrac{6000}{2.0}$

Calculate the force and give the units:  $F = 3000$ N

**Method 2:** Using $F = ma$

Determine the acceleration using $a = \dfrac{\Delta v}{\Delta t}$  $a = \dfrac{6.0 - 0}{2.0} = 3.0$ m/s$^2$

Substitute the values into the equation:  $F = 1000 \times 3.0$

Calculate the force and give the units:  $F = 3000$ N

As mentioned earlier, both methods give the same answer.

The equation $F = \dfrac{\Delta p}{\Delta t}$ helps to illustrate two important ideas:

**1.** For a particular force, there is a greater change in momentum if the force acts for a longer time.

For example, a footballer who follows through when kicking (continues the movement of the leg after making contact with the ball) makes contact with the ball for longer, so there is a greater change in the ball's momentum and the ball flies faster.

**2.** For a particular change in momentum, the longer the change takes, the smaller the force will be.

For example, when a parachutist lands, he bends his knees. This makes the momentum change take a longer time, so the force on the parachutist is smaller. This is also very important in car safety features such as crumple zones – the car is designed to crumple on impact, which makes the momentum change take place over a longer time and reduces the forces on the people in the car.

## Conservation of momentum

In any collision, the total momentum before the collision is the same as the total momentum after the collision. This is called the **principle of conservation of momentum** and is explored in the two worked examples below. It is worth pointing out that this principle applies to all collisions – cars bumping into each other, gas atoms colliding with the walls of a container, a ball being hit by a bat, colliding stars and galaxies in space, and the list goes on.

## WORKED EXAMPLES

**1.** In an experiment, a 2.0 kg trolley travelling at 0.5m/s crashes into, and sticks to, a 3.0 kg trolley that is stationary before the crash. Calculate the velocity $v$ of the pair after the crash.

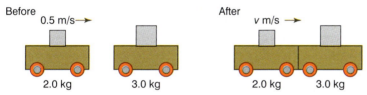

△ Fig. 1.64 Lab trolleys before and after collision.

Use the principle of conservation of momentum.

total momentum before collision = total momentum after collision

$(2.0 \times 0.5) + (3.0 \times 0) = (5.0 \times v)$

$1.0 + 0 = 5.0v$

final velocity $v = 0.2$ m/s

The direction of the final velocity is to the right – the same as the direction of the initial momentum.

**2.** Two cars collide head-on as shown in the diagram. After the collision both cars are stationary. Calculate the velocity $v$ of the 750 kg car before the collision.

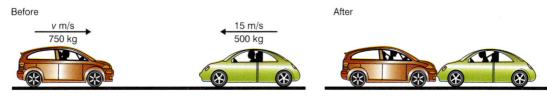

△ Fig. 1.65 Cars before and after collision. The car moving to the right has positive momentum and the car moving to the left has negative momentum.

Use the principle of conservation of momentum. Momentum is a vector quantity – it also has direction. The direction to the right is taken as being positive.

total momentum before collision = total momentum after collision

$(750 \times v) + (500 \times -15) = (750 \times 0) + (500 \times 0)$

$750v - 7500 = 0$

$750v = 7500$

$v = 10$ m/s

---

**SEAT BELTS AND CAR SAFETY**

Momentum changes can be important when considering safety features in cars, such as seat belts. When a vehicle stops suddenly, its passengers tend to keep going until something stops them. Without seat belts, they may stop very suddenly

Δ Fig. 1.66 Seat belts are designed to prevent people in vehicles from continuing to move forwards in the vehicle.

when they hit the windscreen or a passenger in front of them. The seat belt applies a force in the opposite direction to the direction of motion of the vehicle.

Seat belts are designed to stretch a little during a crash. If they did not, they would hold the person in place too strongly, which would make the person stop too quickly and increase the forces. As the seat belt stretches, the momentum change is spread over a longer period of time, which reduces the force experienced by the person. However, because of this stretching, seat belts should be replaced after a collision, since the material will not be able to stretch again in a subsequent accident, so damaged seat belts could cause further injury.

**Challenge Question:** Explain, in terms of the equation $F\Delta t = \Delta(mv)$, why a seat belt must not stop a driver too abruptly.

## QUESTIONS

1. Define momentum. Is it a scalar quantity or a vector quantity?

2. Use ideas about change in momentum to explain why a parachutist should bend their knees when they land.

3. Consider two lab trolleys. Both have a mass of 1.0 kg. The first trolley has a velocity of 5.0 m/s and the second trolley is stationary before the collision. They collide and move off together after the collision as shown in the diagram.

   What is the velocity *v* of the two trolleys after the collision?

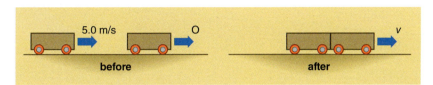

4. A skater of mass 60 kg moving at 6.0 m/s collides with, and holds on to, another stationary skater of mass 30 kg. The pair move off at a velocity *v*. Calculate *v*.

5. A sports car of mass 1000 kg collides with a stationary lorry of mass 3000 kg. They move off together with a velocity of 25 m/s.

   a) Calculate the momentum of the vehicles after the collision.

   b) Calculate the momentum of the vehicles just before the collision.

   c) Calculate the speed of the sports car just before the collision.

# End of topic checklist

## Key terms

principle of conservation of momentum

**SUPPLEMENT** impulse, momentum

## During your study of this topic you should have learned:

◯ Momentum is defined as mass × velocity.

◯ The equation for momentum is $p = mv$.

◯ Impulse of a force is defined as force × time for which force acts:

impulse $= F\Delta t = \Delta(mv)$

◯ Know about the principle of the conservation of momentum.

◯ Resultant force is defined as the change in momentum per unit time:

$$F = \frac{\Delta p}{\Delta t}$$

# End of topic questions

1. A car of mass 500 kg accelerates from 15 m/s to 30 m/s.

   a) Calculate the change in momentum of the car. (1 mark)

   b) If the car takes 5.0 seconds to make this change, calculate the resultant force required. (1 mark)

   c) The actual force provided by the car engine will be larger than the value calculated in part b). Suggest why. (1 mark)

2. Jack is standing on a stationary skateboard. When he steps off the skateboard forwards the skateboard moves backwards. Use the principle of conservation of momentum to explain why this happens. (2 marks)

3. What is the correct expression for the impulse of a force?

   A  impulse = force × time

   B  impulse = kg m/s

   C  impulse = momentum

   D  impulse = N s (1 mark)

△ Fig. 1.67 These moving trams have kinetic energy.

# Energy, work and power

## INTRODUCTION

We tend to use the words energy and **power** as if they were the same. On the news you may hear about a powerful leader, or have a feeling that you have the energy to do your homework. However, to a physicist they each have a very precise meaning. Energy comes in different 'stores'. One of these stores will be familiar to you, and that is **kinetic energy**. A moving object has kinetic energy, which depends on its mass and speed. As you run, you have kinetic energy. When you stop, all this energy is transferred to the ground and your shoes thanks to friction. Forces help to transfer energy between stores. These ideas, and many others, are explored in this topic.

## KNOWLEDGE CHECK

✓ Some everyday uses of energy.
✓ Describe devices that transfer energy from one store to another.

## LEARNING OBJECTIVES

✓ State that energy may be stored as kinetic, gravitational potential, chemical, elastic (strain), nuclear, electrostatic and internal (thermal).
✓ Describe how energy is transferred between stores during events and processes, including examples of transfer by forces (mechanical work done), electrical currents (electrical work done), heating, and by electromagnetic, sound and other waves.
✓ Know the principle of the conservation of energy and apply this principle to simple examples including the interpretation of simple flow diagrams.
✓ **SUPPLEMENT** Recall and use the equation for kinetic energy

$E_k = \frac{1}{2}mv^2$

✓ **SUPPLEMENT** Recall and use the equation for the change in gravitational potential energy $\Delta E_p = mg\Delta h$

✓ **SUPPLEMENT** Know the principle of the conservation of energy and apply this principle to complex examples involving multiple stages, including the interpretation of Sankey diagrams.

✓ Understand that mechanical or electrical work done is equal to the energy transferred.
✓ Recall and use the equation for mechanical working
$W = Fd = \Delta E$

✓ Describe how useful energy may be obtained, or electrical power generated, from: chemical energy stored in fossil fuels, chemical energy stored in biofuels, water, including the energy stored in waves, in tides, and in water behind hydroelectric dams, geothermal resources, nuclear fuel, light from the Sun to generate electrical power (solar cells), and infrared and other electromagnetic waves from the Sun to heat water (solar panels) and be the source of wind energy, including references to a boiler, turbine and generator where they are used.

✓ Describe advantages and disadvantages of each method in terms of renewability, availability, reliability, scale and environmental impact.

✓ Understand, qualitatively, the concept of efficiency of energy transfer.

✓ **SUPPLEMENT** Know that radiation from the Sun is the main source of energy for all our energy resources except geothermal, nuclear and tidal.

✓ **SUPPLEMENT** Know that energy is released by nuclear fusion in the Sun.

✓ **SUPPLEMENT** Know that research is being carried out to investigate how energy released by nuclear fusion can be used to produce electrical energy on a large scale.

✓ **SUPPLEMENT** Define efficiency as:

$$(\%) \text{ efficiency} = \frac{\text{(useful energy output)}}{\text{(total energy input)}} (\times 100\%)$$

$$(\%) \text{ efficiency} = \frac{\text{(useful power output)}}{\text{(total power input)}} (\times 100\%)$$

recall and use these equations.

✓ Define power as work done per unit time and also as energy transferred per unit time; recall and use the equations

(a) $P = \dfrac{W}{t}$

(b) $P = \dfrac{\Delta E}{t}$

## ENERGY STORES

There are many stores of energy. Energy may be stored as kinetic, gravitational potential, chemical, elastic (strain), nuclear, electrostatic and internal (thermal).

Table 1.9 shows some examples of energy stores.

| Energy store | Description | Some examples |
|---|---|---|
| Kinetic | The energy stored by a moving object. Faster moving objects have greater kinetic energy. | Runners, moving cars and planets orbiting the Sun. |
| Gravitational potential | The energy stored by an object due to its height or position. The higher an object is above ground, the greater is this energy. | Bird flying, person in a tall building, a cuckoo clock (see Fig. 1.68) and an aeroplane in the sky. |

| Chemical | The energy stored in chemical bonds, such as those between atoms and molecules. | Electrical battery, muscles, petrol and food. |
|---|---|---|
| Elastic (strain) | The energy stored when an object is squashed or stretched. | An extended rubber band, a compressed spring (see Fig. 1.69) and a blown-up balloon. |
| Nuclear | The energy stored in the nucleus of an atom. | Nuclear power station and glowing stars. |
| Electrostatic | The energy stored when like charges are moved closer or unlike charges are moved further apart. | Thunderclouds and particle accelerators. |
| Internal (thermal). | The total kinetic and potential energy of the atoms (or molecules) of an object. Hotter objects have greater internal, or thermal, energy. | A hot cup of coffee, fires and warm human bodies. |

Δ Table 1.9 Examples of energy stores.

◁ Fig. 1.68 This cuckoo clock stores gravitational potential energy in two weights.

## ENERGY TRANSFERS

Energy can exist in different types of stores. According to the **principle of conservation of energy**, energy cannot be created, or destroyed. It can be transferred, dissipated or just stored in different ways.

Energy can remain in the same store for millions of years, or just for fraction of a second. For example, the **chemical energy** stored in coal has been there for millions of years. Once dug out and burned, this stored energy can be transferred to internal (thermal) energy by burning the coal. Energy is transferred between stores in this process.

For a swinging pendulum, **gravitational potential energy** is transferred into kinetic energy, then this kinetic energy is transferred back into gravitational potential energy, and then the cycle is repeated again. In Fig. 1.70, the pendulum bob has greatest amount of stored gravitational potential energy at positions A and C. At these positions there is no kinetic energy since the pendulum bob is stationary. At position B, the pendulum bob is moving at maximum speed and has the greatest kinetic energy. Energy is transferred between stores in this swinging pendulum.

Δ Fig. 1.69 The spring in this vehicle suspension system has elastic (strain) energy.

Energy is transferred between stores by one of the four types of energy transfers:

- Mechanical **work done** – This is when a force moves an object through a distance.
- Electrical work done – This is when **charges** move (electrical current) due to a **potential difference**.
- Heating – This is due to temperature difference caused either electrically or by chemical reaction.
- Waves – This is due to electromagnetic **radiation**, sound or other waves.

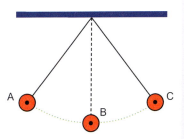

Δ Fig. 1.70 Energy changes in the swing of a pendulum.

The idea of 'work done' is linked to energy transferred by forces, and this is explored later.

### Energy flow diagram

Diagrams are used in physics to show how energy is transferred from one store to another. The energy flow diagram in Fig. 1.71 is for a parachutist falling through the air.

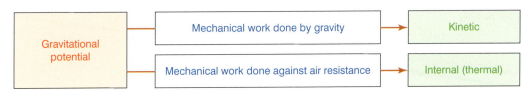

Δ Fig. 1.71 A simple energy flow diagram.

The parachutist has gravitational potential energy and this is transferred to kinetic energy as the speed increases because of mechanical work done by the Earth's gravitational pull. Mechanical work is also done against air resistance, so some energy is also transferred to internal (thermal) energy. The temperature of the air and parachutist will increase.

Fig. 1.72 shows another way to show the flow of energy between stores. This is called a Sankey diagram. On a **Sankey diagram** the energy of each store is shown as numbers, and the width of the arrow is drawn to scale. This makes them useful and easy to interpret.

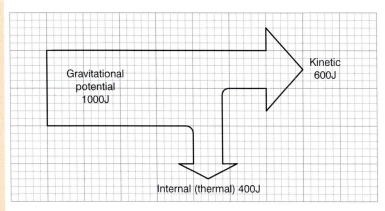

△ Fig. 1.72 Sankey diagram for a falling parachutist.

## QUESTIONS

1. Name any four energy stores.

2. Two runners with the same mass are running at different speeds. Explain which runner has the greater kinetic energy.

3. A falling apple gains kinetic energy. State what causes this energy transfer.

4. SUPPLEMENT Use Fig. 1.72 to determine the percentage of gravitational potential energy transferred to kinetic energy.

### Gravitational potential and kinetic energies

All moving objects have energy stored as **kinetic energy** $E_k$. Kinetic energy depends on the mass $m$ of the object and its speed $v$, and is given by the equation:

$$E_k = \frac{1}{2}mv^2$$

Kinetic energy is measured in **joules** (J), mass is in kg and speed is in m/s.

Any object above the surface of the Earth has energy stored as gravitational potential energy $E_p$. Gravitational potential energy depends on the mass $m$ of the object, its height $h$ above the ground and the acceleration of free fall $g$ which is taken as 9.8 m/s². In physics we often need to know the change in the gravitational potential energy $\Delta E_p$ as an object moves between two positions or heights: for example, a falling apple, a descending parachutist and lifting books onto a shelf. (Remember that the Greek letter delta $\Delta$ is used to mean 'change in …'). The equation for the gravitational potential energy is:

$$\Delta E_p = mg\Delta h$$

Gravitational potential energy is also measured in joules (J), mass is in kg and the change in height $\Delta h$ is in m.

## WORKED EXAMPLE

A skier has a mass of 70 kg and travels up in a ski-lift a vertical height of 300 m. Calculate the change in the skier's gravitational potential energy.

Write down the equation: $\Delta E_p = m\,g\,\Delta h$

Substitute values for $m$, $g$ and $h$: $\Delta E_p = 70 \times 9.8 \times 300$

Work out the answer and write
down the unit: $\Delta E_p = 205\ 800$ J or about 210 kJ

## WORKED EXAMPLE

An ice skater has a mass of 50 kg and travels at a speed of 5.0 m/s. Calculate the ice skater's kinetic energy.

Write down the equation: $E_k = \frac{1}{2}mv^2$

Substitute the values for $m$ and $v$: $E_k = \frac{1}{2} \times 50 \times 5.0^2$

Work out the answer and write down the unit: $E_k = 625$ J

## QUESTIONS

1. Calculate the gravitational potential energy gained when a 5.0 kg mass is lifted through a vertical distance of 2.0 m.

2. Calculate the kinetic energy of a 2.0 kg ball rolling at 2.0 m/s.

# ENERGY AND THE EARTH

Energy and matter are constantly interacting on our planet. Part of this interaction produces volcanoes, glaciers, mountain ranges, oceans and continents. The energy comes from two sources: electromagnetic radiation from the Sun, which keeps the oceans and the atmospheric cycles (such as the water cycle) going; and the **internal energy**, which comes from **radioactive decay** in the Earth's core and is the driving force behind plate tectonics.

**Challenge Question:** The Sun emits an enormous amount of radiant power – about $4 \times 10^{26}$ W. Why does the Earth only receive a fraction of this power?

△ Fig. 1.73 The natural world is full of examples of energy stores thanks to the presence of the Sun. This majestic waterfall has kinetic and gravitational potential stores thanks to the Sun.

## SUPPLEMENT

You can use the principle of the conservation of energy to calculate what happens when energy is transferred from a kinetic to a gravitational store.

As long as negligible energy is transferred to other stores $mg\Delta h = \frac{1}{2} mv^2$.

## WORKED EXAMPLE

A stone is thrown vertically upwards and reaches a height of 6.0 m above the hand of the thrower. What speed was the stone travelling at when it left the person's hand?

decrease in kinetic energy of the stone as it rises = the increase in the gravitational potential energy of the stone

At the top of the flight, the stone is stationary, so it has zero kinetic energy.

Write down the equation: $\frac{1}{2}mv^2 = mg\Delta h$

$$\frac{1}{2}v^2 = g\Delta h$$

Note that the mass has cancelled out; the mass does not matter in this case.

Substitute values for $g$ and $h$: $v^2 = 2\,g\Delta h$
$$= 2 \times 9.8 \times 6.0$$
$$= 117.6$$

Work out the answer and write down the unit:
$$v = \sqrt{117.6}$$
$$= 10.8 \text{ m/s}$$

△ Fig. 1.74 The path of a stone when it is thrown.

The kinetic energy given to the stone when it is thrown is transferred to gravitational potential energy as it gains height and slows down. At the top of its flight a large part of the kinetic energy will have been transferred to stored gravitational potential energy. A small amount is stored as internal (thermal) energy because of work done against air resistance. The stone and the air become slightly warmer.

## ENERGY RESOURCES

### Fossil fuels

Most of the energy we use is obtained from **fossil fuels** – coal, oil and natural gas. Chemical energy is stored in fossil fuels.

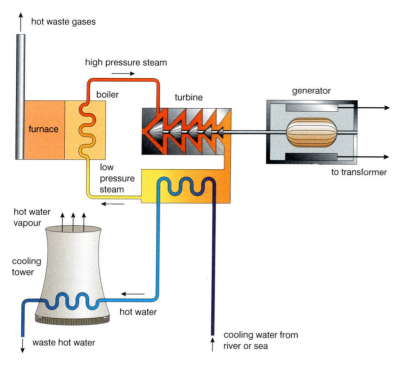

△ Fig. 1.75 How a power station works. The most common fuels used in power stations are coal, oil and gas.

Many power stations use fossil fuels (coal, oil, natural gas) to produce electricity that is supplied to homes and factories. Other power stations burn alternative fuels to produce this electricity, but the basic method of producing power is generally the same:

- Fuel is burned and steam is produced in a boiler.
- The steam turns a **turbine**.
- The turbine drives a generator.
- The generator produces electricity.
- The electricity is supplied to homes, industry, etc.

Once supplies of fossil fuels have been used up they cannot be replaced – they are **non-renewable**. At current levels of use, oil and gas supplies will probably last for about another 40 years, and coal supplies for no more than a few hundred years from now. The development of **renewable** sources of energy is therefore becoming increasingly important.

The biggest advantage of using fossil fuels at present is that they are relatively cheap, but with dwindling supplies in the future, this may not always be the case. Fossil fuels are non-renewable energy resources – they will eventually run out. The major disadvantage of using fossil fuels such as coal and oil, is that they release sulfur dioxide and carbon dioxide when burned. Sulfur dioxide contributes to acid rain and can cause breathing problems for all living creatures, including us humans. Carbon dioxide from burning fossil fuels increases the levels of carbon in our atmosphere, which may contribute to the greenhouse effect and make the Earth hotter in years to come.

### Biofuels

**Biofuels** are produced from natural products – often plants or food waste. Just as in fossil fuels, chemical energy is stored in biofuels. The major difference is that plants are a renewable source of energy, and as such, they are not responsible for creating extra carbon that may be the cause of global warming.

Some biofuels are produced by using microorganisms. For example, in some countries such as Brazil and Indonesia, yeast is added to sugar cane, which ferments directly into ethanol. Biodiesel, a fuel for cars, can be made by fermenting sugar and wheat. Biodiesel cannot be easily used in cars without modifications.

Growing plants for biofuels require a lot of land. In some countries, forests are being destroyed to grow plants used for biofuels. This affects many animals that rely on the forest; some species will become extinct with the continuation of deforestation. The major advantages of biofuels are that they are cheap renewable resource, produce less carbon dioxide when burned than absorbed during the growth of the plants and they reduce our dependence of fossil fuels.

## Energy from wind

The wind is used to turn windmill-like turbines that generate electricity directly from the rotating motion of their blades. Modern wind turbines are efficient, but it takes about one thousand of them to produce the same amount of energy as a modern gas, coal or oil-burning power station, and that is only when the wind is blowing favourably. It is worth remembering that the source of wind energy on the Earth is from the electromagnetic waves, mainly infrared, from the Sun. The infrared waves warm up the surface of the Earth, and stir its atmosphere to produce pressure changes and wind.

Wind power is a renewable energy resource. It will be there as long as we have the Sun. There are no polluting gases produced from wind turbines and, also, they require no fuel. Once set up, the wind turbines are very cheap to run. Wind power does have disadvantages – it can be quite expensive to set up a large cluster of wind turbines, the wind turbines can spoil the view (visual pollution) and can be very noisy. We can only get energy from the wind turbines on windy days, so we cannot just rely of them to produce all our energy needs.

Δ Fig. 1.76 On a windy day a very large wind turbine generates 2000 kW of electricity. That's enough to meet the needs of about 1200 homes.

### Developing practical skills

You are going to plan an investigation to evaluate wind power as an energy source. You have the following equipment:

- model wind turbine
- multimeter to measure the voltage generated
- anemometer to measure wind speed
- hair dryer to generate wind power (note: set hair dryer setting to cool)
- metre ruler to measure distance.

### Energy from water

Dams can be used to store water, which is allowed to fall in a controlled way that generates electricity. This is particularly useful in hilly regions for generating hydroelectric power. When demand for electricity is low, surplus electricity can be used to pump water back up into the high dam for use in times of high demand.

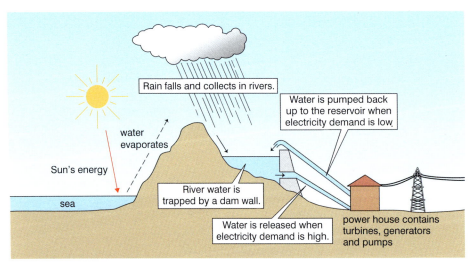

△ Fig. 1.77. Gravitational potential energy is stored by the water behind the dam wall.

The energy stored in waves can be used to move large floats and generate electricity. Similarly, a very large number of floats are needed to produce a significant amount of electricity. It is worth mentioning that the energy stored in waves ultimately comes from the Sun's infrared radiation falling on the surface of the Earth.

◁ Fig. 1.78 A wave generator.

Dams on tidal estuaries trap the water at high tide. When the water is allowed to flow back at low tide, tidal power can be generated. This obviously limits the use of the estuary for shipping and can cause environmental damage along the shoreline.

Water power in all its forms is a renewable energy resource. Thanks to the energy from the electromagnetic waves from the Sun, waves and wind are free – there are no costs for fuel. Unlike burning fossil fuels, there are no polluting gases released into the atmosphere. Water power can be easily switched on depending on the demand. There are some disadvantages of water power – the energy from tidal systems is relatively small, farmland and homes may have to be flooded when setting up hydroelectric dams and the floats used in tidal systems can destroy the habitat of birds and animals, and be a nuisance for fisherman in their boats.

## Energy from the Sun

Solar cells can be used to transfer light energy from the Sun directly into electricity. This electricity can be stored, often in batteries, to be used when convenient. Electricity generated in this way uses a renewable source. These panels are commonly referred to as solar PV (photovoltaic) panels to distinguish them from solar heating panels.

△ Fig. 1.79 Solar (photovoltaic) panels on a roof.

In solar panels, the infrared waves from the Sun are used simply to heat water that is pumped through black pipes in a panel, often on the roof of a house. Heating the water in this way reduces the demand on other energy resources. The energy can be stored in the water as internal (thermal) energy.

The biggest advantage of solar energy is that there are no fuel costs and it's a renewable energy resource. There are no harmful polluting gases produced. Solar cells and solar panels are expensive to set up for the customers, and at present, the cost of the electricity produced is more than from burning fossil fuel. The major disadvantage of solar energy is that it there is no energy produced at night. If night-time energy is required by customers, then expensive backup battery systems have to be installed – the batteries charge up during the day, and release energy at night.

## Geothermal resources

Geothermal power is obtained using the internal (thermal) energy of the Earth. In certain parts of the world, water forms hot springs that can be used directly for heating. Water can also be pumped deep into the ground to be heated.

Geothermal energy is a renewable energy resource – there are no fuel costs. There are no harmful gases produced. Geothermal energy is not available everywhere on the surface of the Earth.

## Nuclear fuel

A nuclear power station uses the heat generated by a controlled fission process to convert water to steam. This drives a turbine as in a conventional power station. Uranium is the most commonly used fuel, but plutonium is also used.

Nuclear fuel produces far more energy per unit mass than fossil fuels. It would take many million kilograms of coal to produce the same energy as a few grams of uranium. Nuclear fuel does not produce any polluting gases such as carbon dioxide. However, a working nuclear power station can produce an abundance of radioactive waste product. Some of the waste material can be radioactive for thousands of years – affecting future generations. Nuclear waste cannot be burned or destroyed. It has to be stored safely, often deep underground and far away from any animals and people. Nuclear power stations are generally safe, but accidents have happened in the past with radioactive material released into the atmosphere. Nuclear power stations simply have to be sited far away from towns and cities.

Δ Fig. 1.80 A nuclear power station in the Czech Republic.

SUPPLEMENT

The Sun releases vast amounts of energy into space from fusion reactions within its core. The Sun is the main source of most of the energy resources available on the Earth.

The electromagnetic radiation from the Sun is responsible for the chemical stores for fossil fuel and in the plants used in biofuels. The Sun's energy is responsible for churning the atmosphere to produce ocean and sea waves and also wind.

Geothermal, nuclear and tidal resources are the only ones not directly linked to the Sun. The tides are produced by the motion of the Moon around the Sun. The internal (thermal) energy stored within the Earth has been there since its creation many billions of years ago and is also the result of radioactive decay.

Scientists have been trying to mimic what the Sun does here on the Earth. There are many projects around the world, where fusion reactions are being used to potentially produce electrical energy on a very large scale. Fig. 1.81 shows one possible fusion reactor known as Tokamak.

△ Fig. 1.81 This fusion reactor (Tokamak) could produce electrical energy in the future.

## QUESTIONS

1. State the energy transfers that take place in a solar cell.

2. What is the energy store in fossil fuels and biofuels?

   **A** kinetic   **B** elastic   **C** thermal   **D** chemical

3. Describe the process used to generate electricity in fossil-fuelled power stations.

4. State the energy store for geothermal resource.

### WORK

**Work** is done when the application of a force results in movement. The amount of work done depends on the magnitude of the force and the distance moved in the direction of the force. Work can only be done when the object or system has energy. When work is done, energy is transferred.

Look at Fig. 1.82. In this position the gymnast is not doing any work against his body weight – he is not moving.

The gymnast in Fig. 1.83 is doing work. He is moving upwards against his weight. Energy is being transferred as he does the work.

△ Fig. 1.82 A gymnast.

△ Fig. 1.83 A gymnast doing work against his own body weight.

The work done can be either electrical or mechanical. Work done is equal to the amount of energy transferred. The equation for mechanical work done is:

work done = force × distance moved in the direction of the force
           = energy transferred

$$W = F \times d = \Delta E$$

Where: $W$ = work done in joules (J)

       $F$ = force in newtons (N)

       $d$ = distance moved in the direction of the force in metres (m)

       $\Delta E$ = energy transferred in joules (J)

1 joule is the energy transferred (or the work done) when a force of 1 newton moves a distance of 1 metre in the direction of the force.

## WORKED EXAMPLES

1. A cyclist pedals along a flat road. He exerts a force of 60 N on the road surface and travels 150 m. Calculate the work done by the cyclist.

   Write down the equation:                     $W = F \times d$

   Substitute the values for $F$ and $d$:      $W = 60 \times 150$

   Work out the answer and write down the unit:   $W = 9000$ J

   It is worth mentioning that the energy transferred is also equal to 9000 J. The store for this energy would be chemical from the food eaten by the cyclist.

2. A person does 3000 J of work in pushing a supermarket trolley 50 m across a level car park. What force was the person exerting on the trolley?

   Write down the equation with $F$ as the subject: $F = \dfrac{W}{d}$

   Substitute the values for $W$ and $d$:         $F = \dfrac{3000}{50}$

   Work out the answer and write down the unit:   $F = 60$ N

When something slows down because of friction, work is done. The kinetic energy of the motion is transferred to internal (thermal) energy as the frictional forces slow down the object. For example, if you are riding your bike and you brake, the kinetic energy from your motion is transferred to internal (thermal) in the brake blocks, and these blocks become very hot as a result of this process.

## QUESTIONS

1. Calculate the work done when a 50 N force moves an object 5.0 m in the direction of the force.

2. Calculate the force required to move an object through a distance of 8.0 by transferring 4000 J of energy.

3. Calculate the work done when a force of 40 N moves a block 2.0 m in the direction of the force.

4. How far does an object move when the force on it is 6.0 N and the work done is 300 J?

5. What force is needed to move a piano a distance of 2.0 m when the work done is 800 J?

6. **SUPPLEMENT** A 1.2 kg book is lifted through a vertical height of 0.90 m. Calculate the work done against gravity.

7. **SUPPLEMENT** A 900 kg car starts from rest. After travelling a distance of 100 m it has a speed 8.0 m/s. Calculate the resultant force acting on the car. (Hint: The work done by the force is equal to the change in the kinetic energy of the car.)

### POWER

There are many situations where it is important to know how *quickly* the energy is being transferred – a kettle is no use if it takes 5 hours to deliver the energy to heat some water. For this we need to introduce the concept of **power**.

A powerful engine in a car can take you up a road to the top of a mountain more quickly than a less-powerful engine. Both engines can do the same amount of work, given enough time, but the powerful engine can do the work more quickly. In the same way, a powerful electric motor on a cooling fan will move the air in the room more quickly; and a 'powerfully built' athlete will, by transferring more kinetic energy to it as it is launched, throw a javelin further.

Power is defined as the work done per unit time or the energy transferred per unit time. The more powerful a machine is, the quicker it does a fixed amount of work or transfers a fixed amount of energy.

Since power is the work done per unit time or the energy transferred by unit time, power can be calculated using the equations:

$$\text{power} = \frac{\text{work done}}{\text{time taken}} = \frac{\text{energy transferred}}{\text{time taken}}$$

$$P = \frac{W}{t} \text{ or } P = \frac{\Delta E}{t}$$

Where: $P$ = power in joules per second or watts (W)

$\Delta E$ = energy transferred in joules (J)

$W$ = work done in joules (J)

$t$ = time taken in seconds (s)

1 **watt** of power is 1 joule of work being done per second.

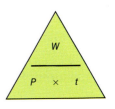

△ Fig. 1.84 The equation triangle for work done, power and time. You can use this triangle to help you rearrange the equation.

## WORKED EXAMPLES

1. The work done by a crane in lifting a girder is 20 000 J in 40 s. Calculate the output power of the motor of the crane.

   Write down the equation: $P = \dfrac{W}{t}$

   Substitute the values for $W$ and $t$: $P = \dfrac{20\ 000}{40}$

   Work out the answer and write down the unit: $P = 500$ W

2. A student with a weight of 600 N runs up the flight of stairs, a vertical distance of 5.0 m, shown in the diagram (right) in 6.0 s. Calculate the student's power.

   Write down the equation for work done: $W = F\,d$

   Substitute the values for $F$ and $d$: $W = 600 \times 5.0 = 3000$ J

   Write down the equation for power: $P = \dfrac{W}{t}$

   Substitute the values for $W$ and $t$: $P = \dfrac{3000}{6.0}$

   Work out the answer and write down the unit:
   $P = 500$ W

△ Fig. 1.85 A student running up a flight of stairs.

### REMEMBER

The student is lifting his body against the force of gravity, which acts in a vertical direction. The distance measured must be in the direction of the force (that is, the vertical height).

1. A man (70 kg) and a boy (35 kg) run up a set of stairs in the same time. Explain why the man is twice as powerful.

2. When a machine is called 'powerful', what does it mean?

3. State the unit of power.

4. Calculate the power of a motor that transfers 1200 J of energy every 5.0 s.

5. a) A crane lifts a mass of 60 kg to a height of 5.0 m. Calculate the work done by the crane.

   b) The crane takes 1.0 minute to do this. Calculate the output power of the crane.

## EFFICIENCY

Energy is always conserved – the total amount of energy after the transfer must be the same as the total amount of energy before the transfer. Unfortunately, in nearly all energy transfers some of the energy will end up as unusable internal (thermal) energy stored within objects or the surrounding air.

### SUPPLEMENT

In a power station only some of the energy originally produced from the fuel is transferred to useful electrical output. **Efficiency** can be calculated from the following equations:

$$\text{efficiency} = \frac{\text{useful energy output}}{\text{total energy input}} \times 100\%$$

or

$$\text{efficiency} = \frac{\text{useful power output}}{\text{total power input}} \times 100\%$$

For example, the electric motor that is used to power a train may take in 10 kW of electricity, and give out 9.5 kW of kinetic energy.

The useful power output is 9.5 kW and the power input is 10 kW.

$$\text{efficiency} = \frac{\text{useful power output}}{\text{total power input}} \times 100\%$$

$$\text{efficiency} = \frac{9.5}{10} \times 100\% = 95\%$$

The efficiency can also be expressed as 0.95, rather than 95%.

The other 5% of energy ends up increasing the temperature of the motor and passes to the surrounding air. This energy is wasted, and the motor may need cooling fans to prevent it from overheating.

A diesel engine is more efficient than a petrol engine, and can give out 200 kJ of kinetic energy from 500 kJ of stored chemical energy of diesel fuel. This equates to an efficiency of 40%. You will note that the engine will have dissipated 300 kJ to internal (thermal) energy – much of it down the exhaust pipe.

In a power station, as much as 70% of the energy transfers may not produce useful energy. This would mean that the power station was only 30% efficient.

Scientists are working hard to increase the efficiency of power stations. Many power stations are now trying to make use of the large amounts of internal (thermal) energy in the hot water produced by power stations. In some cities, the houses of whole regions of the city are heated by hot water from a nearby power station. Some of the most modern fossil-fuelled power stations have efficiencies nearer to 40%. This may not seem much, but if all power stations in the world could use 25% less fuel, it would save millions of tonnes of coal or gas per year.

## Developing practical skills

A student investigates the efficiency of a small electric motor. She uses a motor to lift a mass through a constant distance of 1.0 m. She times how long it takes to lift the masses and makes a record of the potential difference and the current of the motor. The student's data is shown in the table.

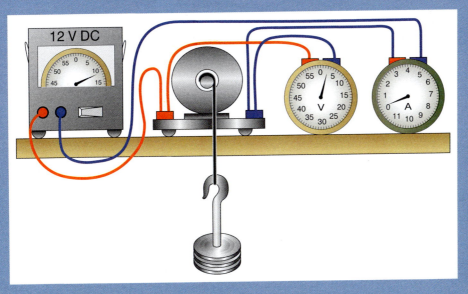

△ Fig. 1.86 Apparatus for the investigation.

| Mass lifted/kg | Distance lifted/m | Useful work done/J | Voltage of motor/V | Current in motor/A | Time to lift the mass/s | Electrical energy supplied/J |
|---|---|---|---|---|---|---|
| 0.01 | 1.0 | | 2.4 | 0.20 | 22.0 | |
| 0.03 | 1.0 | | 2.4 | 0.22 | 24.4 | |
| 0.05 | 1.0 | | 2.4 | 0.25 | 26.5 | |
| 0.07 | 1.0 | | 2.3 | 0.28 | 27.6 | |
| 0.09 | 1.0 | | 2.3 | 0.29 | 28.7 | |

## Planning experiments and investigations

**1.** What quantities would be measured and what measuring instruments would the student need to measure them for this investigation?

**2.** The timer measured to 0.01 s, but the student decided to record values to a precision of 0.1 s. Suggest why she did this. Was the student correct to do this?

## Observing, measuring and recording data

**1.** Copy and complete the table to show the useful energy output and the total energy input. (Take $g$ = 10 N/kg.) The electrical energy supplied can be calculated using the equation: electrical energy = voltage × current × time.

**2.** Use your data to plot a graph of useful energy output ($y$-axis) against total energy input ($x$-axis).

**3.** Describe the pattern (if any) shown by the graph.

## Evaluating methods

**1.** If you were to take more measurements with this equipment, what value(s) of mass would you choose? Explain your answer.

# End of topic checklist

## Key terms

biofuels, boiler, chemical energy, efficiency, elastic (strain) energy, electrostatic energy, internal (thermal) energy, energy, fossil fuels, generator, geothermal resources, gravitational potential energy, heating, hydroelectric dams, kinetic energy, nuclear energy, power, principle of conservation of energy, renewable, solar cells, solar panels, turbine, work done

**SUPPLEMENT** Sankey diagram

## During your study of this topic you should have learned:

○ Energy 'stores' are: kinetic, gravitational potential, chemical, elastic (strain), nuclear, electrostatic and internal (thermal).

○ Energy is transferred between stores during events and processes.

○ Energy is transferred by forces (mechanical work done), electrical currents (electrical work done), heating, and by electromagnetic, sound and other waves.

○ Know the principle of the conservation of energy.

○ Know about simple energy flow diagrams.

○ **SUPPLEMENT** The equation for kinetic energy is: $E_k = \frac{1}{2}mv^2$.

○ **SUPPLEMENT** The equation for change in gravitational potential energy is: $\Delta Ep = mg\Delta h$.

○ **SUPPLEMENT** Know about Sankey diagrams.

○ Mechanical or electrical work done is equal to the energy transferred.

○ The equation for (mechanical) work done is: $W = Fd = \Delta E$

○ Useful energy may be obtained, or electrical power generated, from: fossil fuels, biofuels, water (waves, tides and dams), geothermal resources, nuclear fuel, light from the Sun (solar cells), infrared and other **electromagnetic waves** from the Sun (solar panels) and wind.

○ Know how boilers, turbines and generators are used to generate electricity.

○ Know the advantages and disadvantages of power generation in terms of renewability, availability, reliability, scale and environmental impact.

○ Understand the idea of efficiency.

○ **SUPPLEMENT** Know that radiation from the Sun is the main source of energy for all our energy resources except geothermal, nuclear and tidal.

○ **SUPPLEMENT** Energy is released by nuclear fusion in the Sun.

# End of topic checklist continued

○ **SUPPLEMENT** Know that nuclear fusion can be used to produce electrical energy on a large scale.

○ **SUPPLEMENT** Efficiency is defined by the equations:

$$\text{efficiency} = \frac{(\text{useful energy output})}{(\text{total energy input})} \, (\times\, 100\%) \text{ and}$$

$$\text{efficiency} = \frac{(\text{useful power output})}{(\text{total power input})} \, (\times\, 100\%)$$

○ Power is defined as work done per unit time and also as energy transferred per unit time.

○ The equations for power are: $P = \dfrac{W}{t}$ and $P = \dfrac{\Delta E}{t}$

# End of topic questions

*Note: the marks in brackets give an indication of the level of detail you should include in your answers.*

**1.** What is the unit of work done?

    **A** newton     **B** joule     **C** watt     **D** kilogram     (1 mark)

**2.** A student is carrying out a personal fitness test. She steps on and off the 'step' 200 times. She transfers 30 J of energy each time she steps up. Calculate the energy transferred during the test.     (3 marks)

**3. SUPPLEMENT** A child of mass 35 kg climbed a 30 m high snow-covered hill.

    **a)** Calculate the change in the child's potential gravitational energy.     (3 marks)

    **b)** The child then climbed onto a lightweight sledge and slid down the hill. Calculate the child's maximum speed at the bottom of the hill. (Ignore the mass of the sledge.)     (3 marks)

    **c)** Explain why the actual speed at the bottom of the hill is likely to be less than the value calculated in part **b)**.     (3 marks)

**4.** Use the relationship between the work done, force and distance to complete the table.

| Work done/J | Force/N | Distance/m |
|---|---|---|
| | 100 | 2.0 |
| 750 | | 375 |
| 9 000 | 120 | |
| | 450 | 200 |
| 3 000 | | 30 |
| 60 000 | 150 | |

    (6 marks)

**5. SUPPLEMENT** Calculate the energy transferred when a piano of mass 300 kg lifted through a vertical height of 9.0 m.     (3 marks)

**6. SUPPLEMENT** Calculate the height climbed up a ladder when the person's mass is 70 kg and the gravitational potential energy gained is 2800 J.     (3 marks)

**7. SUPPLEMENT** A 1500 kg helicopter gains gravitational potential energy of 1.35 MJ in climbing from the ground. Calculate its height.     (3 marks)

**8. SUPPLEMENT** Use the relationship between kinetic energy, mass and speed to complete the table.

| Kinetic energy/J | Mass/kg | Speed/m/s |
|---|---|---|
| | 84 | 9.0 |
| 196 | | 1.4 |
| 50 | 1.0 | |
| | 950 | 13 |
| 62 500 | | 250 |
| 6000 | 3000 | |

(6 marks)

9. **SUPPLEMENT** Calculate the kinetic energy of a bird of mass 200 g flying at 6.0 m/s. (3 marks)

10. **SUPPLEMENT** Calculate the speed of a car of mass 1500 kg with a kinetic energy of 450 kJ. (3 marks)

11. **SUPPLEMENT** A skateboarder of mass 60 kg is 3.15 m above ground level travelling at 1.0 m/s. (3 marks)

   a) What is his kinetic energy?

   b) What is the change in the gravitational potential energy of the skateboarder in part a)? (3 marks)

   c) What is the total energy (kinetic + gravitational) of the skateboarder in parts a) and b)? (2 marks)

   d) Assuming that energy is transferred between gravitational potential and kinetic stores in the descent, show that the skateboarder is travelling at about 7.9 m/s on reaching ground level after the descent down the 3.15 m slope. (3 marks)

12. a) What is meant by a non-renewable energy source? (2 marks)

   b) Name three non-renewable energy sources. (2 marks)

   c) Which non-renewable energy source is likely to last the longest? (2 marks)

13. Draw up a table to compare renewable energy resources and non-renewables. Add columns to your table to describe at least one advantage and one disadvantage for each energy resource when it is used to provide large-scale electricity production. (6 marks)

14. Coal-fired power stations and nuclear power stations have environmental impact.

   a) Which of these power stations releases carbon into the atmosphere? (1 mark)

   b) Which of the fuels used in these power stations, will run out first? (1 mark)

15. Power stations need to be located on suitable sites. Suggest three factors that a company may consider before choosing a site for a coal-fired power station. (3 marks)

16. **SUPPLEMENT** The input to an electric motor is 5000 J. 1500 J of the energy is transferred to internal (thermal) energy in the engine and the surrounding air.

**a)** How much energy is usefully transferred? (3 marks)

**b) SUPPLEMENT** What is the efficiency of the motor? (3 marks)

17. **SUPPLEMENT** A fan has 50 J input, 30 J used to spin the fan, 15 J as internal (thermal) energy and 5.0 J as sound. How much energy is not useful? (3 marks)

18. **SUPPLEMENT** Some energy is useful and some energy is wasted in energy transformations. Copy the table and fill in the gaps.

| Object | Input energy/J | Useful energy/J | Wasted energy/J | Efficiency/% |
|---|---|---|---|---|
| Light bulb | 100 | 10 | | |
| Torch | 70 | 55 | | |
| Radio | 250 | 210 | | |

(6 marks)

19. **SUPPLEMENT** State the equation used to calculate efficiency. (2 marks)

20. **SUPPLEMENT** A crane does 650 J of useful work for every 1000 J of energy put in. Calculate its efficiency. (3 marks)

21. **SUPPLEMENT** An engine has 1000 J energy input. It produces 400 J of useful energy. Calculate its efficiency. (3 marks)

22. **SUPPLEMENT** 1000 J is put into a device that is 40% efficient. How much energy is wasted? (3 marks)

23. **SUPPLEMENT** Which is the least efficient of these two engines: a petrol engine that wastes 70 J for every 100 J input, or a steam–diesel hybrid engine that gives 20 J useful energy for every 80 J input? (3 marks)

24. **SUPPLEMENT** Jumana and Maria went up the hill. Jumana's weight is 500 N and Maria's weight is 450 N. Explain who did most work to climb the hill. (3 marks)

25. **SUPPLEMENT** Explain why, however long you have been sitting writing, you have hardly done any mechanical work at all. (3 marks)

26. **SUPPLEMENT** A man pushes a wheelbarrow up a 5.0 m long ramp onto a surface 1.6 m higher than his starting level. The weight of the barrow is 300 N.

**a)** How much work has been done in raising the barrow 1.6 m? (3 marks)

**b)** The force he needed to push the barrow along the ramp is 100 N. How much work did he do? (3 marks)

**c)** Why are the numbers in parts **a)** and **b)** different? (2 marks)

27. **SUPPLEMENT** Peter and Paul walk home from school together up a hill. Peter is heavier than Paul.

**a)** Who does most work? (2 marks)

**b)** Who produces most power? (2 marks)

28. **SUPPLEMENT** A crane takes 10 s to lift a load of 5000 N a vertical distance of 20 m. Calculate the output power of the crane. (4 marks)

29. **SUPPLEMENT** Calculate the work done by a 75 kW tractor in 20 s. (3 marks)

Δ Fig. 1.87 The skis underneath stop the snowmobile from sinking into deep snow.

# Pressure

## INTRODUCTION

A snowmobile can travel over soft snow because its weight is spread over a large area of snow by the skis. If the rider got off and stood on the snow, he would probably sink into it up to his knees, even though he is much lighter than the snowmobile.

If a pair of shoes has narrow heels, the wearer can easily damage a wooden floor by making dents in it. You can push a drawing pin into a soft board using the **pressure** your thumb exerts at the sharp end of the pin.

In this topic you will find out why these things happen. In each case, the question is not just what force is used, but also what area it is spread over.

### KNOWLEDGE CHECK

✓ How to calculate areas of regular shapes, such as squares and rectangles.
✓ How to calculate the volume of regular objects, such as cubes and cylinders.
✓ The concept of force.
✓ The concept of density.

### LEARNING OBJECTIVES

✓ Define pressure as force per unit area; recall and use the equation
  $p = \dfrac{F}{A}$.
✓ Describe how pressure varies with force and area in the context of everyday examples.
✓ Describe, qualitatively, how the pressure beneath the surface of a liquid changes with depth and density of the liquid.

✓ **SUPPLEMENT** Recall and use the equation for the change in pressure beneath the surface of a liquid:
  $\Delta p = \rho g \Delta h$.

## MEASURING PRESSURE

**Pressure** is defined as force per unit area. Where we have a large force over a small area we have a high pressure, and a small force over a large area gives us a low pressure.

Δ Fig. 1.88 When a drawing pin is placed pin-side down, the pressure on the surface is much greater than when it is placed head-side down.

Pressure is measured in newtons per square metre ($N/m^2$), usually called pascals (Pa). So 1 Pa = 1 $N/m^2$.

In order to measure how 'spread out' a force is, use this equation:

$$\text{pressure} = \frac{\text{force}}{\text{area}}$$

$$p = \frac{F}{A}$$

Where: $p$ = pressure in pascals, Pa ($N/m^2$)

$F$ = force in newtons (N)

$A$ = area in m$^2$

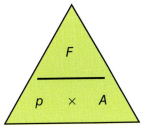

△ Fig. 1.89 the equation triangle for force, pressure and area.

## WORKED EXAMPLE

Calculate the pressure on the snow a snowmobile exerts when it has a weight of 800 N and the runners have an area of 0.20 m$^2$.

Write down the equation: $p = \dfrac{F}{A}$

Confirm that $F$ is in N and $A$ is in m$^2$.

Substitute the values for $F$ and $A$: $p = \dfrac{800}{0.20}$

Work out the answer and write down the units: $p = 4000$ N/m$^2$ or 4.0 kPa

Note that 4.0 kPa is a very low pressure. When you stand on the ground in basketball shoes, the pressure on the ground will be around 20 kPa. The Earth's atmosphere exerts a pressure of about 100 kPa on its surface. This atmospheric pressure is exerted on all objects on the Earth. The wheel of a car generates a pressure on the ground of around 200 kPa. Pressures can be quite high, so the kPa is often used.

## QUESTIONS

1. Explain why you can push a drawing pin into a surface using your thumb but you cannot push your thumb into the same surface.

2. Calculate the pressure exerted by a 100 N force acting on an area of 0.20 m$^2$.

3. A pressure of 40 Pa is exerted over an area of 2.0 m$^2$. Calculate the force involved.

4. A force of 500 N produces a pressure of 640 Pa. Calculate the area this force is spread over.

## Developing practical skills

A student has been reading about how scientists can gain information about the mass of dinosaurs from the depth of their fossilised footprints. He decides to investigate how far a wooden block sinks into sand when the pressure on it changes. The student loads 100 g masses onto the block one at a time (to a maximum of six masses) and measures how deeply the block is pushed into some sand.

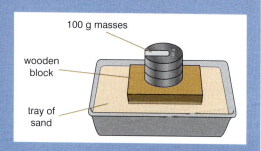

△ Fig. 1.90 Apparatus for the investigation.

The student finds very little evidence of a pattern in his measurements. He feels this is because the block tends to tip over, rather than standing straight, which means that the sand is not equally pushed down. He also feels that the sand does not push down very much anyway – it just gets pushed to the side.

To extend his experiment, the student has an idea about investigating if the 'wetness' of the sand makes a difference to the way the block behaves, but he has not yet devised a plan to test this.

### Planning experiments and investigations

1. Explain how using the block in different ways and using different numbers of 100 g masses allows the student to test a variety of different pressures.

2. Devise a method to measure the depth to which the block sinks in the sand. You should name any equipment needed. Remember that the block may not sink equally in all directions.

3. What is the independent variable in this investigation? What is the dependent variable?

### Observing, measuring and recording data

4. Use ideas about particles to explain the student's observation that the sand 'just gets pushed to the side'.

### Interpreting and evaluating data

5. Suggest how the student could measure the 'wetness' of the sand in a reliable way.

6. Give an example of a situation where the idea of pressure can be used to explain why an object does not sink into a material such as sand.

## PRESSURE IN FLUIDS

Because particles in a liquid or gas (fluid) are constantly in random motion, they are constantly colliding with each other and the walls of the container.

This causes a force on the other particles and the container walls. Usually this force is described in terms of the pressure it causes on a particular area. The pressure at a point in a gas or liquid which is at rest acts equally in all directions.

## PRESSURE DIFFERENCE, HEIGHT AND DENSITY

If you dive below the water, the height of the water above you will exert pressure on you. At a depth of 10 m of water, the pressure has increased by 100 kPa, and for each further 10 m of depth the pressure increases by another 100 kPa. The rapid increase in pressure explains why scuba divers cannot go down more than 20 m without taking extra precautions.

The increase in pressure below the surface of a liquid depends on

- the depth below the surface
- the density of the liquid.

So the pressure will be much higher at a certain depth below the surface of mercury than it is below the surface of water. Note in particular that the pressure does not depend on the area of the water. When a diver goes to inspect a well, the pressure 10 m below the surface is the same as the pressure 10 m below the surface of a large lake. See Fig. 1.92.

For a dam, the walls retaining the water, have to be wider as the depth of water increases because of increased pressure with depth.

Scuba divers breathe compressed air at high pressure to prevent their lungs collapsing due to the high pressure from the water above them. This is a safe sport, but only because first-time divers are trained to a very high standard before they are allowed to dive.

Δ Fig. 1.91 These scuba divers breathe compressed air at high pressure to prevent their lungs collapsing due to the high pressure from the water above them.

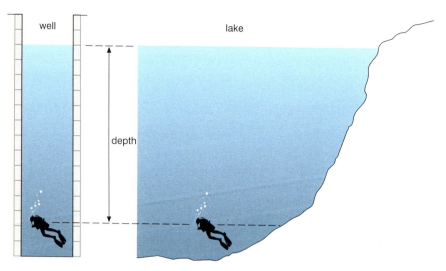

△ Fig. 1.92 The pressure on the diver is the same in the well and in the lake. In both cases it depends only on the density of the liquid and the depth of the diver.

## PRESSURE AND SUBMARINES

Early submarines had underwater endurance limited by battery capacity, so these submersibles actually spent most of their time on the surface, with hull designs that balanced the need for a relatively streamlined structure with the ability to move on the surface.

△ Fig. 1. 93 Submarines experience great pressure from the surrounding water.

Submarines actually have two hulls. The external hull, which forms the visible shape of the submarine, is called the casing, which hides external ballast tanks to give buoyancy on the surface, and is free-flooding when dived. It is made of steel only 2–4 mm thick. The pressure hull, which is inside the casing, is designed to withstand the pressure outside it from the water around the submarine, and has normal atmospheric pressure inside it, which allows the crew of the submarine to breathe normally. The dive depth (the maximum depth at which the submarine can operate) is dependent on the strength of the hull.

The Challenger deep is the deepest point in the Pacific Ocean. In 2019, a team lead by Vescovo took about 4 hours to descend in a small submersible to reach the record-breaking depth of 10.9 km. The pressure at this depth is about 1100 times greater than that at sea-level. The team found extraordinary sea creatures close to the flat, silt-covered seabed. Sadly, they also found a plastic bag and sweet wrappers.

**Challenge Question:** The pressure at sea-level is about 100 kPa. What is the vertical force on a sweet wrapper of area 4.0 cm$^2$ lying on the horizontal sea bed at a depth of 10.9 km?

The pressure below the surface of a fluid, and in fact between any two points in the fluid, can be calculated by the following equation:

change in pressure
= density × gravitational field strength × change in depth

$$\Delta p = \rho g \Delta h$$

Where:  $\Delta p$ = pressure difference in pascals (Pa)

$\rho$ = density in kilograms per cubic metre (kg/m³)

$g$ = gravitational field strength (N/kg)

$\Delta h$ = change in height in metres

Note that the density $\rho$ must be in kg/m³. When it is quoted in g/cm³, you must convert it. Remember that 1 g/cm³ = 1000 kg/m³. The value of $g$ is 9.8 N/kg.

There is one major cause of confusion: the difference between total pressure and additional pressure. Consider the pressure on scuba divers. Before they jump in, the pressure on them is already 100 kPa due to atmospheric pressure. When they have dived down 10 m, the pressure on them increases by about 100 kPa, so the total pressure is now 200 kPa. At 20 m, the total pressure on them is about 300 kPa, and so on.

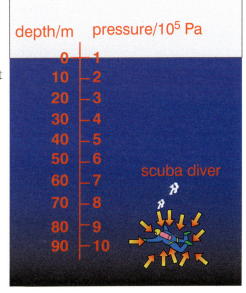

△ Fig. 1.94 How the pressure on a diver varies with depth.

## WORKED EXAMPLE

An aquarium has a tunnel through a tank of water at a depth of 5.0 m below the surface. The manufacturer guarantees the tunnel to a pressure difference of 200 kPa. Is the tunnel safe? The density of water = 1000 kg/m³.

Write down the equation: $\Delta p = \rho g \Delta h$

Substitute the values into the equation: $\Delta p = 1000 \times 9.8 \times 5.0$

Work out the answer and write down the unit: $\Delta p = 49\,000$ Pa or 49 kPa

The tunnel is safe.

Note that the total pressure on the outside of the tunnel is 49 kPa from the water, plus 100 kPa from the air pushing on top of the water, giving 149 kPa. However, the tunnel is also full of air, which is pushing outwards with a pressure of 100 kPa. So the tunnel only has to withstand a pressure difference of 49 kPa.

1. State two factors that pressure in a fluid depends on.

2. **SUPPLEMENT** Calculate the increase in pressure as you dive from the surface of a lake to a depth of 8.0 m.
   density of water = 1000 kg/m$^3$

3. **SUPPLEMENT** Calculate the pressure difference at 100 m below sea level.
   density of sea water = 1030 kg/m$^3$

4. **SUPPLEMENT** Calculate the total pressure on a scuba diver at a depth of 30 m. Take atmospheric pressure at sea-level as 100 kPa.

5. **SUPPLEMENT** Calculate the total pressure at the bottom of a column of mercury of height 15 cm.
   density of mercury = 13 600 kg/m$^3$
   atmospheric pressure = 100 kPa

# End of topic checklist

## Key terms

pressure

## During your study of this topic you should have learned:

○ Pressure is defined as force per unit area, and measured in N/m².

○ The equation for pressure is: $p = \dfrac{F}{A}$.

○ Pressure beneath the surface of a liquid changes with depth and density of the liquid.

○ **SUPPLEMENT** The change in pressure beneath the surface of a liquid is given by the equation: $\Delta p = \rho g \Delta h$.

# End of topic questions

*Note: the marks in brackets give an indication of the level of detail you should include in your answers.*

**1. a)** Calculate the pressure on the floor caused by:

    **i)** an ordinary shoe heel (person of mass 40 kg, heel 5.0 cm × 5.0 cm) when all the person's weight is on one heel
    *(2 marks)*

    **ii)** an elephant (mass 500 kg, area of one foot 300 cm$^2$) when all four feet are on the ground
    *(2 marks)*

    **iii)** a high-heeled shoe (worn by a person of mass 40 kg, heel area 0.50 cm$^2$) when all the person's weight is on one heel.
    *(2 marks)*

**b)** Which of the situations in part **a)** will damage a wooden floor that starts to dent at a pressure of 4000 kPa?
*(2 marks)*

(Note: to convert from cm$^2$ to m$^2$ you need to divide by 10 000.)

**2. SUPPLEMENT** The density of fresh water is 1000 kg/m$^3$. The pressure gauge on a submarine in a river was reading 100 kPa when it was at the surface. A sailor notices that the gauge is now reading 250 kPa.

**a)** Calculate the depth of the submarine.
*(2 marks)*

**b)** Suggest how your answer to part **a)** will change in slightly denser sea-water.
*(1 mark)*

**3. SUPPLEMENT** A space probe on Saturn's moon Titan is 50 m below the surface of a lake of liquid methane. Calculate the increase in pressure on the space probe. The density of liquid methane is 420 kg/m$^3$. The gravitational field strength on Titan is 1.4 N/kg.
*(2 marks)*

**4. a)** A skater glides on one skate. The mass of the skater is 65 kg and the area of the skate is $9.0 \times 10^{-4}$ m$^2$. Calculate the pressure exerted on the ice by the skate.
*(2 marks)*

**b)** Which row contains the correct force expression and the correct unit of pressure?
*(1 mark)*

|   | Expression for force | Unit for pressure |
|---|---|---|
| **A** | force = pressure × area | Pa/m$^2$ |
| **B** | force = pressure / area | N/m$^2$ |
| **C** | force = pressure × area | Pa |
| **D** | force = pressure / area | Nm$^2$ |

**5. SUPPLEMENT** An oil well is 1500 m deep and filled with oil of density 960 kg/m$^3$. Calculate the pressure due to the fluid at the bottom of the well.
*(2 marks)*

6. **SUPPLEMENT** A diver is exploring a sunken ship and notes that the pressure is $2.96 \times 10^5$ Pa at the ship compared to $1.00 \times 10^5$ Pa at the surface. Taking the density of water to be 1000 kg/m³, calculate the depth that the diver is at.   (3 marks)

7. **a)** Describe how the pressure in a liquid depends on the depth of the liquid and the density of the liquid.   (2 marks)

   **b)** A container has a cross-sectional area of 4.0 m² and is filled with water of density 1000 kg/m³. Calculate the pressure due to the water at a depth of 0.50 m.   (2 marks)

8. **SUPPLEMENT** The air pressure at the base of a mountain is $1.01 \times 10^5$ Pa. At the top of the mountain, the air pressure is measured at $0.80 \times 10^5$ Pa. Given that the density of air is 1.2 kg/m³, calculate the height of the mountain.   (2 marks)

9. **SUPPLEMENT** The density of water in a lake is $1.02 \times 10^3$ kg/m³. Atmospheric pressure is $1.01 \times 10^5$ Pa. Calculate the total pressure at a depth of 12 m below the surface of the lake.   (2 marks)

10. **SUPPLEMENT** A fish is swimming at a depth of 10.4 m in water of density $1.03 \times 10^3$ kg/m³. Calculate the pressure at this depth caused by the water.   (2 marks)

# Exam-style questions

*Note: exam-style questions, sample answers and comments have been written by the authors. The marks awarded for these questions indicate the level of detail required in the answers. In examinations, the way marks are awarded may be different. References to assessment and/or assessment preparation are the publisher's interpretation of the syllabus requirements and may not fully reflect the approach of Cambridge Assessment International Education.*

## Example answers

### Question 1

The diagram shows a car travelling to the right.

The arrows represent four forces on the car as it moves.

The arrows are not drawn to scale.

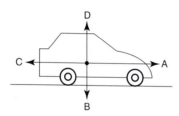

**a) i)** Which arrow represents the weight of the car?

*B* ✓ ①  [1]

**ii)** Which arrow represents the driving force acting on the car?

*A* ✓ ①  [1]

**b) SUPPLEMENT** The horizontal forces on the car are unbalanced.

**i)** State the equation linking resultant force, mass and acceleration.

*F=ma* ✓ ①  [1]

The car accelerates at 2.0 m/s² and it has a mass of 1500 kg.

COMMENTS

**1) a) i)** and **ii)** The first two questions are straightforward, recalling and applying simple ideas in a familiar situation.

**b) i)** and **ii)** The mathematical parts of the question are good. Working has been shown and the answer is correct.

**iii)** The answer refers to the direction of force as 'horizontally'. This should be clearer and specify forwards ('horizontally' could also mean backwards which is incorrect). This is an easy mistake to make. It is important to check through answers to spot mistakes like this.

**iv)** The answer is vague and does not address the point of the question. It is still in part b) and that is the clue that the answer is still related to $F = ma$. The question asks about forces so the answer should also refer to the resultant force on the car being the difference between the force provided by the engine and air resistance.

**c)** 'Bigger' is too vague. The answer needed to mention 'larger mass', as the question is still linked to $F = ma$. The answer does then go on to link force to acceleration correctly. The idea of more air resistance is a sensible suggestion.

**ii)** Calculate the magnitude of the resultant force on the car.

$1500 \times 2$ ✔ ①  $= 3000$

$Force = 3000\ N$ ✔ ①  [2]

**iii)** Which direction does this force act in?

*Horizontal* ✗  [1]

**iv)** The force provided by the car engine is larger than the value you have calculated. Suggest why.

*The car is speeding up and energy is lost to the surroundings, so the engine has to give a bigger force.* ✗ ✗  [2]

**c)** A truck tries to keep up with the car as it accelerates.

The truck falls behind, even though the engine in the truck provides a bigger force than the engine in the car.

Suggest why the truck falls behind.

*The truck is bigger, so it has to have a bigger force to get the same acceleration because there will be more air resistance.* ✗ ✔ ✔ ① ①  [3]

(Total 11 marks)

 7/11

## Question 2

In 2009, Usain Bolt set the world record for 100 m at 9.58 s.

**a) i)** State the equation linking average speed, distance moved and time taken. [1]

  **ii)** Calculate the average speed for Usain Bolt's run.

   Give your answer to an appropriate number of significant figures. [3]

  **iii)** At some part of the race, Usain Bolt must have run faster than this.

   Explain why. [3]

**b)** At the start of the race, it is counted as a false start when a runner moves before 0.10 s after the starter has fired the starting gun. Suggest why. [3]

(Total 10 marks)

## Question 3

The graph shows how the speed of a cyclist varies with time.

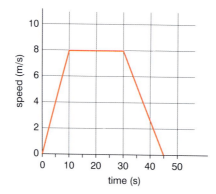

**a) i)** Determine the times when the cyclist was travelling at a constant speed. [1]

  **ii)** How can you tell from the graph that the speed is constant? [1]

**b) SUPPLEMENT** Calculate the acceleration of the cyclist during the first 10 s. [3]

**c)** Use the graph to find the total distance travelled by the cyclist. [3]

(Total 8 marks)

## Question 4

A student is planning to investigate air resistance.

He makes a number of paper parachutes of different sizes and attaches them one at a time to a small mass.

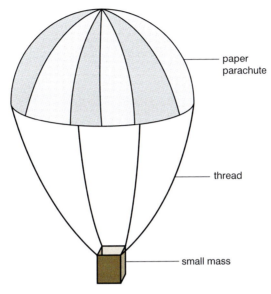

a) Describe how the student should carry out his investigation.
   You should include:

   **i)** what other equipment the student should use

   **ii)** what measurements the student should make

   **iii)** how the student should use his measurements to draw a conclusion.          [5]

b) **SUPPLEMENT** Use ideas about the forces acting on falling objects to explain how a falling object can reach a terminal velocity.          [5]

(Total 10 marks)

## Question 5

A crane at a building site is lifting a container.

The point labelled C is the centre of gravity of the container.

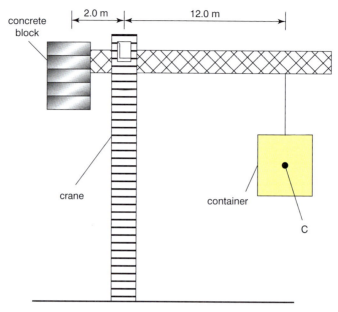

The container has a mass of 2000 kg.

**a)** State the equation linking weight, mass and acceleration of free fall $g$.          [1]

**b)** Calculate the weight of the container.          [2]

**c)** Use ideas about moments to explain the purpose of the concrete block.          [3]

**d)** In the diagram, the crane is balanced horizontally.

   Calculate a suitable value for the mass of the concrete block.          [4]

(Total 10 marks)

## Question 6

A student investigates stretching a spring.

The student hangs masses onto the spring one at a time and measures the length of the spring.

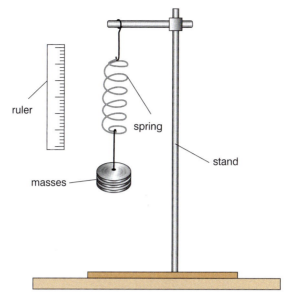

**a)** Describe how the student should use a ruler to obtain accurate measurements for the length of the spring. [3]

**b)** Suggest one safety precaution the student should take during the investigation. [1]

The student calculates the extension in the spring for each weight attached.

The table shows the results.

| Load/N | Extension/cm |
|--------|--------------|
| 0      | 0.0          |
| 1.0    | 3.1          |
| 2.0    | 6.0          |
| 3.0    | 8.8          |
| 4.0    | 13.7         |
| 5.0    | 14.9         |

**c)** **i)** Draw a graph of load against extension. [5]

**ii)** Is there any evidence that the student made a mistake in the measurements? Explain your answer. [2]

**iii)** Describe whether the spring shows a linear behaviour with the extension being directly proportional to the load. [3]

(Total 14 marks)

A child climbs to the top of a slide at a playground.

The child has a mass of 30 kg and the top of the slide is 3.0 m above the ground.

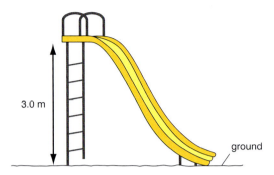

**a)** State the equation linking gravitational potential energy, mass, $g$ and height. [1]

**b)** Calculate the gravitational potential energy gained by the child when he climbs to the top of the slide. [2]

**c)** State the link between the gravitational potential energy gained and the work done by the child. [1]

**d)** To calculate the power of the child as he climbs to the top of the slide, what other measurement would be needed? [1]

**e)** The child rides down the slide. Assuming energy is transferred just between gravitational potential and kinetic stores, calculate the speed of the child at the bottom of the slide. [4]

(Total 9 marks)

## Question 8

Two students want to find the density of clay.

They each have a sample of clay.

**a)** State the equation linking density, mass and volume. [1]

The students suggest different methods to find the volume of their sample of clay.

**b)** The first student shapes his sample of clay into a regular cube shape.

Then he measures the length of the sides.

He finds the volume by doing a calculation with his measurements.

**i)** How should the student choose his equipment to make his measurement of volume as precise as possible? [2]

**ii)** Describe a feature of this method that may lead to inaccurate results. [1]

**c)** The second student decides to find the volume of her sample of clay using a measuring cylinder. Describe how she should do this. [4]

**d)** Describe how the students can use an electronic balance to find the mass of their samples of clay. [1]

**i)** If the electronic balance is incorrectly calibrated, how will this affect their measurements? [1]

**ii)** Suggest how the students can check the calibration of the electronic balance. [2]

(Total 12 marks)

Most things in the world are either a solid, a liquid or a gas. These are the three main states of matter. Substances can change from a solid to a liquid in a process called melting, and from liquid to gas in a process called evaporation. Gases change to liquids by condensation and liquids change to solids in solidification.

You are probably most familiar with these changes for water. It is possible for the states to exist at the same time: for example, there is a temperature at which ice, water and steam are all present. This is called the triple point of water The triple point of pure water is at 0.01 °C (273.16 K, 32.01 °F) at a pressure of 611.2 Pa.

## STARTING POINTS

**1.** What happens to the particles when a solid melts?

**2.** Explain what happens when a solid dissolves in a liquid.

**3.** What happens to the speed of gas molecules as temperature increases?

## SYLLABUS SECTIONS COVERED

**2.1** Kinetic particle model of matter

**2.2** Thermal properties and temperature

**2.3** Transfer of thermal energy

# 2 Thermal physics

Δ Water exists as a solid, a liquid and a gas in the world around us.

Δ Fig. 2.1 Water in all three states of matter.

# Kinetic particle model of matter

## INTRODUCTION

Almost all matter can be classified as a solid, a liquid or a gas. These are called the three states of matter.

The fourth state of matter is called 'plasma'. It only exists at high temperatures rarely seen on Earth, so we won't consider it further here, even though most of the matter in the Universe and most stars are made of plasma.

### KNOWLEDGE CHECK

✓ The effects of heating a solid, liquid or gas.
✓ The effects of cooling a solid, liquid or gas.
✓ Matter is made of particles (atoms and molecules).
✓ Define and calculate and calculate pressure.
✓ Everyday properties of gases – for example that they expand when heated and they exert a pressure on container walls.

### LEARNING OBJECTIVES

✓ Know the distinguishing properties of solids, liquids and gases.
✓ Know the terms for the changes in state between solids, liquids and gases (gas to solid and solid to gas transfers are **not** required).
✓ Describe the particle structure of solids, liquids and gases in terms of the arrangement, separation and motion of the particles, and represent these states using simple particle diagrams.
✓ Describe the relationship between the motion of particles and temperature, including the idea that there is a lowest possible temperature (−273 °C), known as absolute zero, where the particles have least kinetic energy.
✓ Describe the pressure and the changes in pressure of a gas in terms of the motion of its particles and their collisions with a surface.
✓ Know that the random motion of microscopic particles in a suspension is evidence for the kinetic particle model of matter.
✓ Describe and explain this motion (sometimes known as Brownian motion) in terms of random collisions between the microscopic particles in a suspension and the particles of the gas or liquid.
✓ **SUPPLEMENT** Know that the forces and distances between particles (atoms, molecules, ions and electrons) and the motion of the particles affects the properties of solids, liquids and gases.
✓ **SUPPLEMENT** Describe the pressure and the changes in pressure of a gas in terms of the forces exerted by particles colliding with surfaces, creating a force per unit area.

✓ **SUPPLEMENT** Know that microscopic particles may be moved by collisions with light fast-moving molecules and correctly use the terms atoms or molecules as distinct from microscopic particles.

✓ Describe qualitatively, in terms of particles, the effect on the pressure of a fixed mass of gas of: a change of temperature at constant volume and a change of volume at constant temperature.

✓ Convert temperatures between kelvin and degrees Celsius; recall and use the equation:
$T$ (in K) = $\theta$ (in C) + 273

✓ **SUPPLEMENT** Recall and use the equation pV = constant for a fixed mass of gas at constant temperature, including a graphical representation of this relationship.

## STATES OF MATTER

The three states of matter each have different properties:

- A solid has a fixed volume and shape, is not easily compressed and does not flow easily.
- A liquid assumes the shape of the part of the container that it occupies, usually occupying the lowest level, is not easily compressed and flows easily.
- A gas assumes the shape and volume of its container, occupying the whole volume, can be compressed and flows easily.

Matter can change state between solid, liquid and gas. A solid changing to liquid is called **melting**; liquid to gas is called **evaporation**. A gas changing into liquid is called **condensation**; liquid to solid is called **solidification**.

For example, ice can be melted into water by heating it. The water can then be turned into gas (steam) by further heating. The reverse can also happen when energy is removed from matter. Steam can be condensed into water, and the water can be frozen back into ice. When you next get caught in rain, just remember it is all about change of state from gas (clouds) to water.

## MOLECULAR MODEL

In this topic, these properties of matter are explained in terms of the particle structure of the three states.

◁ Fig. 2.2 The main body of this rocket is filled with liquid oxygen and liquid hydrogen, which have to be kept at extremely low temperatures to prevent them from heating up and turning back into gas. If the fuel were made colder it would turn into a solid.

We now know that all materials are made of tiny particles (atoms, ions and molecules) that can exert electrostatic forces of attraction, and repulsion, on each other. The particles in a solid are locked together by the forces between them. However, even in a solid, the particles are not completely still. They vibrate constantly about their fixed positions. When the solid is heated, it is given more internal energy, its temperature increases, and the particles vibrate faster and further about their fixed positions.

When the temperature is increased further, the vibrations of the particles increase to the point at which the forces are no longer strong enough to hold the structure together in the rigid order of a solid. The forces can no longer prevent the particles from moving around, but they do prevent them from flying apart from each other. This is what makes a liquid. The volume of the liquid is the volume occupied by the particles from which it is made.

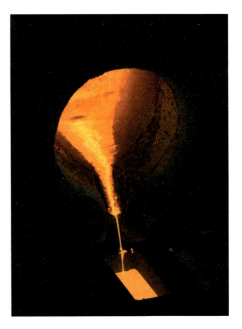

△ Fig. 2.3 The molten iron can be poured into a mould before it cools down and turns back into a solid.

When the temperature of the liquid is increased even further, then the particles do fly apart from each other. The liquid has changed state by becoming a gas. The particles fly around at high speed – several hundred kilometres per hour. If they are in a container, they travel all over it, bouncing off the walls. The volume of a gas is not fixed – it just depends on the size of the container that the gas is put into. We use the **kinetic particle model** to explain the behaviour of solids, liquids and gases. Table 2.1 summarises this model.

| | Solid | Liquid | Gas |
|---|---|---|---|
| Arrangement and separation of particles | Regular pattern, very closely packed together, particles held in place | Randomly arranged, closely packed together, particles able to move past each other | Randomly arranged, widely spaced, particles able to move freely |
| Diagram | | | |
| Motion of particles | Vibrate around fixed positions | Move around each other in a random motion | Move faster and randomly (range of speeds in all different directions) |

△ Table 2.1 The kinetic particle model of matter.

The arrangement of particles can be used to explain the properties of solids, liquids and gases that you met earlier.

Solids:

- retain a fixed shape and volume because the particles are locked into place in the lattice by strong attractive electrostatic forces
- are not easily compressed or expanded when temperature changes because there is little free space between the particles
- do not flow because the particles are fixed.

Liquids:

- assume the shape of the part of the container that they occupy because the particles can move around each other
- are not easily compressed or expanded when temperature changes because there is little free space between the particles
- flow easily because the particles can move around each other.

Gases:

- assume the shape and volume of their container because the particles move past one another continuously with negligible electrostatic forces acting between them (unless they collide with each other or the container walls)
- can be compressed or expanded when temperature changes because there is lots of free space between the particles
- have particles that can move randomly and easily past one another.

## QUESTIONS

1. Describe what happens to the motion of atoms as the temperature increases.

2. Explain why it is easier to compress a gas than a liquid.

3. Describe the arrangement of particles in: a) a solid; b) a liquid; c) a gas.

4. What does the volume of a gas depend on?

    **A** volume of container

    **B** temperature

    **C** pressure

    **D** random motion

### What are particles that make up matter?

The particles of matter can be single atoms. There are materials like this, for example, helium gas, and all metals such as copper and gold. In most materials, especially liquids and gases, the particles are atoms grouped together to form molecules. A water molecule is $H_2O$ and a nitrogen molecule is $N_2$. This means that the particles moving around in liquid or gaseous water each consist of two hydrogen atoms and one oxygen atom. In liquid nitrogen or in nitrogen gas, the particles each consist of two nitrogen atoms.

Taking the idea of particles one step further, you can start to apply your knowledge of forces and motion to the particles of a gas. This step is building up a theory – the kinetic theory of matter – to see if the predictions that come from our ideas match what happens when we experiment with gases.

The kinetic particle model of gases builds up a set of ideas based on molecules moving around randomly with their speeds dependent on the temperature of the gas – the higher the temperature, the faster the molecules move.

Gases exert pressure. This can be explained in terms of the kinetic particle model applied to gases. Imagine holding an air-filled balloon in your hand. The air molecules within the balloon move quickly in all directions, and all

△ Fig. 2.4 The air within this hot-air balloon is heated with a burner. The air molecules within this balloon move faster than the cooler air molecules outside the balloon.

of them will eventually collide with the inside surface of the balloon. A tiny force is exerted on the balloon with every collision made by the molecules within the balloon. There are so many molecules within the balloon that, overall, the total force exerted by all the colliding molecules with the balloon can be felt by your hand. Squeezing the balloon will increase the force exerted by the molecules because the rate at which they collide with the inside of the balloon will increase. The pressure exerted by the colliding molecules on the inside of the balloon is the force acting on the balloon per unit area. Therefore, the pressure you feel from an inflated balloon is the results of molecules colliding with the surface of the balloon.

Table 2.2 summarises how kinetic theory of matter links with our observations of a gas.

| Observation of a gas | Ideas from the kinetic particle model |
|---|---|
| Gases have a mass that can be measured. | The total mass of a gas is the sum of the masses of the individual molecules. |
| Gases have a temperature that can be measured. | The individual molecules are always moving. The faster they move, the more kinetic energy they have, the higher the temperature of the gas. |

| Observation of a gas | Ideas from the kinetic particle model |
| --- | --- |
| Gases have a pressure that can be measured. | When the molecules hit the walls of the container they exert a force on it. It is this force per unit area of the container wall that we observe when measuring pressure. **SUPPLEMENT** As molecules strike the walls of a container, their momentum changes. As momentum changes, a force is created and can be calculated using $F = \dfrac{\Delta p}{\Delta t}$ (see section 1.6). |
| Gases have a volume that can be measured. | Although the volume of each molecule is extremely tiny, they are always moving about and spread out throughout the container. |
| Temperature has an **absolute zero**. | As the temperature falls, the speed of the molecules (and their kinetic energy) becomes less. At absolute zero the molecules would have stopped moving. |

Δ Table 2.2 What happens inside a gas.

Absolute zero is a temperature of −273 °C. This the lowest possible temperature of matter. At this temperature, the particles of matter stop moving, and have zero kinetic energy. All gases turn to liquid and then solid before reaching this temperature. For example, helium becomes liquid at −269 °C, then a solid below this temperature.

## QUESTIONS

1. Explain how the kinetic theory explains the measurable volume of a gas.

2. State the lowest possible temperature of matter.

3. Explain what happens to particles within matter at absolute zero.

### Brownian motion

Evidence for the kinetic particle model of matter comes from observations such as **Brownian motion**. When viewed under a microscope, small microscopic particles, such as pollen grains suspended in water or fine smoke particles in air, can be seen to have random motion. The explanation is that these microscopic particles are constantly being hit by even smaller particles, which are too small to see directly. We know these smaller particles as water molecule or air molecules.

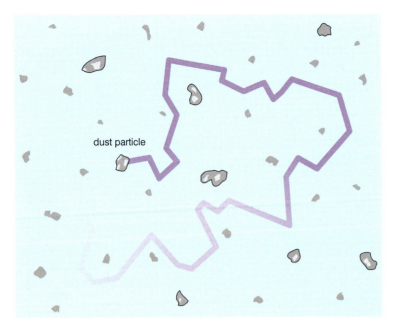

△ Fig. 2.5 Brownian motion as seen in dust particles. Every dust particle has a random (haphazard) motion as shown by the zig-zag path.

Microscopic particles (pollen grain, dust particles and smoke particles) can be moved by collisions with fast-moving molecules of fluids. The microscopic particles can be seen as tiny specks of light, whereas the molecules are far too small to be seen individually. The evidence from Brownian motion is that gas molecules themselves must have random motion. The gas molecules have less mass and move faster than the microscopic particles.

### Pressure and gas particles

According to the kinetic particle model, the pressure on the walls of a container is caused by the collisions made by the speeding gas molecules. The colliding molecules exert a force on the piston. The force per unit area of the piston is the pressure exerted on the piston. You can feel this pressure if you try to hold a bicycle pump in the pushed-in position while blocking the air outlet with your finger as shown in Fig. 2.6. If the pump is broken and allows the air to escape, this does not work.

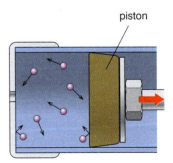

△ Fig. 2.6 The molecules of the gas are colliding with the piston and trying to push it out.

In Fig. 2.6 the piston is not moving. However, there is a force trying to push it out. If the molecules travel faster, then they will hit the piston in the pump more often and with greater force. The pressure on the piston and on the walls will go up. This is exactly what will happen when the temperature of the air inside the pump is increased.

The molecules will also hit each other as well as the walls of the container. At normal pressures they travel a lot less than 1 mm between collisions. This does not affect the way that the model works.

△ Fig. 2.7 The tyre has been pumped up with air. It is the pressure caused by the movement of the air molecules inside that keeps it inflated.

## QUESTIONS

1. State what is meant by Brownian motion.

2. Explain how the kinetic theory explains Brownian motion.

3. **SUPPLEMENT** Explain how pressure is exerted on the walls of a container.

## GASES AND THE ABSOLUTE SCALE OF TEMPERATURE

### Pressure and temperature at constant volume

When the volume of the gas stays constant, then the pressure exerted by the gas increases as the temperature increases. This can be explained in terms of the kinetic theory of matter. Gas molecules move faster and have greater kinetic energy when the temperature goes up. The gas molecules collide with greater force with the container walls. This in turn means greater pressure on the walls because pressure $= \dfrac{\text{force}}{\text{area}}$.

## Pressure and volume at constant temperature

When the piston of a bicycle pump is pushed in with the air outlet blocked, then the more you push it in, the harder and harder it gets to push it further. The pressure in the container goes up as its volume gets smaller.

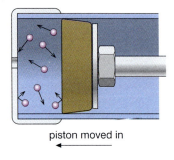

piston moved in

△ Fig. 2.8 The pressure increases when the volume is reduced.

According to the kinetic particle model there is the same number of molecules in the container travelling at the same speed. However, because the molecules are now packed in more densely, there will be more collisions with the walls (and with the piston) per second. When the volume is halved, then the number of collisions per second with the walls and with the piston will double, and the pressure on the piston will double.

## Temperature in kelvin

The lowest temperature for matter is – 273 °C. There is no temperature below this value. This is why this temperature is known as absolute zero. Since there is an absolute zero, there is another system of measuring temperature in which the temperature at absolute zero is given the number 0. This temperature scale is known as the Kelvin scale of temperature – named after the British physicist and engineer Lord Kelvin (1824–1907).

The Kelvin scale is linked closely to the Celsius scale. A temperature change of 1 kelvin (K) is the same as a temperature change of 1 °C. The temperature $T$ in K, is related to the temperature $\theta$ in °C by the equation:

$T$ (in K) = $\theta$ (in °C) + 273

To change temperature

- from K to °C, you add 273
- from °C to K, you subtract 273

It is worth pointing out that there is no 'degree' symbol when you have temperature in K.

## QUESTIONS

**1.** Convert the following to kelvin (K):

**a)** 0 °C (freezing point of ice)

**b)** 100 °C (boiling point of pure water)

**c)** 400 °C

**2.** Convert the following to °C:

**a)** 600 K

**b)** 100 K

**c)** 3 K

A fixed amount of gas in a sealed container at constant temperature obeys the following equation:

pressure × volume = constant

$$pV = \text{constant}$$

where: $p$ = pressure in Pa (or N/m²)

$V$ = volume in m³

Pascals and newtons per square metre are the same thing. When using this equation, you can use whichever units you like so long as you continue to use the same ones.

The pressure exerted by the gas is inversely proportional to its volume, as long as the temperature remains the same. (This is sometimes known as Boyle's law.) In simple terms, this means the pressure exerted by the gas will double when its volume is halved, see Fig. 2.9. You can easily demonstrate this using a blown-up balloon. Pressure exerted by the air inside the balloon will increase when you gently squeeze the balloon. It best not to overdo this, because the balloon can burst - wear safety glasses if you intend to do this.

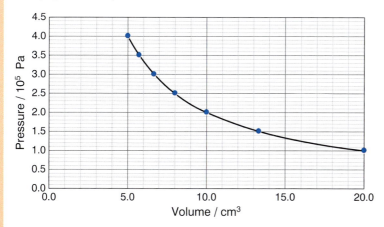

Δ Fig. 2.9 The pressure exerted by a gas at constant temperature is inversely proportional to its volume. $pV$ = constant for any data point on this graph.

So, in an experiment you can write the initial values of pressure and volume multiplied together, $p_1 \times V_1$ and the final values of pressure and volume multiplied together, $p_2 \times V_2$, and equate them.

$$p_1V_1 = \text{constant} = p_2V_2$$

or

$$p_1V_1 = p_2V_2$$

## WORKED EXAMPLE

A bicycle pump contains 400 cm³ of air at atmospheric pressure of 100 kPa. The air is compressed slowly. Calculate the pressure when the volume of the air is compressed to 125 cm³.

Write down equation: $$p_1 V_1 = p_2 V_2$$

Substitute values into the equation: $100 \times 400 = p_2 \times 125$

$$p_2 \times 125 = 40\,000$$

Rearrange the equation to calculate the final pressure: $p_2 = \dfrac{40\,000}{125}$

Work out the answer and write down the unit: $p_2 = 320$ kPa

The volumes are both in cm$^3$ and the pressures are both in kPa. The equation can be used in any consistent units.

## QUESTIONS

1. State the link between the pressure of a gas and its volume at constant temperature.

2. State how the pressure exerted by a gas at constant volume depends on its temperature.

3. **SUPPLEMENT** An aerosol can has a volume of 150 cm$^3$. It contains gas at a pressure of 350 kPa. Calculate the volume of this gas when all of it is allowed to expand into the atmosphere at a pressure of 100 kPa. Assume the temperature remains constant.

---

**SCIENCE IN CONTEXT**

## COOL PHYSICS

There is a strange story about absolute zero. Its exact value of −273.15 °C can never be reached. Matter can be cooled close to 0 K, but never 0 K. This idea is enshrined in the so-called laws of thermodynamics.

How do physicists cool matter to very low temperatures? Well, they cannot use ordinary fridges. Instead, they use powerful lasers focussed on a thin metal sheet, which have the effect of reducing the vibration of the atoms to almost standstill. The amount of kinetic energy the atoms have is linked to temperature. No vibrations would mean 0 K. Records are constantly being broken, but in 2017 a research team in America lowered the temperature of an aluminium wafer 100 micrometres thick to just 0.00036 K.

Low temperatures are important in science. For example, liquid helium at about 4 K (−269 °C) is used in the superconducting magnets used in MRI scanners in hospitals. In the future, the hope is that at temperatures close to 0 K, supercomputers can operate at incredible speed.

**Challenge Question:** Give examples of other applications where very low temperatures are useful.

# End of topic checklist

## Key terms

absolute zero, atoms, Brownian motion, kelvin (temperature), kinetic particle model, microscopic particles, molecules, states of matter

## During your study of this topic you should have learned:

○ The three states of matter are: solids, liquids and gases.

○ A solid changing to liquid is called melting; liquid to gas is called evaporation.

○ A gas changing into liquid is called condensation; liquid to solid is called solidification.

○ Know the particle structure of solids, liquids and gases in terms of the arrangement, separation and motion of the particles.

○ Particles move faster, or vibrate more, when temperature increases.

○ The lowest possible temperature (−273 °C) is known as absolute zero.

○ At absolute zero, particles have zero kinetic energy.

○ Pressure is exerted by particles colliding with container walls.

○ The random motion of microscopic particles (pollen grain, dust particles, etc) in a suspension is evidence for the kinetic particle model of matter.

○ Brownian motion is evidence of random collisions between the microscopic particles in a suspension and the particles (atoms or molecules) of the gas or liquid

○ **SUPPLEMENT** Pressure exerted by a gas is because of forces exerted by particles colliding with surfaces, and pressure defined as force per unit area.

○ **SUPPLEMENT** Microscopic particles (pollen grain, dust particles, etc) may be moved by collisions with light fast-moving molecules.

○ For a fixed mass of gas, at constant volume, pressure increases when temperature increases because particles move faster and collide often with container walls.

○ For a fixed mass of gas, pressure increases when volume decreases because particles move at the same speed but collide often with container walls.

○ **SUPPLEMENT** Temperature can be measured in kelvin, with $T$ (in K) = $\theta$ (in °C) + 273.

○ **SUPPLEMENT** For a fixed mass of gas at constant temperature, $pV$ = constant.

# End of topic questions

*Note: the marks in brackets give an indication of the level of detail you should include in your answers.*

**1.** Give an example of a material for each state of matter that demonstrates the properties of that state. (3 marks)

**2.** Use ideas about particles to explain why:

**a)** solids keep their shape, but liquids and gases do not (3 marks)

**b)** solids and liquids have a fixed volume, but gases fill their container. (3 marks)

**3.** Describe how the kinetic theory of matter explains the existence of absolute zero. (3 marks)

**4.** What is absolute zero in Kelvins (K)?

   **A** −273 K       **B** 100 K       **C** 0 K       **D** 273 K    (1 mark)

**5.** How does the kinetic theory explain the fact that gases exert a pressure on their container? (2 marks)

**6.** **SUPPLEMENT** A student blows up a balloon. At room temperature, 20 °C, she measures the volume of the balloon as 1500 cm³. Then she puts the balloon in a freezer where the temperature is −13 °C. Assuming the pressure stays constant, work out the new volume of the balloon. (3 marks)

**7.** **SUPPLEMENT** A sample of gas is sealed in a 20 cm³ metal container at a pressure of $1.0 \times 10^5$ Pa. Calculate the new pressure of the gas when the metal container is slowly crushed to a volume of 5.0 cm³ at the same temperature. (3 marks)

**8.** **SUPPLEMENT** The volume of a cylinder is 0.05 m³. 1.4 m³ of air at atmospheric pressure ($1.0 \times 10^5$ Pa) is pumped into the tyre. Calculate the pressure in the cylinder. Assume that the temperature remains constant. (3 marks)

**9.** **SUPPLEMENT** The correct pressure in a tyre should be $2.4 \times 10^5$ Pa. A driver has checked the pressure and it is $1.5 \times 10^5$ Pa. What volume of air at atmospheric pressure ($1.0 \times 10^5$ Pa) should the driver pump into the tyre to increase it to the correct pressure? The volume of the tyre is 0.013 m³. (4 marks)

# Thermal properties and temperature

## INTRODUCTION

Some things expand when they are heated. In this topic you will find out why.

The expansion of a liquid (mercury) in a capillary tube is used to make a simple thermometer that you can use to measure temperatures in the laboratory. Expansion can be useful. However, when designing a bridge that is made in sections, it is important to leave gaps to prevent buckling in hot weather, see Fig. 2.10. The same idea is used in railway tracks. The gaps are important between the sections of the track, even though they may produce unwanted 'clickety-clack' noise.

Δ Fig. 2.10 This expansion joint on a bridge stops the bridge from buckling when it expands in hot weather.

## KNOWLEDGE CHECK

✓ The kinetic particle model for states of matter.

## LEARNING OBJECTIVES

✓ Describe, qualitatively, the thermal expansion of solids, liquids and gases at constant pressure.
✓ Describe some of the everyday applications and consequences of thermal expansion.
✓ **SUPPLEMENT** Explain, in terms of the motion and arrangement of particles, the relative order of magnitudes of the expansion of solids, liquids and gases as their temperatures rise.
✓ Know that a rise in the temperature of an object increases its internal energy.
✓ **SUPPLEMENT** Describe an increase in temperature of an object in terms of an increase in the average kinetic energies of all of the particles in the object.
✓ **SUPPLEMENT** Define specific heat capacity as the energy required per unit mass per unit temperature increase; recall and use the equation:

$$c = \frac{\Delta E}{m \Delta \theta}.$$

✓ **SUPPLEMENT** Describe experiments to measure the specific heat capacity of a solid and a liquid.
✓ Describe melting and boiling in terms of energy input without a change in temperature.
✓ Know the melting and boiling temperatures for water at standard atmospheric pressure.
✓ Describe condensation and solidification in terms of particles.
✓ Describe evaporation in terms of the escape of more-energetic particles from the surface of a liquid.

✓ Know that evaporation causes cooling of a liquid.
✓ **SUPPLEMENT** Describe the differences between boiling and evaporation.
✓ **SUPPLEMENT** Describe how temperature, surface area and air movement over a surface affect evaporation.
✓ **SUPPLEMENT** Explain the cooling of an object in contact with an evaporating liquid.

## THERMAL EXPANSION OF SOLIDS, LIQUIDS AND GASES

With only a few exceptions, all materials (solids, liquids and gases) expand as they become warmer.

Solids, and liquids, will expand in all directions. The effect is small but not trivial. A metre rule that is heated from 0 °C to 100 °C will increase in length by 1–2 mm depending on what material it is made of. Some plastics do not make good metre rules as they can get up to several millimetres longer when heated.

On a hot day, a 1000 km railway track can possibly become more than 300 m longer. In the case of a track that has joints, there is a gap of a few millimetres every 20 m, to allow the rails to expand. Modern long welded tracks have no expansion gaps of this type, although as can be seen in Fig. 2.11 the track has to be held extremely firmly to stop it moving.

Liquids also expand in all directions. This means that the volume of the liquid, which continues to be incompressible, will increase as its temperature increases. For example, the volume of water can increase by about 4% as its temperature changes from 0 °C to 100 °C.

△ Fig. 2.11 This track has to be held very firmly to stop it from bending sideways when it gets hot.

It is impossible to restrict the thermal expansion of solids and liquids, as very large forces will be created in the material if it is not allowed to expand. This is why a large bridge is always built with expansion joints to allow it to get longer on hot days (Fig. 2.12).

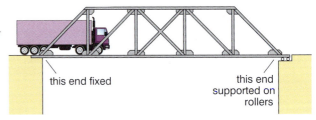

this end fixed                    this end supported on rollers

△ Fig. 2.12 Expansion joints on a bridge.

Gases behave completely differently. Firstly, there is no need to allow the gas to expand if it gets hotter; if you put it in a sealed container, then you can just allow the pressure to increase instead.

The properties of water are very strange. Not only does it require a great deal of heat to change its temperature, it is also unique in that it expands as it freezes. This makes ice less dense than liquid water, so ice floats on water. This has been vital to evolution – life can survive at the bottom of ponds, where in very cold weather the water stays liquid, even when the surface has frozen.

SUPPLEMENT

How can we explain the expansion of materials using the kinetic theory model?

All matter (solid, liquid and gas) expands when heated – the volume occupied by the particles (atoms or molecules) increases. It is worth noting that the actual volume of each particle remains unaffected by changes in temperature.

When solids are heated, the relative increase in their size is very small. The explanation for this is that the particles in a solid are held in their fixed positions by strong attractive electric forces which prevent the particles from moving apart too much. An increase in temperature makes the particles vibrate faster. External pressure acting on a solid has no effect on its expansion. Steel is used in railway tracks and in buildings. To prevent damage, we would not like steel to expand too much during hot days. For every 1 °C increase in temperature of steel, its volume only increases by about 0.004%.

Liquids also expand when heated. The particles of a liquid move faster around each other when the temperature is increased. The relative increase in their separation is a bit more than in solids because the attractive electric forces are less than those for solids. Just as for solids, external pressure has no significant effect on the expansion of liquids. Mercury is a liquid-metal used in some thermometers. For every 1 °C increase in the temperature of mercury, its volume increases by about 0.018%.

Gases will only expand if allowed to do so by the container. Increasing the temperature will increase the speed, and kinetic energy of the particles. The volume of the gas will simply be the volume of the container it is in. However, if the pressure acting on the gas is constant, then increasing the temperature will increase the volume. This can only happen if the container is flexible, and allowed to change its volume, e.g. a balloon.

**1.** Explain why gaps are left between railway tracks.

**2.** The volume of water increases by about 4% from 0 °C to 100 °C. The volume of water in a beaker at 0 °C is 200 cm³. Estimate its volume at 100 °C.

**3.** **SUPPLEMENT** Describe in terms of particles why solids expand when temperature is increased.

**4.** **SUPPLEMENT** Describe in terms of particles why liquids expand when temperature is increased.

## INCREASING INTERNAL ENERGY IN OBJECTS

You make things hotter by heating them or by rubbing them or shaking them. For example, rubbing your hands together helps to warm them up on a cold day. The kinetic energy of the movement is transferred to internal (thermal) energy in your hands. A rise in temperature of an object shows that its internal energy has increased.

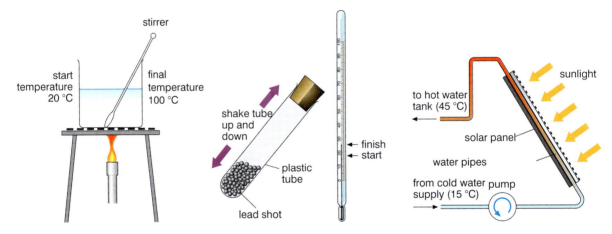

△ Fig. 2.13 Some examples of how to make things hotter – heating water, shaking lead shot and infrared warming water.

The larger the amount of material, the more energy you need to heat it up. All materials are made up of tiny particles. The larger the mass of the material, the more particles there are to share the added energy, so the smaller the temperature rise. Some materials are harder to heat up than others.

## Particles and internal energy

As a material is heated, the particles gain internal energy. So a rise in temperature of a material is related to a rise in internal energy of the material. Increasing the temperature of an object simply increases the average kinetic energies of all the particles (atoms, ions and molecules).

## Specific heat capacity

Different objects need different amounts of energy to change temperature. The amount of energy needed depends on:

- the mass of the object
- the material (e.g. water, copper, etc) of the object
- the temperature change required.

It takes 4200 J of energy to change the temperature of 1.0 kg of water by 1 °C. For a 1.0 kg block of lead, it takes 190 J of energy to change the temperature by 1 °C. It would be easier heat up lead than water. On the other hand, water will take longer to lose its thermal energy. During night times, the seas around the world will stay warmer than the land. The amount of energy required to change the temperature of a material depends on its **specific heat capacity**.

The specific heat capacity $c$ of a material is defined as the energy required by the material per unit mass per unit change in temperature. You can use the following equation to calculate specific heat capacity:

$$c = \frac{\Delta E}{m \Delta \theta}$$

where $\Delta \theta$ is the change in energy in joules (J), $m$ is the mass in kilograms (kg) and $\Delta E$ is the change in temperature (°C). Specific heat capacity has units J / kg °C.

Table 2.3 shows the specific heat capacities of some materials.

| Material | Specific heat capacity in J/kg °C |
|---|---|
| Copper | 390 |
| Coal ash | 900 |
| Aluminium | 910 |
| Brick | 800 |
| Pyrex glass | 780 |
| Steel | 510 |
| Concrete | 3350 |
| Vegetable oil | 1500 |
| Pure water | 4200 |

△ Table 2.3 The specific heat capacity of some materials.

### WORKED EXAMPLE

Calculate the energy required to change the temperature of 0.50 kg of water from 20 °C to 100 °C. The specific heat capacity of water is 4200 J / kg°C.

| | |
|---|---|
| Rearrange the equation: | $\Delta E = mc\Delta \theta$ |
| Substitute values: | $\Delta E = 0.50 \times 4200 \times (100 - 20)$ |
| Calculate the value, and include the unit: | $\Delta E = 168\,000$ J or 168 kJ |

This is an enormous amount of energy for just 0.50 kg of water. If the water is being heated in a kettle, then the actual energy supplied will be more than this because of additional energy transferred to the material of the kettle, and also the surroundings (table and air).

## Determining specific heat capacity

To determine the specific heat capacity of a substance, we just need to measure the change in temperature using a thermometer, the mass of the substance using a top-pan balance, somehow work out the energy supplied to the substance and then use the equation: $c = \dfrac{\Delta E}{m\Delta\theta}$.

The energy can be supplied by a heater of known power output, e.g. 50 W. All you need to know then is the time the heater was switched on. For example, in a time of 100 s, this heater will supply 5000 J of energy.

In all experiments, you need to make sure that all the energy supplied by the heater goes to the substance. When water is being heated in a beaker, it would be best to have a lid on the beaker, and also to lag the beaker to minimise the energy transfer to the surroundings.

## Developing practical skills

## Specific heat capacity of metal

A student investigates the specific heat capacity of different metal blocks. The student compares blocks of the same mass, 1.0 kg.

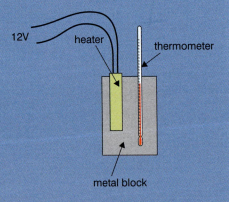

The student heats up an aluminium block with a 50 W electrical heater. The heater slots into the larger hole in the aluminium block and the thermometer slots into the smaller hole. The student uses a stopwatch to measure the time taken for the temperature to rise by 10 °C.

△ Fig. 2.14 Apparatus used to determine the specific heat of a metal.

The student repeats the experiment for different metals. The data collected is shown in the table.

| Type of metal | Temperature rise / °C | Power of heater / W | Time taken to increase the temperature by 10°C / s | Energy transferred by the heater / J |
|---|---|---|---|---|
| Aluminium | 10 | 50 | 221.0 | |
| Copper | 10 | 50 | 90.0 | |
| Steel | 10 | 50 | 120.0 | |

**Planning experiments and investigations**

**1.** The heater has a power rating of 50 W or 50 J/s. Use the data to calculate the energy transferred by the heater for each metal. Complete the table with your answers.

**2.** A small amount of oil is put in the hole to surround the thermometer. Suggest reasons why oil is used.

**3.** Name two control variables in this experiment.

**Interpreting and evaluating data**

**4.** Determine the specific heat capacity of each material.

**Evaluating methods**

**5.** How do his experimental results compare to the accepted values given in Table 2.3? Suggest reasons for any differences.

**6.** Suggest how the student could improve his method to get more accurate results.

## QUESTIONS

**1.** State the units of specific heat capacity.

**2.** Use Table 2.3 to deduce which material would be the most difficult to heat up.

**3.** An aluminium pan has mass 2.0 kg. It has 3.0 kg of water. Calculate the total energy needed to raise the temperature of the water and the pan by 80°C. (Use the data in Table 2.3.)

**4.** A 50 W heater is placed in oil and switched on for 480 s. The mass of the oil is 300 g and the change in temperature is 53 °C. Determine the specific heat capacity of the oil.

## MELTING, BOILING AND EVAPORATION

We experience melting and boiling many times in everyday life. This section explores what happens at the particle level when materials melt and boil.

During melting, or boiling, energy is supplied to substance without any change in the temperature. For example, pure ice will melt at a temperature of 0 °C. Pure water, at a standard atmospheric pressure of 100 kPa, will boil at 100 °C. These two temperatures can easily be reproducible. This is how liquid-in-glass thermometers are calibrated on the Celsius scale.

The **melting point** of a substance is the temperature at which it changes from a solid to a liquid. **Solidification** is when a substance changes from a liquid to a solid. The particles in the substance come close together. The **boiling point** of a substance is the temperature at which it changes from a liquid to a gas. The particles in the substance get further apart. **Condensation** is when a substance changes from a gas to a liquid. The particles in the substance come close together.

## EVAPORATION

When particles break away from the surface of a liquid and form a **vapour**, this is known as **evaporation**. The more energetic molecules of the liquid escape from the surface as shown in Fig. 2.15. This reduces the average energy of the molecules remaining in the liquid, and so the temperature of the liquid falls.

Evaporation causes cooling. The evaporation of sweat helps to keep your body cool in hot weather. The more energetic molecules of liquid sweat escape from the surface of your skin and so the average energy and therefore temperature of the remaining molecules falls and your skin cools down. This is what happens when any body is in contact with an evaporating liquid. The body cools down. The cooling in a refrigerator is also due to evaporation of a special liquid inside the freezing compartment at the top of the refrigerator. The vapour is collected and compressed back into liquid inside the condenser behind the refrigerator. The liquid is circulated by an electric pump and recycled.

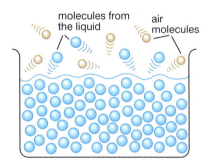

△ Fig. 2.15 Evaporation.

The rate of evaporation is increased at higher temperatures. It is also increased by a strong flow of air across the surface of the liquid, as in this way the evaporating molecules are carried away quickly. A certain amount of water will also evaporate more quickly when you increase its surface area. Tea or coffee in a shallow, wide cup cools down much more quickly than in a tall, narrow mug because the larger surface area of the cup allows more evaporation.

## QUESTIONS

1. State what happens to the temperature of an evaporating liquid.

2. **SUPPLEMENT** State the factors that will increase the rate of evaporation.

3. **SUPPLEMENT** Explain why hot water in a beaker poured over a large tray will cool down faster.

## Water is strange

Water has a surprisingly high specific heat capacity. This means that a lot of energy has to be transferred to change the temperature of water significantly. This is important in several ways:

- Water makes an excellent **coolant** for machines such as car engines. It can remove a lot of heat energy from the machine without boiling.
- The temperature of the seas and oceans remains fairly steady, as huge energy transfers are needed to significantly change the temperature of that much water. This helps keep the planet at a fairly even temperature, which is good for living things.

SUPPLEMENT

The words 'evaporation' and 'boiling' also cause confusion. When a liquid evaporates it loses molecules from its surface. This will occur in an open container of water at any temperature. For example, water from a hot drink left in a cup will eventually evaporate. The molecules of water in the cup will have a range of energies, and even at room temperature the molecules with the highest energies will leave the surface.

A liquid **boils** when its temperature reaches boiling point. At this temperature the molecules have enough energy to leave the liquid in large quantities, even those inside the liquid. These molecules collect to form large bubbles of vapour and cause the liquid to bubble violently.

Many solids evaporate slowly, which is why you can smell dry food – coffee beans, for example. Some people even claim to be able to smell a sheet of zinc metal, even though the evaporation rate is incredibly low.

## QUESTIONS

1. Explain in terms of energy and temperature what happens when a substance boils.

2. At boiling point, explain what happens to the molecules of a liquid.

3. Explain what happens when a liquid evaporates.

# End of topic checklist

## Key terms

boiling, condensation, evaporation, melting, solidification

**SUPPLEMENT** specific heat capacity

## During your study of this topic you should have learned:

○ Most solids, liquids and gases at constant pressure expand when temperature increases.

○ Thermal expansion has applications (e.g. thermometers) and consequences (e.g. buckling bridges).

○ **SUPPLEMENT** Solids and liquids expand with temperature because the average separation between particles increases.

○ **SUPPLEMENT** Increasing temperature increases the kinetic energy of the particles, but its volume is the volume of the container it is in.

○ A rise in the temperature of an object increases its internal energy.

○ **SUPPLEMENT** An increase in temperature of an object increases the average kinetic energies of all of the particles in the object.

○ **SUPPLEMENT** Specific heat capacity of a material is defined as the energy required per unit mass per unit temperature increase.

○ **SUPPLEMENT** The equation for specific heat capacity is: $c = \dfrac{\Delta E}{m\Delta\theta}$

○ **SUPPLEMENT** Know about experiments used to determine the specific heat capacity of a solid and a liquid.

○ In melting and boiling, energy is supplied without a change in temperature.

○ The melting point (temperature) of pure ice is 0 °C.

○ The boiling point (temperatures) for water at standard atmospheric pressure of 100 kPa is 100 °C.

○ Condensation is a term used when a gas changes to a liquid.

○ Solidification is a term used when a liquid changes to a solid.

○ Evaporation occurs when the more energetic particles leave from the surface of a liquid.

○ Evaporation causes cooling of a liquid.

○ **SUPPLEMENT** Boiling occurs at a specific temperature and evaporation can take place at all temperatures.

○ **SUPPLEMENT** Rate of evaporation increases with increasing temperature, increasing surface area and air movement over the surface of a liquid.

○ **SUPPLEMENT** An object in contact with an evaporating liquid cools down because internal energy is removed from the object.

# End of topic questions

*Note: the marks in brackets give an indication of the level of detail you should include in your answers.*

**1.** **a)** State one example where thermal expansion of metal is a disadvantage. (1 mark)

   **b)** **SUPPLEMENT** Explain the expansion of a solid in terms of particles. (2 marks)

**2.** **a)** Give one example of evaporation of water. (1 marks)

   **b)** Explain in terms of particles, how a shallow lake in a hot country dries out. (2 marks)

   **c)** State the melting and boiling temperatures of pure water. (2 marks)

   **d)** **SUPPLEMENT** State one difference between boiling and evaporation. (1 mark)

**3.** What is the correct name of the process in which a liquid changes into a solid?

   **A** boiling

   **B** condensation

   **C** evaporation

   **D** solidification (1 mark)

**4.** **SUPPLEMENT** 100 g of glass is heated until its temperature rises from 19 °C to 33 °C. The specific heat capacity of glass is 840 J/kg °C. Calculate the energy supplied to the glass. (2 marks)

**5.** **SUPPLEMENT** 250 g of the brick inside a storage heater (specific heat capacity = 910 J/kg °C) absorbs 5000 joules of energy. Calculate the temperature rise of the brick. (2 marks)

**6.** **SUPPLEMENT** A student is doing an experiment to determine the specific heat capacity of vegetable oil in a beaker. The beaker has a lid, and is covered with cotton wool. A 40 W heater is placed in the oil. The mass of oil is 400 g.

   **a)** Explain the purpose of the lid and the cotton wool. (2 marks)

   **b)** The heater is switched on for 3.0 minutes. The temperature of the oil increases from 30 °C to 42 °C. The oil is stirred when the temperatures are measured.

   **i)** Suggest the reason for stirring the oil. (1 marks)

   **ii)** Calculate the energy supplied to the oil by the heater. (2 marks)

   **iii)** Calculate the specific heat capacity of the oil. (2 marks)

△ Fig. 2.16 These paragliders stay in the air longer by using convection currents in the atmosphere to take them higher.

# Transfer of thermal energy

### INTRODUCTION

Thermal energy can flow by **conduction**, convection or radiation. It always flows from a region of high temperature to a region of low temperature, i.e. from hot to cold. The explanation of this energy flow requires an understanding of the roles of particles (atoms, ions and molecules), including **electrons**.

Convection currents in the air created by the hot ground are being used by the paragliders in Fig. 2.17 to lift them higher. Metal pans are used to warm up food because they are good at conducting thermal energy. Thermal radiation is transferred through space by infrared waves from the Sun.

In this topic we examine all three methods of heat transfer.

### KNOWLEDGE CHECK

✓ The particle structure of solids, liquids and gases.
✓ Energy can exist in different stores, including internal (thermal) energy.
✓ Energy can be transferred from one place to another.

### LEARNING OBJECTIVES

✓ Describe experiments to demonstrate the properties of good thermal conductors and bad thermal conductors (thermal insulators).
✓ **SUPPLEMENT** Describe thermal conduction in all solids in terms of atomic or molecular lattice vibrations and also in terms of the movement of free (delocalised) electrons in metallic conductors.
✓ **SUPPLEMENT** Describe, in terms of particles, why thermal conduction is bad in gases and most liquids.
✓ **SUPPLEMENT** Know that there are many solids that conduct thermal energy better than thermal insulators but do so less well than good thermal conductors.
✓ Know that convection is an important method of thermal energy transfer in liquids and gases.
✓ Explain convection in liquids and gases in terms of density changes and describe experiments to illustrate convection.
✓ Know that thermal radiation is infrared radiation and that all objects emit this radiation.
✓ Know that thermal energy transfer by thermal radiation does not require a medium.

✓ Describe the effect of surface colour (black or white) and texture (dull or shiny) on the emission, absorption and reflection of infrared radiation.

✓ **SUPPLEMENT** Know that for an object to be at a constant temperature it needs to transfer energy away from the object at the same rate that it receives energy.

✓ **SUPPLEMENT** Know what happens to an object if the rate at which it receives energy is less or more than the rate at which it transfers energy away from the object.

✓ **SUPPLEMENT** Know how the temperature of the Earth is affected by factors controlling the balance between incoming radiation and radiation emitted from the Earth's surface.

✓ **SUPPLEMENT** Describe experiments to distinguish between good and bad emitters of infrared radiation.

✓ **SUPPLEMENT** Describe experiments to distinguish between good and bad absorbers of infrared radiation.

✓ **SUPPLEMENT** Describe how the rate of emission of radiation depends on the surface temperature and surface area of an object.

✓ Explain some of the basic everyday applications and consequences of conduction, convection and radiation, including: heating objects such as kitchen pans and heating a room by convection.

✓ **SUPPLEMENT** Explain some of the complex applications and consequences of conduction, convection and radiation where more than one type of thermal energy transfer is significant, including: a fire burning wood or coal and a radiator in a car.

## CONDUCTION

Materials that allow thermal energy to transfer through them quickly are called **thermal conductors**. Those that do not are called **thermal insulators**.

Metals are excellent thermal conductors. This is why pans for cooking food over fires are made from metals (e.g. copper, aluminium, steel). Wood, plastic, glass and cotton wool are examples of bad thermal conductors.

If one end of a conductor is heated, the atoms, or molecules, that make up its lattice structure start to vibrate more vigorously. As the atoms in a solid are linked together by chemical bonds, the increased vibrations can be passed on to other atoms. The energy of movement (kinetic energy) passes through the whole material.

Metals are particularly good thermal conductors because they contain free, or delocalised, electrons that transfer energy very rapidly. (The term delocalised is used to mean that electrons are free from the atoms, and can roam easily within the material.) The atoms of a metal are surrounded by a sea of these free (delocalised) electrons.

As the electrons travel through the piece of metal, they take the thermal energy with them. This is in addition to the thermal energy that is transferred by vibrations of the atoms making up the structure of the metal. Fig. 2.17 shows conduction in a solid. Atoms in the hot part of a solid (left) vibrate further and faster than atoms in the cold part (right). The vibrations are passed on through the bonds from atom to atom. The free electrons gain kinetic energy at the hot end and transfer this energy by colliding with the atoms at the cooler end. It is the movement of the free electrons that makes metals act as good thermal conductors.

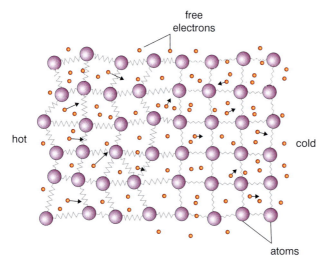

△ Fig. 2.17 Conduction in a solid.

Conduction cannot occur when there are no particles present, so a vacuum is a perfect insulator. Liquids are poor conductors because of weaker chemical bonds between particles and also fewer free electrons per unit volume than conductors. Gases are very poor conductors, because the particles are further apart and therefore, they exert negligible forces on each other.

Conduction can be demonstrated using the equipment shown in Fig. 2.18.

◁ Fig. 2.18 In this experiment to show conduction, the rods are made of different materials (e.g. copper, brass, aluminium, glass and wood), so the heat conducts along them at different rates. The better the conductor, the quicker the wax at the end of the rod melts.

Another way to demonstrate the properties of good and bad conductors of thermal energy is to wrap a piece of paper around a bar made of wood on one side and copper on the other side. The bar is then held just above a Bunsen flame. The paper only chars on the wood side of the bar, as copper is a good thermal conductor so thermal energy travels away from the paper on the copper side. Wood is a thermal insulator so does not conduct the thermal energy away.

Another example is the fact that metal handlebars of a bike always feel colder than the plastic grips – thermal energy is conducted away from your hands by the metal but not by the plastic.

## QUESTIONS

1. Which of the following is a bad thermal conductor?

   **A** glass      **B** copper      **C** gold      **D** steel

2. Name two good thermal conductors.

3. **SUPPLEMENT** State two ways in which thermal energy is conducted in metals.

4. Suggest why wood is a poorer thermal conductor compared with metals.

5. **SUPPLEMENT** Explain why liquids are poorer thermal conductors than metals.

## CONVECTION

Convection is the main method of thermal transfer in fluids.

Convection occurs in liquids and gases because these materials flow (they are fluids). The particles in a fluid move all the time. When a fluid is heated, energy is transferred to the particles, causing them to move faster and further apart. This makes the heated fluid less dense than the unheated fluid. The less dense, warmer fluid rises above the more dense, colder fluid, causing the fluid to circulate as shown in Fig. 2.19. This **convection current** is how the thermal energy is transferred.

◁ Fig. 2.19 Potassium manganate(VII) crystals in water demonstrate convection currents. The warmer water expands, becomes less dense and rises, making a trail as some of the dissolved potassium permanganate is carried along as well. Colder water sinks and replaces the warmer water that has risen.

If the movement of a fluid is restricted, energy cannot be transferred. That is why many insulators, such as ceiling tiles and woollen clothes, contain trapped air pockets. Wall cavities in some houses are filled with fibre to prevent air from circulating and transferring thermal energy by convection.

## QUESTIONS

1. Explain why convection only occurs in liquids and gases.

2. Explain why warm air rises.

3. Explain why a small paper windmill held above a hot table lamp will spin.

4. Describe how cavity-wall insulation in houses reduces heat loss by convection.

### RADIATION

Radiation, unlike conduction and convection, *does not need particles* to transfer thermal energy from one place to another. Radiation can travel through a vacuum. This is clearly shown by the radiation that arrives at the Earth from the Sun. This is why we can feel the warmth of the Sun even though it is 150 billion metres away. Radiated thermal radiation is carried mainly by **infrared radiation**, which is part of the **electromagnetic spectrum**. Infrared radiation has **wavelengths** longer than that of visible light.

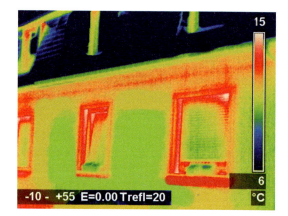

△ Fig. 2.20 Thermogram of a house. The red colours show greater amounts of infrared radiation.

All objects absorb and emit infrared radiation all the time. An object will emit infrared radiation if its temperature is above absolute zero (−273 °C or 0 K). Hot objects radiate more infrared radiation than cold objects. The amount of radiation emitted or absorbed by an object depends on its temperature and on its surface. Figure 2.20 shows a thermogram. Thermograms give a visual representation of the amount of infrared radiation that is given out by an object at any particular moment. The amount of infrared radiation absorbed or emitted or reflected depends on the surface colour (black or white) of the object and its texture (dull or shiny).

Shiny white surfaces are excellent reflectors of thermal radiation. Table 2.4 shows more information on the emission and absorption properties of different types of surfaces.

| Type of surface | As an emitter of radiation | As an absorber of radiation | Examples |
|---|---|---|---|
| Dull black | Good | Good | Emitter: cooling fins on the back of a refrigerator are dull black to radiate away more energy.<br><br>Absorber: the surface of a black bitumen road gets far hotter on a sunny day than the surface of a white concrete one. |
| White shiny | Poor | Poor | Emitter: marathon runners, at the end of a race, wrap themselves in shiny blankets to prevent them from cooling down too quickly by radiation (and convection).<br><br>Absorber: fuel storage tanks are sprayed with shiny silver or white paint to reflect infrared radiation from the Sun. |

Δ Table 2.4 Comparison of different surfaces as emitters or absorbers of infrared radiation.

## Good emitters

Fig. 2.21 shows an arrangement that can be used to show that objects with dark surfaces are better emitters than objects with white surfaces. The two cans (e.g. fizzy drink cans) are identical, except one is painted black (B) and the other is painted white (W). Both are filled to the top with hot water at the same temperature. The temperature of water in each can is measured using identical thermometers. After a fixed amount of time, the temperatures are measured and recorded.

The temperature of the water in can B will be less than the temperature of the water in can W. This is because a greater amount of infrared radiation is emitted from the black surface of can B. The black can is a good emitter of infrared radiation and the white can is a bad emitter of infrared radiation.

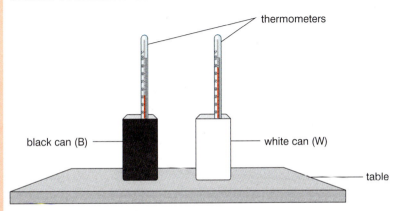

Δ Fig. 2.21 The black-coloured can emits more infrared radiation than the white-coloured can in the same time interval.

## Good absorbers

Fig. 2.22 shows the same two cans from the experiment above. This time, each can is filled with cool water at the same temperature. The cans are placed the same distance away from a heater. After a fixed time interval, the temperature of the water in can B will be *greater* than the temperature of the water in can W. This is because a greater amount of infrared radiation is absorbed by the black surface of can B. The black can is a good absorber of infrared radiation and the white can is a bad absorber of infrared radiation.

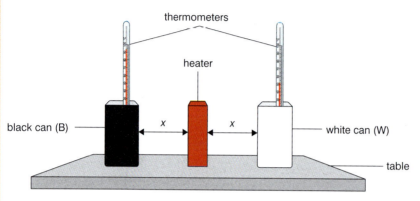

△ Fig. 2.22 The black-coloured can absorbs more infrared radiation than the white-coloured can in the same time interval. Each can is at the same distance x from the heater.

## Earth as an absorber and emitter of radiation

Imagine a table lamp pointed towards a cool table. After some time, the surface of the table will become warmer, but its temperature will be constant. This is because the rate at which infrared radiation energy is supplied by the lamp onto the surface of the table is the same as the rate of infrared radiation energy emitted by the warmer table. For example, if 1.5 W of power is absorbed by the table, then it would emit 1.5 W of power.

If an object receives energy at a greater rate than it transfers away, then its temperature will go up. The opposite is also true. The temperature of the object will go down if it emits energy at a greater rate than it receives. All of this is very important for our Earth.

The only way the Earth receives energy is from the infrared radiation from the Sun. The Earth absorbs this energy and would get hot. It does not continue to get hotter because it radiates infrared radiation into space. The atmosphere of the Earth would prevent some of this radiation escaping, especially the greenhouse gases (e.g. carbon dioxide, methane). These gases absorb the energy radiated from the Earth, then release it in all directions, which keeps the Earth warm. Scientists believe that the average temperature of the Earth has been increasing for some time because of increased amounts of greenhouse gases pumped into the atmosphere by cars, industries, etc.

The rate of emission of infrared radiation of an object depends on two factors; its surface temperature and its surface area. The rate of energy emitted is greater when

- surface temperature of the object is larger
- surface area of the object is larger.

**SCIENCE IN CONTEXT**

## THE PLANET VENUS

Venus has similar size and mass to our Earth, yet its surface temperature is about 460 °C. At this temperature, a space probe made of lead landing on its surface would simply melt.

△ Fig. 2.23 The surface of Venus is inhospitable at 460 °C.

The main reason for its higher temperature is its atmosphere – which is mainly the greenhouse gas carbon dioxide. About 96% of the atmosphere of Venus has carbon dioxide; the Earth's atmosphere by comparison has about 0.04%. The carbon dioxide absorbs the infrared radiation emitted from the surface of Venus, and re-emits some of it back to Venus, making Venus hotter than it would have been without the carbon dioxide.

**Challenge Question:** What other gases in our atmosphere would absorb infrared radiation?

## QUESTIONS

1. Describe the difference between conduction and convection.

2. **SUPPLEMENT** State which is the better emitter of infrared radiation: an object at 300 K, or an object at 0 °C.

3. State two factors that affect the rate of thermal radiation emitted by an object.

4. Two metal discs are removed from a hot oven. Both discs are identical apart from their colours – one is dull black and the other shiny white. Explain which disc will emit the greater rate of thermal radiation.

5. Explain the benefits of painting houses white in very hot countries.

## CONSEQUENCES OF ENERGY TRANSFER

This part of the topic considers some everyday consequences of energy transfer.

### Radiators

Radiators are used to heat homes in countries that have cool winters. A radiator does radiate some heat, and if you stand near a hot radiator your hands can feel the infrared radiation being emitted. However, this is only around one quarter of the heat being released by the radiator. Three quarters of the thermal energy is taken away by the hot air that rises from the radiator. Colder air from the room flows in to replace this hot air, and a convection current is formed as shown in Fig. 2.24. So a 'radiator' is mainly a convection heater.

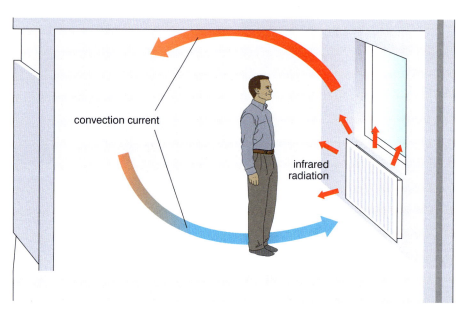

convection current

infrared radiation

Δ Fig. 2.24 A side view of a room with a hot-water radiator below the window. You will see from this that the convection current is far more efficient at heating the top of the room than it is at heating the person standing in front of the radiator.

### Vacuum flask

Another example of thermal transfers in everyday life is a vacuum flask (Fig. 2.25). A vacuum flask will keep a hot drink hot or a cold drink cold for hours by almost completely eliminating the flow of heat out or in.

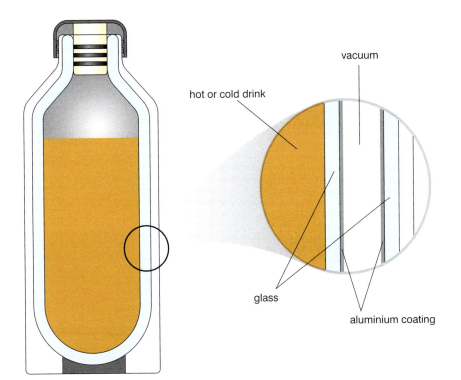

△ Fig. 2.25 A vacuum flask.

Conduction is almost entirely eliminated by making sure that any heat flowing out must travel along the glass of the neck of the flask. The path is a long one, the glass is thin, and glass is a very poor conductor of heat. Energy cannot be lost by conduction across the vacuum space between the two walls of the glass flask. The bung in the top of the flask must also be a very poor conductor of heat – cork or expanded polystyrene are good materials to use.

Convection is eliminated because the space between the inner wall and the outer wall of the flask is evacuated so that there is no air to form convection currents.

When the contents are hot, radiation is greatly reduced because the inner walls of the flask are coated with pure aluminium. Because the aluminium is in a vacuum, it stays extremely shiny forever, so the wall in contact with the hot liquid emits very little infrared radiation.

When the contents are cold, the shiny outer surface of the aluminium-coated glass reflects almost all the infrared radiation falling on it, so hardly any is absorbed.

### Kitchen pan

Most kitchen pans are made from metal – metal is an excellent conductor of thermal energy. Some pans have a copper bottom because copper is a better conductor than aluminium or steel. It is also important to have metal pans and pots that are chemically inactive – you do not want to alter the taste of the food being made.

The pan-handles are often made of wood or plastic, because both are poor thermal conductors.

## Car radiators

A car radiator is definitely not used for its radiating properties. It is designed to transfer thermal energy from the hot water circulating around the car engine away by blowing air over it. In most cars, the air is blown by electric fans, but some cars use the wind from the moving car.

The radiators are often made from aluminium, and have 'fins' to increase the surface area. This helps to increase the rate at which thermal energy is removed.

Δ Fig. 2.26 Car radiators have a greater surface area, which helps with the removal of thermal energy.

## Fire burning wood or coal

You do not need to stand too close to a wood fire to appreciate the intense thermal energy emitted by infrared radiation. Directly above the fire, a significant amount of thermal energy is removed by convection. This thermal energy would be useful if a cooking pot is placed above the fire.

## QUESTIONS

1. State the main method of heat transfer in a room radiator.

2. For a vacuum flask, describe which features reduce the energy transfer by:

   a) conduction

   b) convection

   c) radiation.

3. SUPPLEMENT a) Explain the function of a car radiator.

   b) You are standing a few metres away from a wood fire, and feel warm. State the main thermal transfer.

## Developing practical skills

A student heats water in a beaker until it is just boiling. As the water cools, the student measures its temperature and obtains the results shown in the graph.

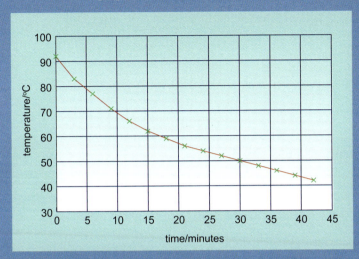

△ Fig. 2.27 Results of measuring the water temperature as it cools.

## Observing, measuring and recording data

**1.** Why should the student record the room temperature as well?

**2.** How often did the student measure the temperature of the water?

**3.** How would the graph have changed if the student had measured the temperature:

   **a)** more frequently

   **b)** less frequently?

## Evaluating methods

**3.** How could the student have reduced the rate of cooling of the water?

**4.** How could the student investigate the hypothesis 'the bigger the temperature difference between an object and its surroundings, the greater the rate of energy transfer between them'?

# End of topic checklist

## Key terms

conduction, convection, infrared radiation, thermal conductor, thermal insulators, thermal radiation

**SUPPLEMENT** free (delocalised) electrons

## During your study of this topic you should have learned:

○ Thermal conductors transfer heat better than thermal insulators in solids.

○ **SUPPLEMENT** Thermal conduction in all solids happens because of atomic or molecular lattice vibrations, and also movement of free (delocalised) electrons in metallic conductors.

○ **SUPPLEMENT** Thermal conduction is bad in gases and most liquids because there are fewer free electrons and the forces between atoms are weaker.

○ Convection is how thermal energy is transferred in liquids and gases (fluids).

○ Convection in fluids happens because of density changes, and how this can be demonstrated by experiments.

○ Thermal radiation is infrared radiation and this is emitted by all objects.

○ Thermal energy transfer by thermal radiation does not require a medium; it can travel through a vacuum.

○ Dull black objects are good emitters and absorbers of infrared radiation.

○ Shiny white objects are poor emitters and absorbers of infrared radiation but they are good reflectors of this radiation.

○ **SUPPLEMENT** An object has a constant temperature because it transfers energy away from the object at the same rate that it receives energy.

○ **SUPPLEMENT** An object will get hotter when the rate at which it receives energy is more than the rate at which it transfers energy away.

○ **SUPPLEMENT** An object will get cooler when the rate at which it receives energy is less than the rate at which it transfers energy away.

○ **SUPPLEMENT** The temperature of the Earth is affected by factors controlling the balance between incoming radiation and radiation emitted from the Earth's surface.

○ **SUPPLEMENT** Know about experiments used to distinguish between good and bad emitters and good and bad absorbers of infrared radiation.

○ **SUPPLEMENT** The rate of emission of radiation depends on the surface temperature and surface area of an object.

○ Know about applications of conduction, convection and radiation in the home, for example, cooking food or heating a room.

○ **SUPPLEMENT** Know about heat transfers that occur when burning wood or coal, and in a radiator in a car.

# End of topic questions

*Note: the marks in brackets give an indication of the level of detail you should include in your answers.*

1. Explain why several thin layers of clothing are more likely to reduce thermal transfer than one thick layer of clothing. (3 marks)

2. The diagram shows a cross-section of a steel radiator positioned in a room next to a wall.

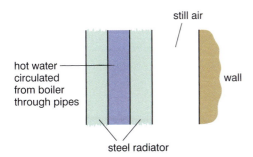

hot water circulated from boiler through pipes

still air

wall

steel radiator

   Describe how energy from the hot water reaches the wall behind the radiator. (6 marks)

3. Suggest a colour for a fire fighter's uniform. Explain your choice. (3 marks)

4. **SUPPLEMENT** Discuss how you might design a solar cooker to heat water using infrared radiation from the Sun. (3 marks)

5. Imagine you are a local inspector. You are deciding whether or not to give grants for installing home insulation. Discuss all the factors you would consider and what other information you would need before making a decision. (6 marks)

6. Explain why solids transfer energy mainly by conduction. (3 marks)

7. **a)** Thermal energy can be transferred by convection in which one of the following materials?

   **A** brass     **B** concrete     **C** water     **D** wood     (1 mark)

   **b)** Describe how a convection heater warms a room. (4 marks)

8. Using conduction in your answer, suggest why serving dishes are usually made from glass. (3 marks)

9. Explain why energy transfer from the Sun to us cannot be by conduction or convection. (2 marks)

10. Explain how the temperature of the Earth is affected by its atmosphere. (3 marks)

11. Two neighbours in a hot country have identical houses. One is painted black and the other white. Explain which house you would prefer to be in. (3 marks)

# Exam-style questions

*Note: exam-style questions, sample answers and comments have been written by the authors. The marks awarded for these questions indicate the level of detail required in the answers. In examinations, the way marks are awarded may be different. References to assessment and/or assessment preparation are the publisher's interpretation of the syllabus requirements and may not fully reflect the approach of Cambridge Assessment International Education.*

## Example answers

## Question 1

This question is about particles.

**a)** Brownian motion is often used as evidence supporting the particle model of matter.

**i)** State what is Brownian motion.

<u>*Atoms in a gas moving about*</u> ✗        (2)

**ii)** How does the explanation of Brownian motion support the particle model of matter?

<u>*The particles move about*</u>

<u>*very fast*</u> ✗ ✗ ✗        (3)

**b)** The photo shows bubbles rising in water.

**b) i)** These parts of the question are answered well.

**ii)** The answer makes good use of the relevant equations saving a lot of descriptive writing.

The bubbles increase in volume as they move towards the surface of the water.

**i)** Explain why the bubbles rise to the surface.

*The bubbles are less dense than the* ✔ ①. *so the forces on them are water unbalanced and they float upwards.* ✔ ①

(2)

**ii) SUPPLEMENT** Explain why the volume of the bubbles increases as they rise.

*The pressure = depth x density xg,* ✔ ①
*so the pressure gets less as the
bubbles move upwards.* ✔ ① *Also, pressure x volume is constant,
so if the pressure decreases then the volume increases.* ✔ ①
*So as the pressure on the bubbles decreases their volume will
increase and the bubbles will get bigger.* ✔ ①

(4)

(Total 11 marks)

## Question 2

A student investigates the effect of insulation on cooling.

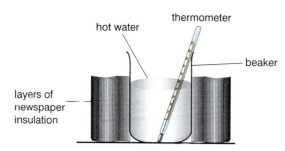

The student puts some hot water into a beaker and measures the temperature drop in 20 minutes.

He repeats the experiment using layers of paper as insulation.

His results are shown in the table.

| Number of layers of insulation | Temperature drop in 20 minutes/°C |
|---|---|
| 0 | 21 |
| 5 | 20 |
| 10 | 18 |
| 15 | 17 |
| 20 | 18 |

**a)** Draw a suitable graph of these results. (5)

**b)** The student concludes that the graph shows that thicker insulation reduces heat loss.

Is this a correct conclusion from this data? Explain your answer. (2)

(Total 7 marks)

## Question 3

Two experiments are carried out to investigate energy transfer in water.

In Experiment 1, cold water is gently heated at the top of a glass boiling tube. A block of ice trapped at the bottom remains solid even when the water at the top begins to boil.

In Experiment 2, cold water is gently heated at the bottom of the tube. Ice at the top of the tube melts before the water boils.

**a)** State the process by which thermal energy travels through the glass. (1)

**b) i)** What is the principal process in Experiment 2 that takes the energy from the water at the bottom to the ice at the top? (1)

   **ii)** Describe how the process in **b) i)** occurs. (2)

**c)** Suggest two reasons why the ice in Experiment 1 does not melt, even when the water at the top begins to boil. (2)

(Total 6 marks)

## Question 4 SUPPLEMENT

**a)** Explain why copper is a better thermal conductor than air. (3)

**b)** The radiant power incident on an object is 20 W. The object itself emits power at a rate of 15 W. Explain what will happen to the object. (3)

Two identical thermometers are placed in bright sunshine. The bulb of one thermometer is painted black and the other white. The surface areas of both bulbs are also the same. The thermometers are left in the sunshine for about 30 minutes.

**c)** Explain, whether or not both will show the same readings. (2)

(Total 8 marks)

What is the connection between the waves you see on water and light? Light is a wave that behaves in a similar way to water waves. Sound is another type of wave, as you will learn later in this section. Studying the behaviour of waves will help you to understand many of your everyday experiences, ranging from how you see objects to how you hear sounds.

## STARTING POINTS

**1.** Explain why a red object looks red.

**2.** Describe the pitch and loudness of the sound you hear when the sound wave has a large amplitude and the frequency is low.

**3.** How does light travel through space?

**4.** Draw a diagram to show how light is reflected by a plane mirror.

## SYLLABUS SECTIONS COVERED

**3.1** General properties of waves

**3.2** Light

**3.3** Electromagnetic spectrum

**3.4** Sound

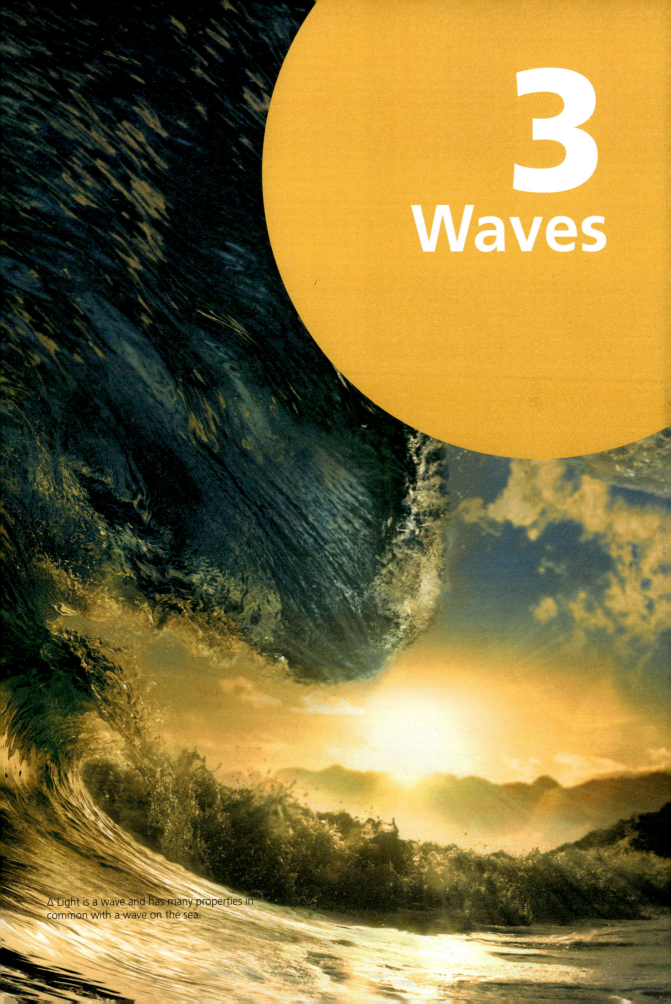

# 3
# Waves

△ Light is a wave and has many properties in common with a wave on the sea.

△ Fig. 3.1 This photo shows many examples of waves in action.

# General properties of waves

### INTRODUCTION

The behaviour of waves affects us in every moment of our lives. Waves are reaching us constantly: sound waves, light waves, infrared waves, television and mobile-phone microwave signals, and **radio waves**, the list goes on. The study of waves is an important part of physics.

The woman in Fig. 3.1 is surrounded by waves: she can feel the infrared waves from the Sun coming in through the windows; she can hear the sound waves of her friend on the phone; the phone uses microwaves; and she can see around her with light waves.

### KNOWLEDGE CHECK

✓ Light and sound are both waves.
✓ Sound and light waves can be reflected off surfaces.

### LEARNING OBJECTIVES

✓ Know that waves transfer energy without transferring matter.
✓ Describe what is meant by wave motion as illustrated by vibrations in ropes and springs, and by experiments using water waves.
✓ Describe the features of a wave in terms of wavefront, wavelength, frequency, crest (peak), trough, amplitude and wave speed.
✓ Recall and use the equation for wave speed
  $v = f \lambda$.
✓ Know that for a transverse wave, the direction of vibration is at right angles to the direction of propagation and understand that electromagnetic radiation, water waves and seismic S-waves (secondary) can be modelled as transverse.
✓ Know that for a longitudinal wave, the direction of vibration is parallel to the direction of propagation and understand that sound waves and seismic P-waves (primary) can be modelled as longitudinal.
✓ Describe how waves can undergo: reflection at a plane surface, refraction due to a change of speed and diffraction through a narrow gap.
✓ Describe the use of a ripple tank to show: reflection at a plane surface, refraction due to a change in speed caused by a change in depth, diffraction due to a gap and diffraction due to an edge.
✓ **SUPPLEMENT** Describe how wavelength and gap size affects diffraction through a gap.
✓ **SUPPLEMENT** Describe how wavelength affects diffraction at an edge.

## LONGITUDINAL AND TRANSVERSE WAVES

All waves transfer energy without transferring matter. Wave motion can be illustrated by vibrations in ropes and springs. Fig. 3.2 shows two types of wave motion illustrated by a spring.

In a **longitudinal wave,** the vibrations are parallel to the direction in which the wave propagates or travels. This type of wave can be shown by pushing and pulling a spring. The spring stretches in places and squashes in others.

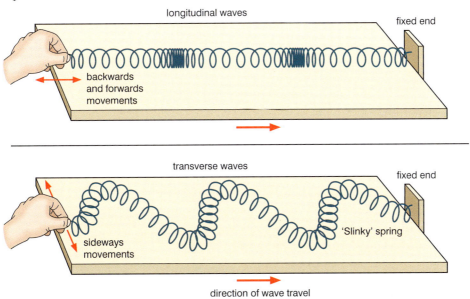

△ Fig. 3.2 Longitudinal and transverse waves are made by vibrations. Both types of wave have a repeating shape or pattern.

Sound and seismic P-waves (primary) are examples of longitudinal waves.

In a **transverse wave,** the vibrations are at right angles to the direction of propagation. All electromagnetic waves (e.g. light, radio waves), water waves and seismic S-waves (secondary) are transverse waves. As shown in Fig. 3.2, a transverse wave can be produced on a spring, by sideways movement of one end. You can also use a stretched-out rope to create transverse waves. Water waves can be produced on the surface of water in a tank or tray by constantly dipping your finger in and out of the water. Alternatively, a ripple tank can be used with the waves created by a 'paddle' attached to an electric motor.

Longitudinal and transverse waves are made by vibrations. Both types of wave have a repeating shape or pattern.

All waves transfer energy from one place to another without transferring matter. In the case of electromagnetic waves, it requires no material at all and it can travel through a vacuum.

## Features of a wave

The important features of a wave are its wavelength ($\lambda$), **frequency** ($f$) and speed ($v$). A wave also has a series of peaks (crests), and troughs. See Fig. 3.3.

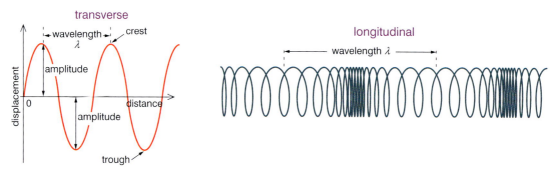

△ Fig. 3.3 The wavelength and amplitude of a transverse wave and the wavelength of a longitudinal wave.

- The **wavelength** is the distance between two adjacent peaks or, if you prefer, the distance between two adjacent (neighbouring) troughs of the wave. In the case of longitudinal waves, it is the distance between two adjacent points of maximum squashed region, or the distance between two adjacent points of maximum stretched regions. Wavelength is measured in metres (m), or centimetres (cm) and millimetres (mm).
- The **frequency** is the number of complete waves that go past a point per unit time. Frequency is measured in hertz (Hz), where 1 Hz = 1 complete wave per unit second. You can also think of frequency as the number of complete oscillations of a point in the medium per unit time.
- The **amplitude** is the maximum particle displacement of the wave from the undisturbed position. (Displacement is the distance in a certain direction from the undisturbed position.) In transverse waves, this is half the crest-to-trough height. Amplitude is measured in m, cm or mm.
- The **speed** of the wave is the distance travelled by the wave per unit time. Speed is measured in m/s, cm/s or mm/s. The speed depends on the substance or medium the wave is passing through.
- A **wavefront** is a line drawn to represent the peaks of a wave in two-dimensions. The distance between two adjacent wavefronts is equal to the wavelength of the wave. Wavefronts are very helpful when showing some of the properties of the waves, for example **reflection** and **diffraction** (spreading of a wave).

The largest ocean wave recorded had a wavelength of 340 m, a frequency of 0.067 Hz (that is to say one peak every 15 s), and a speed of 23 m/s. The amplitude of the wave was 17 m, so the ship that was measuring the wave was going 17 m above the level of a smooth sea and then 17 m below. The wave went down 34 m from crest to trough.

## Waves transfer energy

A wave transfers energy, and can also carry information. You can feel the thermal energy of infrared waves from the Sun; you can see the energy contained in the ocean waves from a typhoon as they reach the coast after travelling hundreds of miles. And you can see the information contained in the light reaching your eyes from this page, or from a laptop screen.

Note that in none of these cases has any object or matter travelled by vibrations from the source of the waves to the destination. Instead, the wave is passed on from point to point along the route taken by the wave. One good example is a piece of wood or a seabird on the sea. They are shaken up and down, and side to side, by a wave, but after the wave has passed they end up where they were before.

## QUESTIONS

1. Describe the direction of vibrations in:

   **a)** a longitudinal wave

   **b)** a transverse wave.

2. For a wave, define: **a)** wavelength, **b)** frequency, **c)** amplitude.

3. Calculate the distance travelled by a wave in 3.0 s given its speed is 5.0 m/s.

4. What do all waves transfer?

   **A** energy    **B** frequency    **C** wavelength    **D** amplitude

## Relationship between speed, frequency and wavelength

The speed of a wave in a given medium is constant. When you change the wavelength, the frequency *will* change as well. If you imagine that some waves are going past you on a spring or on a rope, then they will be going at a constant speed. When the waves get closer together, then more waves must go past you per second, and that means that the frequency has gone up.

The **wave speed**, frequency and wavelength of a wave are related by the equation:

wave speed = frequency × wavelength

$$v = f \times \lambda$$

Where:   $v$ = wave speed

$f$ = frequency

$\lambda$ = wavelength

## WORKED EXAMPLES

**1.** A loudspeaker emits sound waves of frequency 300 Hz. The waves have wavelength 1.13 m. Calculate the speed of the sound in air.

Write down the equation:   $v = f \times \lambda$

Substitute the values for $f$ and $\lambda$:   $v = 300 \times 1.13$

Calculate the answer and write down the unit:   $v = 339$ m/s

△ Fig. 3.4 The equation triangle for wave speed, frequency and wavelength.

**2.** A radio station broadcasts radio waves of wavelength 250 m. The speed of the radio waves is $3.0 \times 10^8$ m/s. Calculate the frequency.

Write down the equation for $f$   $f = \dfrac{v}{\lambda}$

Substitute the values for $v$ and $\lambda$:   $f = \dfrac{3.0 \times 10^8}{250}$

Calculate the answer and write down the unit: $f = 1\,200\,000$ Hz or 1200 kHz

## Using water waves to show reflection, refraction and diffraction

All waves can be reflected, refracted and diffracted.

Reflection is the bouncing-off of a wave at a surface, such as a wall for sound waves or a mirror for visible light. **Refraction** is when the direction of a wave changes because of a change in its speed. Refraction will happen for light as it travels from air into water, or glass. Diffraction is the spreading out of a wave at a narrow gap or at an edge. For example, sound waves can be diffracted by a narrow gap when the door is left slightly opened – this is why you can hear a conversation on the other side of the door.

A ripple tank can be used to show reflection, refraction and diffraction of water waves, see Fig. 3.5.

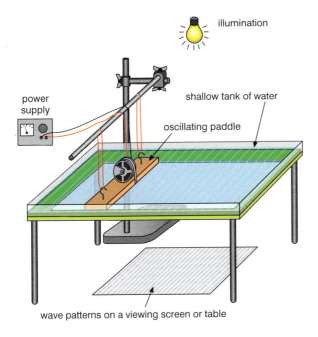

illumination

power supply

shallow tank of water

oscillating paddle

wave patterns on a viewing screen or table

◁ Fig. 3.5 A ripple tank.

To show **reflection**, you put a plane surface in the tank some distance from the paddle. To show **refraction**, you put a thin glass sheet in the water to change the depth of the water in a given region, hence the speed of the water waves. To show **diffraction**, you put a plane surface with a gap approximately the same width as the wavelength of the water waves. Diffraction also occurs around an edge; this can be demonstrated by placing a straight-edge block into the water.

Fig. 3.6 shows how water waves can be used to explain reflection (see Reflection of light) at a plane surface. Waves hit a barrier at an angle of incidence, $i$. The waves bounce off with the angle of incidence, $i$, equal to the angle of reflection, $r$. The reflected wave is the same plane as the incident wave.

When a wave moves from one medium into another, it will either speed up or slow down. For example, a wave going along a rope will speed up if the rope becomes thinner. And sound waves going from cold air to hotter air will speed up. When a wave slows down, the wavefronts crowd together – the wavelength gets smaller.

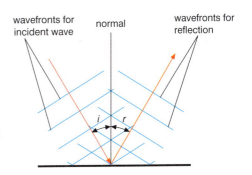

wavefronts for incident wave    normal    wavefronts for reflection

$i$  $r$

△ Fig. 3.6 Reflection at a plane surface. The angle of incidence $i$ is equal to the angle of reflection $r$. All angles are measured from the normal.

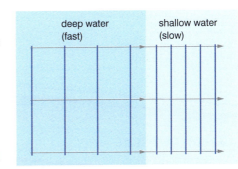

deep water (fast)    shallow water (slow)

△ Fig. 3.7 When waves slow down, their wavelength gets shorter. Remember that the separation between adjacent wavefronts is equal to one whole wavelength.

Fig. 3.7 shows this happening as water waves moves from deep water to shallow water. The wave slows down as it travels across the boundary. The frequency of the wave does not change as it crosses the boundary, so if the speed decreases and the frequency stays the same, the wavelength must also decrease. When a wave speeds up, the wavefronts spread out – the wavelength gets larger. If the speed increases but the frequency stays the same, then the wavelength must also increase.

When waves slow down, their wavelength gets shorter. When a wave enters a new medium at an angle then the wavefronts also change direction. This is known as refraction (see Refraction of light in the following topic). The amount that the wave is bent by depends on the change in speed. Water waves are slower in shallower water than in deep water, so water waves will refract when the depth changes as shown in Fig. 3.8.

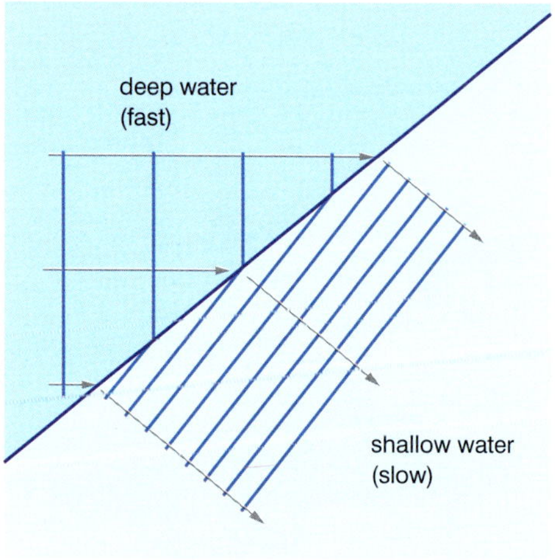

△ Fig. 3.8 If waves cross into a new medium at an angle, their wavelength and direction change.

**SUPPLEMENT**

Wavefronts change shape when they pass the edge of an obstacle or go through a gap (Fig. 3.9). This process is known as diffraction. Diffraction is most noticeable when the width of the gap is similar in size to the wavelength of the waves. At an edge, longer wavelength waves spread out the most. This is shown in Fig. 3.10.

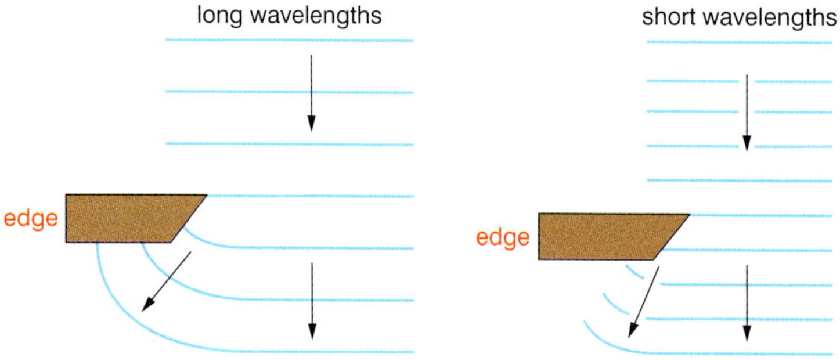

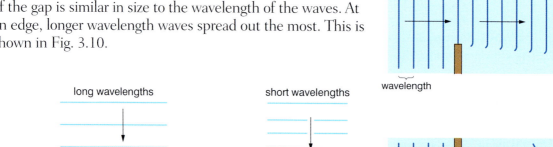

long wavelengths    short wavelengths

edge    edge

△ Fig. 3.10  At an edge, long wavelength waves are diffracted more than shorter wavelength waves.

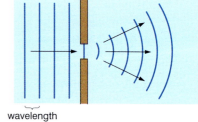

wavelength

wavelength

△ Fig. 3.9 Diffraction of a wave at a gap.

## QUESTIONS

1. Compare transverse and longitudinal waves, and give one example of each.

2. State three things that all waves do.

3. A student is using a ripple tank to demonstrate the diffraction of water waves at a gap. The waves have frequency 10 Hz and wavelength 2.0 cm.

   a) Calculate the speed of the waves in cm/s.

   b) **SUPPLEMENT** Suggest a suitable value of the width of the gap in order to see lots of diffraction at the gap.

# End of topic checklist

## Key terms

amplitude, diffraction, longitudinal wave, frequency, refraction, reflection, transverse wave, wave, wave speed, wavelength

## During your study of this topic you should have learned:

○ A wave transfers energy without transferring matter.

○ Wave motion can be shown by vibrations in ropes and springs, and vibrations of water.

○ A wavefront is a line in two dimensions showing the crests of a wave.

○ Wavelength is the distance between adjacent peaks (or troughs) – it is measured in m, cm and mm.

○ Frequency is the number of complete waves passing a point per unit time, or the number of oscillations per unit time at a point – it is measured in Hz.

○ Wave speed is the speed of a wave in one direction – it is measured in m/s, cm/s or mm/s.

○ The equation of wave speed is: $v = f\lambda$.

○ A transverse wave has vibrations at right angles to the direction of propagation (examples: electromagnetic radiation, water waves and seismic S-waves (secondary)).

○ A longitudinal wave has vibrations parallel to the direction of propagation (examples: sound waves, seismic P-waves (primary)).

○ All waves undergo reflection at a plane surface, refraction due to a change of speed and diffraction through a narrow gap.

○ A ripple tank can be used to demonstrate reflection at a plane surface, refraction due to a change in speed caused by a change in depth, diffraction due to a gap and diffraction due to an edge.

○ **SUPPLEMENT** Significant diffraction occurs at a gap when the wavelength is about the same as the width of the gap.

○ **SUPPLEMENT** Longer wavelength waves are diffracted more around an edge.

# End of topic questions

*Note: the marks in brackets give an indication of the level of detail you should include in your answers.*

1. A wave has amplitude 2.0 mm, wavelength 0.50 m and frequency 680 Hz.

    **a)** State the number of wave oscillations in a time interval of 1.0 s. (1 mark)

    **b)** State the distance between two adjacent peaks. (1 mark)

    **c)** Show that the speed of the wave is 340 m/s. (3 marks)

    **d)** Calculate the distance travelled by the wave in 10 s. (2 marks)

2. Radio waves of frequency 900 MHz are used to send information to and from a mobile (cell) phone. The speed of the waves is $3.0 \times 10^8$ m/s. Calculate the wavelength of the waves. (1 MHz = $10^6$ Hz) (2 marks)

3. **a)** Calculate the wavelength of waves of speed $3.0 \times 10^8$ m/s and frequency 400 MHz. (2 marks)

    **b)** **SUPPLEMENT** For the waves in part **a)** to diffract, about how wide should the opening be? (2 marks)

4. Calculate the frequency of waves of speed 60 m/s and wavelength 0.10 m. (2 marks)

5. Calculate the speed in cm/s of water waves in a ripple tank given the wavelength is 3.0 cm and the paddle is vibrating in the water at 8.0 Hz. (2 marks)

6. **SUPPLEMENT** Microwaves of wavelength 3.0 cm and radio waves of wavelength 100 cm are incident on a metal plate with a sharp edge. Explain which of these waves will show more diffraction at the edge. (2 marks)

7. **SUPPLEMENT** In a ripple tank experiment, an object with a gap of 0.50 cm is placed in the water. Water waves of frequency 40 Hz and speed 20 cm/s are incident on this object. With the help of a calculation, explain whether or not these waves will diffract significantly at the gap. (4 marks)

8. What is being observed in the photograph of water waves passing through a gap in a shallow lagoon?

   **A** amplitude     **B** diffraction     **C** reflection     **D** refraction

# Light

## INTRODUCTION

Visible light is just part of the electromagnetic spectrum; without it our lives, and of all the animals in the world, would be difficult to imagine. There are different processes involved in seeing the world around us, including reflection and refraction. You may already know that, as light enters your eyes, it is refracted by the lens in your eye and brought to a focus on your retina.

△ Fig. 3.11 Vision is important to us humans, and animals alike. Eyes use light to make sense of the world.

## KNOWLEDGE CHECK

✓ All waves have wavelength, amplitude and frequency.
✓ Longitudinal and transverse waves are two types of wave motion.
✓ Wavefronts can be used to show reflection, refraction and diffraction.

## LEARNING OBJECTIVES

✓ Define and use the terms normal, angle of incidence and angle of reflection.
✓ Describe the formation of an optical image by a plane mirror, and give its characteristics, i.e. same size, same distance from mirror, virtual.
✓ State that for reflection, the angle of incidence is equal to the angle of reflection; recall and use this relationship.
✓ **SUPPLEMENT** Use simple constructions, measurements and calculations for reflection by plane mirrors.

✓ Define and use the terms normal, angle of incidence and angle of refraction.
✓ Describe an experiment to show refraction of light by transparent blocks of different shapes.
✓ Describe the passage of light through a transparent material (limited to the boundaries between two media only).
✓ State the meaning of critical angle.
✓ Describe internal reflection and total internal reflection using both experimental and everyday examples.

✓ **SUPPLEMENT** Define refractive index, $n$, as the ratio of the speeds of a wave in two different regions.

✓ **SUPPLEMENT** Recall and use the equation $n = \dfrac{\sin i}{\sin r}$.

✓ **SUPPLEMENT** Recall and use the equation $n = \dfrac{1}{\sin c}$.

✓ **SUPPLEMENT** Describe the use of optical fibres, particularly in telecommunications.

✓ Describe the action of thin converging and thin diverging lenses on a parallel beam of light.
✓ Define and use the terms focal length, principal axis and principal focus (focal point).

✓ Draw and use ray diagrams for the formation of a real image by a converging lens.

✓ Describe the characteristics of an image using the terms enlarged/same size/ diminished, upright/inverted and real/virtual.

✓ Know that a virtual image is formed when diverging rays are extrapolated backwards and does not form a visible projection on a screen.

✓ **SUPPLEMENT** Draw and use ray diagrams for the formation of a virtual image by a converging lens.

✓ **SUPPLEMENT** Describe the use of a single lens as a magnifying glass.

✓ **SUPPLEMENT** Describe the use of converging and diverging lenses to correct long-sightedness and short-sightedness.

✓ Describe the dispersion of light as illustrated by the refraction of white light by a glass prism.

✓ Know the traditional seven colours of the visible spectrum in order of frequency and in order of wavelength.

✓ **SUPPLEMENT** Recall that visible light of a single frequency is described as monochromatic.

## REFLECTION OF LIGHT

Perhaps the most familiar type of wave in everyday life is light. Light does not need a medium to travel through as it is an electromagnetic wave.

Light waves have all of the properties of waves. You have already learned about their speed, frequency and wavelength. Most importantly, light, like all electromagnetic waves, is a **transverse wave**.

Like all other waves, light can be reflected, refracted and diffracted. Reflection and refraction are easy to demonstrate with a mirror and a glass of water. The effects caused by diffraction of light waves are very hard to see. The effects are small because the wavelength of light is about 0.00050 mm, and we rarely look through such tiny gaps.

### Reflection of light and ray diagrams

When you look in a plane mirror you see an image of yourself (Fig. 3.12).

- The image is laterally inverted because when you raise your right hand your image raises what you would call its left hand.
- The image is formed as far behind the mirror as you are in front of it and is the same size as you.
- The image cannot be projected onto a screen. It is known as a **virtual image.**

△ Fig. 3.12 As you look at the face of the girl and her image in the mirror, you can see that every part of her face is directly opposite its image in the mirror, and that each part is the same distance away from the mirror as its image.

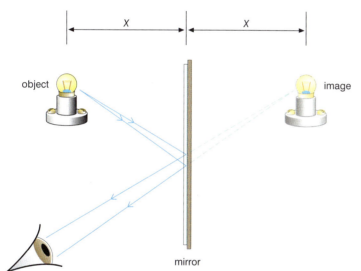

◁ Fig. 3.13 Rays of light travel outwards from the lamp in all directions. Here, just two rays are drawn to show how light goes from the lamp to the observer's eye. After the rays have reflected from the mirror, they travel along lines that *look* as if they started from the image. The eye is tricked into thinking that the light really did start from the image.

A ray of light is a line drawn to show the path that the light waves take. We need to study what happens when an incident light ray hits a mirror and is reflected off. Light rays are reflected from mirrors in such a way that

angle of incidence ($i$) = angle of reflection ($r$)

The angles are measured to an imaginary line at 90° to the surface of the mirror. This line is called the **normal**.

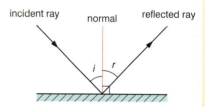

△ Fig. 3.14 The angles of incidence and reflection are the same when a mirror reflects light.

The image in a plane mirror is virtual. A virtual image cannot be projected onto a screen, and as such, it is an illusion. A virtual image is formed when diverging rays are extrapolated backwards. When you are given the position of the object, then you can construct a diagram to show the position of the image. The diagrams in Fig. 3.15 show you how. Notice that in each case the angle of incidence is the same as the angle of reflection.

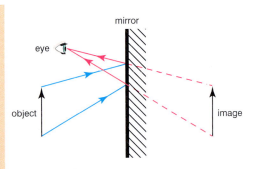 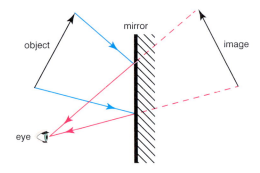

△ Fig. 3.15 Determining the position of an image. The blue rays are the incident rays and the red rays are the reflected rays. You can calculate the position of the image – it is the same distance behind the mirror, as is the object in front.

In a plane mirror the image is always the same size as the object. Examples of plane mirrors include household 'dressing' mirrors, security mirrors for checking under vehicles, and periscopes.

## SUPPLEMENT

An image formed by a plane mirror, such as the one in Fig. 3.15, is:

- virtual
- laterally inverted
- the same size as the object
- the same distance behind the mirror as the object is in front of the mirror.

Note that the image is never formed on the surface of the mirror. This is a common mistake.

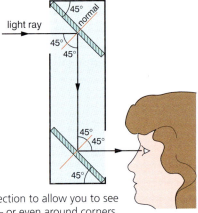

▷ Fig. 3.16 A periscope uses reflection to allow you to see above your normal line of vision – or even around corners.

## Developing practical skills

A student wants to find the position of an image in a plane mirror. To do this she sets up a plane mirror with an object pin placed vertically a few centimetres in front of it (Fig. 3.17). To find the image, the student looks into the mirror at an angle a little further along the mirror. She can see the image of the object pin in the mirror and she places two 'sighting pins' in line with the image in the mirror. The student repeats this process from a slightly different angle, again putting in two sighting pins.

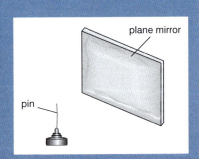

△ Fig. 3.17 The apparatus needed for the investigation.

## Planning experiments and investigations

**1.** How can the student use the positions of these sighting pins to find the position of the image?

**2.** How can the student use the positions of the sighting pins to show that the angle of incidence is equal to the angle of reflection for light reflecting off the mirror?

## Observing, measuring and recording data

**3.** Draw a plan view diagram to show this experiment. Include the object pin, sighting pins and position of the image.

**4.** On your diagram, check that the image is as far behind the mirror as the object is in front. Check also that the line joining the object and image cuts through the mirror at 90°.

## Interpreting and evaluating data

**5.** Apart from checking the measurements as in your diagram, how could the student check that she has marked the position of the image correctly?

**6.** Would this method for finding the image work with a curved mirror? Explain your answer.

## REFRACTION OF LIGHT

The view through some windows is deliberately obscure – the image that you see is distorted. This is because the glass has a different thickness in different places. Rays of light passing through the window are bent to a different extent. Plain windows in some houses can give slightly distorted images because it used to be much harder to make large, flat panes of glass.

The bending of light is the phenomenon known as refraction. Look closely around you, and you will see many examples of refraction of light. Fig. 3.18 shows an optical illusion. The pencil is not broken at all, but it looks as if it is because of light refracted through the water and the glass.

◁ Fig. 3.18 Refraction of light makes this pencil look broken.

Light waves *slow down* when they travel from air into glass. When they are at an angle to the glass, light rays bend *towards* the normal as they enter the glass. When the light rays travel out of the glass into the air, their speed increases and they bend *away* from the normal. When the block of glass has parallel sides, the light resumes its original direction after passing through. This is why a sheet of window glass has so little effect on the view beyond. However, the view is shifted slightly sideways when you look through the glass at an angle.

Fig. 3.19 shows how you can demonstrate the refraction of light through a glass block.

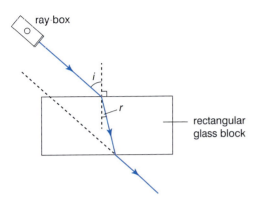

△ Fig. 3.19 Refraction of light by a rectangular glass block.

The angle of incidence, $i$, is the angle between the incident light ray and the normal to the surface in the air. The angle of refraction, $r$, is the angle between the refracted light ray and the normal to the surface inside the material (e.g. glass).

(Note that unfortunately, the letter $r$ is used both for the angle of reflection and the angle of refraction. It should be clear from the context whether it is reflection or refraction.)

## QUESTIONS

1. Explain why a pond, or a swimming pool, will look shallower when viewed at an angle.

2. The speed of sound in air is about 340 m/s and in helium about 1000 m/s. Explain what would happen to sound waves travelling from air into a helium balloon at an angle.

## Refractive index

The **refractive index** of a material indicates how much the material changes the direction of the light. It is calculated using the following equation:

refractive index $n = \dfrac{\sin i}{\sin r}$

Where:     $i$ = angle of incidence

     $r$ = angle of refraction

The refractive index of a vacuum is exactly 1 and the refractive index of air is fractionally higher, but we will take it as 1.00. Other common refractive indices are water 1.3; glass 1.5; sapphire 1.8; diamond 2.4.

The refractive index $n$ can also be defined as:

$$n = \dfrac{\text{speed of light in vacuum (or air)}}{\text{speed of light in the material}}$$

## WORKED EXAMPLES

**1.** The speed of light in a vacuum is 300 000 000 m/s.
What is the speed of light in glass with a refractive index of 1.5?

Write down the equation:     $n = \dfrac{\text{speed of light in vacuum (or air)}}{\text{speed of light in the material}}$

Rearrange the equation:     $\text{speed in material} = \dfrac{\text{speed in vacuum}}{n}$

Substitute the values:     $\text{speed in material} = \dfrac{300\,000\,000}{1.5}$

Calculate the answer and write down the unit:
     speed in material = 200 000 000 m/s
     $= 2.0 \times 10^8$ m/s

**2.** A light ray approaches a block of plastic at an angle of incidence of 60°. The refractive index of the plastic is 1.4. Calculate the angle of refraction.

Write down the equation: $n = \dfrac{\sin i}{\sin r}$

When $i = 60°$, $\sin i = 0.866$

Rearrange the equation:     $\sin r = \dfrac{\sin i}{n}$

Substitute the values:     $\sin r = \dfrac{0.866}{1.4}$

Calculate $\sin r$:     $\sin r = 0.619$

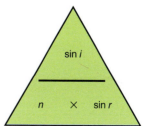

△ Fig. 3.20 The equation triangle for $n = \dfrac{\sin i}{\sin r}$.

From a calculator, when $\sin r = 0.619$, then $r = 38.2°$
The angle of refraction is about 38°.

1. The refractive index of a particular glass is 1.5 and the angle of incidence is 50°. Calculate the angle of refraction.

2. The angle of refraction for a ray of light in a block of plastic with refractive index 1.4 is 25°. Calculate the angle of incidence.

3. The angle of incidence of a ray of light is 55°. The angle of refraction in the material is 35°. Calculate the refractive index of the material.

4. Light travels at different speeds in different materials. The refractive index of a material indicates the speed of light in the material. Here is a table of refractive indices for some materials.

| Material | Refractive index $n$ |
|----------|----------------------|
| Water | 1.33 |
| Glass | 1.52 |
| Diamond | 2.42 |

a) Deduce whether light travels faster or more slowly in water than it does in vacuum.

b) State and explain through which of these materials you think light will travel slowest.

c) Calculate the speed of light in each of the materials in the table and confirm (or otherwise) your prediction from part b)

## Developing practical skills

A student wants to find the refractive index of a rectangular block of glass. He draws around the block and marks the position of a ray of light that travels through the block. With the block removed, the student can draw in a normal line and then measure the angle of incidence and the angle of refraction. The student repeats this process for different angles of incidence. His measurements are shown in the table.

△ Fig. 3.21 Ray of light being refracted by a glass block.

| Angle of incidence $i/°$ | Angle of refraction $r/°$ |
| --- | --- |
| 10 | 6.5 |
| 20 | 13 |
| 30 | 20 |
| 40 | 25 |
| 50 | 32 |
| 60 | 35 |

## Observing, measuring and recording data

**1.** Draw a diagram to show the measurements the student needs to make.

**2.** How should the student mark the normal line during the experiment?

## Interpreting and evaluating data

**3.** What was the independent variable in this investigation? What was the dependent variable?

**4.** State the equation linking refractive index, sin i and sin r.

**5.** Draw a graph of sin i (y-axis) against sin r (x-axis).

**6.** Use your graph to find a value for the refractive index of the block.

## Evaluating methods

**7.** Describe two possible reasons why the measurements may not be completely accurate.

**8.** What difference would it make to the results if light of a different colour was used in the experiment?

## Total internal reflection and the critical angle

The speed of light in glass is about $2.0 \times 10^8$ m/s and in air about $3.0 \times 10^8$ m/s. So, when light travels from glass to air, it speeds up, and this will make the light refract away from the normal. Fig. 3.22 shows what happens when the angle of incidence $i$ within the glass is slowly increased. The angle of refraction is $r$. The angle $c$ is something special, and will be discussed further soon.

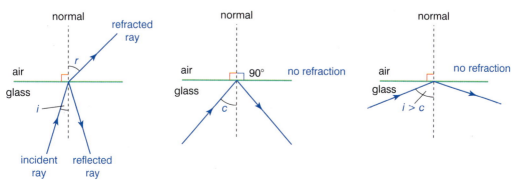

△ Fig. 3.22 Light travelling from glass to air at different angles of incidence.

- *i* less than *c*: There is a weak internal reflection at the glass–air boundary, and a strongly refracted ray out from the glass. Notice that *r* is more than *i*.
- *i* is equal to *c*: The angle of incidence *i* is equal to *c* and angle of refraction is equal to 90°. The angle of incidence when the angle of refraction is 90° is called the **critical angle** *c*.
- i more than *c*: The angle of refraction cannot be more than 90°. In this case, there is no refraction, just a strong reflection at the glass–air boundary. This reflection is known as **total internal reflection** (TIR).

Total internal reflection only occurs when:

- light attempts to travel into a material with *lower* refractive index, e.g. from glass to air or water to air
- the angle of incidence is greater than the critical angle.

Fig. 3.23 shows an underwater photograph of fish in a shallow river in the Amazon rainforest in Brazil. You can see the total internal reflection of light at the surface of the water – there are mirror images of the fish and the riverbed at the top of the photograph.

△ Fig. 3.23 The surface of the river behaves like a perfect mirror.

3.24 shows an arrangement with a semi-circular glass block that can be used to demonstrate critical angle and total internal reflection. The ray from the projector passes straight through the glass without any change in direction because the angle of incidence is 0°. This ray travels through the glass and makes an angle of incidence *i* within the glass. The light is internally reflected at the glass-air boundary and strongly refracted into the air, making an angle of refraction *r*. When *i* = critical angle, *r* = 90° and when *i* is more than the critical angle, total internal reflection takes place at the glass–air boundary.

The critical angle for glass is about 42° and for water about 49°.

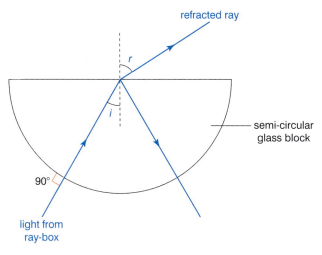

refracted ray

r

i

90°

semi-circular
glass block

light from
ray-box

△ Fig. 3.24 A semi-circular block of glass can be used to demonstrate critical angle and total internal reflection.

## Calculating critical angle

You can calculate the critical angle $c$ from the refractive index $n$ of a transparent material using the equation:

$$n = \frac{1}{\sin c}$$

For example, for glass, $n = 1.5$. Therefore:

$$1.5 = \frac{1}{\sin c}$$

$$\sin c = \frac{1}{1.5} = 0.667$$

$$c = \sin^{-1}(0.667) = 42°$$

A ray of light making an angle greater than 42° in glass will undergo total internal reflection.

Total internal reflection is used in optical fibre cables. An optical fibre is a thin rod of high-quality glass or plastic, which absorbs or scatters very little light. Light entering one end of the fibre undergoes repeated total internal reflections as it travels along the length of the fibre and emerges at the other end. Light can be channelled along the fibre even when it is bent.

Telecommunication systems rely increasingly on optical fibres instead of the more traditional copper cables. Cables made from optical fibres do not use electricity – the signals are carried by light or infrared waves. The signals are very clear because they do not suffer from electrical interference. Other advantages are that the optical fibres are cheaper than copper cables and can carry thousands of different signals down the same fibre at the same time.

Bundles of several thousand optical fibres are used in medical endoscopes for internal examination of the body. The bundle carries an image from one end of the bundle to the other, each optical fibre carrying one tiny part of the image.

△ Fig. 3.25 A single optical fibre.

## QUESTIONS

1. Define critical angle for a material such as glass.

2. Explain why light cannot undergo total internal reflection when travelling from air to glass.

3. **SUPPLEMENT** Calculate the critical angle for the following transparent materials:

   **a)** ruby $n = 1.71$

   **b)** sugar solution $n = 1.49$

   **c)** pure ice $n = 1.31$

**SCIENCE IN CONTEXT**   **APPLICATIONS OF TOTAL INTERNAL REFLECTION**

### Bicycle reflectors

Unlike glass mirrors, which can provide multiple and blurred images, prisms provide perfect reflections and images. No wonder that you will find them used in optical instruments such as cameras and binoculars. Fig. 3.26 shows total internal reflection in a glass prism, and where you may find prisms in a pair of binoculars.

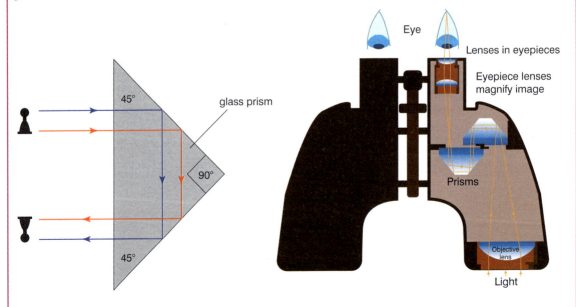

△ Fig. 3. 26 Total internal reflection by prisms is used in binoculars.

Total internal reflection has also provided safety for cyclists with 'reflectors'. Fig. 3.27 shows the basic construction of such a reflector.

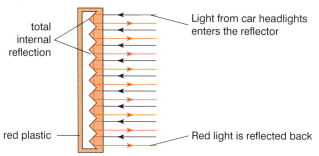

total internal reflection

Light from car headlights enters the reflector

red plastic

Red light is reflected back

△ Fig. 3.27 A bicycle reflector.

A bicycle reflector is smooth on the outside but the plastic is angled like 90° prisms on the inside. Light from the headlights of a car travel straight through the flat outside surface. On the inside, the light is totally internally reflected, and returned in the same direction from which it came. The car driver will see the reflection of their own headlights, but the important thing is that the driver knows that the cyclist is there.

**Challenge Question:** What is the main property of the image produced when the single prism shown in Fig. 3.26 is used?

## THIN LENSES

A **converging lens,** also known as a convex lens, makes parallel rays of light to converge (Fig. 3.28). The light rays are bent by refraction. The amount of refraction increases from the middle of the lens (where there is no refraction) to a maximum at the outer edge of the lens. The point where the parallel light rays arriving along the principal axis of the lens all cross over is known as the **principal focus (focal point)**, F. This distance between the principal focus and the centre of the lens is the **focal length** of the lens. The smaller the focal length, the greater the amount of light refracted by the lens. Note that there are two principal foci. The word 'foci' is the plural of 'focus'. The foci are on each side of the lens and at the same distance away from the centre of the lens.

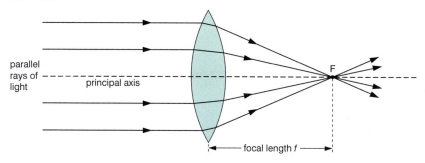

parallel rays of light

principal axis

F

focal length $f$

△ Fig. 3.28 Rays through a convex lens converge to a focus.

The **principal** axis is defined as the line of symmetry passing through the centre of the lens. The principal foci lie on this line.

Converging lenses are used to form images by magnifying glasses, cameras, mobile (cell) phones, telescopes, binoculars, microscopes, film projectors and also in spectacles for correcting vision for long-sighted people.

### Determining the position of an image

To find the position of the image of an object formed by a converging lens, you can draw a ray diagram. In all of the diagrams, we will assume that the lenses are thin – so the refraction can be taken almost along a line vertical to the principal axis.

There are three standard rays that you can use to do this. A standard ray is one whose complete path you know. In ray diagrams, you need any two of the standard rays to find the position and size of the image. In addition, it is a wise precaution to draw the third ray to check the accuracy with which you drew the first two.

For convenience, ray diagrams are usually drawn with the bottom of the object on the principal axis. This means that the bottom of the image is also on the principal axis, and you need only locate the top of the image. Figs. 3.29, 3.30 and 3.31 show the standard rays.

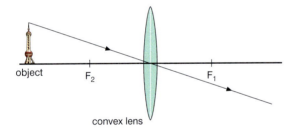

◁ Fig. 3.29 A ray from the top of the object, straight through the centre of the lens.

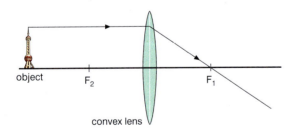

◁ Fig. 3.30 A ray from the top of the object, parallel to the principal axis until it reaches the lens, and then down through the principal focus $F_1$ on the far side of the lens.

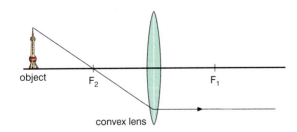

◁ Fig. 3.31 A ray from the top of the object through the principal focus $F_2$ on the near side of the lens, down to the lens and then parallel to the axis.

You can use a suitable combination of these three rays to locate images, and identify their characteristics. Three examples are given here.

**Example 1:** Object placed at a distance greater than 2f from the lens

Fig. 3.32 shows an object placed at a distance greater than twice the focal length f of the lens. The image has the following characteristics:

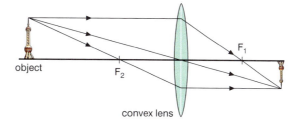

- it is diminished (smaller than object)
- inverted (upside down)
- closer to the lens than the object
- real image.

△ Fig. 3.32 The object is a long way from the lens (more than twice the focal length).

A real image is one that can be projected onto a suitable screen. Examples of the formation of this type of image are in the eye and in a camera.

**Example 2:** Object placed between f and 2f from the lens

Fig. 3.33 shows an object placed between f and 2f from the lens. The image has the following characteristics:

- it is enlarged (larger than object)
- inverted
- further from the lens than the object
- real image.

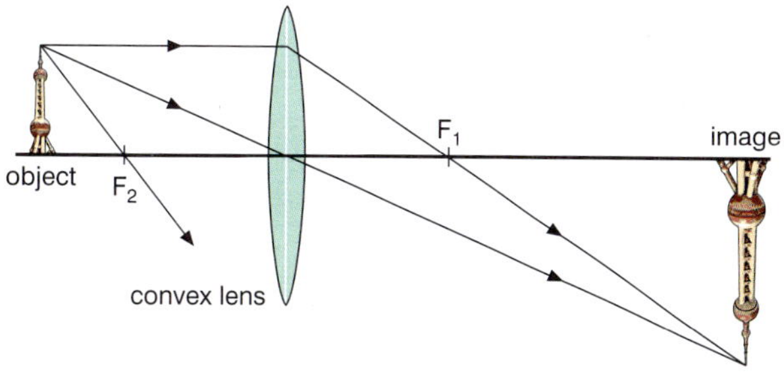

△ Fig. 3.33 The object is closer to the lens (between ×1 and ×2 the focal length).

Examples of the formation of this type of image are in a film projector and in a photographic enlarger.

SUPPLEMENT

**Example 3:** Object placed at a distance less than f from the lens

Fig. 3.34 shows an object placed within the principal focus and the lens.

The image has the following characteristics:

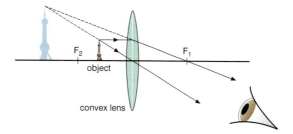

- it is enlarged (larger than object)
- upright
- further from the lens than the object, and on the same side as the object
- virtual image.

△ Fig. 3.34 The object is closer to the lens than the focal length. This single lens is being used as a magnifying glass.

To see the image, you have to look through the lens. This single lens is being used as a **magnifying glass.**

A virtual image is formed when the diverging rays are extrapolated backwards, and it cannot be projected onto a screen.

### Diverging lens

A diverging lens, also known as a concave lens, is thinner in the middle than it is at the edges. Fig. 3.35 shows rays passing through a thin diverging lens.

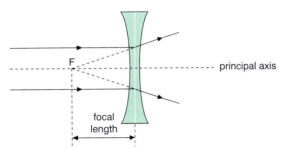

△ Fig. 3.35 A diverging lens. The principal focus F is a virtual one.

After passing through the lens, the parallel rays of light appear to come from a point on the principal axis. This point F is still called the principal focus, and the distance between the centre of the lens and the principal focus is the focal length of the lens.

SUPPLEMENT

Fig. 3.36 shows the image formed by a thin diverging lens.

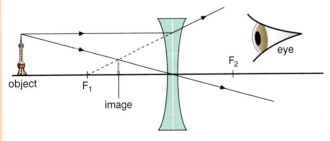

△ Fig. 3.36 Image formed by a diverging lens.

No matter where the object is placed, the image formed by this type of lens has the following characteristics:

• diminished (smaller than object)

• upright

• closer to the lens than the object, and the same side as the object

• virtual image.

Unlike converging lenses, diverging lens have fewer uses. They are commonly used in spectacles for correcting vision for short-sightedness.

## Using lens to correct vision

Short-sightedness is a condition of the eyes where people cannot clearly see distant objects, but they can see close objects. Each of our eyes has a converging lens that can change shape, and alter its focal length. People with this condition cannot make the lens form an image on the back of the eye (retina) when looking at distant objects. Instead, the image is formed in front of the retina, so what people see is a blurred image. This condition is corrected by using a diverging lens (Fig. 3.37).

△ Fig. 3.37 Short-sightedness is corrected by using a diverging lens.

Long-sightedness is a condition of the eyes where people cannot clearly see closer objects, but they can see distant objects. The eye lens forms an image beyond the retina when looking at closer objects – the image seen is blurred. This condition is corrected by using a converging lens (Fig. 3.38).

△ Fig. 3.38 Long-sightedness is corrected by using a converging lens.

## QUESTIONS

1. Explain the term principal focus for a converging lens.

2. An object is placed at a distance of 2*f* from the centre of a converging lens, where *f* is the focal length.

   **a)** Draw a ray diagram for the image.

   **b)** State the properties of the image.

3. A parallel beam of light is incident on a lens. Explain how you can deduce whether the lens is a converging lens or a diverging lens.

4. **SUPPLEMENT** Describe the condition of short-sightedness, and state the type of lens that can be used to correct the vision.

## DISPERSION OF LIGHT

When white light is passed through a triangular glass or plastic prism, it is split into a spectrum of different colours. See Fig. 3.39.

This is called **dispersion**. The refractive index of the glass (or plastic) is slightly different for each colour of light, so each colour is refracted by a different amount. The light rays are bent or refracted twice: once as they enter the prism,

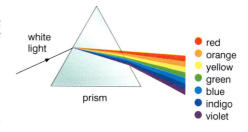

white light

prism

- red
- orange
- yellow
- green
- blue
- indigo
- violet

△ Fig. 3.39 Dispersion of light by a prism. Wavelengths progressively decrease from red to blue, and the frequency progressively increases from red to blue.

and again in the same direction as they leave it. The dispersion increases each time, which is why the colours are separated so much. Red is always bent least and violet is bent most.

White light is therefore a mixture of seven different colours: red, orange, yellow, green, blue, indigo and violet. (You can remember this as *ROYGBIV*). The light of each colour travels through air at the same speed, but has different wavelengths and frequencies. The wavelength of red light is about 0.0007 mm, and the wavelength progressively decreases through the colours with blue light having the shortest wavelength of about 0.0004 mm. As we go through the colours from red to blue, the frequency increases.

## SUPPLEMENT

Visible light of a single wavelength or frequency is known as **monochromatic** light. We would see monochromatic light as having a unique colour. The band of red colour from the splitting of white light by a prism has a range of wavelengths, but you can get a unique wavelength from a laser. Laser light is monochromatic.

## QUESTIONS

1. State which colour within white light has the shortest wavelength.

2. Describe how the frequency changes from violet light to red light.

3. **SUPPLEMENT** Describe the properties of monochromatic light.

# End of topic checklist

## Key terms

angle of incidence, angle of reflection, angle of refraction, converging lens, critical angle, diminished image, dispersion, diverging lens, enlarged image, inverted image, normal, optical fibres, principal axis, principal focus, real image, total internal reflection, upright image, virtual image

**SUPPLEMENT** long-sightedness, magnifying glass, refractive index, short-sightedness

## During your study of this topic you should have learned:

○ Normal is a line drawn at right angles between the boundary of two materials.

○ The angle of incidence is the angle made by the incident ray to the normal.

○ The angle of reflection is the angle made by the reflected ray to the normal.

○ The image formed by a plane mirror has the following characteristics: same size, same distance from mirror, and virtual.

○ That the law of reflection states that the angle of incidence is equal to the angle of reflection.

○ **SUPPLEMENT** How to use simple constructions, measurements and calculations for reflection by plane mirrors.

○ The angle of refraction is the angle made by the refracted ray to the normal.

○ Describe an experiment to show refraction of light by transparent blocks of different shapes.

○ Describe the passage of light through a transparent material.

○ The critical angle is the angle made to the normal in the denser material when the angle of refraction is 90°.

○ Describe internal reflection and total internal reflection.

○ **SUPPLEMENT** Refractive index, $n$, is defined as the ratio of the speeds of a wave in two different regions.

○ **SUPPLEMENT** The equation for refractive index is: $n = \dfrac{\sin i}{\sin r}$.

○ **SUPPLEMENT** The equation for critical angle is: $n = \dfrac{1}{\sin c}$.

○ **SUPPLEMENT** Describe the use of optical fibres, particularly in telecommunications.

○ A thin converging lens converges a parallel beam of light.

○ A thin diverging lens diverges a parallel beam of light.

# End of topic checklist continued

○ Principal focus (focal point) is the point on the principal axis where parallel rays passing through the lens meet.

○ The principal axis is a line of symmetry passing through the centre of the lens.

○ The focal length is the distance from the centre of the lens to the principal focus.

○ How to draw and use ray diagrams for the formation of a real image by a converging lens.

○ Describe the characteristics of an image using the terms enlarged/same size/ diminished, upright/inverted and real/virtual.

○ Know that a virtual image is formed when diverging rays are extrapolated backwards and does not form a visible projection on a screen.

○ **SUPPLEMENT** Draw and use ray diagrams for the formation of a virtual image by a converging lens.

○ **SUPPLEMENT** Describe the use of a single lens as a magnifying glass.

○ **SUPPLEMENT** A converging lens is used to correct long-sightedness.

○ **SUPPLEMENT** A diverging lens is used to correct short-sightedness.

○ The dispersion of light as shown by the refraction of white light passing through a glass prism.

○ Know the seven colours (red, orange, yellow, green, blue, indigo and violet) of white light, and that frequency increases from red to violet and wavelength decreases from red to blue.

○ **SUPPLEMENT** Visible light of a single frequency or wavelength is described as monochromatic.

# End of topic questions

*Note: the marks in brackets give an indication of the level of detail you should include in your answers.*

**1.** State four characteristics of an image formed by a plane mirror. (4 marks)

**2. a)** Rays of light can be reflected and refracted. State one difference between reflection and refraction. (1 mark)

**b)** The diagram shows a glass block and two rays of light.

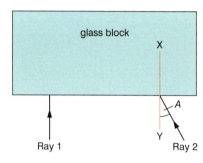

    **a)** Copy the diagram and complete the paths of the two rays as they pass into and then out of the glass block. (2 marks)

       **i)** Name the angle marked as *A*. (1 mark)

      **ii)** State the name of the line marked as XY. (1 mark)

**3.** The diagram shows light entering a prism. Total internal reflection takes place at the inner surfaces of the prism.

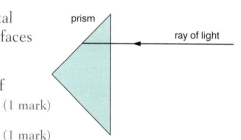

    **a)** Copy the diagram and complete the path of the ray. (1 mark)

    **b)** Suggest one use for a prism like this. (1 mark)

    **c)** Copy and complete the table about total internal reflection by glass. Use T for total internal reflection or R for refraction.

| Angle of incidence at the second face/° | Total internal reflection (T) or refraction (R) |
| --- | --- |
| 36 | |
| 42 (critical angle) | |
| 46 | |

(3 marks)

**4. SUPPLEMENT** A student traces the path of a narrow beam of red light through a rectangular block of plastic, and finds that the angle of incidence is 50.0 and the angle of refraction is 21.7°.

    **a)** Calculate the refractive index of the plastic.     (3 marks)

    **b)** Calculate the critical angle for the plastic block.     (3 marks)

**5. SUPPLEMENT** An object is 2.0 cm tall and placed 2.0 cm from a converging lens that has a focal length of 4.0 cm. Draw the ray diagram. Complete the rays backwards as dotted lines to draw the image.     (3 marks)

**6.** Which statement correctly describes a property of a virtual image?

    **A** It can be projected onto a screen.

    **B** It is always inverted.

    **C** It is always magnified.

    **D** It is formed when looking into a mirror.     (1 mark)

**7.** Explain why dispersion occurs.     (6 marks)

**8.** White light passing through a glass prism shows dispersion.

    **a)** State the seven colours present in white light.     (1 mark)

    **b)** State whether red light or green light has the shorter wavelength.     (1 mark)

    **c)** State whether orange light or yellow light has the higher frequency.     (1 mark)

**9. SUPPLEMENT** The speed of light in sugar solution is $2.5 \times 10^8$ m/s and in vacuum it is $3.0 \times 10^8$ m/s.

    **a)** Calculate the refractive index of the sugar solution.     (3 marks)

    **b)** Light travels from vacuum into the sugar solution at an angle of incidence of 45°. Calculate the angle of refraction in the sugar solution.     (3 marks)

# Electromagnetic spectrum

△ Fig. 3.40 Microwaves can be used to make tasty popcorn in a microwave oven.

## INTRODUCTION

Electromagnetic waves are all around us. Our eyes can only respond to a tiny section of the electromagnetic spectrum, which spans from radio waves to **gamma rays**.

Humans have been inventive enough to make good use of electromagnetic waves. Imagine a world without microwaves – there would be no television, no text messaging, no making of popcorn in a microwave oven and no sending images between mobile (cell) phones using Bluetooth. Electromagnetic waves have harmful effects too. Our knowledge of these waves helps us to minimise any harmful effects: for example, using sunblock to stop **ultraviolet** radiation from the Sun damaging our skin.

## KNOWLEDGE CHECK

✓ All waves have speed, wavelength and frequency.
✓ Light can travel through a vacuum.

## LEARNING OBJECTIVES

✓ Know the main regions of the electromagnetic spectrum in order of frequency and in order of wavelength.
✓ Know that all electromagnetic waves travel at the same high speed in a vacuum.
✓ Describe typical uses of the different regions of the electromagnetic spectrum including: (a) radio waves; radio and television transmissions, astronomy, radio frequency identification (RFID), (b) microwaves; satellite television, mobile phones (cell phones), microwave ovens, (c) infrared; electric grills, short range communications such as remote controllers for televisions, intruder alarms, thermal imaging, optical fibres, (d) visible light; vision, photography, illumination, (e) ultraviolet; security marking, detecting fake bank notes, sterilising water, (f) X-rays; medical scanning, security scanners and (g) gamma rays; sterilising food and medical equipment, detection of cancer and its treatment.
✓ Describe the harmful effects on people of excessive exposure to electromagnetic radiation, including: (a) microwaves; internal heating of body cells, (b) infrared; skin burns, (c) ultraviolet; damage to surface cells and eyes, leading to skin cancer and eye conditions and (d) X-rays and gamma rays; mutation or damage to cells in the body.
✓ Know that communication with artificial satellites is mainly by microwaves: some satellite phones use low orbit artificial satellites and some satellite phones and direct broadcast satellite television use geostationary satellites.

✓ **SUPPLEMENT**  Know that the speed of electromagnetic waves in a vacuum is $3.0 \times 10^8$ m / s and is approximately the same in air.

✓ **SUPPLEMENT**  Know that many important systems of communications rely on electromagnetic radiation including: (a) mobile phones (cell phones) and wireless internet use microwaves because microwaves can penetrate some walls and only require a short aerial for transmission and reception; (b) Bluetooth uses radio waves because radio waves pass through walls but the signal is weakened on doing so; and (c) optical fibres (visible light or infrared) are used for cable television and high-speed broadband because glass is transparent to visible light and some infrared; visible light and short wavelength infrared can carry high rates of data.

✓ **SUPPLEMENT**  Know the difference between a digital and analogue signal.

✓ **SUPPLEMENT**  Know that a sound can be transmitted as a digital or analogue signal.

✓ **SUPPLEMENT**  Explain the benefits of digital signaling including increased rate of transmission of data and increased range due to accurate signal regeneration.

## ELECTROMAGNETIC WAVES

Electromagnetic (EM) waves are transverse waves – visible light, infrared and radio waves are three examples. Electromagnetic waves are special because they can travel through a vacuum. Other waves, such as sound waves, cannot travel through a vacuum. We can feel the warmth from the Sun's infrared waves because they can travel to us through the emptiness of space before reaching us.

Electromagnetic waves travel at the same high speed through vacuum and air. For example, it would take less than a few hundredths of a second for radio waves to travel between China and Australia.

### SUPPLEMENT

The speed of all electromagnetic waves is the same in a vacuum; 300 000 000 m/s or $3.0 \times 10^8$ m/s. In air, the speed is also about the same. Since all electromagnetic waves have the same speed, and since *speed = frequency × wavelength*, this implies that the frequency of electromagnetic waves is inversely proportional to its wavelength – the shorter the wavelength, the larger is the frequency. Radio waves have the longest wavelength and therefore the lowest frequency.

## ELECTROMAGNETIC SPECTRUM

Electromagnetic waves form a continuous spectrum of waves. The **electromagnetic spectrum** is separated into seven main regions or groups: radio waves, microwaves, infrared, visible light, ultraviolet, X-rays and gamma rays, as shown in Fig. 3.41. The waves have different wavelengths and frequencies. Radio waves have the longest wavelength and the wavelengths progressively get *shorter* as we move towards the gamma rays end of the spectrum. Radio waves can have wavelengths the size of a tall building, whereas gamma rays have wavelengths about the size of atomic nuclei. The frequency of the waves *increases* as we go from radio waves to gamma rays.

wavelength / m

$10^{-12}$  $10^{-9}$  $10^{-6}$  $10^{-3}$  $10^{0}$  $10^{3}$

X-ray

Gamma rays     ultraviolet    infrared    Microwave    radio waves

frequency

△ Fig. 3.41 The electromagnetic spectrum.

## QUESTIONS

**1.** State one thing that is the same for radio waves and light travelling through a vacuum.

**2.** What type of waves are electromagnetic waves?

   **A** sound      **B** longitudinal      **C** transverse      **D** water waves

**3.** Describe the main difference between gamma rays and radio waves.

**4.** Put these following electromagnetic waves into order of increasing wavelength.

   microwaves     gamma rays     infrared     visible light     ultraviolet

**5.** **SUPPLEMENT a)** State the speed in m/s of electromagnetic waves in air.

   **b)** Calculate the distance travelled by light in air in a time of 2.0 s.

---

**SCIENCE IN CONTEXT**      **DISCOVERY OF INFRARED**

We feel the warmth from a hot object because of infrared waves. These waves are invisible to us. William Herschel (1738–1822) was the first person to discover that these invisible waves were a continuation of the visible spectrum. We now know that both visible light and infrared waves are part of the larger electromagnetic spectrum. Fig. 3.42 shows the arrangement of his experiment.

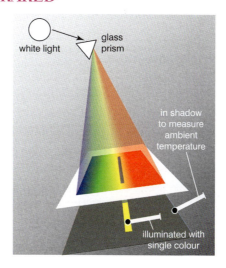

white light      glass prism

in shadow to measure ambient temperature

illuminated with single colour

△ Fig. 3.42 Herschel's experiment.

ELECTROMAGNETIC SPECTRUM

In a darkened room, a beam of white sunlight was passed through a prism. The dispersed light from the prism formed a rainbow of colours on a piece of cardboard that had a single slit. The slit was wide enough to let a single colour pass through to a glass thermometer with its bulb blackened. The rise in temperature, compared with a control thermometer in shadow, was recorded for the various colours. For each measurement, he waited for about 10 minutes before recording the stable temperature. A revised version of his results, with temperatures converted to °C, is shown in Fig. 3.43.

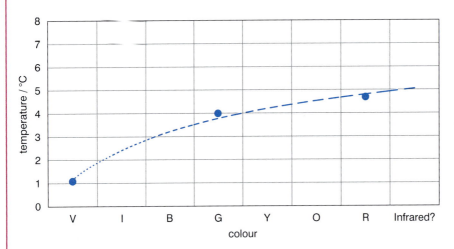

△ Fig. 3.43 The data shows a trend, with temperature rise greater beyond the red end of the visible spectrum.

Fig. 3.43 clearly shows that the trend would give a greater temperature rise in the region beyond the red. This is exactly what Herschel found. He had discovered the infrared region of the electromagnetic spectrum.

**Challenge Question:** If you were repeating this experiment, what additional controls would you have?

## USES OF ELECTROMAGNETIC WAVES

### Radio waves

Radio waves were first discovered by Heinrich Hertz in 1886. Soon after, Guglielmo Marconi successfully transmitted radio waves across the Atlantic Ocean. We are now very familiar with radio waves being used for communication – for radio and television.

Distant objects in space, such as galaxies, some rotating stars, and even blackholes, emit radio waves. Astronomers use giant radio telescopes, like the one shown in Fig. 3.44, to detect and image these objects.

Radio frequency identification (RFID) uses radio waves to identify and tracks tags attached to objects (see Fig. 3.45). The objects could be objects in a factory or store, or domestic animals in a farm. RFID tags are also used in some shops for security to prevent customers from stealing items.

△ Fig. 3.44 Astronomers use giant radio telescopes to search for distant galaxies and blackholes.

△ Fig. 3.45 An RFID tag.

## Microwaves

Microwaves are effectively high-frequency radio waves. Microwaves are used in radar to find the position of planes, ships, and even rain clouds. All of these objects reflect these waves. The distance of the objects can be determined from the time taken between the microwave signal being received after reflection and being sent. The next time you see weather maps with rain clouds on your mobile (cell) phone or television, just remember that the information came from using microwaves.

Microwaves are also used for cooking in microwave-ovens. Molecules in the food absorb the energy carried by microwaves. The internal (thermal) energy of the food increases, making it hotter.

Microwaves can easily pass through the atmosphere of the Earth. This makes them ideal for sending microwave signals between the surface of the Earth and artificial satellites orbiting high above its surface. Satellites are used by mobile (cell) phones companies. We can now instantly communicate with people on the other side of the Earth with the help of these orbiting satellites.

## Infrared

The hotter an object, the more infrared waves it gives out.

Thermograms are images that show the infrared waves given out from objects – useful for detecting people in the dark. Fig. 3.46 shows an infrared thermometer, which directly measures the temperature of a person without making any physical contact.

Infrared electric grills are used for cooking. Infrared waves are used in short-range communication with television, and other electronic gadgets, using remote control. Since we cannot see infrared waves, they are used as part of intruder alarm systems. An intruder breaks a hidden beam of infrared, which sets off the alarm. Infrared waves are also used in sending information along optical fibres.

△ Fig. 3.46 With an infrared thermometer you can check someone's temperature without getting too close.

## Visible light

Visible light is important to all humans and animals on the Earth. Light provides illumination and helps us to see the world around us. Seeing the pages of this book is only possible because of light. We cannot help ourselves from taking photographs with cameras and mobile (cell) phones – they provide us with treasured memories.

## Ultraviolet

Fluorescent materials absorb energy from ultraviolet waves, and re-emit the energy as visible light. Fluorescent materials come in a variety of forms. They can be liquid (paint and ink) or powder.

You can use security marking pens for your valuables. The markings will show up under an ultraviolet source. Fluorescent materials are also used on bank notes to help detect any fakes. Ultraviolet waves can damage the cells in our bodies. This is why some people use sunblock to reduce the ultraviolet energy penetrating to their skins. However, this harmful effect of the waves can be used to sterilise water by killing off any bacteria (germs).

## X-rays

X-rays are more harmful to humans than ultraviolet waves. In medical scans, patients are irradiated with X-rays for a very short time. X-ray scans of the body can help to identify broken bones and torn muscles. X-rays can easily pass through flesh, but not bones. X-rays are also used in security scanners at many airports, see Fig. 3.47.

△ Fig. 3.47 X-ray scan of baggage at an airport.

## Gamma rays

Gamma rays are produced by changes taking place in the nuclei of some atoms, e.g. cobalt-60. Gamma rays are as harmful as X-rays. Gamma rays are used for sterilising food and medical equipment. Gamma rays are also used in sophisticated scanners for the detection and treatment of some cancers. In the treatment known as radiotherapy, gamma rays are used to kill off cancerous cells.

## HARMFUL EFFECTS OF ELECTROMAGNETIC WAVES

Apart from radio waves, all other electromagnetic waves can be harmful to us humans. Even long exposure to intense sunlight can damage the cells in our eyes. This is why it is best to wear sunglasses on very sunny days.

Table 3.1 shows the harmful effect of all other electromagnetic waves, especially for long exposures.

| Electromagnetic waves | Harmful effects |
|---|---|
| Microwaves | • Internal heating of cells in our bodies. |
| Infrared | • Skin burns and rashes. |
| Ultraviolet | • Damage to surface cells that can lead to skin cancer.<br>• Damage to the eyes and can lead to eye conditions such as cataracts and macular degeneration. |
| X-rays and gamma rays | • Body cells can be permanently damaged or mutated. |

△ Table 3.1 Harmful effects of electromagnetic waves.

## QUESTIONS

1. State three uses of radio waves.

2. Name three types of electromagnetic waves that are harmful to humans.

3. Which electromagnetic waves are used in TV remote controllers?

   **A** infrared    **B** gamma rays    **C** radio waves
   **D** visible light

4. Name all types of electromagnetic waves that either damage or mutate cells.

5. Suggest the harm a 'leaky' microwave may do to a person.

## COMMUNICATIONS WITH MICROWAVES

Artificial satellites orbiting high above the Earth use microwaves for communications. Microwaves have the ability to travel through the Earth's atmosphere without too much absorption or reflection. The satellites used for communications orbit in one of the two orbits:

• low Earth orbit (LEO)

• geostationary orbit.

A satellite in a low Earth orbit (LEO), as the name suggests, can be relatively close to the surface of the Earth – between 160 km and 1000 km above the surface of the Earth. There are thousands of satellites in such orbits travelling at speeds of about 8 km/s. They are cheap to build and launch using rockets from all around the world. Satellites in low orbits are used for satellite-phones.

Satellites in geostationary orbits are at a height of about 36 000 km above the equator of the Earth. Geostationary satellites take exactly 24 hours to orbit the Earth and travel from west to east. This means that the satellite remains above the same point above the rotating Earth. The coverage of the Earth's surface area can be immense, and it can offer services to remote areas of the Earth. There are a few hundred of these satellites travelling at speeds of about 3 km/s and forming a ring above the equator. The major drawback of these satellites is the cost to build them, and also to launch them because big, and expensive, fuel-carrying rockets are required.

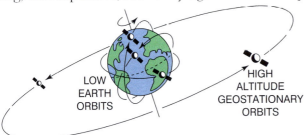

LOW EARTH ORBITS

HIGH ALTITUDE GEOSTATIONARY ORBITS

△ Fig. 3.48 Satellites can be in low Earth orbits or in geostationary orbits.

## OTHER COMMUNICATION SYSTEMS

### Mobile phones and wireless internet

Mobile (cell) phones and wireless internet use microwaves. Microwaves can penetrate some walls, which greatly helps with having wireless internet in homes and work places. The wavelength of the microwaves used is about a few centimetres. This means that the aerials used for transmission and reception can be short. Look around a mobile (cell) phone and you will not see a large aerial sticking out from it.

### Bluetooth

Bluetooth technology uses radio waves for sharing information between fixed and mobile devices over short distances. It was first developed by the Ericsson Mobile company in Sweden some 30 years ago. The radio waves have a frequency of about 2.4 GHz, and a wavelength of about 13 cm. Laptops, speakers and mobile (cell) phones are just a few examples of devices using this type of technology. No cables are necessary, and the radio waves used can travel through walls and furniture, but the signal can lose strength. Although Bluetooth has a low setting-up cost, it does have a low level of security and the rate at which information can be transferred is low compared with wireless internet.

### Optical fibres

Optical fibres use either visible or infrared for transmitting information for cable-television and high-speed internet broadband systems. The short wavelength of both these waves makes it possible to carry high rates of data. Optical fibres allow data to be transmitted without loss of signal or any electromagnetic interference. The major drawback of optical fibres is cost – they are more expensive to set up than traditional copper cables.

## Digital and analogue signals

Electrical signals come in two forms – **analogue** and **digital**. See Fig. 3.49. The output signal from a microphone picking up sound will be analogue. An analogue signal varies continuously with time. Devices such as laptops and mobile (cell) phones use digital signals. A digital signal has two possible values – high and low. This type of signal is simplistic, but devices can store and process information accurately using digital signals. Digital signals are easier to process, and transmit at high speed over vast distances. Unlike analogue signals, which can alter shape when external 'noise' signals are also picked up, digital signals with their just two values of 'high' and 'low' are easier to restore or regenerate by electronic circuits. The range of the transmission can be increased because digital signals can be regenerated.

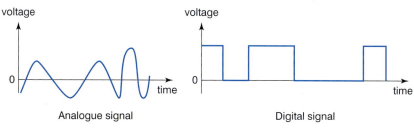

△ Fig. 3.49 Analogue and digital signals.

## QUESTIONS

1. Name two types of satellite-orbits used for communications.

2. **SUPPLEMENT** State the type of waves used by Bluetooth.

3. **SUPPLEMENT** Describe some of the properties of microwaves that make them ideal for wireless internet.

4. **SUPPLEMENT** List the benefits of using digital signals rather than analogue signals in communications.

# End of topic checklist

## Key terms

artificial satellite, digital signal, electromagnetic waves, gamma rays, geostationary satellite, infrared, low orbit satellite, microwaves, optical fibres, radio waves, ultraviolet, visible light, X-rays

**SUPPLEMENT** analogue signal, Bluetooth, regeneration (of signal)

## During your study of this topic you should have learned:

○ The main regions of the electromagnetic spectrum in order of increasing frequency and in order of decreasing wavelength are: radio waves, microwaves, infrared, visible light, ultraviolet, X-rays and gamma rays.

○ Uses of radio waves include: radio and television transmissions, astronomy and radio frequency identification (RFID).

○ Uses of microwaves are: satellite television, mobile phones (cell phones) and microwave ovens.

○ Uses of infrared include: electric grills, short range communications such as remote controllers for televisions, intruder alarms, thermal imaging and optical fibres.

○ Uses of visible light include: vision, photography and illumination.

○ Uses of ultraviolet include: security marking, detecting fake bank notes and sterilising water.

○ Uses of X-rays include: medical scanning and security scanners.

○ Use of gamma rays include: sterilising food and medical equipment and detection of cancer and its treatment.

○ The harmful effects of microwaves include: internal heating of body cells.

○ The harmful effects of microwaves and infrared include: skin burns and rashes.

○ The harmful effects of ultraviolet include: damage to surface cells and eyes, skin cancer and eye conditions.

○ The harmful effects of X-rays and gamma rays include: mutation of cells and damage to cells in the body.

○ Communication with artificial satellites is mainly by microwaves.

○ Satellite phones use low orbit artificial satellites.

○ Satellite phones and direct broadcast satellite television use geostationary satellites.

# End of topic checklist continued

○ **SUPPLEMENT** The speed of electromagnetic waves in a vacuum is $3.0 \times 10^8$ m/s and is approximately the same in air.

○ **SUPPLEMENT** Mobile phones (cell phones) and wireless internet use microwaves because microwaves can penetrate some walls and only require a short aerial for transmission and reception.

○ **SUPPLEMENT** Bluetooth uses radio waves because radio waves pass through walls but the signal is weakened on doing so.

○ **SUPPLEMENT** Optical fibres (visible light or infrared) are used for cable television and high-speed broadband.

○ **SUPPLEMENT** Optical fibres use glass because it is transparent to visible light and some infrared.

○ **SUPPLEMENT** Visible light and short wavelength infrared can carry high rates of data.

○ **SUPPLEMENT** Digital signals have only two values, and analogue signal is a continuous signal.

○ **SUPPLEMENT** Information on sound can be transmitted as a digital or analogue signal.

○ **SUPPLEMENT** The benefits of digital signaling include: increased rate of transmission of data and increased range due to accurate signal regeneration.

# End of topic questions

*Note: the marks in brackets give an indication of the level of detail you should include in your answers.*

1. Ultraviolet waves are part of the electromagnetic spectrum.

   a) Name any two other electromagnetic waves that have frequency lower than that of ultraviolet waves. (2 marks)

   b) Describe the harmful effects of excessive exposure to ultraviolet waves. (3 marks)

   c) Explain how ultraviolet waves can be helpful in the treatment of water. (2 marks)

2. Infrared waves are used in optical fibres. The length of the optical fibre is 520 m. The infrared waves have speed $2.6 \times 10^8$ m/s and wavelength $1.3 \times 10^{-6}$ m.

   a) Other than optical fibres, state one other application of infrared waves. (1 mark)

   b) Calculate the time it takes for these waves to travel the length of the fibre. (3 marks)

   c) Calculate the frequency of the infrared waves. (3 marks)

3. a) Explain the characteristics of a geostationary satellite. (3 marks)

   b) Describe two practical uses of these satellites in communications. (2 marks)

   c) Suggest one major advantage of having a satellite in a geostationary orbit. (1 mark)

4. **SUPPLEMENT** A baby monitor system transmits and receives information using Bluetooth.

   a) State the types of electromagnetic waves used by Bluetooth. (1 mark)

   b) The information transmitted by the system as digital signals.
      i) Describe some of the advantages of having digital signals. (2 marks)
      ii) Explain what are digital signals. (1 mark)

5. Which statement is correct?

   A Fake bank notes can be identified using infrared waves.

   B Mobile phones use microwaves.

   C Remote controllers for televisions emit X-rays.

   D Visible light is used to sterilise water. (1 mark)

# Sound

△ Fig. 3.50 Sound is important to us all.

## INTRODUCTION

The human ear detects sound in the frequency range 20 Hz to 20 000 Hz. Young people have a better response to higher frequencies. Our ears convert the sound waves into electrical signals that our brains can process. It would be difficult to imagine life without sound – no music, no conversation, no sounds of nature. In this section, you will learn more about sound, and also some applications of ultrasounds.

### KNOWLEDGE CHECK

✓ All waves have speed, wavelength, amplitude and frequency.
✓ There are two types of waves: longitudinal and transverse waves.
✓ All waves show reflection, refraction and diffraction.

### LEARNING OBJECTIVES

✓ Describe the production of sound by vibrating sources.
✓ Describe the longitudinal nature of sound waves.
✓ State the approximate range of frequencies audible to humans as 20 Hz to 20 000 Hz.
✓ Know that a medium is needed to transmit sound waves.
✓ Know that the speed of sound in air is approximately 330–350 m / s.
✓ Describe a method involving a measurement of distance and time for determining the speed of sound in air.
✓ Describe how changes in amplitude and frequency affect the loudness and pitch of sound waves.
✓ Describe an echo as the reflection of sound waves.
✓ Define ultrasound as sound with a frequency higher than 20 kHz.
✓ **SUPPLEMENT** Describe compression and rarefaction.
✓ **SUPPLEMENT** Know that, in general, sound travels faster in solids than in liquids and faster in liquids than in gases.
✓ **SUPPLEMENT** Describe the uses of ultrasound in non-destructive testing of materials, medical scanning of soft tissue and sonar including calculation of depth or distance from time and wave speed.

## The basics of sound

Sound waves are produced in air by any vibrating object. Any vibrating object will do, for example your larynx (voice box) when you talk, the strings of a guitar and the engine of a car.

Sound waves are longitudinal waves and they need a medium to travel through. Sound waves can also travel through liquids and solids. The speed of sound in air depends on its temperature and density. Speed of sound in air is approximately 330 m/s to 350 m/s. The speed of sound is different in other gases and in other materials.

Human ears respond to sound waves in the frequency range 20 Hz to 20 000 Hz; this is the audible range for humans. Animals ears respond differently to sounds. For example, dogs can hear frequencies higher than 20 000 Hz and elephants can hear low frequency sounds. Low frequency sounds can travel further than high frequency sounds. Elephants can hear each other over several kilometres.

Sound of frequency greater than 20 000 Hz is referred to as ultrasound. Ultrasound, like all other waves, can be reflected, refracted and diffracted. Bats use ultrasound to catch their prey at night.

### SUPPLEMENT

Sound waves propagate through the air as a series of pressure regions called compressions and rarefactions. In a compression region, the air pressure is slightly higher than normal pressure with air molecules squashed together. In a rarefaction region, the air pressure is slightly lower than normal pressure with air molecules further apart. The distance between two adjacent rarefactions, or compressions, is equal to the wavelength of sound.

In general, sound travels faster in solids than in liquids, and faster in liquids than in gases. For example, the speed of sound in carbon-dioxide is about 270 m/s, in water about 1400 m/s and in aluminium about 6300 m/s.

△ Fig. 3.51 The vibrating strings of this guitar will produce sound in the air.

## QUESTIONS

**1.** Explain what are compressions.

**2.** The wavelength of a sound wave is 20 cm.

    **a)** State the distance between two neighbouring rarefactions.

    **b)** SUPPLEMENT Suggest the distance between a rarefaction and the next compression.

**3.** State and explain whether we can hear sound of frequency 15 Hz.

**4.** SUPPLEMENT The speed of sound in a material is 2000 m/s. Suggest what the material could be.

# Determining the speed of sound in air

The simplest method to determining the speed of sound in air uses two microphones and a fast recording device such as a digital storage oscilloscope or a data-logger connected to a computer.

**1.** A sound source and the two microphones are arranged in a straight line, with the sound source beyond the first microphone.

**2.** The distance $x$ between the microphones is measured using a ruler.

**3.** The time $t$ taken by the sound to travel the distance between the two microphones is measured.

**4.** Then speed of sound $= \dfrac{x}{t}$

The following results were recorded by a student carrying out this experiment.

$x = 1.50$ m     $t = 4.4$ ms

We can use the data above to determine the speed $v$ of the sound waves.

$$v = \frac{1.50}{0.0044}$$
$$v = 340 \text{ m/s}$$

This value is within the range 330 m/s to 350 m/s given earlier.

## Pitch, frequency, amplitude and loudness

Sounds with a high **pitch** have a high frequency. Examples of high-pitch sounds include birdsong and whistles. Low-pitch sounds have a low frequency. Examples of low-pitch sounds include the horn of a large ship and a bass guitar.

Loud sounds have large amplitude, whereas quiet sounds have small amplitude. Typical sound wave patterns are shown in Fig. 3.52 as displacement of sound against time graphs.

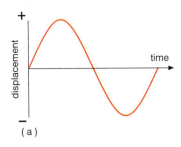
(a)

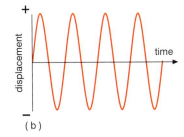
(b)

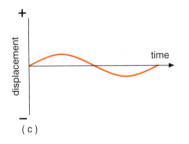
(c)

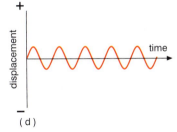
(d)

△ Fig. 3.52 Wave sound patterns.

Higher frequency sound will have shorter times between adjacent peaks.

Here is a quick analysis of the sound waves in Fig. 3.52:

- (a) shows a loud sound of low pitch or frequency. The pitch of sound in both (a) and (c) is the same.
- The sound shown in (b) is as loud as the sound in (a), but of higher pitch or frequency than the sound in (a). The sounds shown in (b) and (d) have the same pitch.
- The sound in (c) has the same pitch as the sound in (a), but a quieter sound than both the sounds shown in (a) and (b).
- Finally, the sound in (d) has the same loudness as the sound in (c) and the same pitch or frequency as the sound in (b).

### Echoes

Hard surfaces reflect sound waves. An **echo** is a sound that has been reflected before you hear it. For an echo to be clearly heard, the obstacle needs to be large compared with the wavelength of the sound. You will hear an echo when you make a loud noise when you are far away from a brick wall or a cliff.

### Determining the speed of sound by an echo method

The following worked example illustrates how echoes may be used to determine the speed of sound.

### WORKED EXAMPLE

Two students stand side by side at a distance of 480 m from the school wall. Student A has two flat pieces of wood, which make a loud sound when clapped together. Student B has a stopwatch.

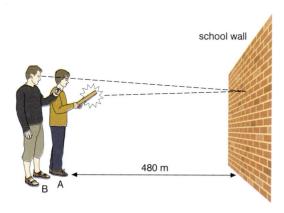

△ Fig. 3.53 Two students carrying out investigations into the speed of sound.

As student A claps the pieces of wood together, student B starts the stopwatch. When student B hears the echo, he stops the stopwatch. The time recorded on the stopwatch is 2.9 s.

Calculate the speed of sound.

Write down the equation:    speed of sound  $= \dfrac{\text{distance travelled}}{\text{time taken}}$

Work out the total distance: distance to wall $= 2 \times 480 = 960$ m
and back

Record the time the sound took to travel to the wall and back:

$$\text{time} = 2.9 \text{ s}$$

Substitute in the equation:  speed of sound  $= \dfrac{960}{2.9} = 330$ m/s

The answer is written to 2 significant figures (SF) to indicate the accuracy of this experiment. The distance and time are recorded to 2 SF, the final answer should reflect that as well. The experiment can be repeated, and an average value for the speed found.

## USES OF ULTRASOUND

Ultrasound is sound of frequency greater than 20 000 Hz, or 20 kHz. Ultrasound can travel through gases, liquids and solids.

### SUPPLEMENT

### Sonar

Ultrasound can be used to locate objects in deep water. Ultrasound has been used to map the seabed, locate buried shipwrecks and treasure and even locate shoals of fish. The technique of locating objects under water is simple. Send a pulse of ultrasound, measure the time it takes to come back after being reflected and then use the equation:

speed of ultrasound $= \dfrac{\text{total distance}}{\text{time taken}}$

to determine the depth of the object. The technique outlined above is known as sonar, or echolocation.

Ultrasound is preferred to ordinary sound because it can travel further in water without too much absorption. The preferred frequency for ultrasound is about 50 kHz. The speed of ultrasound in water is about 1500 m/s. The worked example below shows how the depth of seabed can be determined using sonar. You will see the obvious similarities with the worked example above to determine the speed of sound in air – both techniques use echoes.

### WORKED EXAMPLE

Fig. 3.54 shows a ship with a transmitter and detector of ultrasound on its underside. The depth of the seabed is $d$. A pulse of ultrasound is emitted and is detected 0.10 s later. The speed of sound in the seawater is 1500 m/s. Calculate $d$.

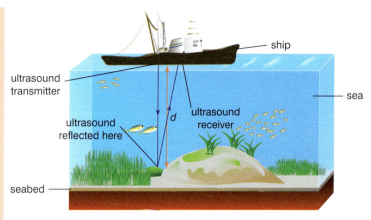

△ Fig. 3.54 Using ultrasound to measure the depth of the seabed.

Write down the equation for speed: $\text{speed} = \dfrac{\text{total distance}}{\text{time taken}}$

Work out the total distance travelled by the ultrasound:

$\text{total distance} = \text{speed} \times \text{time taken}$

$\text{total distance} = 1500 \times 0.10 = 150 \text{ m}$

The total distance is twice the depth $d$.

Calculate $d$ by dividing the total distance by 2: $\qquad d = \dfrac{150}{2}$

$$d = 75 \text{ m}$$

Therefore, the depth of the seabed is 75 m. A common mistake made by students is to leave the answer as 150 m without dividing by 2.

## Medical scanning

Ultrasound can safely pass through humans. This makes it ideal for medical scanning of soft tissues, including foetal scans. Ultrasound will reflect at the boundary between two different materials, and the amount reflected depends on the density of the two materials.

An ultrasound transducer is placed on the patient. The transducer is a special device that can emit ultrasound and detect it too. A special gel is applied between the patient's skin and the transducer to make sure that all the ultrasound enters the patient. The ultrasound will be reflected at the boundaries between tissues. The reflected ultrasound is detected by the same transducer. From the 'delay' time, just like the echolocation system of sonar, the depth of the boundaries can be determined using computer software. The display shows all the boundaries between various tissues and muscles within the patient.

Some examples of medical scanning are: foetal scan, scan of torn ligaments and muscles, and eye scans.

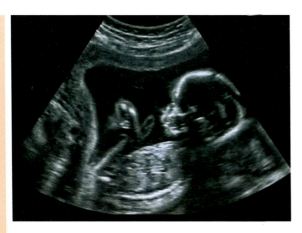

△ Fig. 3.55 Ultrasound scan of a baby in its mother's womb.

## Material testing

Ultrasound can be used to detect cracks in materials, including pipes and building structures. The technique for locating the cracks is similar to both sonar and medical scanning. Ultrasound will reflect at the crack, and once again, the time measured after sending the ultrasound can be used to determine the depth of the crack below the surface of a material.

## QUESTIONS

1. Explain whether or not sound of frequency 32 kHz is ultrasound.

2. State what affects the loudness of a sound wave.

3. State what affects the pitch of the sound we hear.

4. **SUPPLEMENT** A scientist is testing for cracks in a concrete pillar supporting a bridge. A pulse of ultrasound is sent into the pillar. The pulse is detected 0.00015 s later. The speed of ultrasound in the concrete is 4000 m/s. Calculate the depth of the crack.

## Developing practical skills

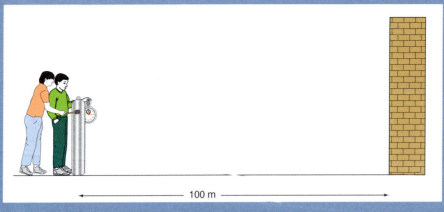

△ Fig. 3.56 Two students measuring the speed of sound.

Two students are finding the speed of sound. They stand 100 m from a large wall. The first student strikes a piece of metal with a hammer. The sound this makes reflects back from the wall and the student hears an echo. The student hits the metal again in time with the echo and continues to do so, tapping out a steady rhythm.

The second student is in charge of timing. He knows that in between each sound that the first student makes the sound travels 200 m (to the wall and back again). By timing the interval for a number of strikes, the second student can record the data he needs.

### Observing, measuring and recording data

**1.** Explain whether the students should repeat their measurements for this experiment.

**2.** The students stand 100 m away from the wall that provides the echo. Explain why this is a suitable distance to use.

**3.** The students measure a time of 2.3 s from striking the metal to striking the metal at the fourth following echo. Calculate the speed of sound given by this measurement.

**4.** A better way to find the speed of sound would be through the use of a graph. Describe how the students could collect suitable data and how a graph could be used to find the speed of sound.

**5.** Explain why using a graph to find the speed of sound would improve the accuracy of the experiment.

### Interpreting and evaluating data

**6.** What effect will reaction time have on the measurements made?

**7.** Suggest how the timing in this experiment could be improved.

# End of topic checklist

## Key terms

amplitude, echo, frequency, longitudinal waves, loudness, pitch, ultrasound

**SUPPLEMENT** compression, rarefaction

## During your study of this topic you should have learned:

○ Sound is produced by vibrating sources.

○ Sound is a longitudinal wave.

○ The approximate range of frequencies audible to humans is 20 Hz to 20 000 Hz.

○ A medium is needed to transmit sound waves.

○ The speed of sound in air is approximately 330–350 m/s.

○ Describe a method for determining the speed of sound in air.

○ The larger the amplitude, the louder is the sound.

○ The higher the frequency, the higher is the pitch.

○ An echo is a reflection of sound waves.

○ Ultrasound is sound with a frequency higher than 20 kHz.

○ **SUPPLEMENT** Compressions are regions of high pressure and rarefactions are regions of low pressure.

○ **SUPPLEMENT** Sound travels faster in solids than in liquids and faster in liquids than in gases.

○ **SUPPLEMENT** Describe the uses of ultrasound in testing of materials, medical scanning of soft tissue and sonar including calculation of depth or distance from time and wave speed.

# End of topic questions

*Note: the marks in brackets give an indication of the level of detail you should include in your answers.*

**1. a) i)** Explain what causes a sound. (2 marks)

   **ii)** Describe how sound travels through the air. (2 marks)

   **b)** Astronauts in space cannot talk directly to each other – they have to speak to each other by radio. Explain why this is so. (3 marks)

   **c)** What type of wave is sound?

   **A** electromagnetic    **B** longitudinal    **C** seismic    **D** transverse    (1 mark)

**2.** Ayesha and Salma are doing an experiment to measure the speed of sound. They stand 150 m apart.

Ayesha starts the stopwatch when she sees Salma make a sound and she stops it when she hears the sound herself. She measures the time as 0.44 s. Calculate the speed of sound in air from this data. (3 marks)

**3.** The speed of sound in air is approximately 340 m/s.

   **a)** Calculate the wavelength of the musical note middle C, which has a frequency of 256 Hz. (3 marks)

   **b)** A student hears two echoes when she claps her hands. One echo is 0.5 s after the clap, and one echo is 1.0 s after the clap. She decides that the two echoes are from two buildings in front of her. How far apart are the buildings? (3 marks)

**4.** Sound from a loudspeaker has a low frequency and is very quiet. Describe how the sound can be made louder and higher pitch. (2 marks)

**5.** A polystyrene ball is suspended so it is touching the prongs of a vibrating tuning fork. The ball kicks away from the tuning fork and then moves back to it.

Explain the behaviour of the ball by:

   **a)** describing how the prongs of the tuning fork move (2 marks)

   **b)** describing how a sound wave is created by the tuning fork. (2 marks)

**6. SUPPLEMENT** A geologist is searching for an oil lake underground. He sends a pulse of ultrasound into the ground. The pulse is detected 0.16 s later. The speed of ultrasound in the ground is about 6000 m/s. Calculate the depth of the oil lake.

## COMMENTS

**a) i)** This answer does not address the question. The question clearly asks for the name of the missing regions. 'UV' is not a name, nor a standard symbol.

**ii)** This is correct.

**b) i)** Stating 'in a hospital' is too vague to be a 'situation' as the question asks.

**ii)** This describes the correct use so 'imaging' should have been given as a specific situation in i).

**c) i)** A situation has not been described.

# Exam-style questions

*Note: exam-style questions, sample answers and comments have been written by the authors. The marks awarded for these questions indicate the level of detail required in the answers. In examinations, the way marks are awarded may be different. References to assessment and/or assessment preparation are the publisher's interpretation of the syllabus requirements and may not fully reflect the approach of Cambridge Assessment International Education.*

## Example answers

## Question 1

The table shows some of the regions of the electromagnetic spectrum.

| Gamma | X-rays | A | Visible | Infrared | B | Radio waves |
|-------|--------|---|---------|----------|---|-------------|

**a) i)** Complete the chart by writing the names of the missing regions (A and B) of the spectrum.

*A: UV* ✗ [1]

*B: microwaves* ✓ ① [1]

**ii)** The table lists the spectrum in what order?

**A.** increasing amplitude

**B.** increasing density

**C.** increasing frequency

**D.** increasing wavelength

*D* ✓ ① [1]

**b) i)** Describe one situation in which X-rays are useful.

*in a hospital* ✗ [1]

**ii)** Explain why X-rays are useful in the example you have given.

*X-rays can show broken bones because they will pass through the skin and flesh* ✓ ① [1]

*but there will be a shadow where the bones are.* ✓ ① [1]

## Exam-style questions continued

**c) i)** Describe one situation in which X-rays can be harmful.

*When they get into your body.* ✗ [1]

**ii)** Describe how X-rays can be harmful and how the risks can be reduced.

*They can damage body cells* ✓ ① [1]

*and cause some cells to become cancer cells.* ✗ [1]

**d)** A remote control for a television uses infrared signals.

The human body detects infrared radiation as heat.

Suggest why the infrared signal from a television remote control does not make your skin feel hot.

*The signal from the remote is not strong enough to make you feel hot.* ✗

*There is not enough energy to burn you.* ✓ ① [2]

(Total 11 marks)

**ii)** There are two valid points about how X-rays can be harmful but there is no description of how the risks can be reduced. Always read the question carefully and answer each point.

**d)** 'Not strong enough' is too vague. The correct term 'amplitude' should be used. The second part of the answer correctly links to energy but has not been expanded to make the link from 'strong' to 'amplitude'.

This part of the question test basic definitions and these should be learned thoroughly.

## Question 2

The diagram shows some waves on the surface of water in a ripple tank.

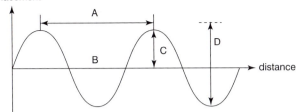

a)  i) State which letter represents the wavelength of the wave. [1]

   ii) State which letter represents the amplitude of the waves. [1]

b)  i) The waves in the water are transverse waves. Give another example
       of a transverse wave. [1]

   ii) Describe the difference between transverse waves and longitudinal waves. [2]

c) A student makes some observation about the water waves in the ripple tank.

   *number of complete waves passing by in 6.0 seconds – 10*

   *distance between adjacent crests – 5.0 cm*

   i) State the equation linking wave speed, frequency and wavelength. [1]

   ii) Calculate the wave speed of these waves in m/s. [2]

   (Total 8 marks)

## Question 3

a) Describe an experiment to find the refractive index of glass, using a glass block.
   You should include:

   the equipment needed

   a diagram of how the equipment will be used

   what measurements should be made

   how the measurements will be used to find the refractive index. [6]

b) Use ideas about reflection and refraction to explain how information can be sent
   along optical fibres.

   You may use diagrams to help your explanation. [5]

   [Total 11 marks]

## Question 4

a) State one difference between sound and ultrasound. [1]

b) Sound can be diffracted by small gaps. Explain what is meant by diffraction. [1]

c) A ship sounds its foghorn. An echo from a nearby cliff is heard 4.8 s later. The
   speed of sound in the air is 350 m/s.
   Calculate how far the ship is from the cliff. [4]

   [Total 6 marks]

You will probably have experienced magnetism in simple toys and in bar magnets. The magnetic field around a bar magnet, when plotted, looks very similar to the one around the Earth. However, it is the existence of electromagnetism that really makes a difference to your life.

Without electromagnetism, the generation of electricity would not happen in the way that it does. Without electromagnetism, the high voltages transmitted down power lines could not be transformed into the lower voltages that you need in your home. Electricity is something that many people use every day – for lighting, heating, cooking and to power many different items of equipment. However, it can be dangerous.

## STARTING POINTS

**1.** How can electromagnets be made stronger?

**2.** Describe some similarities and differences between magnets and electromagnets.

**3.** How could you investigate the magnetic field pattern for: a) a permanent bar magnet; b) the field between two bar magnets?

**4.** What is an electric circuit?

## SYLLABUS SECTIONS COVERED

**4.1** Simple phenomena of magnetism

**4.2** Electrical quantities

**4.3** Electric circuits

**4.4** Electrical safety

**4.5** Electromagnetic effects

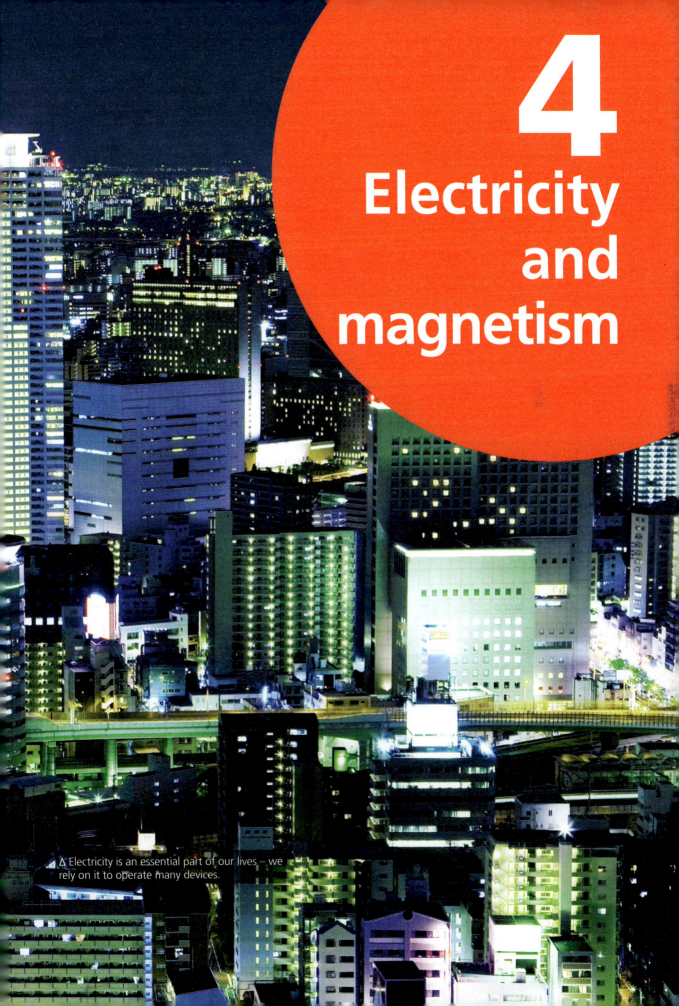

# 4
# Electricity and magnetism

△ Electricity is an essential part of our lives – we rely on it to operate many devices.

△ Fig. 4.1 A compass.

# Simple phenomena of magnetism

## INTRODUCTION

The property of magnetism has been known for many centuries. Ancient travellers used naturally magnetic rocks such as lodestone to guide their journeys. Lodestone, which is magnetic, points towards the north when suspended. The development of the compass made it possible to make long sea voyages of discovery, whereas previously ships had stayed within sight of land. There is evidence that some animals, such as birds, can sense the **magnetic field** of the Earth and that they have their own 'in-built compass', which may help navigation during long migrations.

The magnetic field of the Earth has a wider importance. It acts as a shield, protecting the surface of the Earth from many charged particles emitted from the Sun. The Earth would have been a much hotter and inhabitable place without this protection from the Earth's magnetic fields. A study of magnetism helps us to understand our Earth better and will be crucial when we start to learn about electromagnetism later in this section.

## KNOWLEDGE CHECK

✓ The ends of a bar magnet are called poles and that is where the magnetic field is strongest.
✓ Not all materials are magnetic.
✓ The Earth has a magnetic field, which is how compasses are able to point to the north.

## LEARNING OBJECTIVES

✓ Describe the forces between magnetic poles and between magnets and magnetic materials, including the use of the terms north pole (N pole), south pole (S pole), attraction and repulsion, magnetised and unmagnetised.
✓ Describe induced magnetism.
✓ State the differences between the properties of temporary magnets (made of soft iron) and the properties of permanent magnets (made of steel).
✓ State the difference between magnetic and non-magnetic materials.
✓ Describe a magnetic field as a region in which a magnetic pole experiences a force.

✓ Draw the pattern and direction of magnetic field lines around a bar magnet.

✓ State that the direction of a magnetic field at a point is the direction of the force on the N pole of a magnet at that point.

✓ Describe the plotting of magnetic field lines with a compass or iron filings and the use of a compass to determine the direction of the magnetic field.

✓ Describe the uses of permanent magnets and electromagnets.

✓ **SUPPLEMENT** Explain that magnetic forces are due to interactions between magnetic fields.

✓ **SUPPLEMENT** Know that the relative strength of a magnetic field is represented by the spacing of the magnetic field lines.

## MAGNETS REPEL AND ATTRACT

When a permanent magnet is suspended and allowed to swing, it will line up approximately north–south. The two ends of a magnet, which are the most strongly magnetic parts, are called the north pole and the south pole, often labelled N and S. For the suspended magnet, the N pole points approximately towards the north, and the S pole points approximately towards the south.

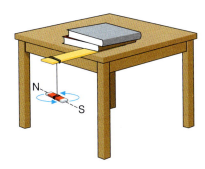

△ Fig. 4.2 A bar magnet aligns itself with the Earth's magnetic field when it is suspended – it is being used as a compass.

There are forces between magnets, and between magnets and **magnetic materials**.

When two north poles from different magnets are brought together, there will be a repulsion between them. This also happens when two south poles are used. Two like poles (N–N or S–S) repel. However, when a north pole and a south pole are brought together, there will be an *attraction*. Two unlike poles (N–S or S–N) attract. Magnets will also attract magnetic materials that can be magnetised by the magnet such as iron, nickel and cobalt.

## QUESTIONS

1. You are provided with a bar magnet with its north pole marked. Describe how you can deduce the poles of another magnet.

2. The north pole of a compass points towards the Earth's north pole. Suggest the magnetic polarity of the Earth's north pole.

## Magnetically hard and soft materials

Several elements are magnetic, the most important of which are iron, cobalt and nickel. Scientists have developed alloys and ceramics made from combinations of elements to get the exact properties that they want. Some of these materials are magnetically hard (such as steel, which is an alloy of iron and other elements such as carbon or tungsten). This means that they stay magnetic once they have been magnetised. This is what you would want from a permanent magnet.

When we refer to a 'magnet', we mean a **permanent magnet** that is made of magnetically hard materials. Permanent magnets are used in computer hard drives, electric motors, phones, microphones and loudspeakers.

Other materials are magnetically soft (such as pure iron), which means that they cannot be permanently magnetised. This is particularly useful in some electromagnetic devices such as the electromagnet and the relay. In these cases, magnetism is only needed under particular circumstances, such as when a switch is closed. Pure iron used in an electromagnet is an example of a temporary magnet.

A magnetic material is defined as a material that can be magnetised, either temporarily or permanently. Examples of this include soft iron, steel, nickel and cobalt. A non-magnetic material is one that cannot be magnetised – basically the opposite of a magnetic material. A non-magnetic material will not be attracted to a strong magnet. Examples of non-magnetic materials include copper, aluminium, gold and silver.

Δ Fig. 4.3 Some microphones use permanent magnets.

## QUESTIONS

1. Name a material that may be used to make temporary magnets.

2. Name a material that may be used to make permanent magnets.

3. State the difference between a magnetic material and a non-magnetic material.

## Magnetic induction

When a soft magnetic material is brought near to a magnet it will be attracted. It has had magnetism induced in it; it has become magnetised. When the magnet is taken away, the material loses its magnetism again – it becomes unmagnetised. The magnet will continue to attract the soft magnetic material even when the material is turned around. This is the opposite behaviour to two magnets, as two magnets will repel each other in certain orientations. This simple method enables you to work out whether you are holding two magnets or one magnet and one piece of magnetic material.

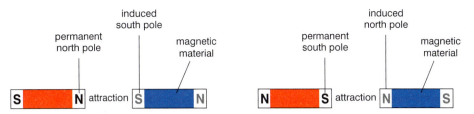

△ Fig. 4.4 The pole of a permanent magnet always induces the opposite pole in an unmagnetised piece of magnetic material. The permanent magnet will always *attract* the magnetic material.

1. Describe how a permanent magnet can be used to identify an object made from:

   **a)** non magnetic material

   **b)** soft iron.

2. The N pole of a magnet is brought close to the end of a soft iron rod. Explain why there is a magnetic force of attraction between the magnet and the rod.

## Magnetic fields

Magnets have a **magnetic field** around them. A magnetic field is a region in which a magnetic pole experiences a force. We describe magnetic fields using **magnetic field lines**. Magnetic field lines come out from the N pole of a magnet and go into its S pole. The direction of the magnetic field is shown by arrows on these lines. The direction of the field at a point is the direction in which a free north pole would move. Fig. 4.5 shows the magnetic field around a permanent bar magnet.

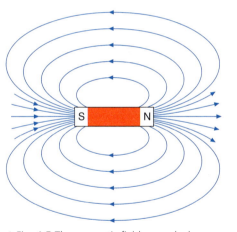

△ Fig. 4.5 The magnetic field around a bar magnet.

The spacing between the field lines represents the strength of the magnetic field. Closer field lines indicate a stronger magnetic field. In Fig. 4.5, you will notice that the field lines are closer together at the two poles – this is where the magnetic field is the strongest.

Magnets repel or attract each other because their magnetic fields interact. This is best shown by the two magnets in Fig. 4.6. The magnetic field lines of the magnets change. You can almost sense the repulsion between the two magnets with the bunching together of the field lines between the south poles.

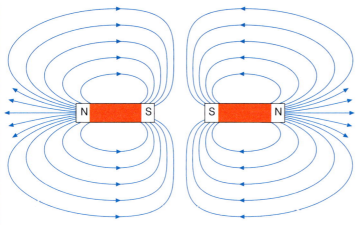

△ Fig. 4.6 Interacting magnetic fields of two repelling magnets.

You can either use iron-filings or a compass to plot magnetic field lines. The tiny pieces of iron line up along the magnetic field lines, as shown in Fig. 4.7.

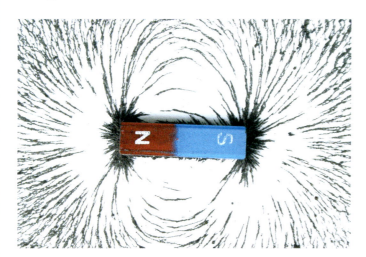

◁ Fig. 4.7 The iron filings show the magnetic field lines around a bar magnet.

A compass contains a tiny bar magnet on a pivot so that it can rotate in the horizontal plane. The compass needle shows the direction of the magnetic field at any point around a magnet. The N pole of the needle of a compass will always point towards the south pole of the magnet. Small plotting compasses can be used to plot the magnetic field around a magnet, see Fig. 4.8. This is the procedure:

1. Place a magnet on a piece of paper, and trace the outline of the magnet.

2. Place a plotting compass at one pole of the magnet.

3. Mark a dot on the paper, next to the compass, where the N pole of the compass points.

4. Move the compass so that its S pole is at the dot marked. Now mark a new dot as outlined in point 3.

**5.** Keep doing this until you reach the other end of the magnet.

**6.** Connect all the dots. This gives you one of the field lines. Mark the direction of the magnetic field on this line.

**7.** Repeat this process by starting at different points around the magnet.

It worth mentioning that:

• magnetic field lines never cross
• and the direction of the field is from north to south.

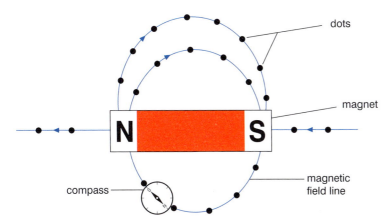

△ Fig. 4.8 Plotting magnetic field lines using a plotting compass.

## Permanent magnets and electromagnets

A permanent magnet never loses its magnetism. In contrast, an electromagnet is only magnetic when there is an **electric current** in the coil (see the topic on Electromagnetic effects). **Electromagnets** are useful in applications when magnetism is needed for a short period of time, such as in scrap yards, where they can be used to lift scrap metal that is magnetic.

## QUESTIONS

**1.** Define magnetic field.

**2.** State the direction of a magnetic field.

**3.** State two methods you can use to plot magnetic field lines.

**4.** SUPPLEMENT In Fig. 4.5, how can you deduce where the magnetic field is the strongest?

# STRONG MAGNETS

The strongest magnets are made from alloys that contain rare earth elements such as neodymium (Nd), samarium (Sc) and yttrium (Y). For example, neodymium magnets are made from an alloy of neodymium, iron and boron. Such magnets retain their magnetism for a very long time, and are found in electric motors in cordless tools and computer hard disk drives. Neodymium magnets can even be used at high temperatures of 200 °C.

Our Earth has a magnetic field, and this can be detected using a simple compass. Neodymium magnets are about 100 thousand times stronger than the Earth's magnetic field. However, this is nothing compared with the magnetic fields that can be created by super-cooled electromagnets carrying large current. The strongest electromagnet in the world can provide a magnetic field that that is about one million times that of the Earth. The useful thing about electromagnets is that you can switch off the magnetic field by turning off the current.

**Challenge Question:** A space probe is being used to investigate the surface of Venus. The temperatures on Venus are extremely high. Why do you think it was sensible for the probe to use a drill machine made from rare-Earth element magnets?

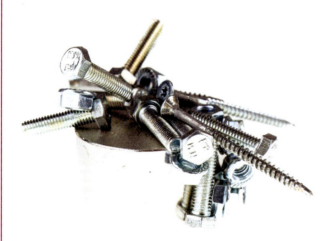

Δ Fig. 4.9 Neodymium magnets are strong.

# End of topic checklist

## Key terms

induced magnetism, magnetic field, magnetic field line, magnetic poles, north pole (N pole), permanent magnet, south pole (S pole), temporary magnet

## During your study of this topic you should have learned:

○ A magnet has a north pole (N pole) and a south pole (S pole).

○ The magnetism is strongest at the poles.

○ Like poles repel, and unlike poles attract.

○ A magnetic material is defined as a material that can be magnetised, either temporarily or permanently.

○ A non-magnetic material will not be attracted to a strong magnet.

○ Magnetism can be induced in magnetic materials.

○ Permanent magnets remain magnetic (e.g. steel), whereas temporary magnets lose their magnetism (soft iron).

○ A magnetic field is a region in which a magnetic pole experiences a force.

○ The direction of a magnetic field at a point is the direction of the force on the N pole of a magnet at that point.

○ Know about the pattern and direction of magnetic field lines around a bar magnet.

○ Magnetic field lines can be plotted using a compass or iron filings.

○ Describe the uses of permanent magnets and electromagnets.

○ **SUPPLEMENT** Magnetic forces are due to interactions between magnetic fields.

○ **SUPPLEMENT** The relative strength of a magnetic field is represented by the spacing of the magnetic field lines – closer field lines imply a stronger field.

# End of topic questions

*Note: the marks in brackets give an indication of the level of detail you should include in your answers.*

1. Describe the difference between a temporary magnet and a permanent magnet. Give an example of each. (4 marks)

2. A student has a piece of metal that he thinks is a magnet. He holds it near another magnet and it is attracted. He says this proves his metal is a magnet. Explain why the student may be wrong. (3 marks)

3. **a)** Sketch the magnetic field lines for a bar magnet. (2 marks)

   **b) SUPPLEMENT** Use the magnetic field lines for the bar magnet to explain where the field is strongest. (2 marks)

4. You are given two bar magnets. Describe how you would investigate the field pattern between them. (4 marks)

5. Describe the difference between a permanent magnet and an electromagnet. (2 marks)

6. Which statement is correct about magnetic poles?

   **A** A bar magnet has two south poles.

   **B** Like poles attract.

   **C** Magnetism is strongest at the poles.

   **D** Unlike poles repel. (1 mark)

# Electrical quantities

## INTRODUCTION

Have you ever brushed your hair and seen individual hairs standing on end and wondered why this happens? Would you like to know how to stick a balloon to a surface without glue? This section explores how and why these things happen. They are both the result of movement of electric charge.

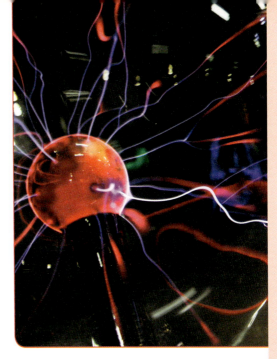

△ Fig. 4.9 A plasma globe. The blue and red light is caused by a flow of electric charge.

In this topic you will learn the basic theory behind current electricity. You will also learn how electrical quantities such as charge, current, electromotive force, potential difference and **resistance** are related.

## KNOWLEDGE CHECK

✓ Forces can be attractive or repulsive.

## LEARNING OBJECTIVES

✓ State that there are positive and negative charges.
✓ State that positive charges repel other positive charges, negative charges repel other negative charges, but positive charges attract negative charges.
✓ Describe simple experiments to show the production of electrostatic charges by friction and to show the detection of electrostatic charges.
✓ Explain that charging of solids by friction involves only a transfer of negative charge (electrons).
✓ Describe an experiment to distinguish between electrical conductors and insulators.
✓ Recall and use a simple electron model to explain the difference between electrical conductors and insulators and give typical examples.
✓ **SUPPLEMENT** State that charge is measured in coulombs.
✓ **SUPPLEMENT** Describe an electric field as a region in which an electric charge experiences a force.
✓ **SUPPLEMENT** State that the direction of an electric field at a point is the direction of the force on a positive charge at that point.
✓ **SUPPLEMENT** Describe simple electric field patterns, including the direction of the field: around a point charge, around a charged conducting sphere and between two oppositely charged parallel conducting plates (end effects will **not** be examined).
✓ Know that electric current is related to the flow of charge.
✓ Describe the use of ammeters (analogue and digital) with different ranges.
✓ Describe electrical conduction in metals in terms of the movement of free electrons.

✓ Know the difference between direct current (d.c.) and alternating current (a.c.).

✓ **SUPPLEMENT** Define electric current as the charge passing a point per unit time; recall and use the equation

$$I = \frac{Q}{t}.$$

✓ **SUPPLEMENT** State that conventional current is from positive to negative and that the flow of free electrons is from negative to positive.

✓ Define electromotive force (e.m.f.) as the electrical work done by a source in moving a unit charge around a complete circuit.

✓ Know that e.m.f. is measured in volts (V).

✓ Define potential difference (p.d.) as the work done by a unit charge passing through a component.

✓ Know that the p.d. between two points is measured in volts (V).

✓ Describe the use of voltmeters (analogue and digital) with different ranges.

✓ **SUPPLEMENT** Recall and use the equation for e.m.f.

$$E = \frac{W}{Q}$$

✓ **SUPPLEMENT** Recall and use the equation for p.d.

$$V = \frac{W}{Q}$$

✓ Recall and use the equation for resistance

$$R = \frac{V}{I}$$

✓ Describe an experiment to determine resistance using a voltmeter and an ammeter and do the appropriate calculations.

✓ State, qualitatively, the relationship of the resistance of a metallic wire to its length and to its cross-sectional area.

✓ **SUPPLEMENT** Sketch and explain the current–voltage graphs of a resistor of constant resistance, a filament lamp and a diode.

✓ **SUPPLEMENT** Recall and use the following relationships for a metallic electrical conductor: resistance is directly proportional to length and resistance is inversely proportional to cross-sectional area

✓ Understand that electric circuits transfer energy from a source of electrical energy, such as an electrical cell or mains supply, to the circuit components and then into the surroundings.

✓ Recall and use the equation for electrical power
$P = IV$

✓ Recall and use the equation for electrical energy
$E = IVt$

✓ Define the kilowatt-hour (kW h) and calculate the cost of using electrical appliances where the energy unit is the kW h.

## ELECTRIC CHARGE

Individual hairs stand on end after brushing, and balloons stick to certain surfaces without glue as a result of the transfer of negatively charged particles called electrons.

Electrical charge is either positive (+) or negative (−). Opposite (unlike) charges will attract one another when close together, whereas like charges will repel each other. Therefore:

• two positive charges repel
• two negative charges repel
• a positive charge and a negative charge will attract.

# Electrical conductors and insulators

Substances that easily allow electric charge to pass through them are called **conductors**; those that do not are called **insulators**.

Metals are conductors. In a metal structure, the metal atoms exist as positive ions surrounded by an electron cloud (Fig. 4.10).

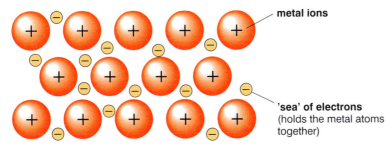

△ Fig. 4.10  In a metal structure the metal ions are surrounded by a cloud or 'sea' of electrons.

You can do a simple experiment to determine whether a given material is a conductor or an insulator. Fig.4.11 shows a cell connected to a small lamp with two leads. The material is placed between the two leads. If the lamp lights, the material is an electrical conductor, and if not, the material is an insulator.

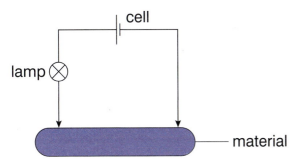

△ Fig. 4.11  Testing whether a material is a conductor or an insulator.

When a conductor is  connected to a battery, electrons within the conductor can move freely along the length of the conductor. The movement of electrons gives rise to an electrical current. For conductors, this current is often large. This is why the lamp in Fig. 4.11 will light up. All metals are good electrical conductors.

In an insulator, there are fewer electrons in a given volume. This implies that the current in the insulator is very small – perhaps even too small to be detected or measured. This is why the lamp in Fig. 4.11 will not light up. Glass, rubber and plastic are excellent electrical insulators.

Table 4.1 lists materials ranging from the best electrical conductor to the best insulator. Silver is about $10^{27}$ times better at conducting charges than the plastic Teflon®. So to replace a 1 mm diameter wire of silver or copper in an electrical circuit, you would need a bar of Teflon far larger in diameter than the Moon's orbit around the Earth.

| Name | Metal or non-metal | Conductor or insulator |
|---|---|---|
| Silver | Metal | Conductor (best) |
| Copper | Metal | Conductor |
| Aluminium | Metal | Conductor |
| Iron | Metal | Conductor |
| Graphite | Non-Metal | Conductor |
| Silicon | Non-Metal | Semiconductor |
| Most Plastics | Non-Metal | Insulator |
| Oil | Non-Metal | Insulator |
| Glass | Non-Metal | Insulator |
| Teflon® | Non-Metal | Insulator (best) |

Table 4.1 Comparison of conductors and insulators.

## Charging insulators by friction

Materials such as glass, acetate and polythene can only become charged when they are rubbed. This is because they are insulators. Electrons do not move easily through insulating materials, so when extra electrons are added, they stay on the surface instead of flowing away, and the surface stays negatively charged. Similarly, when electrons are removed, electrons from other parts of the material do not flow in to replace them, so the surface stays positively charged. Conductors, such as metals, cannot be charged by rubbing.

## Charge as the loss or gain of electrons

All atoms are made up of three main kinds of particles, called electrons, **protons** and neutrons. Electrons are the tiniest of these and have a negative charge. Protons and **neutrons** have about the same mass, but protons are positively charged while neutrons have no charge. Protons and neutrons are found in the **nucleus** of the atom and electrons are found as a cloud surrounding the nucleus, as shown in Fig. 4.12.

In most atoms there are as many electrons as protons. So normally an atom has no overall charge because the total positive charge of all the protons is equal to the total negative charge of all the electrons. When there are more electrons than protons, the atom carries an overall negative charge.

Fig. 4.13 shows a simplified negatively charged object: a lithium atom that has become a negative **ion**.

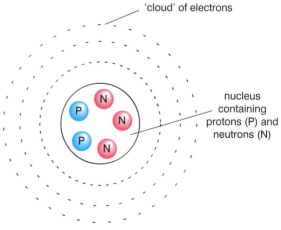

△ Fig. 4.12 Structure of an atom.

A lithium atom normally has three electrons, but the one in Fig. 4.13 has gained an extra electron. It now has three protons but four electrons. When there are more electrons than protons, there is an overall negative charge. The atom has become a negatively charged lithium ion.

Fig. 4.14 shows a simplified positively charged lithium ion. In this ion there are three protons but two electrons.

When you charge an insulator by rubbing it with another insulator, you are adding or taking away electrons from the atoms. The overall charge on the two insulators being rubbed together is zero. The total number of electrons and protons has not changed. However, one of the insulators becomes negative because it has picked up electrons from the other insulator, and that insulator becomes positive because it has lost electrons. The rubbing together of the insulators generates friction, and it is this friction that transfers the electrons. Only free electrons are transferred, the positive protons are held firmly within the nuclei.

Here are two examples:

- When you rub a glass or acetate rod with a cloth, electrons from the rod get rubbed onto the cloth. So the cloth becomes negatively charged and the rod is left with an positive charge.
- When you rub a polythene rod with wool, electrons from the wool get transferred to the rod, so the polythene has a negative charge and the wool has a positive charge (Fig. 4.15).

When an unbalanced charge collects on the surface of an insulator, the charge is called electrostatic charge. 'Static' means 'not moving'.

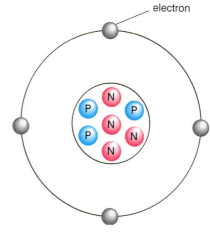

△ Fig. 4.13 A negatively charged ion.

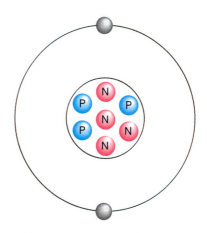

△ Fig. 4.14 A positively charged ion.

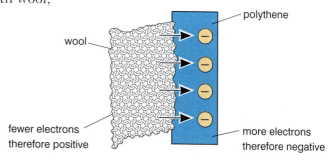

△ Fig. 4.15 Friction transfers electrons from the wool to the polythene rod. The rod becomes negative, and the wool is left with a positive charge. Overall, the charge on the wool and the rod is zero.

## Simple electrostatic experiments

When you suspend charged polythene and acetate rods so they can move freely, and bring the two close together, they will attract each other, since unlike charges attract.

Similarly, when a balloon is rubbed against clothing it will 'stick' to a wall or ceiling. This is because of the attraction between the negative charges on the balloon and the induced positive charges on the ceiling (Fig. 4.16).

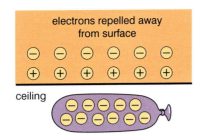

ceiling

negative balloon

△ Fig. 4.16 The balloon induces a charge on the ceiling's surface.

## SUPPLEMENT

The amount of charge on an object is measured in **coulombs** (C). The charge on a single electron is $-1.6 \times 10^{-19}$ C. A proton has numerically the same charge, except it is positive. This is why a neutral atom with the same number of protons and electrons has no overall charge.

A charge of 1 C is equivalent to about $6.3 \times 10^{18}$ protons, and a charge of $-1$ C equivalent to $6.3 \times 10^{18}$ electrons. When charging insulations through friction, there could be many billions of electrons transferred.

## QUESTIONS

1. Two insulators are rubbed together. Friction between the insulators will transfer which of the following particles?

   **A** electrons    **B** ion    **C** neutrons    **D** protons

2. An ion has five protons and six electrons. Explain whether the ion has a positive charge or negative charge.

3. SUPPLEMENT The charge on a rubber balloon is $-0.16$ μC. Calculate the number of electrons responsible for this charge. (Note 1 μC = $10^{-6}$ C.)

4. Storm clouds can become charged, leading to lightning. Suggest how a cloud can become charged.

## SUPPLEMENT

### Attraction and repulsion

Every proton and electron produces an **electric field**. In fact, there is an electric field around any charged object. A balloon, charged by rubbing it on your hair, has an electric field around it.

An electric field is described as a region in which a charge will experience an electric force. The direction of the electric field at a point is the direction of the force experienced by a positive charge at that point. We draw electric field lines to show the direction and strength of an electric field. The closer the field lines, the stronger is the electric field. Fig. 4.17 shows the electric field patterns for two like charges – which repel – and for two unlike charges – which attract.

Why will a proton attract an electron? A proton has an electric field around it. The electron is in this electric field, hence it will experience an electric force – this force happens to be attractive.

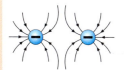 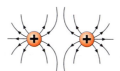
Like charges repel each other.

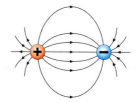
Unlike charges attract each other.

Δ Fig. 4.17 Electric field lines show the shape of an electric field.

◁ Fig. 4.18 Because the static charge on each hair is similar, the hairs repel each other and stick up in all directions.

## SUPPLEMENT

## Simple electric field patterns

The electric fields around a negative point charge (e.g. electron), a positive point charge (e.g. proton) and a positively charged conducting sphere are shown in Fig. 4.19. Notice the electric fields show a 'radial pattern'. When the field lines are extrapolated, they all meet at a single point.

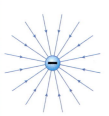
Negative point charge

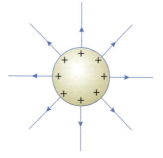
Positive point charge

Positively charged sphere

Δ Fig. 4.19 Some examples of electric fields.

The electric field around two parallel plates with opposite charges is shown in Fig. 4.20. The field lines are evenly spaced between the plates, except at the ends. This means that the strength of the electric field is the same (uniform) between the parallel plates.

The electric field bends around the plates in the same way that it does around two magnets.

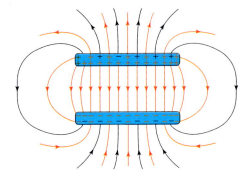

△ Fig. 4.20 Electric field around two parallel oppositely charged parallel plates.

## Developing practical skills

A student is trying to design an experiment to measure how electrostatically charged a plastic rod is. She knows that a charged rod will deflect a stream of water from a tap.

Her plan is to bring a charged rod up to the stream of water and then measure the angle of deflection of the water. She expects that the bigger the angle of deflection is, the greater the charge on the rod will be. She expects to be able to devise a relative scale for how charged different rods are.

charged rod

stream of water deflected by charged rod

△ Fig. 4.21 Water being deflected by a charged rod.

## Planning experiments and investigations

1. How could the student measure the angle of deflection of a stream of water from a tap? Draw a diagram of the arrangement.

2. The student will need to know that the flow from the tap is constant – describe how she could check this.

3. What is the independent variable in this investigation? What is the dependent variable?

## Observing, measuring and recording data

4. The student hopes to 'devise a relative scale for how charged different rods are'. What does 'relative' mean in this sentence?

## Interpreting and evaluating data

5. The student plans to 'bring a charged rod up to the stream of water'. Explain why this part of her plan needs further improvement.

# HAZARDS OF ELECTROSTATICS

The sudden discharge of electrical charge caused by friction between two insulators can cause shocks in everyday situations – for example:

- combing your hair
- pulling clothes over your head
- ironing synthetic fabrics
- getting out of a car.

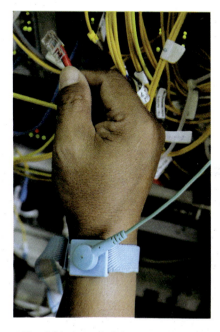

△ Fig. 4.22 An antistatic wrist strap in use.

You may have noticed that you can get a nasty spark from your finger if you touch a metal object after rubbing your feet on a nylon carpet. This is similar to the effect you can sometimes feel if you touch a metal door handle. It is for this reason that workers who make sensitive electronic devices connect themselves to the ground using devices such as antistatic wrist straps (Fig. 4.22), which link to a grounding point (a point that is connected to 0 V) so that any static charge can discharge safely via the wrist strap and not damage the equipment before starting work. Also, to protect against sparks of this type, aircraft are connected to the ground by a special wire before refuelling starts.

Lightning is a spectacular example of electrostatics in action. Scientists believe that the electrical charge is generated by friction when ice particles in clouds collide. One bolt of lightning carries about 5 C of charge. Lightning conductors on buildings usually prevent lightning strikes by discharging the cloud above, but if a strike still occurs the charge should be carried safely to ground.

△ Fig. 4.23 Lightning.

**Challenge Question:** Why do you think workers on oil-rigs wear shoes with metal soles?

## ELECTRIC CURRENT

When there is no current in a conductor, the free electrons move randomly between atoms, with no overall movement along the length of the conductor. When you connect it in an electrical circuit with a power source like a battery, there is a current in the conductor. Now the electrons drift in one direction, while still moving in a random way as well. The drift speed is very slow, often only a few millimetres per second. There can only be a current in a conductor when it is connected in a complete circuit. When the circuit is broken, the current stops. Electrical conduction in metals is due to the movement of free electrons,

The size of an electric current at a point in a circuit depends on the number of electrons that are going past and their drift speed. However, instead of measuring the actual number of electrons we use the total charge carried by the electrons round the circuit per second. So current is related to how quickly, or slowly, charge flows in a circuit.

Electric current is measured in **amperes**, or **amps** (A). Small currents are measured in milliamperes (mA), where 1 mA = 0.001 A.

Current is measured using a device called an **ammeter**. There are generally two types of ammeters – analogue and digital. Fig. 4.24a shows an analogue ammeter and a digital ammeter connected in a simple circuit. The digital ammeter displays a reading of 0.17 A and this requires no special reading skills. The analogue ammeter also shows a reading of 0.17 A, but this time you have to take care with interpreting this reading. To avoid misreading the value of the current due to parallax error, you have to take the measurement at eye-level.

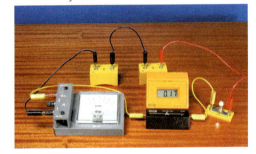

The analogue ammeters have a pointer on a dial, and the digital ammeters are more versatile because you can turn a dial for different ranges. A digital multimeter is shown in Fig. 4.24b. This can be used to measure other electrical quantities too. For example, the dial can be on 200 mA, which means small currents up to 200 milliamperes can be measured.

To measure the current in a component, you must connect the ammeter in **series** with it. When two components are connected in series, you can follow the path of the current through both the components without lifting your finger, or going back over the path you have already taken. Fig. 4.25 shows an electrical circuit with two lamps, three ammeters all connected in series to a battery. All the ammeters will show the same reading - the current in a series circuit is always the same.

△ Fig. 4.24(a) Analogue and digital ammeters connected in a simple series. (b) A digital multimeter can be used to measure current, and other electrical quantities.

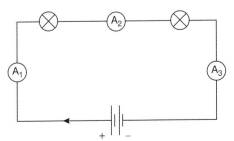

△ Fig. 4.25 In this series circuit, the current will be the same throughout the circuit.

ELECTRICITY AND MAGNETISM

# ALTERNATING CURRENT AND DIRECT CURRENT

A **direct current** (d.c.) will be produced by a battery. The direction of direct current remains the same, even if the magnitude of the current changes over time.

The mains electricity used in the home is quite different. The electrons in the circuit move backwards and forwards. This kind of current is called **alternating current** (a.c.). An alternating current changes direction regularly. Mains current moves forwards and backwards 50 times each second. It has a **frequency** of 50 hertz (Hz).

The advantage of using an a.c. source of electricity rather than a d.c. source is that it can be transmitted from power stations to the home at very high **voltages**, which reduces the amount of energy that is lost in the overhead (transmission) cables.

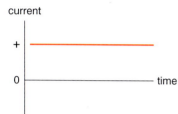

**Direct current (d.c.)**

△ Fig. 4.26 Current-time graph for direct current.

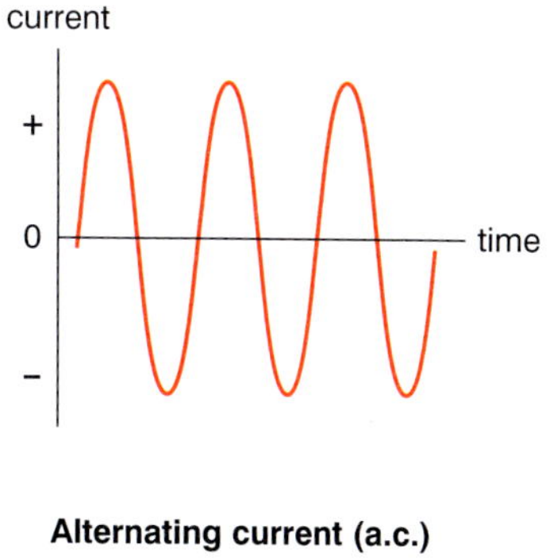

**Alternating current (a.c.)**

△ Fig. 4.27 Current-time graph for alternating current.

**SUPPLEMENT**

Electric current is defined as the charge passing a point in a circuit per unit time. You can calculate the current $I$ using the equation:

$$I = \frac{Q}{t}$$

Where:    $I$ = current in amperes (A)

$Q$ = charge in coulombs (C)

$t$ = time in seconds (s)

Imagine a charge of 12 C flowing past a point in a circuit in a time of 2.0 s. The current $I$ will be:

$$I = \frac{Q}{t} = \frac{12}{2.0}$$

$I = 6.0$ A

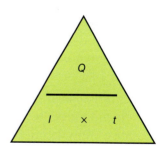

△ Fig. 4.28 Equation triangle for charge, current and time.

Scientists now know that electric current in the wires of a circuit is really a *flow of electrons* around the circuit from negative to positive. Current in metals is due to a flow of electrons. Unfortunately, early scientists guessed the direction of flow incorrectly by assuming that positive charges were responsible for the current. Consequently all diagrams were drawn showing the current flowing from positive to negative. This way of showing the current has not been changed, so the **conventional current** that everyone uses gives the direction in which positive charges would flow – see Fig. 4.29.

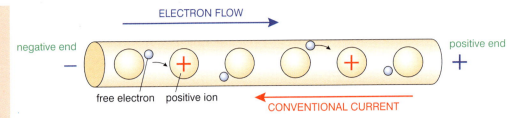

ELECTRON FLOW

negative end                                    positive end

free electron    positive ion

CONVENTIONAL CURRENT

△ Fig. 4.29 Conventional current is drawn in the opposite direction to the electron flow.

## QUESTIONS

1. Calculate the flow of charge in the following:

   **a)** current 3.0 A for 5.0 s

   **b)** current 2.0 A for 10 s

   **c)** current 4.0 A for 23 s

   **d)** current 1.5 A for 0.50 min.

2. A charge of 120 C flows for 4.0 minutes. Calculate the current.

3. A charge of 60 C produces a current of 0.5 A. Calculate how long this takes.

## ELECTROMOTIVE FORCE

The battery in an electrical circuit can be thought of as pushing electrical charge around the circuit to make a current. It also transfers energy to the charges. The **electromotive force** (e.m.f.) of the battery is measured in **volts** (V). Larger e.m.f.s are measured in kilovolts (kV), where 1 kV = 1000 V.

A battery, a solar cell and a bicycle dynamo are all examples of sources of electromotive force. The definition of electromotive force is very precise – e.m.f is defined as the electrical work done by a source in moving a unit charge around a complete circuit.

### SUPPLEMENT

You can use the equation below to calculate the e.m.f. $E$:

$$E = \frac{W}{Q}$$

where: $W$ = the electrical work done in joules (J)

$Q$ = charge flow in coulombs (C)

You can think of 1 volt as 1 joule per coulomb. So, a solar cell of e.m.f. 6.0 V can provide 6.0 J of electrical energy to a charge of 1 C moving around a complete circuit.

## POTENTIAL DIFFERENCE

The electrons moving around a circuit have electrical energy. As electrons pass through the battery, or other source of e.m.f., they gain energy, and as they move around a circuit, they transfer energy to the various components in the circuit. For example, when the electrons move through a lamp they transfer some of their energy to the lamp as thermal (internal) energy, and of course light too. **Potential difference** across a component is an indication of how much energy is transferred by the charges. Potential difference (p.d.) is defined as the work done by a unit charge passing through the component.

Potential difference is measured in volts, so it is often referred to as voltage (Fig. 4.30).

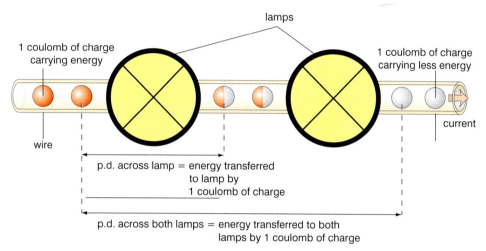

Δ Fig. 4.30 Potential difference (p.d.) is the work done per unit charge, or the energy transferred in the component per unit charge.

Potential difference is measured between two points in a circuit. You can use the equation below to calculate the p.d. $V$:

$$V = \frac{W}{Q}$$

where $W$ = work done or energy transferred in joules (J)

$Q$ = charge flow in coulombs (C)

You can think of a p.d. of 2.0 V across a component as 2.0 J of electrical energy transferred to thermal energy by every 1 C of charge. It is best to think of 1 V as 1 joule per second (J/s).

## Measuring potential difference

Potential difference is measured using a **voltmeter**. When you want to measure the p.d. across a component then the voltmeter must be connected in **parallel** across that component, see Fig. 4.31 and Fig. 4.32. Testing with a voltmeter does not interfere with the circuit provided the voltmeter has a high resistance.

Just like the ammeters, voltmeters can either be analogue or digital. Analogue meters have a dial and pointer, whereas the digital meters give you a reading directly on a display. A multimeter, can provide different ranges and the ability to measure current and resistance too.

A voltmeter can be used to show how the potential difference varies in different parts of a circuit. In a series circuit you find different values of the voltage depending on where you attach the voltmeter. You can assume that energy is only transferred when the current passes through electrical components such as lamps and motors – the energy transfer to thermal energy as the current passes through copper connecting wire is very small indeed. Therefore it is only possible to measure a p.d. or voltage across a component.

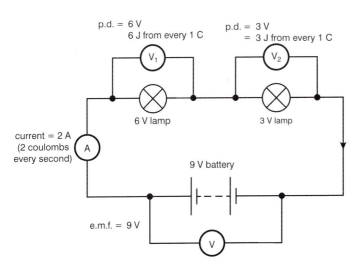

△ Fig. 4.31 A voltmeter is connected in parallel with a component.

△ Fig. 4.32 A voltmeter can be added after the rest of the circuit has been connected.

## RESISTANCE

All components in an electrical circuit have a resistance to the current in them. The relationship between potential difference, current and resistance in electrical circuits is given by this equation:

$V = IR$

where: $V$ = potential difference in volts (V)

$I$ = current in amperes (A)

$R$ = resistance in ohms ($\Omega$).

It is important to be able to rearrange this equation when performing calculations. Use the triangle in Fig. 4.33 to help you. From this equation, you calculate the resistance of a component using the equation:

$R = \dfrac{V}{I}$

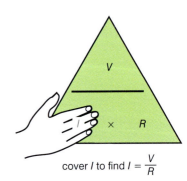

cover $I$ to find $I = \dfrac{V}{R}$

△ Fig. 4.33 Equation triangle for voltage, current and resistance.

## WORKED EXAMPLES

**1.** A heater element is connected to a 230 V supply. The current in the heater is 10 A. Calculate the resistance of the heater.

Write down the equation in terms of $R$: $\qquad R = \dfrac{V}{I}$

Substitute the values for $V$ and $I$: $\qquad R = \dfrac{230}{10}$

Calculate the answer and write down the unit: $R = 23\ \Omega$

**2.** A 6.0 V supply is connected to 1000 $\Omega$ resistor. Calculate the current in the resistor.

Write down the equation in terms of $I$: $\qquad I = \dfrac{V}{R}$

Substitute the values for $V$ and $R$: $\qquad I = \dfrac{6}{1000}$

Calculate the answer and write down the unit: $\quad I = 0.006\ \text{A or } 6.0\ \text{mA}$

## QUESTIONS

**1.** Calculate the potential difference across a 5.0 $\Omega$ resistor, which has a current of 2.0 A in it.

**2.** A lamp has a potential difference of 3.0 V across it and a current of 0.50 A in it.

**a)** Calculate the resistance of the lamp at this current.

**b)** **SUPPLEMENT** Calculate the charge flow in the lamp in a time of 10 s.

**c)** The potential difference across the lamp is increased to 6.0 V. The current is now 0.80 A. Calculate the resistance of the lamp at this current. Comment on your answer.

### Determining resistance

The resistance of a component can be found using the circuit shown in Fig. 4.34. The component (lamp, resistor, **thermistor** or whatever) is placed in a circuit with an ammeter to measure the current in the component and a voltmeter to measure the potential difference across it. To take readings, the circuit is switched on and readings are taken of the p.d. and the current.

The resistance is calculated from the following equation:

$$R = \dfrac{V}{I}$$

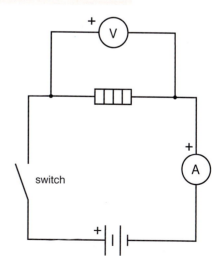

△ Fig. 4.34 Determining the resistance of a component. You just need the current $I$ from the ammeter and the p.d. $V$ across the component from the voltmeter.

Note that the readings may change a little over the first few seconds. If so, this is probably because the component is heating up and its resistance is changing. If this happens, you would have to decide whether to take the readings before the component has heated up, and so determine the resistance at room temperature, or to wait until the readings have stopped changing. This would give you the 'steady-state' resistance with the component at its usual running temperature.

You may wish to change the e.m.f. of the battery by changing the number of cells, or you may adjust the output of the power supply. When the component is a perfect resistor, then you will get the same answer for the resistance. Modern multimeters measure resistance automatically and give a reading in ohms.

SUPPLEMENT

## CURRENT-VOLTAGE GRAPHS

How can we identify components, other than by looking at them? We can plot a graph of current against potential difference (p.d.) for the component. The shape of the graph often helps us to identify the component, and we can also determine its resistance at different currents. A graph of current against potential difference for the component is called the *I-V* characteristic of the component.

Fig. 4.35 shows the circuit you can use to investigate how the current *I* varies with potential difference for a component. The current in the circuit is altered using the **variable resistor**.

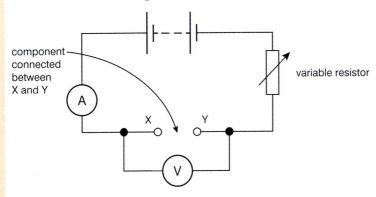

△ Fig. 4.35 Circuit for investigating any component.

Fig. 4.36 shows the *I-V* graphs for a filament lamp, a resistor at constant temperature and a **diode** made from the semiconducting material silicon.

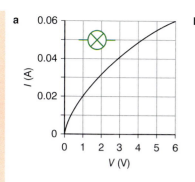

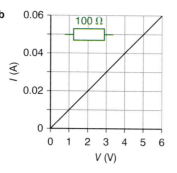

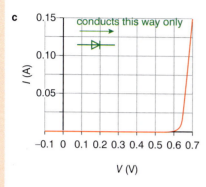

Δ Fig. 4.36 *I-V* graphs for a) filament lamp, b) a fixed resistor, and c) a (silicon) diode.

Analysing the *I-V* graphs:

- **Filament lamp:** The component conducts in both directions. The current increases with the p.d. The current is not directly proportional to the p.d.; we do not have a straight line passing through the origin. The resistance of the filament lamp increases as the current increases; this is because it gets hotter. The free electrons within the filament make more frequent collisions with the vibrating atoms.

- **Resistor at constant temperature:** The component conducts in both directions. The current increases with the p.d. Here, the current is directly proportional to the p.d.; we get a straight line passing through the origin. The resistance of the resistor is constant and does not depend on either the current or the p.d. The gradient of the line is equal to $\frac{I}{R}$, where $R$ is the resistance of the resistor.

- **Diode:** This component, made from a **semiconductor** material such as silicon, conducts in one direction only. When it does not conduct, it has almost an infinite resistance. When it conducts, the resistance is low.

## Developing practical skills

A student decides to find the resistance of a piece of fuse wire. He sets up the circuit in Fig. 4.37 and makes a note of the readings on the ammeter and the voltmeter for five different settings of the variable resistor. His measurements are shown in the table.

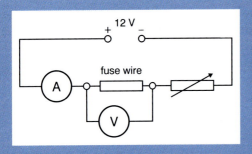

△ Fig. 4.37 A circuit diagram for the investigation.

| Potential difference/V | Current /mA |
|---|---|
| 0.0 | 0 |
| 0.5 | 44 |
| 1.0 | 88.5 |
| 1.5 | 137.5 |
| 2.0 | 181.5 |
| 2.5 | 225.5 |

## Planning experiments and investigations

**1.** The student did not measure the voltage of the supply or the particular settings of the variable resistor. Explain why these measurements were not required.

**2.** The student should check the ammeter and voltmeter for zero errors. What are these?

## Observing, measuring and recording data

**3.** Draw a graph of the student's results.

**4.** Use your graph, with current on the $y$ axis and p.d. on the $x$-axis to determine the resistance of the wire. (Note: The gradient of the best-fit straight line $= \frac{1}{R}$, where $R$ is the resistance of the wire.)

## Interpreting and evaluating data

**5.** Another student suggests that drawing a graph is not necessary. They say that you could use the equation $R = \frac{V}{I}$ for each pair of measurements and then find a mean of these values. Suggest why calculating the gradient of the graph is a better method.

**6.** To get an accurate value for the resistance of the wire, the student needed to avoid any heating effects in the wire. Describe how the student could reduce heating effects when carrying out the experiment.

## Resistance of a metallic wire

The resistance of a metallic wire depends on its length, its cross-sectional area, and the type of metal. Longer wires have greater resistance, and thinner wires have greater resistance.

For a particular metallic wire at a constant temperature, the resistance is directly proportional to its length. The longer the wire, the further the electrons have to travel, the more likely they are to collide with the metal atoms and so the greater the resistance. Therefore, a wire that is twice as long will have twice as much resistance. A graph of resistance $R$ of the wire against its length $L$ will give a straight line graph through the origin. The gradient of the graph depends on the actual material of the wire, e.g. constantan (copper–nickel alloy) or steel.

Resistance is inversely proportional to the cross-sectional area of the wire. The greater the cross-sectional area of the conductor, the more electrons there are available to carry the charge along the length of the wire, so the lower the resistance. Therefore, a wire with twice the cross-sectional area will have half the resistance. A graph of resistance $R$ of the wire against its cross-sectional area $A$ will give a curve.

### REMEMBER

If the wire is of twice the diameter, then its cross-sectional area will be four times bigger, so the resistance of the wire will be one-quarter as much.

## WORKED EXAMPLE

A student is investigating the resistance of a constantan wire for various lengths. Some of his results are shown below:

| Length of wire/cm | p.d. across wire/V | Current in wire/A | Resistance/$\Omega$ |
|---|---|---|---|
| 12.5 | 1.2 | 0.39 | |
| 25.0 | 1.2 | 0.20 | |

Complete the last column in the table above, and deduce the relationship between the resistance $R$ of the wire and its length $L$.

Calculate the resistance of each length using $R = \dfrac{V}{I}$.

For $L = 12.5$ cm, $R = \dfrac{1.2}{0.39} = 3.1\,\Omega$

For $L = 25.0$ cm, $R = \dfrac{1.2}{0.20} = 6.0\,\Omega$

Now analyse the results, and draw a sensible conclusion.

The length has doubled exactly from 12.5 cm to 25.0 cm. The resistance has increased from 3.1 Ω to 6.0 Ω, an increase by a factor of $\frac{6.0}{3.1} = 1.9$. Within the limits of experimental accuracy, this is almost double.

Conclusion: $R$ is directly proportional to $L$.

## QUESTIONS

1. State two factors that affect the resistance of a wire made from the same material at a given temperature.

2. State what would happen to the resistance of a copper wire when its ends are pulled apart, so that it becomes longer and thinner.

3. **SUPPLEMENT** The resistance of a steel wire of length 30 cm is 6.0 Ω. Calculate the resistance of this same wire when its length is cut to 10 cm.

4. **SUPPLEMENT** The resistance of a nichrome wire of cross-sectional area 1.0 mm² is 12 Ω. Calculate the resistance of the same length of nichrome wire but with a cross-sectional area of 2.0 mm².

**SCIENCE IN CONTEXT**

## SUPERCONDUCTORS

In 1908 the Dutch physicist Heike Kamerlingh Onnes became the first person to produce liquid helium, which meant reaching temperatures lower than –269 °C, the boiling point of helium. Having such a cold liquid meant that other low-temperature experiments became possible as he could now cool down the apparatus sufficiently.

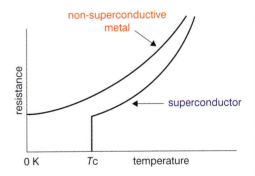

△ Fig 4.38 How resistance varies with temperature in a superconductor and a non-superconductor.

In particular, Kamerlingh Onnes looked at passing electric currents through extremely cold metals, and in 1911 he was measuring the resistance of a sample of mercury. He found that below a particular temperature, called the critical temperature $T_C$, the mercury behaved as if it had no electrical resistance at all – he had discovered superconductivity.

Following this discovery, many more metallic elements were found to have superconducting properties. The search for superconductors has continued, with breakthroughs coming in the study of alloys rather than elements.

A particular milestone came in the discovery of materials that demonstrated superconductivity at temperatures up to −183 °C as this meant that liquid nitrogen could be used as the coolant – and liquid nitrogen is readily available commercially. The search for materials that superconduct at higher temperatures continues.

△ Fig. 4.39 A splash of liquid nitrogen cools a ceramic superconductor, forcing it to float in air below a magnet.

Superconductors are used in a variety of applications. They produce the strong magnetic fields required for MRI scanning in medicine and to confine beams of charged particles in accelerators such as the Large Hadron Collider. They even provide magnetic fields to support Maglev trains that 'float' above the track.

**Challenge Question:** A wind turbine has been produced that generates electricity using superconductors cooled by liquid nitrogen. What do you think is the main advantage of such a wind turbine?

## ELECTRICAL ENERGY AND ELECTRICAL POWER

There are many electrical appliances used in the home that transfer energy from the mains supply to useful stores. For example, an electric kettle will transfer the electrical energy supplied to both useful and wasted energy stores. The useful energy store is the internal energy of the water, and the wasted energy stores will be dissipated to the surroundings. In an electrical circuit, energy may be transferred from the chemical store of the battery to the internal energy of a component, and then into the surroundings.

The rate at which energy is transferred by an appliance, a device or a component, is known as electrical power. Power is measured in watts (W), with 1 watt = 1 joule per second.

The typical power rating of an electric kettle is about 2000 W. This means 2000 J of energy is transferred by the kettle per second. Most of the energy is transferred to heating the water, but some is also transferred to the surroundings.

You can calculate the electrical power $P$ of a device using the equation:

power = current × potential difference

or $P = IV$

where $I$ is the current in the device in amperes (A), and $V$ is the p.d. across the device in volts (V).

Since power is the energy transferred per unit time, the electrical energy $E$ transferred by a device is given by the equation:

energy = power × time

or $E = IVt$

where $t$ is the time in seconds (s).

## WORKED EXAMPLES

**1.** Calculate the electrical power of an appliance with a current of 7.0 A and connected to a 230 V supply.

Write down the equation in terms of $P$: $\qquad P = IV$

Substitute the values: $\qquad\qquad\qquad P = 230 \times 7.0$

Calculate the answer and write down the unit: $P = 1610$ W

**2.** An electric oven has a power rating of 2.0 kW. Calculate the current in the oven when connected to a 230 V supply.

Write down the equation in terms of $I$: $\qquad I = \dfrac{P}{V}$

Substitute the values: $\qquad\qquad\qquad I = \dfrac{2000}{230}$

Calculate the answer and write down the unit: $I = 8.7$ A

**3.** A small electric heater is connected to a 12 V supply. The current in the heater is 0.50 A. Calculate the energy transferred by the heater in a time of 5.0 minutes.

Write down the equation: $\qquad\qquad E = IVt$

Substitute the values: $\qquad\qquad\qquad E = 0.50 \times 12 \times 300$

Remember that the time must be in seconds.

Calculate the answer and write down the unit: $E = 1800$ J

## QUESTIONS

**1.** An appliance has 2.0 A of current in it and operates at 110 V. Calculate the electrical power of this appliance.

**2.** A 20 W lamp has a current of 2.0 A in it. Calculate the potential difference across the lamp.

**3.** Calculate how much electrical energy is transferred in a circuit with a current of 3.0 A and p.d. of 12 V in a time of 1.0 minute.

**4.** A heater runs on 12 V transfers 4800 J of energy in 2.0 minutes. Calculate the current in the heater.

**5.** A lamp transfers 24 J of energy and draws a current of 2.0 A for 1.0 s. Calculate the p.d. across the lamp.

ELECTRICITY AND MAGNETISM

# THE KILOWATT-HOUR

Imagine using a 100 W appliance for a time of 1.0 hour. You can calculate the energy transferred in joules quite simply by multiplying the power in watts by the time in seconds as shown below:

$$energy = power \times time$$

$$energy = 100 \times 3600 = 360\ 000 \text{ J}$$

The energy in joules is quite a big number. This value will be even bigger if the appliance is used for many hours, or even days. Using joules as a measure of energy does not look sensible, especially when paying for the use of domestic energy. Our electricity bills would show energy usage with many zeros. There is a simpler alternative, using **kilowatt-hour** as the unit for energy. The kilowatt-hour is defined as follows:

1 kilowatt-hour is the electrical energy transferred by a 1 kW appliance used for 1 hour.

To calculate the energy in kilowatt-hour (kW h), you can use the equation:

$$energy \text{ in kW h} = power \text{ in kW} \times time \text{ in hours}$$

For the 100 W appliance used for 1.0 hour example above, the energy in kW h would be:

$$energy = 0.100 \times 1.0 = 0.10 \text{ kW h}$$

This value of 0.10 kW h is much simpler and more comprehensible than 360 000 J.

Domestic electricity meters measure the number of kW h of energy used in a home or other building. The more kW h of energy used, the greater the cost. You can calculate the cost using the equation:

$$cost = energy \text{ in kW h} \times cost \text{ per kW h}$$

# WORKED EXAMPLE

A 1500 W heater is used for 2.0 hours. The cost of each kW h is 18 cents.

Calculate the cost of running this heater.

Convert the power into kW:

$$power = 1.5 \text{ kW}$$

Calculate the number of kW h of energy used:

$$energy = 1.5 \times 2.0$$

$$energy = 3.0 \text{ kW h}$$

Now calculate the cost in cents (c):

$$cost = 3.0 \times 18$$

$$cost = 54 \text{ c}$$

In the questions below, assume the cost of a kW h of energy to be 18 cents.

1. A 0.20 kW television is used for 30 minutes. Calculate the energy transformed in kWh and the cost in cents for using the television.

2. A 1500 W electric cooker is used for 4.0 hours. Calculate the energy transformed in kWh and the cost in cents for using the cooker.

3. Explain which of the following items would be more costly:
   - 20 W lamp used for one day
   - 1.92 kW heater used for 15 minutes.

# End of topic checklist

## Key terms

alternating current, ammeter, ampere, charge, conductor (electrical), coulomb, direct current, electric current, electric field, electrical power, electromotive force (e.m.f.), insulator (electrical), kilowatt-hour (kW h), ohm, potential difference (p.d.), resistance, voltmeter, volt, watt, current–voltage graph

**SUPPLEMENT** conventional current, electron flow, free electrons

## During your study of this topic you should have learned:

○ Charges can be either positive or negative.

○ Like charges repel, and unlike charges attract.

○ Objects can be electrostatically charged by friction.

○ Describe simple experiments to show the production of electrostatic charges by friction and to show the detection of electrostatic charges.

○ Charging of solids by friction involves only a transfer of negative charge (free electrons).

○ Describe an experiment to distinguish between electrical conductors and insulators.

○ Good electrical conductors have many more free electrons in a given volume than insulators.

○ **SUPPLEMENT** Charge is measured in coulombs (C).

○ **SUPPLEMENT** An electric field is a region in which an electric charge experiences a force.

○ **SUPPLEMENT** The direction of an electric field at a point is the direction of the force on a positive charge at that point.

○ **SUPPLEMENT** Describe simple electric field patterns, including the direction of the field: around a point charge, around a charged conducting sphere, and between two oppositely charged parallel conduction plates.

○ Electric current is related to the flow of charge.

○ Ammeters (analogue and digital) with different ranges are used to measure current.

○ Electrical conduction in metals is due to the movement of free electrons.

○ Alternating current (a.c.) changes direction, whereas direct current (d.c.) is one direction only.

# End of topic checklist continued

- ○ **SUPPLEMENT** Electric current is defined as the charge passing a point per unit time; $I = \dfrac{Q}{t}$

- ○ **SUPPLEMENT** Conventional current is from positive to negative and that the flow of free electrons is from negative to positive.

- ○ Electromotive force (e.m.f.) is defined as the electrical work done by a source in moving a unit charge around a complete circuit.

- ○ Electromotive force is measured in volts (V).

- ○ Potential difference (p.d.) is defined as the work done by a unit charge passing through a component.

- ○ Potential difference between two points is measured in volts (V).

- ○ Voltmeters (analogue and digital) with different ranges are used to measure potential difference (voltage).

- ○ **SUPPLEMENT** Equation for e.m.f.: $E = \dfrac{W}{Q}$

- ○ **SUPPLEMENT** Equation for p.d.: $V = \dfrac{W}{Q}$

- ○ Resistance can be calculated using the equation: $R = \dfrac{V}{I}$.

- ○ Describe an experiment to determine resistance using a voltmeter and an ammeter.

- ○ The resistance of a metallic wire increases with increasing length.

- ○ The resistance of a metallic wire increases with decreasing cross-sectional area.

- ○ **SUPPLEMENT** Sketch and explain the current–voltage graphs for a resistor of constant resistance, a filament lamp and a diode.

- ○ **SUPPLEMENT** For a metallic electrical conductor: resistance is directly proportional to its length and resistance is inversely proportional to its cross-sectional area.

- ○ Understand that electric circuits transfer energy from a source of electrical energy to the circuit components and then into the surroundings.

- ○ Equation for electrical power: $P = IV$

- ○ Equation for electrical energy: $E = IVt$

- ○ The kilowatt-hour (kWh) is the energy transferred by 1 kW device in a time of 1 hour.

- ○ Calculate the cost of using electrical appliances.

# End of topic questions

*Note: the marks in brackets give an indication of the level of detail you should include in your answers.*

**1.** A plastic rod is rubbed with a cloth.

**a)** Explain how the plastic rod becomes positively charged. (2 marks)

**b)** Describe how you can demonstrate that two positively charged rods repel each other. (2 marks)

**2.** A car stops and one of the passengers gets out. When she touches a metal post she feels an electric shock. Explain why she feels this shock. (2 marks)

**3.** **SUPPLEMENT** **a)** A charge of 10 C flows through a motor in 30 seconds. Calculate the current in the motor. (2 marks)

**b)** The current in a heater is 10 A. Calculate the charge flow through this heater in:

**i)** 1.0 second (2 marks)

**ii)** 1.0 hour. (2 marks)

**4.** Calculate the following:

**a)** the potential difference required to produce a current of 2.0 A in a 12 Ω resistor (2 marks)

**b)** the potential difference required to produce a current of 0.10 A in a 200 Ω resistor (2 marks)

**c)** the current produced when a potential difference of 12 V is applied to a 100 Ω resistor (2 marks)

**d)** the current produced when a potential difference of 230 V is applied to a 10 Ω resistor (2 marks)

**e)** the resistance of a wire with potential difference of 6.0 V and current of 0.10 A (2 marks)

**f)** the resistance of a heater, connected to a 230 V supply and current of 10 A. (2 marks)

**5.** **SUPPLEMENT** An electric motor drives a water pump that lifts water out of a well that is 10 m deep. It can deliver 360 kg of water per minute out of the tap at the top.

**a)** Calculate the gravitational potential energy given to the water per second. Hence, calculate electrical power of the electric motor. Assume that the motor and pump work at 100% efficiency. (4 marks)

**b)** The electric motor is designed to run on 12 V supply. Calculate the current in the motor. (3 marks)

**c)** Calculate the current in the motor if it were to use a 230 V mains supply. (3 marks)

**d)** Suggest one advantage and one disadvantage of the 230 V system over the 12 V system. (2 marks)

6. **SUPPLEMENT** A 1400 W appliance is connected to a 230 V for 30 minutes.

    **a)** Calculate the current in the appliance. (3 marks)

    **b)** The energy usage of the appliance in kW h. (3 marks)

    **c)** The cost of running the appliance, given the cost of each kW h is 18 cents. (2 marks)

7. **SUPPLEMENT** A cell of e.m.f. 1.5 V is connected to a lamp for 20 s. The current in the lamp is 0.10 .

    **a)** Show that the charge passing through the cell is 2.0 C. (2 marks)

    **b)** Calculate the work done on the 2.0 C charge passing through the cell. (2 marks)

8. The current in a component is 2.0 A when the potential difference across it is 10 V.

What is the power dissipated by the component?

**A** 0.20 W

**B** 5.0 W

**C** 10 W

**D** 20 W (1 mark)

# Electric circuits

## INTRODUCTION

Electric circuits can be series or **parallel**, or a combination of the two. Imagine trying to explain a circuit to a friend. You could take a photograph or sketch out the circuit. Physicists and engineers draw circuits using conventional symbols – it is an easier way to communicate ideas. In this section you will learn about different circuits, and do calculations to predict outcomes such as current drawn by a complicated circuit connected to a power supply.

△ Fig. 4.40 You can investigate electrical circuits in the classroom.

## KNOWLEDGE CHECK

✓ Know about electric current, potential difference (p.d.) and the equation $V = IR$.
✓ Using ammeter and voltmeter in circuits.

## LEARNING OBJECTIVES

✓ Draw and interpret circuit diagrams containing cells, batteries, power supplies, generators, potential dividers, switches, resistors (fixed and variable), heaters, thermistors (NTC only), light-dependent resistors (LDRs), lamps, motors, ammeters, voltmeters, magnetising coils, transformers, fuses and relays, and know how these components behave in the circuit.

✓ **SUPPLEMENT** Draw and interpret circuit diagrams containing diodes and light-emitting diodes (LEDs), and know how these components behave in the circuit.

✓ Know that the current at every point in a series circuit is the same.

✓ Know how to construct and use series and parallel circuits.

✓ Calculate the combined e.m.f. of several sources in series.

✓ Calculate the combined resistance of two or more resistors in series.

✓ State that, for a parallel circuit, the current from the source is larger than the current in each branch.

✓ State that the combined resistance of two resistors in parallel is less than that of either resistor by itself.

✓ State the advantages of connecting lamps in parallel in a lighting circuit.

✓ **SUPPLEMENT** Recall and use in calculations, the fact that: the sum of the currents entering a junction in a parallel circuit is equal to the sum of the currents that leave the junction; the total p.d. across the components in a series circuit is equal to the sum of the individual p.d.s across each component; and the p.d. across an arrangement of parallel resistances is the same as the p.d. across one branch in the arrangement of the parallel resistances.

✓ **SUPPLEMENT** Explain that the sum of the currents into a junction is the same as the sum of the currents out of the junction.

✓ **SUPPLEMENT** Calculate the combined resistance of two resistors in parallel.

✓ Know that the p.d. across an electrical conductor increases as its resistance increases for a constant current.

✓ **SUPPLEMENT** Describe the action of a variable potential divider.

✓ **SUPPLEMENT** Recall and use the equation for two resistors used as a potential divider

$$\frac{R_1}{R_2} = \frac{V_1}{V_2}$$

## CIRCUIT DIAGRAMS AND CIRCUIT COMPONENTS

When people started connecting together components and designing circuits, they quickly found that it was not convenient to draw accurate pictures of the circuits that they made. It was much easier to understand how the circuit worked, and to correct any faults, when they used standard symbols for the parts. It was also much easier when the wires were drawn in straight lines, rather than trying to copy the exact route taken.

Study the circuits used in this topic, and learn the symbols and what they represent.

Fig. 4.41 is a simple circuit diagram that shows how a torch is powered by a battery consisting of three cells of e.m.f. 1.5 V, giving a total of 4.5 V.

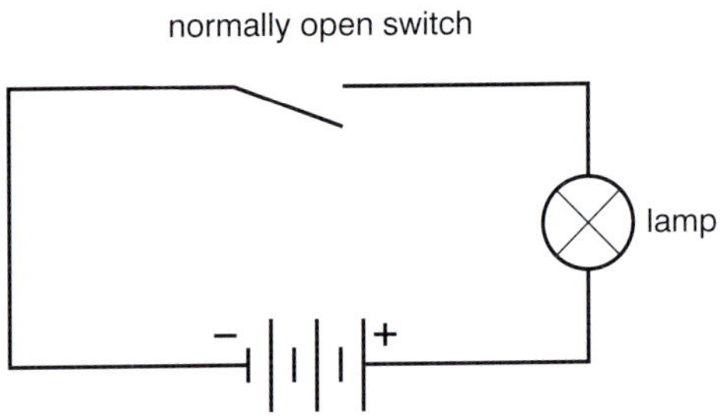

△ Fig. 4.41 A circuit diagram for a torch.

The word battery means an assembly of several cells. To calculate the combined e.m.f. of several sources in series, you add the individual e.m.f.s. The '+' terminal of the cell is indicated by the long thin line, and the '−' terminal by the short thick line. The other symbols in the circuit are the normally open switch, and the lamp.

### SUPPLEMENT

The direction of the current in a lamp does not matter, but a calculator, for instance, could be destroyed if the battery is not inserted correctly. One way to prevent this is to add a **diode** to the circuit. A diode allows current to move in one direction but not in the other.

In Fig. 4.42, the calculator is represented as a resistor. A calculator is far more complicated than that, but it does behave to the battery as if it were a resistor, drawing a small current $I$ from the battery.

The arrow on the diode shows the direction of a conventional current. When the battery is inserted the wrong way round, there is no current. A light-emitting diode (LED) can be used in place of the diode. The LED emits light of a characteristic colour when it is conducting. So, the LED is only lit when the battery is connected correctly to the calculator.

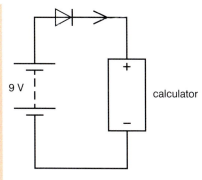

△ Fig. 4.42  A diode only allows current to pass through it in one direction.

You have already met a few of the circuit symbols required for your study. Fig. 4.43 shows some others that you also need to be familiar with. Some may already be familiar to you, others you will meet as you progress through this book.

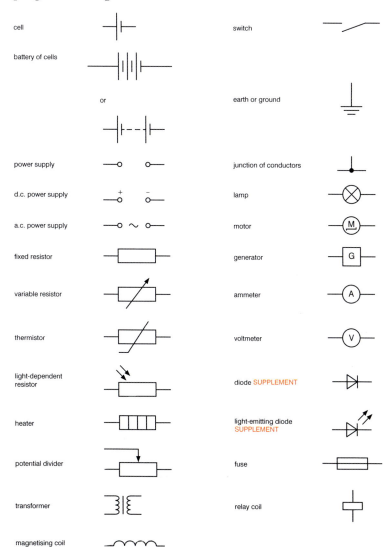

△ Fig. 4.43  Important circuit symbols for you to learn.

## SERIES AND PARALLEL CIRCUITS

Electrical components can be connected together in all sorts of combinations, but most combinations can be broken up into series and parallel combinations.

### Series

In a series circuit, components are connected one after another in a single loop.

When you connect two identical cells, each of e.m.f. 1.5 V, in series, then you will end up with a battery of e.m.f. 3.0 V, see Fig. 4.44. The e.m.f. of the battery is just the sum of the individual e.m.f.s of the cells. Connecting cells in series is useful when you want a larger current.

△ Fig. 4.44 Cells connected in series.

### Lamps in series

Fig. 4.45 shows circuits in which identical lamps are connected to a power supply of the same e.m.f.

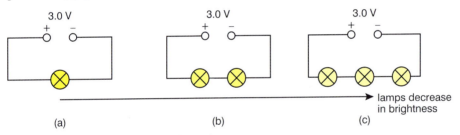

△ Fig. 4.45 Identical lamps connected in series.

The single lamp is the brightest. The brightness of each lamp in the series circuit is the same, but it decreases as we increase the number of lamps. This effectively means that the combined resistance of the circuit increases with more lamps, giving a smaller current in the circuit. The current in each lamp must be the same because they have the same brightness. If an ammeter is connected at any point in the circuit, it will always show the same reading.

It would not be a good idea to have your house lamps all connected in series because if one stopped working, then all the others would go off.

### Resistors in series

Fig. 4.46 shows a resistor of resistance 100 Ω and a resistor of resistance 120 Ω connected in series to a 3.2 V supply. The circuit has two ammeters on either side of the series combination.

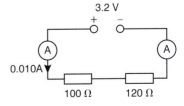

△ Fig. 4.46 Two resistors connected to a power supply.

Both ammeters will show the same reading of 0.010 A. Therefore, the current in a series circuit is the same at all points. This means that the current in each resistor is 0.010 A.

The two resistors in series can be treated as a single resistor with a combined resistance $R_C$ that can be calculated from the e.m.f. 3.2 V and current 0.010 A as follows:

$$R_C = \frac{V}{I} = \frac{3.2}{0.010}$$
$$R_C = 320 \ \Omega$$

The value of 320 $\Omega$ is interesting because it is the sum of the individual resistances. We can generalise the results above for all circuits with the following rules:

- Current in a series circuit is the same.
- The combined resistance $R_C$ of two, or more, resistors is the sum of the individual resistances of the resistors. You can use the equation:

$$R_C = R_1 + R_2 + \dots$$

## SUPPLEMENT

Fig. 4.47 shows a variable resistor and a lamp connected to a 3.00 V supply. Voltmeter 1 measures the potential difference (p.d.) across the lamp, and voltmeter 2 measures the p.d. across the variable resistor.

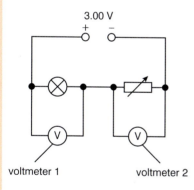

△ Fig. 4.47 The voltmeters measure the p.d.s across the components.

The table below shows the results collected by a student.

| Voltmeter 1 reading/V | Voltmeter 2 reading/V | Sum of the readings/V |
| --- | --- | --- |
| 0.50 | 2.48 | 0.50 + 2.48 = 2.98 |
| 1.51 | 1.50 | 1.51 + 1.50 = 3.01 |
| 2.20 | 0.82 | 2.20 + 0.82 = 3.02 |

The last column is almost 3.00 V; within the limits of experimental accuracy, this is the total p.d. across the components. We can generalise the results above for all circuits with the following rule:

- The total p.d. across components in a series circuit, is equal to the sum of the individual p.d.s across each component.

1. Calculate the combined series resistance in each case:

   a) two identical 330 Ω resistors

   b) a 500 Ω resistor and a 120 Ω resistor.

2. Two 100 Ω and 200 Ω resistors are connected in series to a 3.0 V battery.

   a) Calculate the combined resistance of the circuit.

   b) Calculate the current in the circuit.

3. **SUPPLEMENT** A lamp and a resistor are connected in series to a 5.0 V supply. The current in the circuit is 0.10 A. The p.d. across the resistor is 3.0 V. Calculate:

   a) the p.d. across the lamp

   b) the resistance of the lamp.

## Lamps in parallel

In parallel circuits, electrical components are connected alongside one another, forming extra loops. Fig. 4.48 shows circuits in which identical lamps are connected in parallel to a power supply of the same e.m.f.

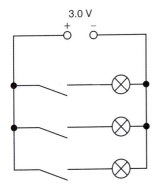

△ Fig. 4.48 Lamps in parallel. Each switch can turn a lamp on or off.

Each lamp can be turned on or off with the help of the switch next to it. The brightness of each lamp is the same when it is lit – this means that the current in each lamp is the same. You can have all three lamps on with all three switches closed. The lamps in your house would be connected in this way. Unlike the series combination, you have control of each lamp. Towns and cities are all lit at night-time using parallel circuits.

△ Fig. 4.49 All of these lights are in parallel. If they were in series then they would all go off if any one of them failed or was switched off.

## Resistors in parallel

Fig. 4.50 shows a resistor of resistance 200 Ω and a resistor of resistance 300 Ω connected in parallel to a 3.0 V supply. The circuit has three ammeters – ammeter $A_1$ measures the current in the 200 Ω resistor, ammeter $A_2$ measures the current in the 300 Ω resistor, and finally ammeter $A_3$ measures the current from the supply.

Here are some results from this circuit.

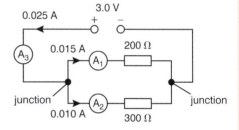

△ Fig. 4.50 Two resistors connected in parallel.

| Ammeter reading $A_1$/A | Ammeter reading $A_2$/A | Ammeter reading $A_3$/A |
|---|---|---|
| 0.015 | 0.010 | 0.025 |

The current from the supply of 0.025 A is larger than any of the other individual currents. The two resistors in parallel can be treated as a single resistor with a combined resistance $R_C$ that can be calculated from 3.0 V and current of 0.025 A from the supply as follows:

$$R_C = \frac{V}{I} = \frac{3.0}{0.025}$$
$$R_C = 120 \ \Omega$$

We can generalise this idea for all components connected in parallel with the following rules:

- The current from the source is always greater than the current in each branch of the parallel circuit.
- The combined resistance of resistors in parallel is always less than the resistance of either of the resistors.

It is worth analysing the parallel circuit shown in Fig. 4.50 in greater detail.

The current from the power supply comes to the junction of the parallel circuit, and splits up. The sum of the currents leaving this junction is equal to the current entering this junction. The same happens at the other end. The currents combine together to produce the same current back to the power supply. This is illustrated in detail in Fig. 4.51.

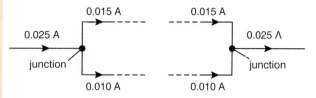

△ Fig. 4.51 Details of what happens at a junction.

We can use the ammeter reading to determine the p.d. across each resistor.

For the 200 Ω resistor: $V = IR = 0.015 \times 200 = 3.0$ V

For the 300 Ω resistor: $V = IR = 0.010 \times 300 = 3.0$ V

The p.d. across each resistor is the same as the 3.0 V from the power supply.

The two resistors behave as a single resistor of combined resistance $R_C$. This value can be calculated as follows:

$$R_C = \frac{V}{I} = \frac{3.0}{0.025} = 120 \ \Omega$$

The combined resistance is less than the resistance of the individual resistors. The equation for determining $R_C$ is not as simple as that for the resistors in series. The combined resistance for two resistors in parallel can be calculated using the equation:

$$R_C = \frac{R_1 R_2}{R_1 + R_2}$$

where $R_1$ and $R_2$ are resistance values of the resistors. We can use this equation to calculate the combined resistance of the two parallel resistors in Fig. 4.48.

$$R_C = \frac{200 \times 300}{200 + 300} = 120 \ \Omega$$

This is exactly what we deduced above.

We can generalise the results above for all circuits with the following rule:

- The sum of the currents entering a junction in a parallel circuit is equal to the sum of the currents that leave the same junction. The reason for this is charge conservation – charge cannot be destroyed. The total charge entering a junction in a given time must be equal to the total charge leaving the same junction.

- The p.d. across each component in a parallel circuit is the same.
- The combined resistance $R_C$ of two resistors in parallel is given by the equation:

$$R_C = \frac{R_1 R_2}{R_1 + R_2}$$

## QUESTIONS

1. State one major advantage of connected lamps in parallel.

2. **SUPPLEMENT** Calculate the combined resistance of:

   **a)** two identical 100 Ω resistors connected in parallel

   **b)** a 10 Ω resistor and a 30 Ω resistor connected in parallel.

3. **SUPPLEMENT** Calculate the current *I* in each case:

   **a)**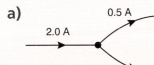

   **b)**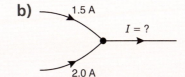

   **c)**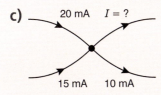

4. **SUPPLEMENT** Two lamps are connected to a 6.0 V battery in parallel. The current in the lamps are 0.10 A and 0.20 A. Calculate the individual resistance of each lamp, and also the combined resistance of the lamps in parallel.

## CHARACTERISTICS AND USE OF SOME CIRCUIT COMPONENTS

Now that you have seen how circuits can be connected, it is time to consider how components may be put together to make useful circuits. You will also have the opportunity of familiarising yourself with a few more circuit symbols. In this section you will consider the properties and use of some electrical components.

### Thermistor and LDR

A **thermistor** is made from a semiconductor. Semiconductors have electrical properties that are between those of conductors and insulators. The resistance of a thermistor depends on its temperature. For a negative temperature coefficient (NTC) thermistor, its resistance decreases as its temperature increases. They are useful components in fire alarms and fridges.

Fig. 4.52 shows a simple temperature-sensing circuit based on a thermistor. As the temperature of the thermistor increases, its resistance decreases and this increases the current in the circuit. The ammeter can be calibrated to indicate temperature.

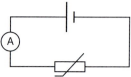

△ Fig. 4.52 A temperature-sensing circuit.

A **light-dependent resistor** (LDR) is also made from a semiconductor – cadmium sulfide is a popular choice. The resistance of an LDR depends on the intensity of light falling on its surface. The resistance of an LDR decreases as the light intensity falling on it increases. They are useful components in street lights and alarm systems.

Fig. 4.53 shows a simple light-sensing circuit based on an LDR for monitoring the brightness in a room. As the intensity of the light increases, its resistance decreases and this increases the current in the circuit. Here too, the ammeter can be calibrated to indicate the brightness.

△ Fig. 4.53 A light-sensing circuit.

## Developing practical skills

A student investigates how the resistance of an NTC thermistor varies with temperature. She uses a multimeter as an ohmmeter. To measure the temperature of the thermistor she immerses it in a water bath. At the start of the experiment she fills the beaker with water at 50 °C. She takes measurements of the temperature and the resistance at various temperatures as the water cools down. The student adds ice to help achieve lower temperatures and stirs the water regularly. The student's measurements are shown in the table.

| Temperature/°C | Resistance/kΩ |
|---|---|
| 50 | 1.12 |
| 45 | 2.11 |
| 40 | 2.79 |
| 35 | 3.54 |
| 30 | 4.25 |
| 25 | 5.45 |
| 20 | 6.61 |
| 15 | 8.47 |
| 10 | 12.62 |

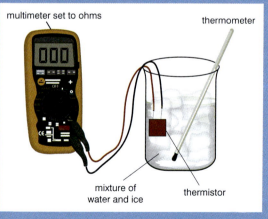

△ Fig. 4.54 Apparatus needed for the investigation.

## Variable resistor

A variable resistor has a length of resistance wire and an adjustable sliding contact. One end of the wire and the contact are connected into the circuit. Because the contact can be moved from one end of the wire to the other, the resistance of the variable resistor can be set to any value from nearly zero to the total resistance of the resistance wire inside the device. The current in a circuit can be controlled by changing the resistance of the circuit using a variable resistor or rheostat. Adjustment of the rheostat changes the length of the wire. Variable resistors are often used, for example, to change the brightness of car lights.

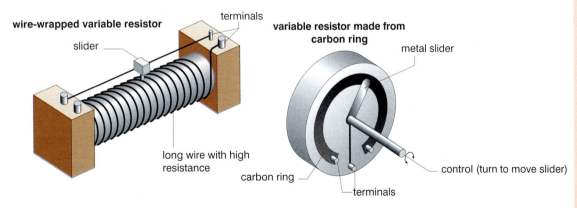

Δ Fig 4.55 Variable resistors are commonly used in electrical equipment, for example in the speed controls of model racing cars or in volume controls on radios and audio systems.

In the circuit in Fig. 4.56 a variable resistor is used to control the speed of an electric motor, which has a resistance of 12 Ω. If it is a 24 V electric motor, and a battery with e.m.f. of 24 V, then with the variable resistor set to 0 Ω, the potential difference (p.d.) across the motor will be 24 V and the motor will run at full speed. The p.d. across the variable resistor will be 0 V. The resistance of the whole circuit is 12 Ω and so the current through the motor will be 2.0 A.

If the variable resistor is set to 12 Ω, then the combined resistance in the circuit is now 24 Ω, and the current $I$ can be calculated:

$$I = \frac{V}{R}$$

$$I = \frac{24}{24}$$

$$I = 1.0 \, \text{A}$$

The current in the motor will have halved and the motor will run slower. Note that we can now work out the p.d. $V$ across the motor.

current in the motor = 1.0 A

resistance of motor = 12 Ω

$$V = I \times R$$
$$V = 1.0 \times 12$$
$$V = 12 \, \text{V}$$

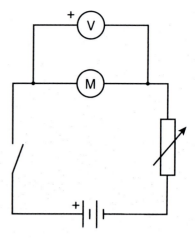

△ Fig. 4.56 The voltmeter can be added after the circuit has been made.

Likewise, the p.d. across the resistor is 12 V and the p.d. values around the circuit add up to 24 V, which is the same as the e.m.f. of the battery, as always.

## Potentiometer

A **potentiometer** is very similar in design to a variable resistor, and in fact the same component can normally be used as either device. In a potentiometer, all three points – both ends of the resistance wire and the adjustable contact – are connected into the circuit. The two ends of the resistance wire are connected to both ends of the battery or power supply, see Fig. 4.57. So when the battery is 5.0 V, then the p.d. across the resistance wire is 5.0 V. When the slider is set to the top at point A, then the p.d., $V_{\text{out}}$, across the two output wires will be 5.0 V. When the slider is set to the bottom at point B, the two output wires are connected to the same point and the p.d. will be 0 V.

This is a major difference between a potentiometer and a variable resistor: the voltage output of the potentiometer can be set to zero. This is one reason why the volume control on most audio equipment is a potentiometer, as it gives full control over the output volume.

The current in the resistance wire is constant. As the slider is B to A, the resistance between the two output contacts will increase, and this increases the output voltage. You can make more sense of this using the equation:

$$V_{\text{out}} = IR$$

where the current $I$ is constant, and the resistance $R$ between the output contacts increases as the length of the resistance wire is increased.

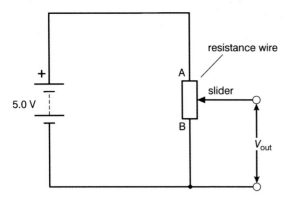

Δ Fig. 4.57 The potentiometer can provide a continuous output voltage from 0 V to 5.0 V.

## VARIABLE POTENTIAL DIVIDER

A variable potential divider, or simply a potential divider and even a voltage divider, is a circuit that does exactly what its name suggest; it divides a supply voltage across two resistors connected in series. Fig. 4.58 shows a potential divider circuit with resistors of resistances $R_1$ and $R_2$. The resistors in series are connected to a supply voltage. The p.d.s across the resistors are $V_1$ and $V_2$ as shown, and the p.d. across both resistors is $V$.

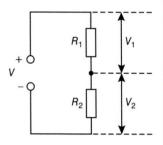

Δ Fig. 4.58 A potential divider circuit.

The current in a series circuit is the same. This implies that the p.d. across the resistor is directly proportional to its resistance. This gives a very useful equation:

$$\frac{R_1}{R_2} = \frac{V_1}{V_2}$$

You can also calculate the p.d. across the resistor of resistance R2 using the equation:

$$V_2 = \frac{R_2}{R_1 + R_2} \times V$$

What happens when both resistors have the same value? $\frac{R_1}{R_2} = 1$,

therefore $\frac{V_1}{V_2} = 1$. The p.d. across the resistor is the same. This can only

mean that the p.d. is half the supply voltage. The actual values of the resistors are not important – it is their relative values that matter. Using two 100 Ω resistor will give the same results as using two 12 kΩ resistors.

Potential divider circuits are useful when one of the components happens to be either a thermistor, or a light-dependent resistor (LDR).

## WORKED EXAMPLE

Calculate the p.d. across the 100 Ω resistor in the potential divider circuit shown.

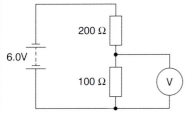

Write down the equation:

$$V_2 = \frac{R_2}{R_1 + R_2} \times V$$

Substitute the values into this equation:

$$V_2 = \frac{100}{200 + 100} \times 6.0$$

Calculate the answer:

$$V_2 = 2.0 \ V$$

The p.d. across the 100 Ω resistor is 2.0 V. Since the p.d.s in a series circuit must add up, the p.d. across the 200 Ω resistor must be 4.0 V. It is worth pointing out that $\frac{R_1}{R_2} = 2.0$ and $\frac{V_1}{V_2} = 2.0$.

### Relay

A **relay** is an electromagnet that can operate one or more switch contacts. For example, the contacts in the relay in Fig. 4.59 join points A and B when the switch is open. When the electromagnet is energised, it attracts a piece of soft iron and joins points A and C. Points B and C are never joined. A relay is useful when you want to want to use a circuit to control a large current in another circuit, e.g. street lights.

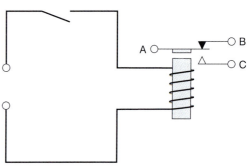

Fig. 4.59 A relay can be used as an output transducer.

### SUPPLEMENT

### Light-operated circuit

In the circuit shown in Fig. 4.60, the relay is not energised so long as the resistance of the LDR stays low. When the illumination reduces, the resistance of the LDR increases and the p.d. across the coil goes up. When the illumination is sufficiently low, the relay will close the contact. Note that the circuit controlled by the relay does not need to have any connection whatsoever to the relay coil circuit. This can be an important safety feature of the circuit.

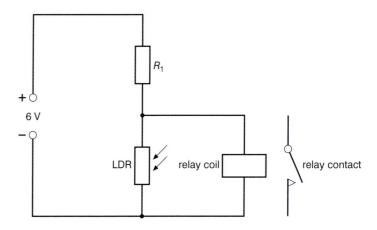

△ Fig. 4.60 The circuit of a light-sensitive switch, using a relay output.

# End of topic checklist

## Key terms

ammeter, battery, cell, light-dependent resistor (LDR),  parallel, relay, resistor, series, thermistor, voltmeter

**SUPPLEMENT** diodes, light-emitting diode (LED), potential divider

## During your study of this topic you should have learned:

◯ How to draw and interpret circuit diagrams using circuit symbols (cells, batteries, power supplies, generators, potential dividers, switches, resistors (fixed and variable), heaters, thermistors, light-dependent resistors (LDRs), lamps, motors, ammeters, voltmeters, magnetising coils, transformers, **fuses** and relays), and know how these components behave in the circuit.

◯ **SUPPLEMENT** How to draw and interpret circuit diagrams containing diodes and light-emitting diodes (LEDs), and know how these components behave in the circuit.

◯ The current at every point in a series circuit is the same.

◯ Know how to construct and use series and parallel circuits.

◯ Calculate the combined e.m.f. of several sources in series.

◯ Calculate the combined resistance of two or more resistors in series using the equation: $R_C = R_1 + R_2 + \ldots$

◯ For a parallel circuit, the current from the source is larger than the current in each branch.

◯ The combined resistance of two resistors in parallel is less than that of either resistor by itself.

◯ Know about the advantages of connecting lamps in parallel in a lighting circuit.

◯ **SUPPLEMENT** The sum of the currents entering a junction in a parallel circuit is equal to the sum of the currents that leave the junction.

◯ **SUPPLEMENT** The total p.d. across the components in a series circuit is equal to the sum of the individual p.d.s across each component.

◯ **SUPPLEMENT** The p.d. across an arrangement of parallel resistances is the same as the p.d. across one branch in the arrangement of the parallel resistances.

◯ **SUPPLEMENT** The sum of the currents into a junction is the same as the sum of the currents out of the junction, and know why this is so.

○ **SUPPLEMENT** Calculate the combined resistance of two resistors in parallel using the equation: $R_C = \dfrac{R_1 R_2}{R_1 + R_2}$

○ The p.d. across a conductor increases as its resistance increases for a constant current.

○ **SUPPLEMENT** Describe the action of a variable potential divider.

○ **SUPPLEMENT** The equation for two resistors used as a potential divider is: $\dfrac{R_1}{R_2} = \dfrac{V_1}{V_2}$

# End of topic questions

*Note: the marks in brackets give an indication of the level of detail you should include in your answers.*

1.  Draw a circuit showing a resistor connected to a thermistor with an ammeter in the circuit and a voltmeter across the resistor. The power supply should be a 9.0 V battery and there should be a switch in the circuit as well. (4 marks)

2.  Look at the following circuit diagrams. They show a number of ammeters and in some cases the readings on these ammeters. All the lamps are identical.

    **a)** For circuit X, state the readings you would expect on ammeters $A_1$ and $A_2$. (2 marks)

    **b) SUPPLEMENT** For circuit Y, state the readings you would expect on ammeters $A_4$ and $A_5$. (4 marks)

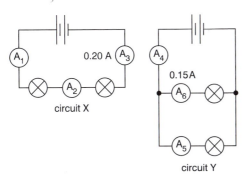

circuit X

circuit Y

3.  Look at the circuit diagram and answer the following questions:

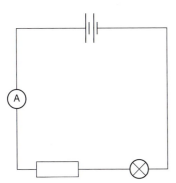

    **a)** What is the source of e.m.f. in this circuit?

    **A** ammeter    **B** battery    **C** lamp    **D** resistor (1 mark)

    **b)** State what will happen to the current if another cell is added. (1 mark)

    **c)** The ammeter reading is 0.30 A and the resistor has resistance 5.0 Ω. Calculate the p.d. across the resistor. (2 marks)

**4.** An engineer was testing the resistance of a component and obtained the table of data shown. The potential difference across the component was altered, and the current in the component was measured using an ammeter.

| Potential difference/V | Current/A |
| --- | --- |
| 0.5 | 0.14 |
| 1.0 | 0.29 |
| 1.5 | 0.43 |
| 3.0 | 0.86 |
| 4.0 | 1.14 |
| 5.0 | 1.43 |
| 5.5 | 1.57 |
| 6.5 | 1.86 |

**a)** Identify the independent variable in this experiment. (1 mark)

**b)** Plot a suitable graph, and use this graph to determine the resistance of the component. (3 marks)

**5.** Copy and complete the following table.

| Potential difference/V | Current/A | Resistance/Ω |
| --- | --- | --- |
|  | 0.15 | 2.0 |
| 6.0 | 0.20 |  |
|  | 0.50 | 12 |
| 12 | 3.00 |  |
| 240 |  | 18.5 |

(5 marks)

**6. a)** Lamps in a house can be connected either in series or in parallel. State one advantage of having them connected in parallel. (1 mark)

**b)** The circuit below is connected by a student.

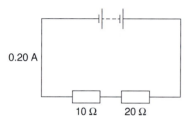

**i)** Calculate the combined resistance of the resistors. (3 marks)

**ii)** The current in the circuit is 0.20 A. Calculate the potential difference across the 10 Ω resistor. (3 marks)

**7.** **SUPPLEMENT** The circuit diagram below shows resistors connected in parallel to a power supply.

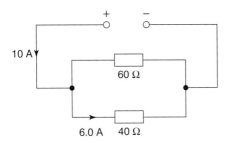

a) Determine the current in the 60 Ω resistor. (1 mark)

b) Calculate the combined resistance of the resistors. (3 marks)

c) Calculate the potential difference across the power supply. (2 marks)

**8.** **SUPPLEMENT** A potential divider circuit is shown below.

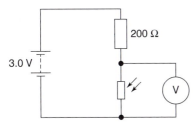

The resistance of the LDR in bright light is 100 Ω.

a) Calculate the p.d. across the LDR in bright light. (3 marks)

b) Calculate the current in the circuit in bright light. (2 marks)

c) Explain what happens to the p.d. across the LDR when it is placed in darkness. (3 marks)

# Electrical safety

Δ Fig. 4.61 Electricity travels from power stations to our homes on pylons like these.

## INTRODUCTION

Electricity is a clean and effective method of generating heat and movement. When a domestic appliance is switched on, a circuit is completed between the local substation and the appliance. Electrical energy travels from the substation to the appliance through the 'live' and 'neutral' wires. Some appliances have a third wire, the **'earth' wire**. This wire does not normally carry any current, but it is there for safety.

### KNOWLEDGE CHECK

✓ Some safety precautions to take when dealing with mains electricity.

### LEARNING OBJECTIVES

✓ State the hazards of: damaged insulation, overheating cables, damp conditions and excess current from overloading of plugs, extension leads, single and multiple sockets when using a mains supply.
✓ Know that a mains circuit consists of a live wire (line wire), a neutral wire and an earth wire and explain why a switch must be connected to the live wire for the circuit to be switched off safely.
✓ Explain the use and operation of trip switches and fuses and choose appropriate fuse ratings and trip switch settings.
✓ Explain why the outer casing of an electrical appliance must be either non-conducting (double-insulated) or earthed.
✓ State that a fuse without an earth wire protects the circuit and the cabling for a double-insulated appliance.

# ELECTRICAL HAZARDS

Electricity can cause hazards in domestic situations. Table 4.2 gives some examples.

| Hazard | Possible consequences |
|---|---|
| Frayed cables | Wiring can become exposed |
| Long trailing cables | These might cause a trip or a fall |
| Damaged plugs | Wiring can become exposed |
| Water around sockets | Water conducts electricity, so can connect a person into the mains supply |
| Pushing metal objects into sockets | This connects the holder to the mains supply and is likely to be lethal |
| Overloading of sockets | Causes too high a current, which might melt the insulation and cause a fire |
| Long, coiled cable to an electric heater | Cable can heat up because of the coiling and start a fire |

Δ Table 4.2 Examples of domestic electrical hazards.

If there is a fault in an electrical appliance, it could take too much electrical current. This might make the appliance itself dangerous, or it could cause the flex between the appliance and the wall to become too hot and start a fire.

## Insulation, fuses and trip switches

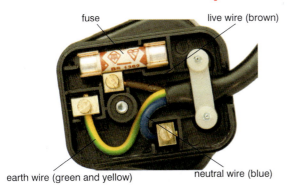

fuse · live wire (brown) · earth wire (green and yellow) · neutral wire (blue)

Δ Fig. 4.62 A three-pin plug has a built-in safety device, the fuse.

There are several ways to make appliances safer to use and to protect the user if a fault should develop. In some countries a **fuse** is fitted into the plug of the appliance. The fuse fits between the brown live wire and the pin. The brown **live wire** or **line wire** and the blue **neutral wire** carry the current. The green and yellow striped **earth wire** is needed to make metal appliances safer.

The laws for the safe use of electricity are constantly being improved by governments, and electricians learn to work to the latest standards. The most important aids to the safe use of electricity are **insulation** and fuses or **trip switches**.

Insulation these days is generally a plastic such as PVC, which is used to cover the copper wires. This prevents them from touching each other, and also prevents the operator from touching them. In parts of appliances where the temperature goes above 100 °C, other plastics, glass or ceramic are used.

The electric current usually has to pass through a fuse or trip switch before it reaches the appliance. If there is a sudden surge in the current, the wire in the fuse will heat up and melt – it 'blows'. This breaks the circuit and stops any further current in. When a trip switch is used, then the trip switch springs open (trips) a switch if there is an excessive current in the circuit. This can be reset easily after the fault in the circuit has been corrected.

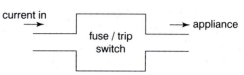

△ Fig. 4.63 How a fuse or trip switch protects an appliance.

In all houses with mains electricity, there is a distribution box (consumer unit) that takes all of the electricity for the house and sends it to the different rooms. In some houses this box may still contain fuses, but in modern installations the box has a type of trip switch called a miniature circuit-breaker, often known as an MCB.

Where a fuse is fitted to a plug, it must have a higher current rating than the appliance needs, but should have the smallest current rating available above this. The most common ratings for plug fuses are 3 A, 5 A and 13 A. Any electrical appliance with a heating element in it should be fitted with a 13 A fuse. An appliance working at 3.5 A should have a 5 A fuse.

Metal-cased appliances, such as washing machines or electric cookers, must have an earth wire as well as a fuse. If the live wire works loose and comes into contact with the metal casing, the casing will become live and the user could be electrocuted.

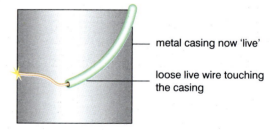

△ Fig. 4.64 A loose live wire can be dangerous if the metal casing of an appliance is not 'earthed'.

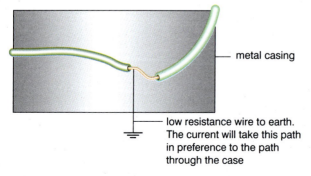

△ Fig. 4.65 An earth wire provides a path for current to flow to ground.

This low resistance means that a large current passes from the live wire to earth, causing the fuse to melt and break the circuit. If the earth wire is not fitted correctly, or if it has broken, the appliance will be extremely dangerous! If there is any doubt about the earthing of the appliance, or of the whole house, it must be checked by an electrician.

Appliances that are made with plastic casing such as electric drills do not have an earth wire in their fuse. This protects the circuit and cabling because the plastic casing acts an insulator and so can never become live. Appliances like this are said to be **double insulated**.

The earth wire provides a very low resistance route to the 0 V earth. This low resistance means that a large current passes from the live wire to earth, causing the fuse to melt and break the circuit. This disconnects the appliance from the live connection, making it safe to touch (Fig. 4.66).

In some situations people may be unexpectedly exposed to electricity: for example, using an electric drill, especially drilling into a wall with hidden power cables, or using power tools out of doors, perhaps in wet conditions. In these cases, a special type of **circuit breaker** called a residual current circuit-breaker (RCCB) must be used in the power socket on the wall. If any of the electricity starts to leak through a short circuit (for example because the device has got wet), the RCCB will turn off the power in 30 ms or less. The RCCB cannot be guaranteed to save the user's life, but it gives them a much better chance of surviving.

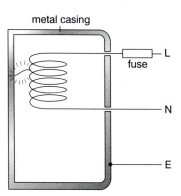

Δ Fig. 4.66 The earth wire and fuse work together to make sure that the metal outer casing of this appliance can never become live and electrocute someone.

## QUESTIONS

1. Describe the wiring of a three-pin plug. You should explain what each of the wires in the plug is connected to and the colour of the insulation.

2. Explain the function of a fuse.

3. A student wants to run an appliance that requires a current of 6.0 A. He chooses a fuse of 5.0 A 'because it's the nearest available'. Explain why this is not a good choice.

4. The earth wire connection to the ground is usually quite a thick piece of copper wire. Suggest why.

5. Explain why appliances with plastic casing do not need to be earthed.

# CURRENT WARS

The American physicist Thomas Alva Edison is often credited with the invention of the electric light bulb. He had the ambition of lighting up the whole of America, and his project began in the late 1800s in Manhattan, New York. Coal-powered stations were used to generate direct current, and expensive cables were laid out to light up his bulbs in some homes. The cables got hot because the large current caused lots of heating. This meant loss of energy generated by the power stations. The power stations had to be located within a few kilometres of customers.

There was an alternative; a better system using alternating current pioneered by Nikola Tesla working for the Westinghouse Electric Corporation. Alternating current could be lowered by stepping up the voltages using **transformers**. Smaller currents in the cables meant less energy losses. This potentially meant fewer power stations and a cleaner environment. Alternating current could not only be used for just lights, but electric motors too – this allowed elevators, drills, pumps and factory machines to be powered by electricity.

Alternating current technology was definitely more versatile than direct current technology. Edison was too stubborn – he believed that his technology was better, without looking at the evidence and the facts. He could have easily worked with Tesla, but chose not to. Scientists are human too; it would be nice to believe that no scientist today would make the same mistake.

**Challenge Question:** Electrical power is transmitted from power stations to towns using overhead cables. What is the main advantage of using alternating current in the cables rather than direct current?

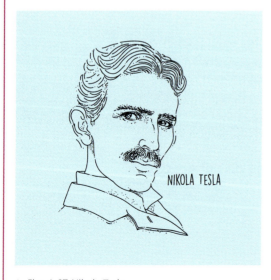

△ Fig. 4.67 Nikola Tesla

# End of topic checklist

## Key terms

double-insulated, earth wire, fuse, insulation, live wire, neutral wire, trip switch

## During your study of this topic you should have learned:

◯ About the hazards of: damaged insulation, overheating cables, damp conditions, excess current from overloading of plugs, extension leads, single and multiple sockets when using a mains supply.

◯ A mains circuit consists of a live wire (line wire), a neutral wire and an earth wire.

◯ Why a switch must be connected to the live wire for the circuit to be switched off safely.

◯ The use and operation of trip switches and fuses and how to choose appropriate fuse ratings and trip switch settings.

◯ Why the outer casing of an electrical appliance must be either non-conducting (**double-insulated**) or earthed.

◯ A fuse without an earth wire protects the circuit and the cabling for a double-insulated appliance.

# End of topic questions

*Note: the marks in brackets give an indication of the level of detail you should include in your answers.*

1.  **a)** A hair dryer works on 230 V mains electricity and takes a current of 4.0 A. Calculate the power of the hair dryer. *(2 marks)*

    **b)** In some countries it is illegal to have power sockets in a bathroom to stop you using electrical devices such as hair dryers near the wash basin or bath. Explain why it would not be sensible to use a hair dryer near to water. *(2 marks)*

2.  A fuse must always placed in series with which of the following wires?

    **A** blue

    **B** earth

    **C** live

    **D** neutral *(1 mark)*

3.  An appliance connected to the mains supply has a power rating of 1400 W. The potential difference of the mains is 230 V. Calculate the approximate current. Explain what size standard fuse you would use. *(3 marks)*

4.  In her living room, Felicity has the following items connected to the mains supply (230 V):

    - three 100 W lamps
    - a TV that takes 2.0 A
    - an audio system that takes 1.0 A
    - a 2.0 kW electric heater
    - a 3.0 kW air conditioning unit.

    The whole room is supplied from a 220 V a.c. power supply through one fuse. Suggest what rating of fuse she should fit, if values of 10 A, 20 A, 30 A, 40 A, 50 A and 60 A are available. *(2 marks)*

5.  Determine the rating of fuse you would use in a microwave of power rating 800 W with:

    **a)** a 240 V mains supply *(2 marks)*

    **b)** a 120 V mains supply. *(2 marks)*

# Electromagnetic effects

## INTRODUCTION

Almost any electrical appliance or tool –
such as electric drills, headphones, CD
players, hair dryers, loudspeakers – must
have a magnet in it somewhere in order to
work. When magnetism is combined with
electricity, it creates a force. It is this
force, which we call the motor effect,
which enables all these devices to work. In
this part of the topic you will learn how
electromagnets are constructed, and also
how magnetic fields are used to generate
electricity.

Δ Fig. 4.68 Part of an electric motor.

## KNOWLEDGE CHECK

✓ An electric current in a wire is due to the motion of electrons.
✓ Current is measured in amperes (A) and potential difference (voltage) in volts (V).
✓ Magnets provide a magnetic field.

## LEARNING OBJECTIVES

✓ Know that a conductor moving across a magnetic field or a changing magnetic field
  linking with a conductor can induce an e.m.f. in the conductor.
✓ Describe an experiment to demonstrate electromagnetic induction.
✓ State the factors affecting the magnitude of an induced e.m.f.
✓ **SUPPLEMENT** Know that the direction of an induced e.m.f. opposes the change
  causing it.
✓ **SUPPLEMENT** State and use the relative directions of force, field and induced
  current.
✓ **SUPPLEMENT** Describe a simple form of a.c. generator (rotating coil or rotating
  magnet) and the use of slip rings and brushes where needed.
✓ **SUPPLEMENT** Sketch and interpret graphs of e.m.f. against time for simple a.c.
  generators and relate the position of the generator coil to the peaks, troughs and
  zeros of the e.m.f.
✓ Describe the pattern and direction of the magnetic field due to currents in straight
  wires and in solenoids.
✓ Describe an experiment to identify the pattern of the magnetic field (including
  direction) due to currents in straight wires and in solenoids.

✓ Describe how the magnetic effect of a current is used in relays and loudspeakers and give examples of their application.

✓ **SUPPLEMENT** State the qualitative variation of the strength of the magnetic field around straight wires and solenoids.

✓ **SUPPLEMENT** Describe the effect on the magnetic field around straight wires and solenoids of changing the magnitude and direction of the current.

✓ Describe an experiment to show that a force acts on a current-carrying conductor in a magnetic field, including the effect of reversing: the current and the direction of the field.

✓ **SUPPLEMENT** Recall and use the relative directions of force, magnetic field and current.

✓ **SUPPLEMENT** Determine the direction of the force on beams of charged particles in a magnetic field.

✓ Know that a current-carrying coil in a magnetic field may experience a turning effect and that the turning effect is increased by increasing: the number of turns on the coil, the current or the strength of the magnetic field.

✓ **SUPPLEMENT** Describe the operation of an electric motor, including the action of a split-ring commutator and brushes.

✓ Describe the construction of a simple transformer with a soft iron core, as used for voltage transformations.

✓ Use the terms primary, secondary, step-up and step-down.

✓ Recall and use the equation

$$\frac{V_p}{V_s} = \frac{N_p}{N_s}$$

where p and s refer to primary and secondary.

✓ Describe the use of transformers in high-voltage transmission of electricity.

✓ State the advantages of high-voltage transmission.

✓ **SUPPLEMENT** Explain the principle of operation of a simple iron-cored transformer.

✓ **SUPPLEMENT** Recall and use the equation for 100% efficiency in a transformer
$$I_p V_p = I_s V_s$$
where $p$ and $s$ refer to primary and secondary.

✓ **SUPPLEMENT** Recall and use the equation:
$$P = I^2 R$$
to explain why power losses in cables are smaller when the voltage is greater.

## ELECTROMAGNETIC INDUCTION

Using the current from a battery is fine if you want to light a torch, but if you want to light a street, or a city, you will need to rely on generating electricity by **electromagnetic induction**. This is the process that power stations use to generate electromotive force (e.m.f.). Whatever the source of the energy, for example coal, wind or nuclear sources, the key process in the generation of electricity makes use of electromagnetic induction. Without it, modern society would look very different indeed.

Solar cells, which convert sunlight directly to electricity, are an exception.

Michael Faraday was the first person to generate electricity from a magnetic field using electromagnetic induction. The large **generators** in power stations generate the electricity we need by using this process.

An electromotive force (e.m.f.). is created across the ends of a conductor when:

- the conductor is moved through a magnetic field ('cutting' the magnetic field lines), or
- the magnetic field is moved past the conductor (again 'cutting' the magnetic field lines), or
- the magnetic field around the conductor changes strength.

△ Fig. 4.69  Generators in a hydroelectric power station.

An e.m.f. created in this way is called induced e.m.f. Fig. 4.70 shows how you can demonstrate that moving a conductor through a magnetic field induces an e.m.f. The conductor is connected across an ammeter, forming a complete circuit. The induced e.m.f. across the ends of the conductor will produce a current, which can be detected by the ammeter.

The faster these changes take place, the larger the induced e.m.f. So, the magnitude of the induced e.m.f. depends on the strength of the magnetic field and the speed with which the conductor is moved through the magnetic field.

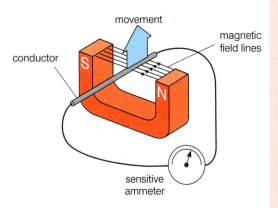

△ Fig. 4.70 Demonstrating electromagnetic induction.

In practice, rather than using a single conductor, a coil of wire with many turns is used. The induced e.m.f. increases as the number of turns are increased.

## SUPPLEMENT

In the arrangement shown in Fig. 4.70, the direction of the induced current is reversed when the conductor is moved through the magnetic field in the opposite direction. The direction of the induced e.m.f., and hence the induced current, is always in a direction that opposes the change producing it. The reasons for this are a bit complicated, but it is all to do with the principle of conservation of energy. A tiny fraction of the kinetic energy of the moving conductor is transferred into electrical energy. Work is always done on the conductor, with attraction between it and the magnetic field of the magnet. If the direction of the induced current was not reversed, then this would violate this very important principle in physics – you cannot gain energy from nowhere.

The direction of the induced current is always at right angles to both the direction of magnetic field and the direction of motion of the conductor. You can use your right hand, as arranged in Fig. 4.71 to predict the direction of the induced current. This rule is also known as Fleming's right-hand rule.

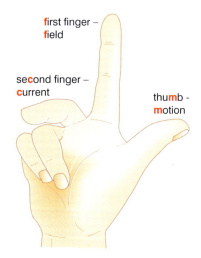

first finger – field

second finger – current

thumb - motion

Δ Fig. 4.71 With the thumb and fingers of your right hand arranged as shown, you can predict the direction of the induced current.

## QUESTIONS

1. Describe how an e.m.f. can be induced in a wire.

2. A wire is held stationary in a strong magnetic field. Explain whether or not an e.m.f. will be induced in the wire.

3. State two factors that affect the magnitude of the induced e.m.f. in a conductor.

4. **SUPPLEMENT** In Fig. 4.70, predict the direction of the induced current in the conductor when it is moved.

**SUPPLEMENT**

## THE A.C. GENERATOR

The electricity generated at power stations is a.c. (alternating current). This is achieved by using a generator, which in simple terms, is a coil that is rotated in a magnetic field, or the magnetic field is rotated around a fixed coil – as long as there is relative motion between the magnetic field and a conductor, an e.m.f. will be induced.

In power stations, the generators have magnetic fields rotating around stationary coils at either a frequency of 50 Hz or 60 Hz, depending on the country. This produces an alternating current of the same frequency. In a much-simplified laboratory version, a coil is rotated between the poles of a strong permanent magnet.

Spinning a coil of wire in a magnetic field produces a continuous, varying e.m.f. much larger than that from a single wire, see Fig. 4.72. The current produced is passed to an external circuit via slip rings, which are rings attached to the coil of wire and to the output circuit. The output is an alternating current.

As the coil rotates clockwise, the direction of the induced current will always be the same next to each of the poles of the magnet. In Fig. 4.72, the current is from A to B, and from C to D. After the coil has rotated half a turn, the current is from D to C, and from B to A. An alternating current has been induced, or an alternating e.m.f. has been induced across the ends of the coil. The slip rings connected to the ends of the coil allow the coil to spin without winding the wire around itself. The brushes, often made of carbon, are contacts that touch the slip rings and complete the circuit.

The induced e.m.f. is:

- maximum when the plane of the coil is parallel to the magnetic field
- zero when the plane of the coil is perpendicular to the magnetic field
- maximum and reversed in direction when the plane of the coil is parallel to the magnetic field after half a revolution.

An e.m.f. is induced across the ends of the rotating coil because the magnetic field linking the coil changes. Rotating the coil faster will increase the size of the maximum induced e.m.f., and also increase the frequency of the alternating current. Using a stronger magnetic field, or increasing the number of turns of the coil, will also increase the size of the maximum induced e.m.f. at a given frequency.

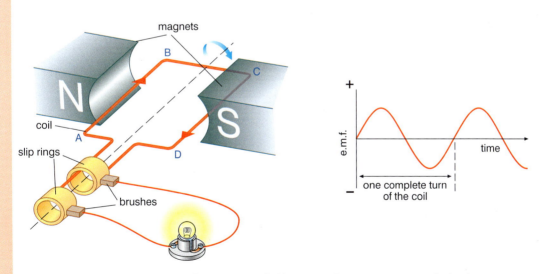

Δ Fig. 4.72 The spinning coil in a uniform magnetic field gives an alternating current in the load (lamp) connected to the generator. The induced e.m.f. against time graph for the generator is also shown.

## Developing practical skills

A student wants to investigate the induced e.m.f. in a coil by a moving magnet. To do this, she hangs a magnet from a spring so that it can oscillate vertically. The student sets the magnet moving so that it oscillates in and out of a coil. To measure the voltage induced, the student connects the coil to a cathode ray oscilloscope (CRO). A CRO gives a voltage–time trace on the screen. The magnitude of the induced e.m.f. can be determined from the vertical height of the trace.

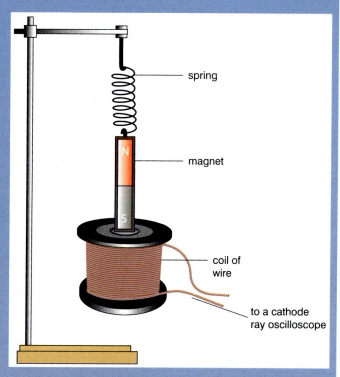

△ Fig. 4.73 The apparatus needed for the investigation.

The student wants to vary the speed of the magnet's motion and measure the maximum e.m.f. induced. However, she cannot think of a way to measure the speed of the magnet. The student adapts her method to a more qualitative approach, simply judging whether or not larger speeds give bigger e.m.f.s.

### Planning experiments and investigations

**1.** The student plans to vary the speed of the magnet by stretching the spring to different lengths before releasing it. Will this method work?

### Observing, measuring and recording data

**2.** The student expects larger e.m.f to be induced when the magnet moves more quickly. How will she be able to judge e.m.f from the CRO screen?

### Interpreting and evaluating data

**3.** The student adapted her plan to a more qualitative approach. What does 'qualitative' mean in this context?

**4.** Suggest how the student could adapt her method to record accurate measurements of the speed of the magnet and the induced e.m.f..

**QUESTIONS**

1. Explain why an e.m.f. is induced in a coil rotating in a uniform magnetic field.

2. State how you can increase the magnitude of the maximum current induced in an a.c. generator rotating at a fixed frequency.

## MAGNETIC EFFECT OF A CURRENT

When a wire is carrying electric current it produces a magnetic field around itself. This is the basis of electromagnetism – moving charges, be it electrons or a beam of positive ions, will create a magnetic field in the space around them. The larger the current, the stronger the magnetic field generated.

By changing the magnitude of the current, you can change the strength of the magnetic field; and by reversing the current you reverse the direction of the magnetic field.

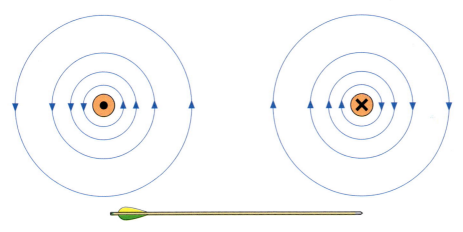

Δ Fig. 4.74 The field pattern for a straight current-carrying conductor. You can use iron-filings or a compass to plot the field patterns.

The dot in the centre of the wire indicates that the current is directed towards you; the cross indicates that the current is directed away. To remember this, think of an arrow. The ● is the tip of the arrow coming towards you, the '✗' is the flights on the tail of the arrow. We are using the conventional current, so remember that the electrons are actually going in the opposite direction.

The magnetic field lines form continuous rings around the wire all along its length. As with magnetic fields from magnets, these field lines never cross. The direction of the field at a point is the direction in which a north pole would move at that point. Just as with bar magnets, the magnetic field patterns can be revealed by using iron-filings or detected using a compass. As with magnets, you can use a small compass to determine the direction of the magnetic field.

Fig. 4.75 shows the magnetic field due to the current in a solenoid. A solenoid consists of a wire coiled up into a spiral shape. A magnetic field is created when a current is passed through the solenoid. The magnetic field resembles that of a permanent magnet – with a north (N) and south (S) pole.

Just as with bar magnets, the pattern of magnetic fields due to currents in straight wires and in solenoids can be identified using iron-filings, and the direction found using a compass – see Magnetic fields in Section 4. Fig. 4.76 shows an experimental arrangement for showing the pattern of the magnetic field around a current-carrying wire. The wire passes through a small hole in a card that is placed at right angles to the wire. Iron-filings are sprinkled around the wire. A gentle tap of the card will reveal the circular field pattern around the wire. The direction of the magnetic field at any point around the wire can be found using a small compass. In this experiment, the current in the wire is fairly large, and the wire gets very hot - so, it is best not to touch the wire. The magnetic field pattern for a solenoid can also be revealed using iron-filings.

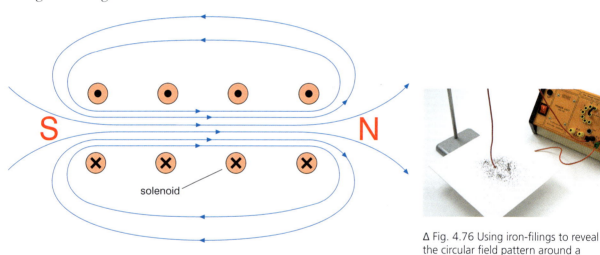

△ Fig. 4.75  Magnetic field in a solenoid.

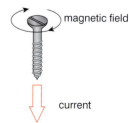

△ Fig. 4.76 Using iron-filings to reveal the circular field pattern around a current-carrying wire.

The closer the magnetic field lines, the stronger is the magnetic field. For a straight current-carrying wire, the strength of the magnetic field decreases as the distance from the wire increases. You can see the field lines get further apart as we move away from the wire.

The strength of the magnetic field also depends on the current itself; larger currents produce stronger magnetic fields.

If the current a straight wire is travelling towards you, the magnetic field lines are going in an anticlockwise direction, and if away from you they are going clockwise. To remember this, think of a woodscrew, see Fig. 4.77. The current is in the direction of travel of the woodscrew, and direction of the magnetic field is in the direction in which you turn the woodscrew.

magnetic field

current

△ Fig. 4.77 A woodscrew can help with predicting the direction of the magnetic field.

You can determine the direction of the magnetic field of the solenoid shown in Fig. 4.75 by using the woodscrew idea applied to a single turn.

The strength of the magnetic field for a straight wire, and a solenoid, can be increased by increasing the current. For a solenoid, the magnetic field within its core is uniform (the field lines are parallel and separation between adjacent lines is the same). It is also worth mentioning that reversing the direction of the electric current will reverse the direction of the magnetic field. You have already seen this in Fig. 4.74.

### Electromagnets

An electric current in a conductor produces a magnetic field around it. **Electromagnets** are made out of a coil of wire wrapped around an iron core. Fig. 4.78 shows an electromagnet when the current is switched on. The strong magnetic field has north (N) and south (S) poles. This field can be turned off by opening the switch. The variable resistor helps to change the current, and hence the strength of the electromagnet. Electromagnets are used in relays and in loudspeakers.

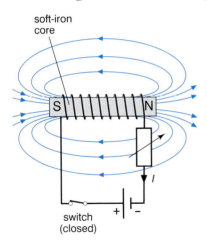

△ Fig. 4.78 The magnetic field produced when a current is passed through the coil.

### Applications of electromagnetism

A **relay** consists of an electromagnet and switch, or switches. A relay is used in circuits where it not possible to have a direct electrical connection between a 'control' circuit and an electrical appliance. Imagine you want to operate a 230 V motor when you shine a bright light onto an LDR. Fig. 4.78 shows how a relay can help.

In the control circuit we have an LDR in a dark enclosure. In darkness, the LDR has a large resistance and the current in this circuit is too small to activate the electromagnet. When a beam of light is incident on the LDR, its resistance decreases, the current in the control circuit is big enough for the electromagnet to produce a magnetic field. This in turn pulls the switch on the motor side of the circuit, switching the motor on. Notice that a small current in the control circuit is helping to switch on a large current in the motor.

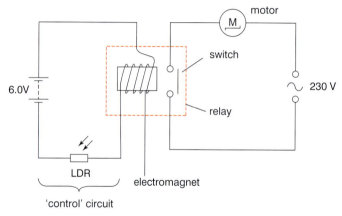

'control' circuit

Δ Fig. 4.79 Using a relay to switch a high-current motor. You cannot directly use a 6.0 V battery to operate the motor – but with the help of a relay, it can be connected to the 230 V source.

In a **loudspeaker**, a varying electric current will cause variations in the magnetic field of a coil mounted onto a magnet, see Fig. 4.80. The coil vibrates because the magnetic field of the magnet and the coil interacts – the coils experience a force (see the section on Force on a current-carrying conductor). As the coil vibrates, so does the cone – which in turns creates changes in the air pressure producing sound.

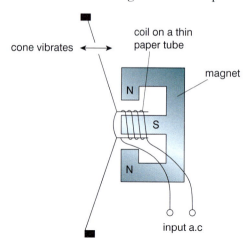

Δ Fig. 4.80 A loudspeaker produces sound because of varying magnetic fields produced by varying currents.

## QUESTIONS

1. Describe how the magnetic fields for a bar magnet and a solenoid are similar.

2. Use Fig. 4.74 to identify where the magnetic field is uniform for a solenoid.

3. a) Describe the construction of a simple electromagnet.

   b) Design a circuit based on a relay for switching on a 230 V fan when the temperature in a room gets too high. Hint: You will need a thermistor, and look at Fig. 4.75 for inspiration.

## Developing practical skills

A student wants to investigate the factors that affect the strength of an electromagnet. He makes the electromagnet by winding a coil of wire around a large soft-iron nail. He then holds the electromagnet vertically in a clamp attached to a clamp stand. He uses a low-voltage power supply to provide the current for the electromagnet.

The student decides to investigate the effect of changing the current in the coil. To measure the strength of the electromagnet he finds out how many paper clips he can hang from the end of the electromagnet. His measurements are shown in the table.

| Current/A | Number of paper clips held |
|-----------|----------------------------|
| 0 | 0 |
| 0.3 | 2 |
| 0.5 | 5 |
| 0.7 | 6 |
| 0.9 | 9 |
| 1.0 | 9 |

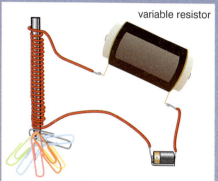

variable resistor

Δ Fig. 4.81 When the circuit is complete, paperclips hang off the nail.

### Planning experiments and investigations

**1.** Describe how the student can vary the current in the electromagnet coil.

**2.** What factors should the student keep constant during the investigation? Why do these factors need to be controlled?

### Observing, measuring and recording data

**3.** Draw a graph of the student's results.

**4.** Describe the pattern (if any) shown by the graph.

### Interpreting and evaluating data

**5.** The student thought of three different ways to hang paper clips on the end of the nail.

   **a)** all the paper clips hanging on the nail together (Fig. 4.81)

   **b)** the paper clips hanging in a line from the end of the nail with the paper clips interlocked

   **c)** the paper clips hanging in a line from the end of the nail, but just held magnetically, not joined together.

### Evaluating methods.

**6.** How could the student change his method so that he could achieve more precise measurements of the strength of the electromagnet?

**7.** The student wants to continue making measurements with higher values of current. Suggest a difficulty he will have as the current increases further.

# FORCE ON A CURRENT-CARRYING CONDUCTOR

A current-carrying current has a magnetic field around it. When this wire is close to a permanent magnet, it should experience a force – this is no different from bringing two magnets close to each other.

A current-carrying wire, placed in a uniform magnetic field, will experience a magnetic force that happens to be perpendicular to both the current and the magnetic field. The force reverses direction when the current is reversed, or the magnetic field is reversed. The size of the force experienced by wire depends on the current and the strength of the magnetic field – larger currents and stronger fields produce bigger forces.

Fleming's left-hand rule, which is shown in Fig. 4.82, predicts the direction of the force. You can demonstrate this using the apparatus in Fig. 4.83. Remember that the current direction is that of the conventional current, and that the electrons are travelling the opposite way.

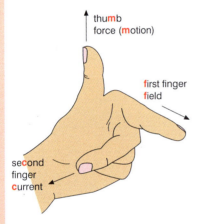

△ Fig. 4.82 Fleming's left-hand rule predicts the direction of the force on a current-carrying wire.

△ Fig. 4.83 Apparatus that can be used to demonstrate that if a wire carrying an electric current is placed in a magnetic field, with the field at right angles to the wire, then the wire will experience a force at right angles both to the wire and to the magnetic field.

When applying Fleming's left-hand rule, you should be able to confirm that if you reverse either the magnetic field, or the current, then the force on the current-carrying wire will be applied in the opposite direction, but that if you reverse both the field and the current then the force stays unchanged.

It is useful to look at the individual and combined magnetic field lines for this arrangement, see Fig. 4.84.

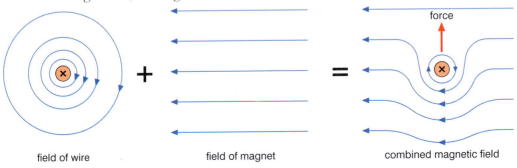

△ Fig. 4.84 How the magnetic field lines are changed by a wire in a uniform magnetic field.

The field lines from the magnet are pushed downwards by the direction of the field lines that are around the wire. If you imagine that the lines are made of stretched elastic, then it is clear why the wire feels an upwards force.

## Force on a beam of charged particles in a magnetic field

When a charged particle, usually an electron, is stationary in a magnetic field, it does not experience any force from the field. So when a copper wire that is full of electrons is placed near a magnet, nothing happens. However, when the charged particles starts to move, then they will experience a force that is at right angles to both the magnetic field and the direction of the current.

Remember that electric current is the flow of charge. So, when a current-carrying wire experiences a force, this must mean that all the moving electrons within the wire must also experience a force. A beam of electrons, not contained by a wire, will deflect in a magnetic field. In fact a beam of any charged particles will deflect in a magnetic field. The direction of the deflected beam can once again be predicted using the left-hand rule. You just need to remember that electron flow is opposite to conventional current.

The deflection of a beam of charged particles in a magnetic field can be demonstrated using the deflection-tube shown in Fig. 4.85.

Δ Fig. 4.85 Electron deflection tube. Large coils provide a magnetic field that deflects the electron beam within the evacuated tube.

## THE D.C. MOTOR

A coil of wire, carrying a direct current, will rotate when placed in a uniform magnetic field. The rotation happens because opposite sections of the coil experience opposite forces. Have a look at the current-carrying coil in Fig. 4.86. The opposite forces will make this coil rotate clockwise.

The motor can be made to rotate faster by increasing:

- the number of turns
- the current
- the strength of the magnetic field.

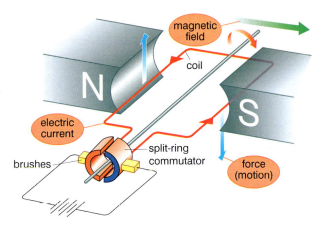

△ Fig. 4.86  An electric motor.

### SUPPLEMENT

The split-ring **commutator** ensures that the motor continues to spin. The split-ring commutator is a split metal ring. The split-ring commutator reverses the direction of the current in the coil, with the wires on the left and the right experiencing forces in the same directions – the net result is that the coil continues with its clockwise rotation.

The brushes, often made from carbon, ensure good electrical contact is maintained with the external circuit and the split-ring commutator as it rotates with the coil. Fig. 4.87 shows the orientations of the split rings as the motor rotates.

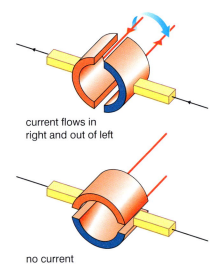

current flows in
right and out of left

no current

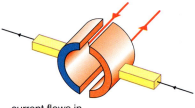

current flows in
right and out of left

△ Fig. 4.87 The split-ring commutator ensures that the coil keeps rotating clockwise. In the vertical position, when the current is zero for a short period, the momentum of the coil takes it over past this position.

**QUESTIONS**

1. State three ways of increasing the speed of a d.c. motor.

2. Explain what makes the coil in Fig. 4.86 rotate.

3. **SUPPLEMENT** Suggest what will happen if a d.c. motor had no split-ring commutator.

4. Describe what would happen to the way a motor would spin when both the current and the magnetic field are reversed at the same time.

## TRANSFORMER

Another use of electromagnetic induction is in transformers. Transformers were first designed by the self-taught English physicist Michael Faraday around 1830. A transformer consists of two coils of wires mounted on a soft-iron core, see Fig. 4.88. The two coils are known as primary and secondary. The primary (p) coil is the 'input' coil, and is connected to a source of alternating current. The secondary (s) coil is the 'output' coil. The ends of this will be connected to whatever circuits you have – lamps, motors, etc. Transformers only work when alternating currents are used.

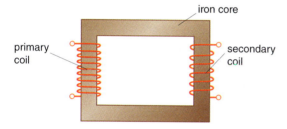

△ Fig. 4.88 The construction of a simple transformer.

There are generally two types of transformers: step-up and step-down. In a step-up transformer, the secondary coil has more turns than the **primary coil**, and this has the effect of increasing the magnitude of the output voltage. Step-up transformers are used in the transmission of electrical power at high-voltage, for example from 12 kV to 400 kV at an electrical power station. At high-voltage the currents in the transmission cables are very small, and the power losses, due to heating of cables, are very small. This is one of the main advantages of transformers – power can be transferred from power stations to towns and cities over vast distances without much loss.

In a step-down transformer, the secondary coil has fewer turns than the primary coil, and this has the effect of decreasing the magnitude of the output voltage. Step-down transformers are used to bring down the 400 kV voltage of transmission cables to 230 V for domestic use.

The operation of a transformer can be explained as follows:

An alternating current in the primary coil produces an alternating magnetic field in this coil. The iron-core increases the strength of this magnetic field, but also links this changing magnetic field to the secondary coil. An e.m.f. is induced in the secondary coil because of the changing magnetic field linking it.

## Turn-ratio equation

For a well-designed transformer, the equation below (often known as the turn-ratio equation) can be used to calculate the output voltage $V_s$:

$$\frac{\text{primary coil voltage } (V_p)}{\text{secondary coil voltage } (V_s)} = \frac{\text{number of primary turns } (N_p)}{\text{number of secondary turns } (N_s)}$$

When the secondary coil has more turns than the primary coil, the voltage increases in the same proportion. This is a **step-up transformer**.

A transformer with fewer turns on the secondary coil than on the primary coil is a **step-down transformer**, and produces a smaller voltage in the secondary coil.

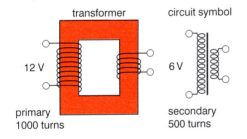

step-down transformer
ratio of number of turns is 2:1
voltage ratio is 2:1

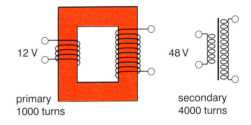

step-up transformer
ratio of number of turns is 1:4
voltage ratio is 1:4

Δ Fig. 4.89 Transformers are widely used to change voltages. They are frequently used in the home to step down the mains voltage of 230 V to 6 V or 12 V.

## WORKED EXAMPLE

Calculate the output voltage from a transformer when the input voltage is 230 V. The number of turns on the primary coil is 2000 and the number of turns on the secondary coil is 100.

Write down the equation:

$$\frac{V_p}{V_s} = \frac{N_p}{N_s}$$

Substitute the known values:

$$\frac{230}{V_s} = \frac{2000}{100}$$

$$\frac{230}{V_s} = 20$$

Rewrite this so that $V_s$ is the subject:

$$V_s = \frac{230}{20}$$

Calculate the answer and write down the unit: $\quad V_s = 11.5 \text{ V}$

The output voltage is smaller than the input voltage; this is a step-down transformer.

## SUPPLEMENT

### Input and output powers

The current used by the transformer must change as well. No transformer is 100% efficient, because all transformers produce some heat when they are working. However if it *were* 100% efficient, then input power to the transformer must be equal to its output power. In other words:

primary coil current ($I_p$) × primary coil voltage ($V_p$) = secondary coil current ($I_s$) × secondary coil voltage ($V_s$)

In simple terms this means that the output current is smaller for a step-up transformer, and larger for a step-down transformer. For the worked example above, the output voltage is 20 times smaller than the input voltage – therefore, the current from the secondary coil can be 20 times larger than the current in the primary coil. It is still worth emphasising that there is no gain in electrical power. The input and output power is the same.

## QUESTIONS

**1.** Describe the difference between a step-up transformer and a step-down transformer.

**2.** A transformer has an input voltage of 2.0 V. There are 20 turns on the primary coil and 200 turns on the secondary coil. Calculate the output voltage.

**3.** A transformer has an input of voltage 1.5 V. There are 60 turns on the primary coil and 240 turns on the secondary coil. Calculate the output voltage.

**4.** A transformer has an input voltage of 2.0 V. There are 50 turns on the primary coil. The secondary coil has 600 turns.

   **a)** Calculate the output voltage.

   **b)** The secondary coil has a resistance of 12 Ω. Calculate the maximum current in this coil.

   **c)** SUPPLEMENT The transformer is 100% efficient. Calculate the current in the primary coil.

## Transmitting electrical power

Most power stations burn fuel to heat water and produce high-pressure steam, which is used to drive a **turbine**. The turbine turns an a.c. generator to produce electrical power.

To minimise the power loss in the transmission cables, the current has to be kept as low as possible. The higher the current, the more the transmission cables will be heated by the current, causing more energy to be wasted as thermal energy.

This is where transformers are useful. This is also the reason that mains electricity is generated as alternating current. When a transformer steps up a voltage, it also steps down the current and vice versa. Power stations generate a voltage of 12 kV. Before this is transmitted, it is converted by a step-up transformer to 400 kV. This is then reduced by a series of step-down transformers to 230 V before it is supplied to homes.

△ Fig. 4.90 A hydroelectric power station doesn't need to burn fuel. This turbine will be turned by water taken from a reservoir behind a dam. The a.c. generator will be fitted to the top of a turbine.

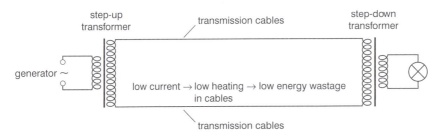

△ Fig. 4.91 Mains electricity is a.c. so that it can be easily stepped up and down. High-voltage, low-current transmission cables waste less energy than low-voltage, high-current cables.

SUPPLEMENT

## Energy losses in cables

With the exception of some lengths of superconducting cable (which has almost zero resistance but needs to be kept at a temperature below −200 °C) the distribution cables used by the electricity companies do not have zero resistance. A typical cable with a length of 100 km may have a resistance of 4.0 Ω. Now consider the problem facing the company when they want to send 4.0 MW of power to a town 100 km away. Since *power = p.d. × current*, they could send either 10 A at 400 000 V, or 160 A at 25 000 V, or 17 400 A at 230 V.

The 230 V solution will not work, the current is simply too large. To send 17 400 A through a cable of resistance 4.0 Ω requires a p.d. across the cable of 68 000 V. More power would be lost from the cables than was put into them by the power station. This would be impossible.

At 25 000 V, the p.d. across the cable would be:

$V = I \times R$

$V = 160 \times 4.0$

$V = 640$ V

The power lost in the cables would be:

$P = V \times I$

$P = 640 \times 160$

$P = 102\ 000$ W

Instead of using the two equations to calculate the power loss, we could have used the single equation below:

power = current² × resistance

$P = I^2R$

$P = 160^2 \times 4.0 = 102\ 000$ W

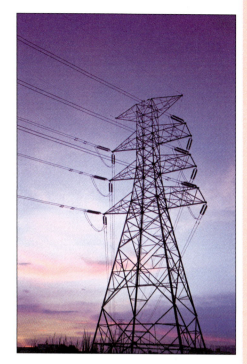

△ Fig. 4.92 A pylon supporting the heavy transmission cables.

Of the 4 000 000 W being sent, this is 2.6%. This is not too bad, as electricity supply companies expect to lose a total of 5–10% of the power generated by the power station.

At 400 000 V, 10 A, the power lost in the cables is just 400 W, which is 0.01% of the power generated. These cables will cost more. Therefore, because the cables will be thicker and heavier, more pylons would be required to support these transmission cables. The electricity company will have to work out which high-voltage solution is best.

## QUESTIONS

**1.** Explain why electrical power is transmitted at high voltages when the distances involved are long.

**2.** Describe how transformers help in the transmission of power at high-voltage.

**3.** **SUPPLEMENT** Practise using the equations given earlier.

    **a)** Calculate how much power would be lost when transmitting at 50 000 V with cable resistance of 4.0 Ω and a current of 80 A?

    **b)** What percentage of the 4.0 MW that the company want to send is this?

# End of topic checklist

## Key terms

d.c. electric motor, electromagnetic induction, induced e.m.f., magnetic field, primary coil, relay, secondary coil, solenoid, step-down, step-up, transformer

**SUPPLEMENT** a.c. generator

## During your study of this topic you should have learned:

○ A conductor moving across a magnetic field, or a changing magnetic field linking with a conductor, can induce an e.m.f. in the conductor.

○ Describe an experiment to demonstrate electromagnetic induction.

○ The magnitude of an induced e.m.f. in a conductor depends on the speed of the conductor and strength of the magnetic field.

○ **SUPPLEMENT** The direction of an induced e.m.f. opposes the change causing it.

○ **SUPPLEMENT** The right-hand rule can be used for the relative directions of force, field and induced current.

○ **SUPPLEMENT** A simple a.c. generator has a rotating coil or rotating magnet, and has slip rings and brushes.

○ **SUPPLEMENT** Sketch and interpret graphs of e.m.f. against time for simple a.c. generators and relate the position of the generator coil to the peaks, troughs and zeros of the e.m.f.

○ The pattern and direction of the magnetic field due to currents in straight wires and in solenoids.

○ Iron-filings and a compass can be used to identify the pattern of the magnetic field due to currents in straight wires and in solenoids.

○ The magnetic effect of a current is used in relays and loudspeakers.

○ **SUPPLEMENT** The strength of the magnetic field around straight wires and solenoids can be deduced from the magnetic field lines.

○ **SUPPLEMENT** Describe the effect on the magnetic field around straight wires and solenoids of changing the magnitude and direction of the current.

○ Describe an experiment to show that a force acts on a current-carrying conductor in a magnetic field, including the effect of reversing: the current and the direction of the field.

○ **SUPPLEMENT** The left-hand rule can be used for the relative directions of the force, magnetic field and current.

○ **SUPPLEMENT** Determine the direction of the force on beams of charged particles in a magnetic field.

○ A current-carrying coil in a magnetic field may experience a turning effect and that the turning effect is increased by increasing: the number of turns on the coil, the current and the strength of the magnetic field.

○ **SUPPLEMENT** Describe the operation of an electric motor, including the action of a split-ring commutator and brushes.

○ Describe the construction of a simple transformer with a soft iron core, as used for voltage transformations.

○ The primary coil is the input coil and the secondary coil is the output coil of a transformer.

○ A transformer can be either step-up or step-down.

○ The equation $\dfrac{V_p}{V_s} = \dfrac{N_p}{N_s}$, where p and s refer to primary and secondary can be applied to transformers.

○ Describe the use of transformers in high-voltage transmission of electricity.

○ State the advantages of high-voltage transmission.

○ **SUPPLEMENT** Explain the principle of operation of a simple iron-cored transformer.

○ **SUPPLEMENT** The equation for 100% efficiency in a transformer is: $I_p V_p = I_s V_s$, where p and s refer to primary and secondary.

○ **SUPPLEMENT** The equation $P = I^2 R$ can be used to explain why power losses in cables are smaller when the voltage is greater.

# End of topic questions

*Note: the marks in brackets give an indication of the level of detail you should include in your answers.*

**1.** Describe what is meant by electromagnetic induction. (4 marks)

**2.** The diagram shows a simple electromagnet made by a student.

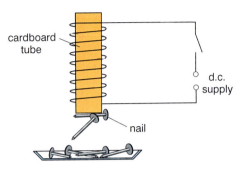

Suggest two ways in which the electromagnet can be made to pick up more iron nails. (2 marks)

**3.** The diagram shows an electric bell.

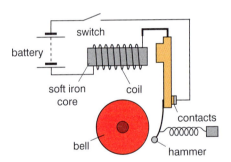

Explain how the bell works when the switch is closed. (4 marks)

**4.** **SUPPLEMENT** Two students are using the equipment shown in the diagram. They cannot decide whether it is an electric motor or a generator. Explain how you would know which it is. (4 marks)

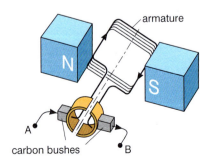

**5.** A householder has asked an engineer to design a small generator to generate electricity when the mains supply fails. After the first design, the householder finds that he is relocating to a country where the mains voltage supplied to houses is lower. Describe how the design could be modified to take this into account.

(4 marks)

**6.** The diagram shows a transformer.

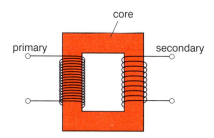

**a)** What material is the core made from?

**A** plastic

**B** brass

**C** soft iron

**D** wood

(1 mark)

**e) SUPPLEMENT** Explain how an output voltage is produced in the secondary coil when the primary coil is connected to an a.c. supply. (3 marks)

**f)** The primary coil has 120 turns, and the secondary coil 70 turns. The output voltage is 14 V. Calculate the input voltage. (3 marks)

**7. a)** A power station generates electricity at a voltage of 25 kV. The power is transmitted at 400 kV. The primary coil has 2000 turns. Calculate the number of turns on the secondary coil. (3 marks)

**b) SUPPLEMENT** Explain why electrical power is transmitted at high-voltage.

(2 marks)

**8. SUPPLEMENT** In each case below, predict the direction of the force on the wire, or the beam of charged particles. The direction of the magnetic field is always into the plane of the paper. (3 marks)

**a)** ⟶ current in a wire

**b)** ⟶ a beam of electrons

**c)** ⟶ a beam of positive particles

# Exam-style questions

*Exam-style questions, sample answers and comments have been written by the authors. The marks awarded for these questions indicate the level of detail required in the answers. In examinations, the way marks are awarded may be different. References to assessment and/or assessment preparation are the publisher's interpretation of the syllabus requirements and may not fully reflect the approach of Cambridge Assessment International Education.*

## Example answers

## Question 1

This question is about electrostatics.

**a)** There are two kinds of electric charge.

Write down the names of both types of electric charge.

*positive and negative* ✓ ① [1]

**b)** Leon wants to charge his plastic comb.

Write down one way he could do this.

*He could rub it.* ✓ ① [2]

**c)** Leon touches a metal radiator. He gets an electric shock.

Describe how Leon gets an electric shock.

*The metal radiator is electric and gives Leon a shock.* ✗ ✗ ✗ [3]

2/6

**[Total 6 marks]**

## COMMENTS

**a)** This is correct. Alternatively the answer could use the symbols '+' and '−'.

**b)** 'By friction' would have been a stronger phrase to use. The response could have been expanded by saying that the comb should be rubbed against an insulator (or could give an example of an insulator, such as cloth). Always check the number of marks available.

**c)** This is a very vague answer. The correct response needs to state that Leon has become charged (perhaps by friction against a carpet) and that these charges move when he touches the radiator, from Leon to the radiator. The correct scientific words need to be used. Relevant words here are: charging, electrons, earth, earthing.

## Question 2

An 1100 W electric iron uses 230 V a.c. supply.

**a)** Explain why an electric current causes the iron to become hot. [2]

   **i)** State the equation linking power, current and voltage. [1]

   **ii)** Calculate the current in the electric iron when it is operating normally. [2]

**b)** The mains plug attached to the iron contains a 13 A fuse.

Describe the purpose of the fuse. [3]

**c)** The mains connection for the iron also contains an earth wire.

   **i)** Explain why an earth wire is needed. [2]

   **ii)** Describe the operation of an earth wire. [3]

**d)** Explain the difference between an alternating current (a.c.) and a direct current (d.c.). [2]

**[Total 15 marks]**

## Question 3

A student investigates how the current varies with potential difference across a filament lamp.

This is the student's circuit diagram.

The lamp is fully lit at 12 V.

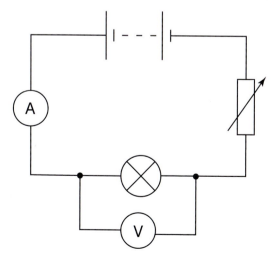

**a)** Describe how the student should use the circuit to carry out the investigation. [2]

  **i)** Sketch the graph the student should obtain if the lamp operates normally. Put the current on the vertical axis and the potential difference $V$ on the horizontal axis. [3]

  **ii)** Describe and explain the shape of the graph you have drawn. [3]

  The student carries out the experiment again using a lamp that is designed to be fully lit at 24 V.

**b)** The variable resistor used in the investigation has a resistance of 15 Ω.

  **i)** State the equation linking voltage, current and resistance. [1]

  **ii)** **SUPPLEMENT** Calculate the current in the variable resistor when the p.d. across it is 3.0 V. [2]

  **iii)** **SUPPLEMENT** Calculate the charge that passes through the variable resistor in 10 minutes when the p.d. across it is 3.0 V. [3]

**[Total 14 marks]**

## Question 4

A student investigates electrostatic charges.

She has some insulating rods made of different types of plastic.

She rubs each one with a cloth to create the electrostatic charge.

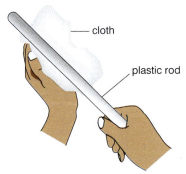

cloth

plastic rod

**a)** **SUPPLEMENT** Using ideas about electrons, explain how an insulating rod can gain a positive or a negative electrostatic charge. [2]

**b)** A metal rod cannot gain an electrostatic charge in this way. Suggest why not. [2]

**c)** Describe an experiment the student could do to find out if two insulating rods had the same charge or opposite charges.

You should describe the equipment the student would need and how she should use it. [4]

**d)** Suggest a situation where electrostatic charges can potentially be dangerous.

You should include:

what the hazard is

how the risk can be reduced. [2]

**[Total 10 marks]**

## Question 5

A student uses a 12 V low-voltage power supply in the classroom.

It plugs into the 230 V mains supply.

**a)** The student realises that the power supply must contain a step-down transformer.

   **i) SUPPLEMENT** Describe the operation of a step-down transformer. [4]

   **ii)** Suggest why the power supply contains a step-down transformer. [1]

**b) SUPPLEMENT** The student wants to use the power supply to provide a current of 3.0 A.

   **i)** Write down the equation linking input power and output power of a transformer, assuming 100% efficiency. [1]

   **ii)** Calculate the input current from the 230 V mains supply if the student is to use an output current of 3.0 A at 12 V. [3]

**[Total 9 marks]**

## Question 6

The diagram shows two bar magnets.

**a)** Copy the diagram. Draw the magnetic field pattern on your diagram. [3]

**b)** Describe how you could plot the magnetic field pattern. [3]

**c)**  **i)** Describe how you can carry out an experiment to show that long, thin sheet of aluminium foil carrying a current experiences a force in a magnetic field. [3]

   **ii)** State and explain how the force on the foil can be increased. [2]

   **iii)** Describe how you can use the same long, thin sheet of aluminium foil to induce an e.m.f. across its ends. [3]

**[Total 14 marks]**

What have treatment for cancer, finding leaks in underground pipes, and dating archaeological specimens got in common? The answer is that they all use radioactivity in some way. Cancer is treated by targeting the tumour with radioactive substances that destroy the cells of the tumour but do minimal damage to the surrounding tissues. Leaks in underground pipes can be detected by adding a radioactive substance to the fluid flowing in the pipe and then using a detector above the ground to trace the amount of radioactivity emitted at any point. Archaeological specimens can be dated using the fact that everything that lives, or once lived, contains some radioactive carbon atoms.

## STARTING POINTS

1. What is an atom?

2. What happens when moving charged particles pass through a magnetic field?

3. What do you understand by the term 'radioactivity'?

## SYLLABUS SECTIONS COVERED

5.1 The nuclear model of the atom

5.2 Radioactivity

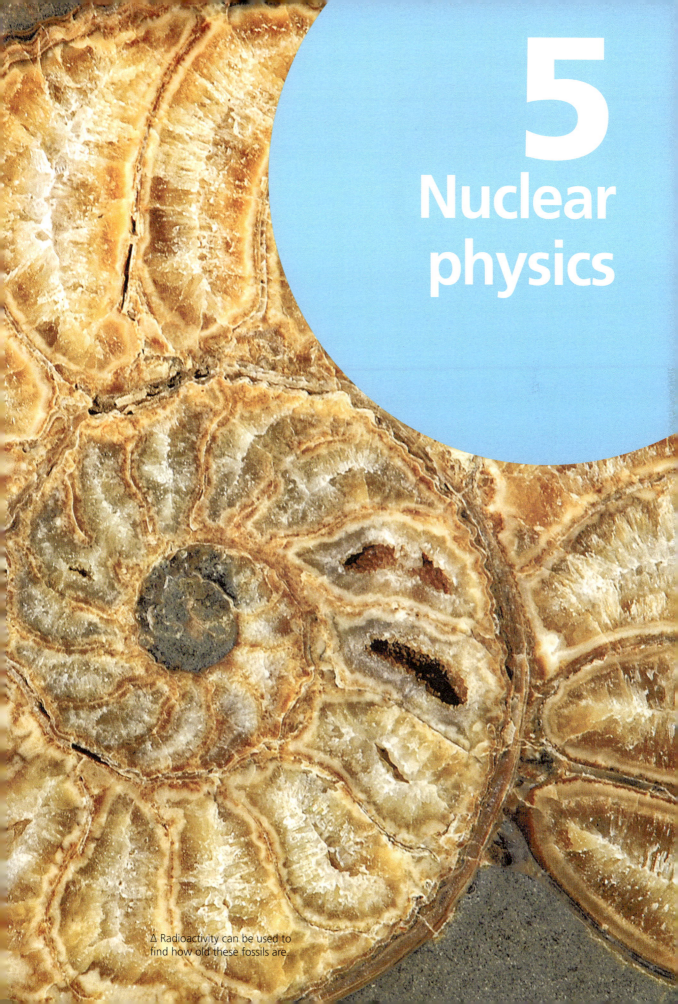

# 5
# Nuclear physics

△ Radioactivity can be used to find how old these fossils are.

△ Fig 5.1 A smoke detector uses a radioactive source to work.

# The nuclear model of the atom

### INTRODUCTION

Ideas about atoms have developed over time by scientists making tiny steps based on experimental evidence. In 1803 John Dalton wrote about atoms as tiny particles of matter that could not be divided. Some 100 years later, J.J. Thomson discovered electrons, which meant atoms could be divided. His model of the atom was a step in the right direction. He imagined the atom to be like a ball of positive charge with electrons embedded in it.

It took experiments from many other scientists to reach a proper understanding of what atoms are. In this section we will explore the modern structure of the atom, and eventually also explain **radioactivity**.

### KNOWLEDGE CHECK

✓ Matter is made from atoms and molecules.

### LEARNING OBJECTIVES

✓ Describe the structure of an atom in terms of a positively charged nucleus and negatively charged electrons in orbit around the nucleus.

✓ Know how atoms may form positive ions by losing electrons or form negative ions by gaining electrons.

✓ **SUPPLEMENT** Describe how the scattering of alpha ($\alpha$-) particles by a sheet of thin metal supports the nuclear model of the atom, by providing evidence for: a very small nucleus surrounded by mostly empty space, a nucleus that contains most of the mass of the atom and a nucleus that is positively charged.

✓ Describe the composition of the nucleus in terms of protons and neutrons.

✓ State the relative charges of protons, neutrons and electrons as +1, 0 and −1 respectively.

✓ Define the terms proton number (atomic number) $Z$ and nucleon number (mass number) $A$ and be able to calculate the number of neutrons in a nucleus.

✓ Use the nuclide notation $^A_Z X$

✓ Explain what is meant by an isotope and state that an element may have more than one isotope.

✓ **SUPPLEMENT** Describe the process of nuclear fission and nuclear fusion, to include the nuclide equation and qualitative description of mass and energy changes without values.

✓ **SUPPLEMENT** Know the relationship between the proton number and the relative charge on a nucleus.

✓ **SUPPLEMENT** Know the relationship between the nucleon number and the relative mass of a nucleus.

## THE ATOM

All matter is made from atoms. The simplest structure of the atom is that it has a tiny positively charged nucleus and the negatively charged electrons orbit around this nucleus. All atoms have this basic structure, see Fig. 5.2.

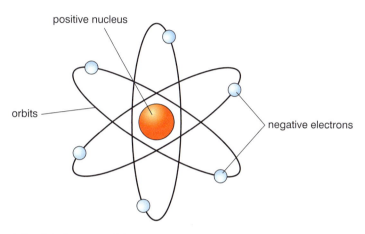

positive nucleus

orbits

negative electrons

△ Fig. 5.2  Structure of the atom.

An atom is electrically neutral because the positive charge on the nucleus is equal to the total charge of all the negative electrons. However, if electrons are removed from an atom, then what is left behind will be a positive atom – which we call a positive **ion**. The converse is also true. Adding extra electrons will make the atom negative – which we refer to as a negative **ion**.

Removing and adding electrons to atoms sounds complicated, but you have already come across this idea when insulators were being charged by rubbing them together. Friction between the insulators was responsible for the transfer of electrons. (See Electric Charge section.)

## SUPPLEMENT

### Alpha-scattering experiment

In the early 1900s, scientists knew that the atom contained positive and negative charges but the structure of the atom remained a mystery. A series of experiments, led by Ernest Rutherford in England, provided clear experimental evidence of the nuclear model of the atom – the idea that the atom has a tiny positive nucleus.

In one of the experiments, Geiger and Marsden, working under Rutherford's guidance, fired alpha ($\alpha$) particles from a radioactive source into thin metal sheets. Gold was preferred, because thin sheets, only a few hundred atoms thick, could be easily made.

The results were unexpected. Most **alpha particles** went straight through the metal (gold) foil, without any deflection, but a few were scattered in different directions. A very small number of alpha particles were even returned back along the path they came from. The undeflected alpha particles could only mean that most of the metal sheet was empty space. The few that were deflected could only be explained in terms of the positively charged alpha particles getting close to the positive nuclei and being repelled, see Fig. 5.3. These were the conclusions from the alpha-scattering experiment:

- Most of the atom is empty space (vacuum), with a very tiny nucleus at the centre.
- Most of the mass of the atom is contained by the nucleus.
- The nucleus is positive.

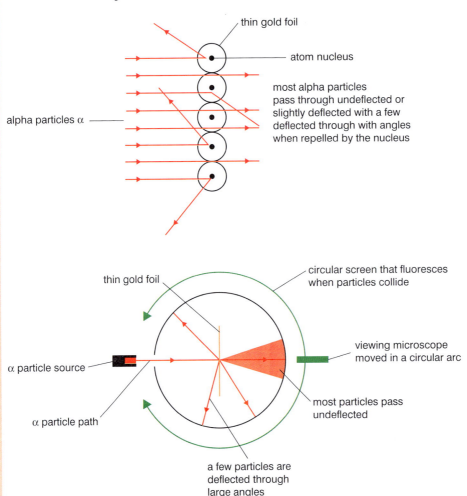

△ Fig. 5.3 The scattering experiment apparatus, with details of scattering of the positive alpha ($\alpha$) particles by the nuclei of the gold atoms.

We are left with the amazing picture in our heads that all solid objects (this book, the Earth below and you) are actually empty space, loosely filled with electrons, with a tiny nucleus at the centre of each atom. The size of the nucleus is really tiny compared with the size of atom. If we represented the nucleus by a 1 cm sphere, then the outermost electron of the atom would be about 1 km away. The electrons themselves are incredibly small – as yet, physicists do not know their actual size.

## QUESTIONS

1. Describe how a neutral atom can be made into a positive ion.

2. **SUPPLEMENT** This question is about the alpha-scattering experiment.

   **a)** State what the alpha particles were fired into.

   **b)** Most of the alpha particles were not scattered at all. State what can be deduced from this observation.

   **c)** List some of the properties of the nucleus.

### THE NUCLEUS

The nucleus of an atom is positive because it has positive particles called protons. The nucleus also has uncharged particles called neutrons. The neutrons and protons are packed tightly within the small space of the nucleus; making the nucleus extremely dense. For a neutral atom, the number of electrons around the nucleus is equal to the number of protons.

Table 5.1 shows the relative charges, and the approximate relative masses of the electron, proton and neutron.

| Particle | Relative charge | Relative mass |
|----------|-----------------|---------------|
| Electron | $-1$ | 0.005 |
| Proton | $+1$ | 1 |
| Neutron | 0 | 1 |

△ Table 5.1 Relative charges, and the approximate relative masses of the electron, proton and neutron.

Protons and electrons have electrical charges that are equal and opposite. The mass of the electron is tiny compared with that of the proton and neutron. Therefore, the mass of the atom is mostly within the nucleus.

The **proton number**, or the **atomic number**, is the total number of protons within the nucleus of an atom. The **nucleon number**, or the **mass number**, is the total number of protons and neutrons within the nucleus. Many physicists use the term nucleon to mean either a proton or a neutron. The complete composition of an atom can be worked out using these two numbers. Fig. 5.4 shows an illustration of a particular lithium atom. This atom has 4 neutrons, 3 protons and 3 electrons. Therefore, its proton number must be 3 and its nucleon number must be 7.

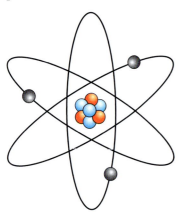

△ Fig. 5.4 A particular neutral atom of lithium.

We can use the **nuclide** notation

$$^A_Z X$$

to describe any nucleus. A nuclide is a nucleus with specific numbers of protons and neutrons. The $A$ is the nucleon number, Z the proton number and X is the chemical symbol for the element. For the lithium nucleus shown in Fig. 5.4, this would be $^7_3$Li. It is worth noting that the number of neutrons can be determined as follows:

$$\text{number of neutrons} = A - Z$$

## Isotopes

Atoms of the same element have one thing in common – each and every nucleus has the same number of protons. Nuclei with the same number of protons, but different number of neutrons are called **isotopes**. The list below shows some of the isotopes of lithium:

$$^5_3\text{Li} \quad ^6_3\text{Li} \quad ^7_3\text{Li} \quad ^8_3\text{Li} \quad ^9_3\text{Li} \quad ^{10}_3\text{Li}$$

Notice that all nuclides have the same number of protons (3), but the number of neutrons is different. The charge on each isotope is the same, but they have different masses. Chemically, all of the lithium atoms above will behave the same because they all have 3 electrons each.

Table 5.2 shows some isotopes of other elements.

| Element | Chemical symbol | Some isotopes | | | | |
|---------|-----------------|---------------|---------------|---------------|---------------|---------------|
| Hydrogen | H | $^1_1$H | $^2_1$H | $^3_1$H | | |
| Carbon | C | $^{10}_6$C | $^{11}_6$C | $^{12}_6$C | $^{13}_6$C | |
| Gold | Au | $^{196}_{79}$Au | $^{197}_{79}$Au | $^{198}_{79}$Au | $^{199}_{79}$Au | |
| Uranium | U | $^{233}_{92}$U | $^{234}_{92}$U | $^{235}_{92}$U | $^{236}_{92}$U | $^{237}_{92}$U |

△ Table 5.2 Some examples of isotopes.

## RELATIVE CHARGE AND RELATIVE MASS OF NUCLEI

As mentioned earlier, the relative charge of the proton is +1. The more protons a nucleus has, the greater its relative charge will be. In fact, the relative charge of a nucleus must be equal to the number of protons. Therefore, the nuclide $^{12}_{6}C$, which has 6 protons, must have a relative charge of +6 and the nuclide $^{198}_{79}Au$ has a relative charge of +79.

The mass of a proton and neutron is about the same. Their relative mass is taken to be approximately 1. The nucleon number is equal to the total number of protons and neutrons within a nucleus. It therefore follows that the relative mass of a nucleus must be equal to the nucleon number. Using the same two examples above, $^{12}_{6}C$ has relative mass of 12 and $^{198}_{79}Au$ has relative mass of 198.

## QUESTIONS

1. Explain why a nucleus of an atom has a positive charge.

2. One of the nuclides of uranium is $^{235}_{92}U$. State its

    a) proton number
    b) nucleon number
    c) number of neutrons.

3. Here are three nuclides: $^{3}_{1}H$, $^{4}_{2}He$, and $^{3}_{2}He$. Explain which two nuclides are isotopes.

4. **SUPPLEMENT** Determine the relative charge and relative mass of the nuclides $^{3}_{1}H$ and $^{235}_{92}U$.

## NUCLEAR FISSION

Many nuclear power stations use uranium as fuel. The energy from the fuel comes through a complicated process. Slow-moving neutrons are absorbed by uranium nuclei. This makes each uranium nucleus unstable, and it splits up into smaller nuclei. Neutrons are also released in this process. These neutrons can go on to produce further reactions with other uranium nuclei. **Nuclear fission** is the splitting of a nucleus. Fig. 5.5 shows a typical fission reaction and the reaction is summarised in the nuclide equation below:

$$^{235}_{92}U + ^{1}_{0}n \rightarrow ^{137}_{56}Ba + ^{97}_{36}Kr + 2^{1}_{0}n$$

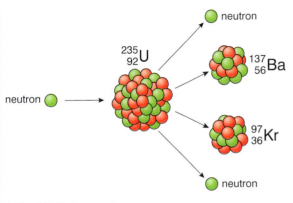

△ Fig. 5.5 Fission reaction.

A neutron $_{0}^{1}n$ is absorbed by a uranium nucleus $_{92}^{235}U$. This makes the new nucleus highly unstable, and it decays almost immediately into nuclei of barium (Ba) and krypton (Kr). In this case, 2 neutrons are also produced. The total mass of the particles after the reaction is less than the total mass of the particles before the reaction – according to the ideas of Albert Einstein, this change in mass is responsible for lots of energy being released. Here the energy appears as kinetic energy of the neutrons and nuclei of barium and krypton.

## NUCLEAR FUSION

All stars, including our Sun, generate energy through fusion reactions. In **nuclear fusion**, lighter nuclei such as hydrogen join together to make a larger nucleus. This is possible in stars because of the high temperatures and pressures. Once again, the mass of the final nucleus is less than the total mass of the particles before the reaction and energy is released.

Fig. 5.6 shows a typical fusion reaction and this reaction is summarised in the nuclide equation below:

$$_{1}^{2}H + {}_{1}^{2}H \rightarrow {}_{2}^{3}He + {}_{0}^{1}n$$

$_{1}^{2}H$    $_{1}^{2}H$       $_{2}^{3}He$   $_{0}^{1}n$

△ Fig. 5.6 Fission reaction.

In this reaction, two hydrogen nuclei $_{1}^{2}H$ join together to make a helium nuclide $_{2}^{3}He$ and a neutron $_{0}^{1}n$.

## QUESTIONS

**1.** State one example where nuclear fission occurs.

**2.** Describe nuclear fusion.

**3.** Explain why energy is released in both nuclear fission and nuclear fusion.

# End of topic checklist

## Key terms

fission, isotope, negative ion, nucleon number, nucleus, nuclide, positive ion, proton number

**SUPPLEMENT** alpha particle, fusion

## During your study of this topic you should have learned:

○ The atom has a positively charged nucleus and negatively charged electrons in orbit around the nucleus.

○ Atoms may form positive ions by losing electrons or form negative ions by gaining electrons.

○ **SUPPLEMENT** The scattering of alpha ($\alpha$) particles by a sheet of thin metal supports the nuclear model of the atom, by providing evidence for: a very small nucleus surrounded by mostly empty space, a nucleus containing most of the mass of the atom, and a nucleus that is positively charged.

○ The nucleus has protons and neutrons inside.

○ The relative charges of a proton, a neutron and an electron are +1, 0 and −1 respectively.

○ The proton number (atomic number) Z is the number of protons inside the nucleus.

○ The nucleon number (mass number) A is the total number of protons and neutrons inside the nucleus.

number of neutrons = A − Z.

○ Use the nuclide notation $^{A}_{Z}X$.

○ An isotope of an element is a nucleus with the same number of protons, and different number of neutrons.

○ An element may have more than one isotope.

○ **SUPPLEMENT** Nuclear fission is the splitting of a nucleus.

○ **SUPPLEMENT** Nuclear fusion is the joining of nuclei.

○ **SUPPLEMENT** In both nuclear fission and fusion energy is released and there is a change in mass.

○ **SUPPLEMENT** The relative mass of a nucleus is approximately equal to its nucleon number.

○ **SUPPLEMENT** The relative charge on a nucleus is equal to the number of protons.

*Note: the marks in brackets give an indication of the level of detail you should include in your answers.*

1. Describe the structure of the atom in terms of its nucleus and electrons.   (4 marks)

2. **SUPPLEMENT** Explain how the scattering of alpha particles provides evidence for the nuclear model of the atom.   (4 marks)

3. **SUPPLEMENT** Give an example of isotopes. Describe how the nuclei of these isotopes differ.   (3 marks)

4. Copy and complete this table to show the particles in the electrically neutral atoms.

| Atom | Symbol | Number of protons | Number of neutrons | Number of electrons |
|---|---|---|---|---|
| hydrogen | $^{1}_{1}H$ | | | |
| carbon | $^{12}_{6}C$ | | | |
| calcium | $^{40}_{20}Ca$ | | | |
| uranium | $^{238}_{92}U$ | | | |

(12 marks)

5. A particular isotope of sodium has a proton number of 11 and a nucleon number of 24. Describe the composition of this nucleus.   (3 marks)

6. **SUPPLEMENT** One of the isotopes of carbon is $^{14}_{6}C$, and one of the isotopes of hydrogen is $^{2}_{1}H$.

   **a)** Determine the relative charge of each nuclide.   (2 marks)

   **b)** Explain why the mass of $^{14}_{6}C$ nucleus 7 times more than the mass of $^{2}_{1}H$ nucleus.   (2 marks)

7. **SUPPLEMENT** The nuclide equation below is for a particular reaction.
   $$^{2}_{1}H + ^{2}_{1}H \rightarrow ^{4}_{2}He$$

   **a)** What type of reaction is this?   (1 mark)

   **b)** Show that the relative charge before and after the reaction remains the same.   (2 marks)

   **c)** What is the correct name for the product in this reaction?

   **A** alpha particle

   **B** electron

   **C** hydrogen nucleus

   **D** uranium nucleus   (1 mark)

# Radioactivity

## INTRODUCTION

The discovery of radioactivity in the late 1800s came at a time of great development in our knowledge of the atom. Far from being the 'fundamental building blocks of nature' as had first been thought, atoms were revealed as collections of particles in many different combinations.

Piecing the whole puzzle together took many years as the properties of unstable atoms were studied and entirely new atoms were discovered. Unfortunately, many of the early experimenters suffered from the harmful effects of radiation before the dangers were recognised.

△ Fig. 5.7 Workers painting luminous watch dials with uranium salts in the early 20th century.

Now that the danger is well understood, radioactive materials are used in a carefully controlled manner in a number of everyday applications such as smoke alarms.

## KNOWLEDGE CHECK

✓ Describe the basic structure of an atom in terms of protons, neutrons and electrons.
✓ Basic knowledge of issues relating to radioactivity in everyday life, such as waste from nuclear power stations.

## LEARNING OBJECTIVES

✓ Know what is meant by background radiation.
✓ Know the sources that make a significant contribution to background radiation including: radon gas (in the air), rocks and buildings, food and drink, and cosmic rays (from the Sun).
✓ Know that ionising nuclear radiation can be measured using a detector connected to a counter.
✓ Use count rate measured in counts/s or counts/minute.
✓ **SUPPLEMENT** Use measurements of background radiation to determine a corrected count rate.
✓ Describe the emission of radiation from a nucleus as spontaneous and random in direction.
✓ Identify alpha ($\alpha$-), beta ($\beta$-) and gamma ($\gamma$-) emissions from the nucleus by recalling: their nature, their relative ionising effects and their relative penetrating abilities ($\beta^+$ are not included, $\beta$-particles will be taken to refer to $\beta^-$).

✓ **SUPPLEMENT** Describe the deflection of α-particles, β-particles and γ radiation in electric fields and magnetic fields.

✓ **SUPPLEMENT** Explain their relative ionising effects with reference to: kinetic energy and electric charge.

✓ Know that radioactive decay is a change in an unstable nucleus that can result in the emission of α, β and γ radiation and know that these changes are spontaneous and random.

✓ State that during alpha (α-) or beta (β-) decay, the nucleus changes to that of a different element.

✓ **SUPPLEMENT** Know that isotopes of an element may be radioactive due to an excess of neutrons in the nucleus and/or the nucleus being too heavy.

✓ **SUPPLEMENT** Describe the effect of alpha (α-), (β-) and gamma (γ-) emissions on the nucleus, including an increase in stability and a reduction in the number of excess neutrons; the following change in the nucleus occurs during beta emission: neutron → proton + electron.

✓ **SUPPLEMENT** Use decay equations, using nuclide notation, to show the emission of α, β and γ radiation.

✓ Define the half-life of a particular isotope as the time taken for half the nuclei of that isotope in any sample to decay; recall and use this definition in simple calculations, which might involve information in tables or decay curves (calculations will not include background radiation).

✓ **SUPPLEMENT** Calculate half-life from data or decay curves from which background radiation has not been subtracted.

✓ **SUPPLEMENT** Explain how the type of radiation emitted and the half-life of an isotope determine which isotope is used for applications including: household fire (smoke) alarms, irradiating food to kill bacteria, sterilisation of equipment using gamma rays, measuring and controlling thicknesses of materials with the choice of radiations used linked to penetration and absorption and diagnosis and treatment of cancer using gamma rays.

✓ State the effects of ionising nuclear radiations on living things, including cell death, mutations and cancer.

✓ Describe how radioactive materials are moved, used and stored in a safe way.

✓ **SUPPLEMENT** Explain safety precautions for all ionising radiation in terms of reducing exposure time, increasing distance between source and living tissue and using shielding to absorb radiation.

## DETECTION OF RADIOACTIVITY

A material is radioactive when some, or all, of the nuclei within the material are unstable, and they release either particles or gamma rays to become stable. These emissions are often referred to as radiation. It is important to understand that these emissions are from within the nuclei, and are nothing at all to do with the electrons of the atoms.

Radioactive materials occur naturally – so we are all exposed to low-level radiation all the time. The radiation comes from a variety of sources; even some of the food we eat is radioactive. Brazil nuts and bananas are slightly radioactive. See Fig. 5.8.

◁ Fig. 5.8 Bananas are a bit radioactive, but very safe to eat because of the low levels of radioactivity.

You do not need to be too concerned, because the levels of radiations are low and cause no harm at all. The main contribution to the **background radiation** comes from radon gas in the air, rocks and buildings, food (and drink) and cosmic rays. Cosmic rays are energetic particles coming from outer space. Fig. 5.9 shows a pie chart illustrating the main contributors to the background radiation.

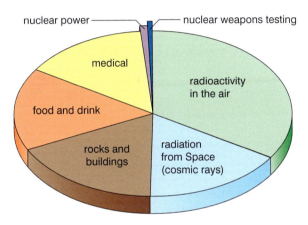

△ Fig. 5.9 Contributions to the background radiation.

Nuclear radiation can be detected by a Geiger–Müller (GM) tube and measured by a radiation counter, see Fig. 5.10 and Fig. 5.11. The count rate is the number of 'particles' detected per unit time; this is often expressed as counts per second or counts per minute – e.g. background count rate is 10 counts/min. The count rate is calculated by taking the counts from the counter and dividing by the time recorded on a stopwatch. For example, for a counter showing 1200 counts in 60 s, the count rate is 20 counts/s.

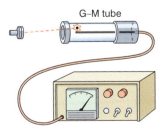

△ Fig. 5.10 Radioactivity is measured using a Geiger–Müller tube connected to a counter.

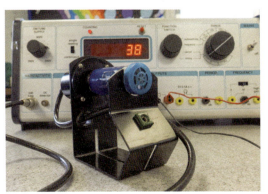

△ Fig. 5.11 Actual laboratory apparatus showing a GM tube connected to a radiation counter.

1. State what contributes the most to the background radiation.

2. State the units for count rate.

3. Brazil nuts are one of the most radioactive foods around. Suggest why this is not serious when you eat these nuts.

4. A student records 4000 counts in a time of 100 s. Calculate the count rate in counts/s.

## THE THREE TYPES OF NUCLEAR EMISSION

An unstable nucleus will emit either particles or gamma rays to become stable. The decay of the nucleus cannot be controlled by external factors such as temperature of pressure. Scientists use the term **spontaneous** to describe this behaviour. Radioactive decay is also a **random** event. This means that the decay of a nucleus is not affected by other nuclei around it. The emitted radiation goes off in random directions.

The three types of radioactive emissions are: alpha ($\alpha$), beta ($\beta$) and gamma ($\gamma$). All of these types radiation produce ionisation. That is, each type of radiation has the ability to remove electrons from atoms and molecules. Alpha particles are the most ionising of the three types of radiation.

Some of the properties of the three types of radiation are summarised in Table. 5.3.

| Radiation | Nature | Relative ionising effect | Relative penetrating ability (see Fig. 5.12) |
|---|---|---|---|
| Alpha ($\alpha$) | • Helium nucleus<br>• Relative charge of +2<br>• Has two protons and two neutrons | • High | • Stopped by skin or paper<br>• Range in air is about 5 cm |
| Beta ($\beta$) | • Electron<br>• Relative charge −1 | • Low | • Stopped by 3 mm of aluminium<br>• Range in air about 1 m |
| Gamma ($\gamma$) | • Short-wavelength electromagnetic waves<br>• Uncharged | • Very low | • Stopped by lead or concrete<br>• Unlimited range in air |

△ Table 5.3 Some properties of the three types of radiation.

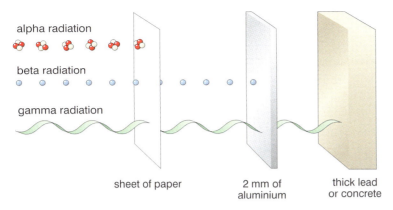

△ Fig. 5.12  Different radiations have different penetration powers.

SUPPLEMENT

## Electric fields

Alpha particles are helium nuclei, and as such have a relative charge of +2. The **beta particles** are just fast-moving electrons, with each having a relative charge −1. Being charged means that both particles can be deflected by electric fields. The positive alpha particles will move away from other positive charges, and the beta particles will do the opposite. Gamma rays are electromagnetic waves, and as such carry no charge. Gamma rays will therefore be unaffected by electric fields.

## Magnetic fields

A beam of either alpha particles or beta particles represents moving charged particles, so both can also be deflected magnetic fields. Gamma rays have no charge – they cannot be deflected by magnetic fields. You can determine the deflection in a magnetic field using the left-hand rule. When using the left-hand rule, do remember that the direction of the current is the direction in which positive charges move. Therefore, if you have beta particles moving to the right, then the 'conventional' current must be to the left. Fig. 5.13 shows the deflections of alpha particles and beta particles in a uniform magnetic field. It is worth pointing out that the alpha particles and beta particles deflect in opposite directions. As mentioned earlier, gamma rays will continue to travel in a straight line because they have no charge.

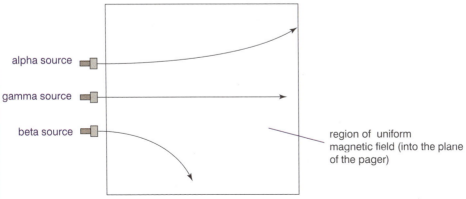

△ Fig. 5.13  Deflection of alpha particles and beta particles in a uniform magnetic field. Gamma rays are not deflected because they have no charge.

## Ionisation

Alpha particles cause the most ionisation because of their greater mass and charge. Alpha particles travel slower than beta particle, but their larger mass implies that they have more kinetic energy than beta particles. Alpha particles can ionise a larger number of air molecules as they fly through the air than beta particles. Beta particles travel much faster than alpha particles, but because of their much smaller mass, they have less kinetic energy than alpha particles. This, together with their smaller charge, makes them less ionising than alpha particles. Gamma rays cause the least amount of ionisation because they have no charge.

### Developing practical skills

A researcher has a radioactive source but does not know what type of radiation the source is emitting.

Plan an investigation to find out what type of radiation the source is emitting. You have the following equipment:

- radioactive source
- GM tube and counter
- sheet of paper
- 2 mm thick sheet of aluminium
- sheet of thick lead

### Planning experiments and investigations

**1.** Plan your experiment, describing clearly the following:

    a) the aim of your investigation

    b) what you will measure

    c) the number and range of readings that you will take.

**2.** Draw out a results table that you would use in your investigation.

## QUESTIONS

**1.** State the most ionising radiation.

**2.** State the radiation that can be stopped by a thin sheet of paper.

**3.** Explain why standing 1 m away from of an alpha-emitting source is safe.

**4.** **SUPPLEMENT** Explain why alpha and beta particles can be deflected by magnetic fields and electric fields.

## RADIOACTIVE DECAY

Ionising radiation is emitted from unstable nuclei in order for them to become more stable. This process is known as radioactive decay. As mentioned earlier, this decay is both spontaneous and random.

In both alpha-decay and beta-decay, the nucleus decays into a nucleus of another element. For example, when nuclei of radium with 226 nucleons (found in rocks) emit alpha particles, they change into nuclei of radon. This is the same radon that contributes towards the background radiation on the surface of the Earth.

Isotopes of an element may be radioactive because there are too many neutrons in the nucleus. In order to become a bit more stable, the isotopes will either eject nucleons (as in the case of alpha-decay), or a neutron may change into a proton to decrease the number of excess neutrons within the nucleus (as in the case of beta-decay).

An alpha particle contains two protons and two neutrons. So, with four nucleons and two protons, it is written as $_2^4\alpha$. It is the same particle as the nucleus of a helium atom, which is written $_2^4He$.

When a nucleus emits an alpha particle it loses 4 nucleons, and its nucleon number decreases by 4. It loses 2 protons and its proton number decreases by 2. In Fig. 5.14, the americium nuclide changes into a nuclide of neptunium after the emission of the alpha particle. There is a change in element, because the proton numbers change. Therefore, whenever there is an alpha decay, the nucleus left behind will be of a different element.

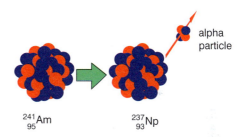

$_{95}^{241}Am$      $_{93}^{237}Np$

△ Fig. 5.14 Alpha decay. In this decay, there is a change of element.

A beta particle is written $_{-1}^{0}\beta$ to show that it is not a nucleon and has a mass so small that it can be ignored and is of exactly the opposite charge to a proton. A beta particle is the same as an electron, and could be written $_{-1}^{0}e$.

When a nucleus emits a beta particle, a neutron inside the nucleus has changed into a proton (that stays in the nucleus) plus an electron. The beta-decay can be summarised as: neutron → proton + electron

The total charge before and after the reaction is unchanged, but the nucleus has lost a neutron and gained a proton. The electron, for reasons too complex to explain, cannot stay within the nucleus and, is emitted as the beta particle, see Fig. 5.15. The nucleon number of the nucleus is unchanged by beta emission, but the proton number increases by 1. The nucleus left behind has greater stability because it now has fewer

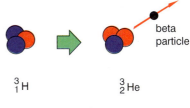

$_1^3H$      $_2^3He$

△ Fig. 5.15 Beta decay.

neutrons. Once again, just as in the case of alpha-decay, the element changes after the decay. In this case, hydrogen changes into helium.

When a nucleus emits a gamma ray, it is just an electromagnetic wave that is emitted as the unstable nucleus reorganises itself internally. No particles are emitted, and so the nucleon number and the proton number do not change, see Fig. 5.16.

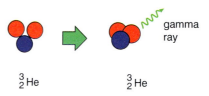

$^{3}_{2}$He  $^{3}_{2}$He

△ Fig. 5.16 Gamma ray emission.

Table 5.4 summarises these changes.

| Nucleus emits | Nucleon number | Proton number |
|---|---|---|
| Alpha particle | Decreases by 4 | Decreases by 2 |
| Beta particle | No change | Increases by 1 |
| Gamma ray | No change | No change |

△ Table 5.4 A summary of changes taking place within radioactive nuclei.

## NUCLEAR EQUATIONS

You can write down nuclear changes as decay equations using the nuclide notation met earlier. The nucleus before the decay is often referred to as the 'parent' nucleus, and the nucleus left after the decay, the 'daughter' nucleus. The rules are as follows:

- The numbers in the top row must be balanced on each side of the equation, because the number of nucleons cannot change.
- The numbers in the lower row must be balanced on each side of the equation, because the total electrical charge will stay unchanged.

Fig. 5.17 shows some examples. In the alpha-decay, radium changes into radon. In the beta-decay, polonium changes into astatine. In gamma-decay, there is no change in either proton or nucleon number – the element remains the same. Note particularly what happens when a beta particle is emitted. Because a neutron has changed into a proton, the proton (atomic) number has increased by 1.

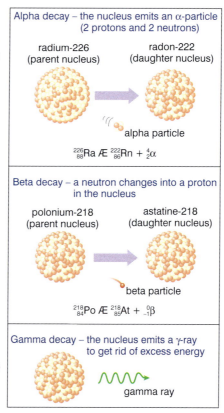

Alpha decay – the nucleus emits an α-particle (2 protons and 2 neutrons)

radium-226 (parent nucleus)    radon-222 (daughter nucleus)

alpha particle

$^{226}_{88}$Ra Æ $^{222}_{86}$Rn + $^{4}_{2}\alpha$

Beta decay – a neutron changes into a proton in the nucleus

polonium-218 (parent nucleus)    astatine-218 (daughter nucleus)

beta particle

$^{218}_{84}$Po Æ $^{218}_{85}$At + $^{0}_{-1}\beta$

Gamma decay – the nucleus emits a γ-ray to get rid of excess energy

gamma ray

△ Fig. 5.17 Examples of radioactive decay.

## QUESTIONS

1. Explain how alpha decay affects a nucleus.

2. Explain how beta decay affects a nucleus.

3. **SUPPLEMENT** A uranium (U) nucleus has 143 neutrons and 92 protons. It decays by alpha-emission into a nucleus of thorium (Th). Write the nuclide equation for this decay.

4. **SUPPLEMENT** In the decay of polonium nuclide shown in Fig.5.17, explain why the nucleus left behind is not of the same element.

### HALF-LIFE

The activity of a radioactive source is the number of ionising particles it emits per unit time. The count rate, measured using a GM tube and a counter, will record a fraction of this activity. Over time, fewer nuclei are left in the source to decay, so the count rate drops. The **half-life** of a particular isotope is the time it takes for half of the nuclei of that isotope in any sample to decay. As it happens, the activity and the count rate from the radioactive source will also halve.

The half-life depends on the isotope of an element, and can be as small as a billionth of a second or as big as billions of years. For example, lithium-12 has a half-life of about one billionth of a second, and rubidium-87 has a half-life of 49 billion years.

The activity of a source is measured in becquerels. A source that is one becquerel, written as 1 Bq, has one nucleus decay per second. A source in a laboratory may be a few hundred Bq, but industrial sources can be several kBq, sometimes MBq or GBq. In the laboratory, we would measure and record the count rate from our GM tube and counter.

Starting with a pure sample of radioactive nuclei of a particular isotope, after one half-life, half the nuclei will have decayed. The remaining undecayed nuclei still have the same chance of decaying as before, so after a second half-life, half of the remaining nuclei will have decayed. After two half-lives a quarter of the nuclei will remain undecayed, see Fig. 5.18.

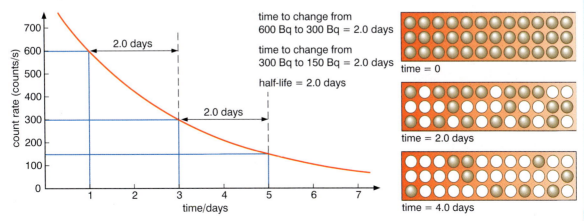

△ Fig. 5.18 A graph of count rate against time. The isotope of the source has a half-life of 2.0 days.

## WORKED EXAMPLE

The radiation from a source is detected by a Geiger–Müller tube and counter as having count rate of 400 counts/min. Three hours later the count rate is 50 counts/min. Calculate the half-life of the isotope of the source.

Write down the count rate and progressively halve it. Each halving of the count rate is one half-life:

| Time | Count rate |
|------|-----------|
| 0 | 400 counts/min |
| 1 half-life | 200 counts/min |
| 2 half-lives | 100 counts/min |
| 3 half-lives | 50 counts/min |

It takes 3 hours to get to 3 half-lives, so 1 half-life is 1 hour.

SUPPLEMENT

## WORKED EXAMPLE

A student is doing an experiment on a radioactive liquid. The half-life of the isotope within the radioactive liquid is 12 minutes. The background radiation in the laboratory is 10 count/min.

At the start of the experiment, the radiation counter records 170 counts in one minute. This is the uncorrected count because it includes the background counts.

Predict the actual counts in one minute recorded by the counter after a time of 24 minutes (two half-lives).

Calculate the corrected count rate:  corrected count rate =
$$170 - 10 = 160 \text{ count/min}$$

After 1 half-life:  corrected count rate = $\dfrac{160}{2}$ = 80 counts/min

After 2 half-lives:  corrected count rate = $\dfrac{80}{2}$ = 40 counts/min

The actual count rate will include the background radiation. Therefore, the total recorded counts in 1 minute will be:
actual count rate = 40 + 10 = 50 count/min

## QUESTIONS

1. Define the half-life of an isotope.

2. A radioactive sample has an isotope with a half-life of 8.0 hours. The count rate at the start is 800 count/s. Calculate the time taken for the count rate to drop to 100 count/s.

**3.** The count rate against time graph for a radioactive source is shown in Fig. 5.19. The count rate includes the background radiation.

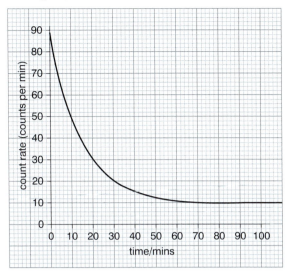

△ Fig. 5.19 Count rate against time graph.

**a)** Suggest why the background count rate must be 10 counts per minute.

**b)** Show that the half-life of the isotope of the radioactive source is about 10 minutes.

---

**SCIENCE IN CONTEXT**

## CARBON DATING

Every living organism (plants, animals and humans) contains the radioactive isotope of carbon-14. Chemically, this is no different from the most abundant and stable isotope of carbon-12. Carbon-14 has a half-life of about 5700 years.

△ Fig. 5.20 The Tollund Man in Denmark is the best example of a body preserved in a bog. Radioactive carbon dating showed that he had been there for more than 2000 years.

When the living material dies, it stops taking in new carbon. The carbon-14 nuclei continue to decay as they always have, and the ratio of carbon-14 nuclei to the non-radioactive carbon-12 nuclei decreases over time. It is this ratio that can be used to estimate the age of the plant or animal material. This method of radioactive carbon dating has been used in dating things such as bone, cloth and wood, see Fig. 5.20.

**Challenge Question:** This technique assumes that the amount of carbon-12 in the atmosphere has remained constant for thousands of years. Can you see a problem with this assumption?

## Developing practical skills

A teacher demonstrates the radioactive decay of protactinium. Before starting the investigation, the teacher makes measurements to allow for background radiation. Then she sets a GM tube alongside a bottle containing the protactinium source. The GM tube is connected to a counter. The teacher starts a stopclock and measures the count rate from the source every 30 seconds for 5.0 minutes. The results are shown in the table.

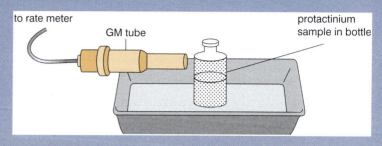

△ Fig. 5.21 Apparatus needed for the investigation.

## Planning experiments and investigations

1. Why does the teacher carry out this experiment, rather than a student?

2. **SUPPLEMENT** What measurements should the teacher make to correct for background radiation?

3. What was the independent variable in this investigation? What was the dependent variable?

| Time/ minutes | Count rate corrected for background radiation/count/s |
|---|---|
| 0 | 80 |
| 0.5 | 60 |
| 1.0 | 44 |
| 1.5 | 35 |
| 2.0 | 28 |
| 2.5 | 21 |
| 3.0 | 16 |
| 3.5 | 14 |
| 4.0 | 10 |
| 4.5 | 7 |
| 5.0 | 6 |

## Observing, measuring and recording data

4. Draw a graph of the results.

5. **SUPPLEMENT** Use your graph to find the half-life of the sample.

## Interpreting and evaluating data

6. Radioactivity is a random process. What does this mean? Is there any evidence from the graph to support the idea?

7. **SUPPLEMENT** Why was it important to correct for background radiation?

8. Would repeating the experiment and taking an average give a more accurate value of the half-life? Explain your answer.

## Application of isotopes

Radioactive isotopes have the same chemistry as non-radioactive isotopes of the same element. This can be very valuable in research as well as medicine.

## Treatment of cancer

In medicine, beta-emitting iodine is used in the treatment of cancer of the thyroid. The thyroid gland can become cancerous and the cancer then spreads through the body. Because the cells of the thyroid absorb far more iodine than other parts of the body, the cancer can be

△ Fig. 5.22 Radioactive isotope of iodine-131 used in thyroid treatment are stored in lead boxes for safety.

targeted by injecting the body with radioactive iodine. The iodine is absorbed by the cancerous cells wherever they are in the body, after which it kills them. The half-life of the iodine isotope used in the treatment of cancer is about 8 days, which is long enough for most of the cancerous cells to be killed off. Using an isotope of much longer half-life would increase the exposure time and unnecessarily damage many healthy cells too.

In radiotherapy, high doses of gamma radiation are fired at cancer cells to kill them. Here, as in the case of X-rays (see topic on light), the radiation that can cause cancer is also an important tool in treating it. Some healthy cells are also damaged by the gamma rays, but these cells can repair themselves much more easily than the cancerous cells are able to.

## Irradiating food and sterilisation

Irradiating food and medical equipment with gamma rays is used for killing off bacteria. Medical equipment used in surgery can be sterilised quickly, and food can be preserved to increase its shelf life. A commonly used isotope is cobalt-60. Gamma rays do not change the chemistry of the items being sterilised. In the case of food items, gamma rays can penetrate deep within the food to kill off any bacteria. Beta and alpha particles would not be suitable because of their poor penetration capabilities, and they can also make the food slightly radioactive.

## Household fire (smoke) alarms

A smoke alarm includes a small radioactive source that emits alpha radiation. The isotope used is usually americium-241. The radiation produces ions in the air, which conduct a small electric current. When smoke absorbs some of the alpha particles, it reduces the number of ions in the air and the current drops. This sets off the alarm. An alpha source is safe, because none of the radiation can penetrate through the plastic casing of the smoke alarm. So that you do not have to change the alarm regularly, the isotope used has a very long half-life. Americium-241 has a half-life of 430 years.

## Thickness control

Beta particles are used to monitor the thickness of paper or metal, see Fig. 5.22. The number of beta particles passing through the material can be used to alter the thickness of the material by adjusting the pressure applied by the rollers. A commonly used isotope is strontium-90. Beta particles are used because they will penetrate through the paper or thin metal sheet. Alpha particles cannot be used because these materials will completely absorb these particles, and gamma rays cannot be used because they would penetrate through the materials without being absorbed. Beta particles are just right to be used for controlling the thickness of paper or thin metal sheet.

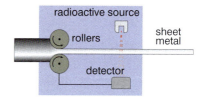

△ Fig. 5.23  Sheet thickness control.

## Other applications

Tracers are radioactive substances with half-lives and radiation types that suit the job they are used for. The half-life must be long enough for the tracer to spread out and be detected, but not so long that it stays in the system and causes irreparable damage.

- Medical tracers are used to detect blockages in vital organs. A gamma camera is used to monitor the passage of the radioactive material through the body. A commonly used isotope is gamma-emitting technetium-99m, which has a short half-life of about 6 hours. The tracer does not stay too long inside the patient. The emitted gamma rays travel through the body of the patient and can be detected by the gamma camera around the patient. Beta- and alpha-emitting sources cannot be used, because most of the radiation will be absorbed by the patient – causing more harm than good.

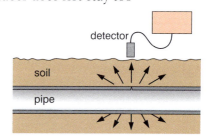

△ Fig. 5.24  Tracers detect leaks.

- Industrial tracers can monitor the flow of liquid and gases through pipes to identify leakages, see Fig. 5.23.  Leaks in underground water pipes can be identified using the isotope sodium-24. This has a half-life of about 15 hours, which is long enough to carry out the tests and locate any leakage into the soil. Sodium-24 is a beta emitter. The leakage of water can be identified from increased count-rate above the soil. An alpha source would not be suitable as a tracer because the alpha particles would be stopped by the pipe and ground – so none would be detected above the ground. Gamma source would also not be suitable because gamma rays can easily penetrate through the material of the pipe and soil – there would be no marked change in count-rate above the soil.

## SAFETY PRECAUTIONS

Alpha, beta and gamma radiation can all damage, kill or mutate living cells. Excessive exposure can also lead to cancer.

Alpha particles, due to their strong ability to ionise other particles, are particularly dangerous to human tissue. However, they cannot penetrate skin, so when alpha sources are outside the body they are relatively harmless. If they are swallowed, inhaled, etc. they cause a lot of cell damage. Gamma radiation is dangerous because of its high penetrating power. This is why such sources are stored away in lead boxes or lead-lined storage cupboards. However, the cell has repair mechanisms that make ordinary levels of gamma radiation relatively harmless.

Nevertheless, radiation can be very useful – it just needs to be used *safely*. Safety precautions for handling radioactive materials include:

- use forceps when moving radioactive sources – don't hold them directly
- do not point radioactive sources at living tissue
- store radioactive materials in lead-lined containers – and lock the containers away securely
- check the surrounding area for radiation levels above normal background levels.

### SUPPLEMENT

Radioactive substances are dangerous to humans because alpha particles, beta particles and gamma rays can all damage or kill off healthy cells. We can only tolerate a small dose of radiation. Any healthy cells damaged in our organs get repaired over time if the energy from the radiation is small.

Some workers, such as radiographers in hospitals, have to use such substances on a regular basis. They can lessen the risks associated with radioactive substances by minimising the dose of energy received from the radiation. This can be done either by reducing the exposure time with the radiation, preventing the radiation from entering the body by either using some form of shielding (e.g. a lead-lined apron) or by keeping far away from radioactive substance.

Imagine a radiographer in a hospital using a beta emitting source. Beta particle are easily absorbed by a few centimetres of air or by few millimetres of metal. So, when necessary, handing the source with either long tongs or wearing metal-lined gloves would be a sensible precaution. However, if the source was technetium-99m or cobalt-60, both of which emit gamma rays, it would be best to wear a lead-lined apron to limit the dose of radiation entering the body. Radiographers often wear special film badges that monitor the dose of radiation they receive over a period of time.

1. Explain why an alpha-source is ideal in a household smoke detector.

2. What radiation is used to sterilise water?

   A   alpha particle      B   beta particles      C   gamma radiation

   D   light

3. List some of the applications of gamma radiation.

4. State the damage ionising radiations can do to living tissue.

5. **SUPPLEMENT** A radiologist uses gamma sources on a regular basis. Describe some of the safety precautions the radiologist may take.

# End of topic checklist

## Key terms

background radiation, ionising radiation, cosmic rays, alpha ($\alpha$) radiation, beta ($\beta$) radiation, gamma ($\gamma$) radiation, half-life

## During your study of this topic you should have learned:

○ Background radiation is radiation emitted from all around us.

○ A significant contribution to background radiation includes: radon gas (in the air), rocks and buildings, food and drink and cosmic rays.

○ Ionising nuclear radiation can be measured using a detector (GM tube) connected to a counter.

○ Count rate is measured in counts/s or counts/minute.

○ **SUPPLEMENT** Corrected count rate takes into account the background radiation.

○ The emission of radiation from a nucleus can be both spontaneous and random.

○ Identify alpha ($\alpha$), beta ($\beta$) and gamma ($\gamma$) emissions from the nucleus by knowing: their nature, their relative ionising effects and their relative penetrating abilities.

○ **SUPPLEMENT** Alpha particles and beta particles can be deflected in electric fields and magnetic fields.

○ **SUPPLEMENT** Gamma rays cannot be deflected in electric fields and magnetic fields.

○ **SUPPLEMENT** Explain relative ionising effects with reference to kinetic energy and electric charge.

○ Radioactive decay is a change in an unstable nucleus that can result in the emission of $\alpha$-particles or $\beta$-particles and/or $\gamma$-radiation.

○ After $\alpha$-decay or $\beta$-decay, the nucleus changes to that of a different element.

○ **SUPPLEMENT** Isotopes of an element may be radioactive due to an excess of neutrons in the nucleus and/or the nucleus being too heavy.

○ **SUPPLEMENT** $\alpha$-decay, $\beta$-decay and $\gamma$-emissions on the nucleus increase the stability of a nucleus.

○ **SUPPLEMENT** $\alpha$-decay and $\beta$-decay both reduce the number of excess neutrons.

○ **SUPPLEMENT** During $\beta$-emission: neutron $\rightarrow$ proton + electron.

○ **SUPPLEMENT** Use decay equations, using nuclide notation, to show the emission of α-particles, β-particles and γ-radiation.

○ Half-life of a particular isotope is the time taken for half the nuclei of that isotope in any sample to decay.

○ How to use the half-life definition in simple calculations.

○ **SUPPLEMENT** Calculate half-life from data or decay curves.

○ **SUPPLEMENT** Radioactive isotopes are used in: household fire (smoke) alarms, irradiating food to kill bacteria, sterilisation of equipment using gamma rays and measuring and controlling thicknesses of materials (e.g. paper) and diagnosis and treatment of cancer using gamma rays.

○ Ionising nuclear radiations can cause cell death, mutate cells and can cause cancer in living things.

○ Radioactive materials are moved, used and stored in a safe way.

○ **SUPPLEMENT** Safety precautions used for all ionising radiation include reducing exposure time, increasing distance between source and living tissue and using shielding to absorb radiation.

# End of topic questions

*Note: the marks in brackets give an indication of the level of detail you should include in your answers.*

**1.** Describe the composition of a neutral atom with atomic number 6 and nucleon number 13. (3 marks)

**2.** **SUPPLEMENT** The diagram illustrates an experiment using some very thin gold foil that was carried out by researchers working for Rutherford.

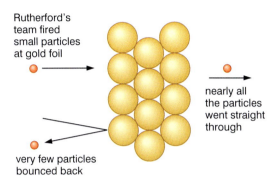

Rutherford's team fired small particles at gold foil

nearly all the particles went straight through

very few particles bounced back

**a)** Name the particles that were fired into the gold foil. (1 mark)

**b)** Describe what Rutherford deduced from the observation that most of the particles passed straight through the foil. (2 marks)

**c)** Describe what Rutherford deduced from the observation that some particles bounced back from the foil. (2 marks)

**3.** **SUPPLEMENT** Scientists sometimes say that 'most matter is empty space'. Explain what this means, using the ideas from the scattering experiment in Question 2. (6 marks)

**4.** **SUPPLEMENT** The following equation shows what happens when a nuclide of sodium-24 decays.
$$^{24}_{11}\text{Na} \rightarrow {}^{x}_{y}\text{Mg} + {}^{0}_{-1}\beta$$

**a)** What type of nuclear radiation is emitted during this reaction?

    **A** alpha

    **B** beta

    **C** gamma

    **D** neutrons (1 mark)

**b)** Determine the values of x and y. (2 marks)

**5.** The graph shows how the count rate of a sample of sodium-24 changes with time. Use the graph to determine the half-life of this sodium isotope. (3 marks)

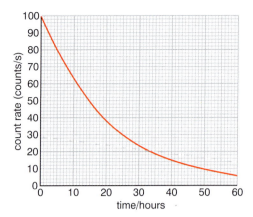

**6.** Describe the properties of beta particles. (3 marks)

**7.** Explain what is meant by ionisation. (2 marks)

**8.** Radon-220 is a radioactive isotope of radon. It decays to polonium-216. Write the nuclear equation for its decay by alpha radiation. The proton (atomic) number of radon is 86 and the proton (atomic) number of polonium is 84. (3 marks)

**9.** A laboratory technician has three radioactive sources: cobalt-60, which is a source of gamma rays, strontium-90, which is a source of beta particles, and americium-241, which is a source of alpha particles.

Suggest how the technician can experimentally identify these three sources. (6 marks)

**10.** A sample of radioactive material has 800 active nuclei.

**a)** Determine the number of active nuclei left after two half-lives. (1 mark)

**b)** Determine how many half-lives it takes to reduce it to 50 active nuclei. (2 marks)

**c)** The isotope within the material has a half-life of 30 minutes. Calculate how long it takes for the number of active nuclei to reduce to 100. (3 marks)

**11.** The isotope of iodine-131 has a half-life of 8.0 days. A sample with this isotope a count rate of 128 counts/minute.

**a)** Determine the count rate after 3 half-lives. (2 marks)

**b)** Calculate the time it will take for the count rate to drop to 4 counts/minute. (2 marks)

## COMMENTS

**a)** Fine – standard definition. Alternatively the answer could be given in terms of atomic number or proton number and mass number or nucleon number.

**b)** Fine – alternatively the answer could be given in terms of protons and neutrons.

**c)** A very common mistake – this answer refers to the radiation given off (the alpha particles) and not the radioactive source itself. Half-life describes how the activity of the source will change over time; the radiation emitted does not decay.

**d)** Both answers here begin correctly but fail to develop the ideas sufficiently.

  **i)** The idea of removing electrons is required.

  **ii)** The consequences of blocking the radiation (no ionisation, no current) are missing.

# Exam-style questions

*Note: exam-style questions, sample answers and comments have been written by the authors. The marks awarded for these questions indicate the level of detail required in the answers. In examinations, the way marks are awarded may be different. References to assessment and/or assessment preparation are the publisher's interpretation of the syllabus requirements and may not fully reflect the approach of Cambridge Assessment International Education.*

## Example answers

### Question 1

Americium-241 is a radioactive isotope that decays by emitting alpha particles.

The isotope has a half-life of 432 years.

**a)** Explain what is meant by isotopes.

*Atoms with the same number of protons* ✓ ①  *but a different number of neutrons.* ✓ ①  **[2]**

**b)** Describe the nature of alpha particles.

*The nucleus* ✓ ①  *of a helium atom.* ✓ ①  **[2]**

**c)** Explain what is meant by 'half-life of 432 years'.

*The radiation loses half its power in 432 years.* ✗ ✗  **[2]**

**d)** Americium-241 is used in smoke detectors. If there is no smoke present, the alpha particles ionise a path through the air and a small current can flow.

  **i)** Describe how alpha particles can ionise particles in the air.

*The alpha particles hit the atoms in the air.* ✗  **[2]**

**ii)** Suggest what happens when particles of smoke enter the detector.

*The smoke* ✔ ① *blocks the radiation*

✗ *so the alarm goes off* ✗ **[3]**

**e)** Radioactive emissions can be harmful to humans.

**i)** Describe one harmful effect that radioactive emissions can have on humans.

*Cause mutations.* ✔ ① **[1]**

**i)** Suggest why it is safe to have a radioactive source in a smoke detector.

*It doesn't last very long* ✗ *and it's on*

*the ceiling.* ✗ **[2]**

(Total 14 marks)

6/14

**e)** **i)** 'Cause mutations' is a bit vague. 'Causes mutations in cells' would be more specific.

**ii)** The point of the question has been missed – it is in part e) for a reason. The idea given in part i) needed to be developed further – in this case explaining why these harmful effects are not caused by the smoke detector. 'It's on the ceiling' gives the correct idea, but more detail is needed.

## Question 2

**a)** A radioactive nucleus emits only alpha particles.

   **i)** Draw a labelled diagram of the apparatus you would use to prove that no beta particles or gamma radiation are emitted from the isotope. [2]

   **ii)** Describe the test you would carry out. [2]

   **iii)** Explain how your results would show that only alpha particles are emitted. [2]

**b) SUPPLEMENT** The diagram shows a stream of alpha particles about to enter the space between the poles of a very strong magnet.

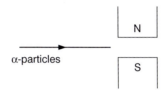

Describe the path of the alpha particles in the space between the magnetic poles. [3]

(Total 9 marks)

## Question 3

**a)** A sodium nucleus decays by the emission of a beta particle to form magnesium (Mg).

   **i) SUPPLEMENT** Copy and complete the decay equation: [2]

$$^{12}_{11}Na \rightarrow Mg +$$

   **ii)** The diagram shows beta particles from a sodium source moving into the space between the poles of a magnet.

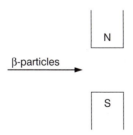

Describe the path of the beta particles between the magnetic poles. [3]

**b)** Very small quantities of a radioactive isotope are used to check the circulation of blood by injecting the isotope into the bloodstream.

Explain why a gamma-emitting isotope is used for this purpose rather than one that emits either alpha particles or beta particles. [2]

(Total 7 marks)

Humans are curious beings. We cannot look at the stars in the night sky, without asking questions. How did the stars get there? Is the Earth the only habitable planet in the Universe? The frontiers of science and technology are being pushed forward all the time. We can now send space probes to distant planets, and even land them on comets hurtling through space. We are learning more about the objects that are close to the Earth. We can use complex telescopes orbiting the Earth to study distant objects in space using not only visible light, but also X-rays. The Chandra X-ray Observatory was launched in 1999, and is still operational and orbiting the Earth. It continues to provide astronomers with stunning images – helping them to test their theories and advance our knowledge and understanding of space.

## STARTING POINTS

**1.** What causes day and night on the Earth?

**2.** What is the name of the force that keeps the Moon in its orbit around the Earth?

**3.** How can you tell if a speck of light in the night sky is a planet and not a star?

**4.** What is a galaxy?

## SYLLABUS SECTIONS COVERED

**6.1** Earth and the Solar System

**6.2** Stars and the Universe

# 6
# Space physics

△ The Chandra X-ray Observatory continues to help astronomers learn about Space.

△ Fig. 6.1 Stunning image of the swirling atmosphere of Jupiter taken from the camera aboard NASA's Juno spacecraft.

# Earth and the Solar System

## INTRODUCTION

Our developing understanding of the Solar System, and the space beyond, has largely come from observations. In the past, these observations were Earth-based and simple instruments were used to measure and record the motion of the planets and our Moon across the night sky. Predictions were made based on these observations – such as the phases of the Moon by the Iranian scholar Al-Biruni some thousand years ago.

We can learn more about our Moon, and the planets beyond, by using powerful telescopes onboard space probes, see Fig. 6.1.

## KNOWLEDGE CHECK

✓ Conservation of energy can be applied to any system.
✓ Gravitational field strength is the force per unit mass.
✓ Gravitational force acts on an object that has mass.
✓ Speed is distance travelled per unit time.
✓ **SUPPLEMENT** Speed of light is $3.0 \times 10^8$ m/s in a vacuum.

## LEARNING OBJECTIVES

✓ Know that the Earth is a planet that rotates on its axis, which is tilted, once in approximately 24 hours, and use this to explain observations of the apparent daily motion of the Sun and the periodic cycle of day and night.
✓ Know that the Earth orbits the Sun once in approximately 365 days and use this to explain the periodic nature of the seasons.
✓ Know that it takes approximately one month for the Moon to orbit the Earth and use this to explain the periodic nature of the Moon's cycle of phases.
✓ **SUPPLEMENT** Define average orbital speed from the equation $v = \dfrac{2\pi r}{T}$ where $r$ is the average radius of the orbit; recall and use this equation.
✓ Describe the Solar System as containing: one star, the Sun; the named planets and know their order from the Sun; dwarf planets that orbit the Sun, including asteroids; moons, that orbit the planets; and smaller Solar System bodies, including comets and natural satellites.
✓ Know that, in comparison to each other, the four planets nearest the Sun are rocky and small and the four planets furthest from the Sun are gaseous and large, and explain this difference by referring to an accretion model for solar system formation to include: the model's dependence on gravity, the presence of many elements in interstellar clouds of gas and dust and the rotation of material in the cloud and the formation of an accretion disc.

✓ Know that the strength of the gravitational field: at the surface of a planet depends on the mass of the planet and around a planet decreases as the distance from the planet increases.

✓ Calculate the time it takes light to travel a significant distance such as between objects in the Solar System.

✓ Know that the Sun contains most of the mass of the Solar System and this explains why the planets orbit the Sun.

✓ Know that the force that keeps an object in orbit around the Sun is the gravitational attraction of the Sun.

✓ **SUPPLEMENT** Know that planets, minor planets and comets have elliptical orbits, and recall that the Sun is not at the centre of the elliptical orbit, except when the orbit is approximately circular.

✓ **SUPPLEMENT** Analyse and interpret planetary data about orbital distance, orbital duration, density, surface temperature and uniform gravitational field strength at the planet's surface.

✓ **SUPPLEMENT** Know that the strength of the Sun's gravitational field decreases and that the orbital speeds of the planets decrease as the distance from the Sun increases.

✓ **SUPPLEMENT** Know that an object in an elliptical orbit travels faster when closer to the Sun and explain this using the conservation of energy.

## THE EARTH

The length of a day and a year is determined by the motion of the Earth through space. A day is the time it takes for the Earth to spin on its axis – this is approximately 24 hours. A year is the time it takes for the Earth to make one orbit around the Sun – this is approximately 365 days.

## Day and night

As Fig. 6.2 shows, it is day-time on the side of the Earth that is directly facing the Sun, and night-time on the opposite side of the Earth. The rotation of the Earth on its axis gives rise to the periodic cycle of day and night. The Earth rotates towards the east. This is why the Sun, Moon, planets and all the stars, rise in the east and move through the sky towards the west.

## The seasons

The Earth's axis of rotation is tilted at 23°. In the winter, the Northern Hemisphere is tilted away from the Sun. The Sun is above the horizon for shorter times each day, so there is less daylight. The Sun is low in the sky and the amount of heat from the Sun is reduced.

Six months later, in the summer, the Earth is on the other side of the Sun and the Northern Hemisphere is tilted towards the Sun. The Sun is high in the sky, there is more daylight and the heat from the Sun is increased.

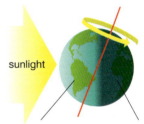

the Earth spins around its axis every 24 hours

sunlight

this side of the Earth is facing towards the Sun – it is day here

this side of the Earth is facing away from the Sun – it is night here

Δ Fig. 6.2 Day and night are caused by the Earth spinning on its axis.

As you can see from Fig. 6.3, the Southern Hemisphere has seasons that are opposite to those in the Northern Hemisphere. Winter in Northern Hemisphere means it is summer in the Southern Hemisphere.

Regions very close to the North Pole experience 24 hours of daylight in the summer time, and 24 hours of darkness in the winter time.

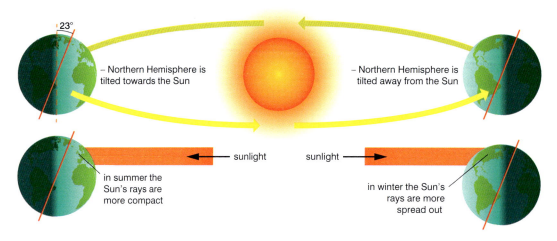

Δ Fig. 6.3 The seasons are caused by the Earth's tilt.

## THE MOON'S CYCLE OF PHASES

The Moon is a natural satellite that orbits the Earth in about 30 days. This period is called a month. The Moon is the second brightest object in the sky (after the Sun) but it does not emit any of its own light. Instead, it reflects the light from the Sun.

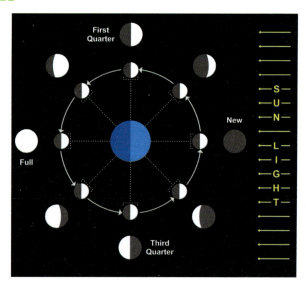

Δ Fig. 6.4 The phases of the Moon.

The Moon's appearance changes at different times of the month. These changes in shape are known as the 'phases' of the Moon. Regardless of its position, one half of the Moon is always illuminated by the Sun. The way we see it depends on how much of the illuminated half we can see from the Earth. When we see all the illuminated half, we see a complete disc, known as a full Moon. When we only see part of the illuminated half, we see an increasing phase (waxing) or decreasing phase (waning) of the Moon. The changing position of the Moon as it orbits the Earth allows us to see the different phases, see Fig. 6.4.

1. It is winter in the Southern Hemisphere. State the season in the Northern Hemisphere.

2. Estimate the time in days between one full Moon and the next half-Moon.

3. Explain why the Sun rises in the east and sets in the west.

## THE SOLAR SYSTEM

The Solar System is the general name for the Sun and all the objects that orbit it. The Sun is a yellow star. It is a hot ball of glowing gases.

The Sun's enormous gravitational pull is responsible for trapping all of the eight planets, minor planets, millions of asteroids and comets in their orbits around it. Some of the planets have smaller objects orbiting them. These are called moons or natural satellites. Our planet Earth has one moon (called the Moon). The two closest planets to the Sun, Mercury and Venus, have no moons. The ringed planet Saturn may have as many as 82 moons.

Some of the stars we see in the night sky may also have their own system of orbiting planets.

### Planets and asteroids

The planets in order of increasing distance from the Sun are: Mercury, Venus, Earth, Mars, Jupiter, Saturn, Uranus and Neptune. Small rocky objects, the asteroids, occupy a region of space mainly between the orbits of Mars and Jupiter. This region is known as the asteroid belt. The largest asteroid, Vesta, is about 500 km in diameter and the smallest asteroids are only a few metres wide. Although spread over a vast region of space, the total mass of all the asteroids is less than the mass of our Moon.

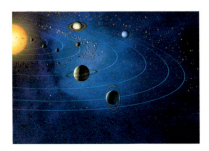

△ Fig.6.5 The Solar System. In order of increasing distance from the Sun we have Mercury, Venus, Earth, Mars, asteroid belt, Jupiter, Saturn, Uranus and Neptune.

A minor planet is an object that orbits around the Sun that is neither a planet nor a comet. Dwarf planets are minor planets. A dwarf planet is an object where its own gravity forms an ellipsoid (spherical or squashed sphere) object.

Currently there are five officially recognised dwarf planets. The most famous of these is Pluto. It was demoted from a planet to a dwarf planet in 2006. The others are Ceres, Eris, Haumea and Makemake. Makemake was discovered in 2015 in the frozen regions beyond the orbit of Neptune. There are many more dwarf planets waiting to be officially recognised by astronomers.

## Comets

Comets are mainly found beyond Neptune, at the frozen outer edges of the Solar System. They move around the Sun in oval-shaped orbits. Comets are small objects made mainly of ice and rock. As a frozen comet gets closer to the hot Sun, it heats up and its icy material turns into gas, creating a long visible tail that points away from the Sun. The most famous comet is Halley's comet. It makes an appearance in the night sky every 75 years, and it has been doing this possibly for billions of years. Many comets are named after their discoverers, like the Churyumov–Gerasimenko comet, which is named after two astronomers Klim Ivanovych Churyumov and Svetlana Ivanovna Gerasimenko. It was the first comet to have a space probe land on its surface in 2014. The landing provided important information on the composition of this comet.

△ Fig. 6.6 Halley's comet with its long tail in the night sky.

△ Fig. 6.7 The space probe Philae landed on the peanut-shaped Churyumov–Gerasimenko comet in 2014.

## QUESTIONS

**1.** Name the most distant planet.

**2.** Name the two closest planets to the Earth.

**3.** State what is a comet.

**4.** Describe the location of most of the asteroids in the Solar System.

### SCIENCE IN CONTEXT   LIFE BEYOND OUR SOLAR SYSTEM

How do astronomers know that some stars may have their own system of orbiting planets? The planets beyond our own Solar System are called exoplanets.

Even the most powerful telescopes on the Earth, or in space, cannot physically see exoplanets. They are just too small and too far away. The brightness of a star, even a dim star, can be accurately measured using large telescopes. Its brightness will show a tiny dip every time an exoplanet crosses over the star, see Fig. 6.8.

In 2017, observations collected by NASA's Spitzer Space Telescope, orbiting high above the Earth's atmosphere, led to the discovery of seven Earth-sized exoplanets around the red star called TRAPPIST-1. All of these exoplanets have the potential of having water on their surface, and hence the potential for life.

**Challenge Question:** Why do you think it is harder to discover exoplanets using telescopes on the Earth's surface?

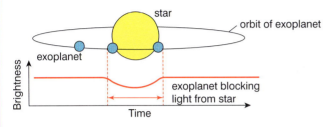

△ Fig. 6.8 The variation in brightness of a star is used to discover an exoplanet.

△ Fig. 6.9 The TRAPPIST-1 system with its exoplanets.

## SUPPLEMENT

## ELLIPTICAL ORBITS

Most objects, including planets, minor planets and comets move around the Sun in elliptical orbits. The model that all planets move in ellipses was first proposed by the Danish mathematician and astronomer Johann Kepler around 1609. The Sun is at one of the two foci of the ellipse. The Sun is not at the centre of the ellipse. You can draw your own ellipse using a length of string, pencil and two thumb tacks, see Fig. 6.10. Comets in our Solar System have the most elliptical orbits.

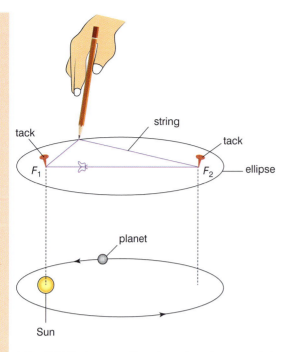

△ Fig. 6.10 To draw an ellipse, loop the string around the tacks (placed at the points $F_1$ and $F_2$ called foci) and move the pencil keeping the string tight. The Sun is at one of the foci of the ellipse – there is nothing at the other foci.

## QUESTIONS

1. **SUPPLEMENT** Which is correct for a planet orbiting the Sun?

   **A** All planets have circular orbits.

   **B** The Sun is at the centre of the elliptical orbit.

   **C** The distance between the Sun and the planet never changes.

   **D** The Sun is at one of the foci of the elliptical orbit.

2. **SUPPLEMENT** Suggest the special name of the eclipse when the foci are on top of each other.

3. **SUPPLEMENT** State the objects orbiting the Sun with the most elliptical orbits.

## FORMATION OF THE SOLAR SYSTEM – ACCRETION MODEL

The Solar System was formed some 4.5 billion years ago from a dense cloud of interstellar gas and dust. The gas in the cloud was mostly hydrogen, with some helium. Interstellar dust is no ordinary dust. It has tiny grains of matter formed from metallic elements such as magnesium, silicon, iron and also molecules such as ammonia, carbon monoxide, methane and nitrogen.

A shockwave from an exploding star (supernova) began the process of this cloud coming together and collapsing under its own gravity. As the cloud collapsed further, it started to swirl and spin faster and faster and also generated lots of heat. Gravity caused most of the gas and dust to form a thin rotating accretion disc. Astronomers use the term accretion to imply the gathering of smaller particles into bigger objects by gravitational attraction. The centre of the accretion disc was bulged because it contained most of the mass of the cloud. High pressure and temperature at the centre of this bulge forced hydrogen nuclei to join (or fuse) together to make helium nuclei. In this process of fusion, enormous energy is released. The centre of the cloud was now a star – our Sun.

Gas and dust further away from the centre of the rotating accretion disc first clumped together into small pieces. These smaller pieces then smashed into each other to make larger pieces. The planets, minor planets and dwarf planets were formed from these larger pieces. The asteroids and comets are the leftover pieces that could not form larger objects. Any remaining gas and dust were gently blown away by the radiant energy of the Sun.

Δ Fig. 6.11 The formation of the Solar System.

## Structure

The four planets nearest to the Sun (Mercury, Venus, Earth and Mars) were formed in the hotter inner parts of the accretion disc where the lumped pieces contained matter with high melting points, such as rocks and iron. The outer cooler regions of the accretion disc had frozen matter such as ammonia, methane, nitrogen and water. These materials produced the gas-giant planets of Jupiter and Saturn and the ice-giant planets of Uranus and Neptune.

## QUESTIONS

1. Name the force responsible for the collapse of the interstellar gas and dust cloud.

2. Name the four 'rocky' planets.

3. Name a material that may be found in the planets beyond Mars.

4. Describe what happened as the gas and dust cloud collapsed to form the accretion disc.

5. Suggest why planets closest to the Sun cannot be made entirely of gas.

## PLANETARY DATA

Through direct observations with telescopes and information collected from space probes, astronomers have managed to gather detailed data on the planets, see Table 6.1.

| Planet | Mass/ $10^{24}$ kg | Mean orbital distance from Sun/$10^6$ km | Closest distance to Sun/ $10^6$ km) | Furthest distance from the Sun/ $10^6$ km | Orbital duration or period/ Earth days | Mean surface temperature/°C | Density/ kg/m³ | Surface gravitational field strength/ N/kg |
|---|---|---|---|---|---|---|---|---|
| Mercury | 0.33 | 57.9 | 46.0 | 69.8 | 88.0 | 167 | 5427 | 3.7 |
| Venus | 4.87 | 108.2 | 107.5 | 108.9 | 224.7 | 464 | 5243 | 8.9 |
| Earth | 5.97 | 149.6 | 147.1 | 152.1 | 365.2 | 15 | 5514 | 9.8 |
| Mars | 0.64 | 227.9 | 206.6 | 249.2 | 687.0 | −65 | 3933 | 3.7 |
| Jupiter | 1900 | 778.6 | 740.5 | 816.6 | 4331 | −110 | 1326 | 23.1 |
| Saturn | 570 | 1433.5 | 1352.6 | 1514.5 | 10 747 | −140 | 687 | 9.0 |
| Uranus | 87 | 2872.5 | 2741.3 | 3003.6 | 30 589 | −195 | 1271 | 8.7 |
| Neptune | 100 | 4495.1 | 4444.5 | 4545.7 | 59 800 | −200 | 1638 | 11.0 |

△ Table 6.1 Some planetary data.

### Average orbital speed

The average **orbital speed** $v$ of any object in an orbit can be calculated using the equation:

$$v = \frac{2\pi r}{T}$$

Where $r$ is the average radius of the orbit and $T$ is the orbital period. This equation may be used for both circular and elliptical orbits. It is worth noting that for a circular orbit, the distance travelled in one period $T$ is the circumference $2\pi r$ of the circle.

### Worked example

The orbital period of the Moon around the Earth is about 30 days. The average radius of its orbit is 380 000 km. Calculate the orbital speed of the Moon in m/s.

First, convert the period into seconds and the radius into metres.

$T = 30$ days $= 30 \times 24 \times 3600 = 2.59 \times 10^6$ s

$r = 380\ 000 \times 10^3 = 3.8 \times 10^8$ m

Now substitute these values into the equation and solve.

$$v = \frac{2\pi r}{T} = \frac{2\pi \times 3.8 \times 10^8}{2.59 \times 10^6} = 920 \text{ m/s}$$

This is almost 1 km per second. Even at this speed it takes 30 days to complete one orbit.

Use Table 6.1 to answer the questions.

1. **SUPPLEMENT** State the relationship between:

   **a)** mean surface temperature of a planet and its mean distance from the Sun

   **b)** orbital duration (period) of a planet and its mean distance from the Sun.

2. **SUPPLEMENT** The density of rocks found on the Earth's surface is about 5000 kg/m³. Identify two other planets with similar density.

3. **SUPPLEMENT** Name the planet with the most elliptical orbit.

4. **SUPPLEMENT** The Earth takes one year to orbit the Sun. Calculate Neptune's orbital period in years.

5. **SUPPLEMENT** The mass of the Sun is $2.0 \times 10^{30}$ kg. Determine:

   **a)** how many times massive is Jupiter than the Earth

   **b)** the total mass of all the planets in the Solar System

   **c)** $\dfrac{\text{total mass of planets}}{\text{mass of the Sun}}$ and comment on your answer.

6. **SUPPLEMENT** Calculate the mean orbital speed in m/s of Mars.

## THE ROLE OF GRAVITY

The surface gravitational field strength of a planet depends on its mass and its radius. The greater the mass, the greater the surface field strength.

The field strength beyond the surface of a planet decreases with increasing distance from its centre. For example, the field strength on the Earth's surface is about 10 N/kg. At a height of about one radius from its surface, this drops to about 2.5 N/kg. At the position of the Moon, the field strength is about 0.0028 N/kg. The field strength is almost zero very far away from the Earth.

The planets orbit the Sun because the Sun has most of the mass in the Solar System. The Sun's gravitational force at the positions of the planets is big enough to make each planet move around the Sun. The Moon only orbits the Earth, and not the Sun, because the Earth's gravitational force on the Moon is much larger than that from the Sun.

**SUPPLEMENT**

## SPEED OF OBJECTS IN THE SOLAR SYSTEM

The gravitational field of the Sun at its surface is about 290 N/kg. The field strength decreases as the distance from the Sun increases. The field strength at Mercury's position is much greater than that at

Neptune's position. This is why the orbital speed of Mercury is much greater than that of Neptune. In summary, as the distance from the Sun increases:

• the Sun's gravitational field strength decreases
• the orbital speed of a planet decreases.

Table 6.2 shows the mean orbital distance from the Sun and the mean orbital speed of all the planets.

| Planet | Mean orbital distance from Sun/$10^6$ km) | Mean orbital speed/km/s |
|---|---|---|
| Mercury | 57.9 | 47.4 |
| Venus | 108.2 | 35.0 |
| Earth | 149.6 | 29.8 |
| Mars | 227.9 | 24.1 |
| Jupiter | 778.6 | 13.1 |
| Saturn | 1433.5 | 9.7 |
| Uranus | 2872.5 | 6.8 |
| Neptune | 4495.1 | 5.4 |

Δ Table 6.2 Orbital speed data for the planets.

All objects travel in elliptical orbits around the Sun.

A planet moves slowest at its most distant point (aphelion) and fastest at its closest point (perihelion). The kinetic energy $E_k$ of a planet, which is directly proportional to speed², increases as it gets closer to the Sun. As kinetic energy increases, the gravitational potential energy $E_p$ of the planet decreases. The sum of the kinetic and potential energies remains constant – as required by the principle of conservation of energy, see Fig. 6.12. The change in speeds is much more dramatic for the comets because of their very elliptical orbits.

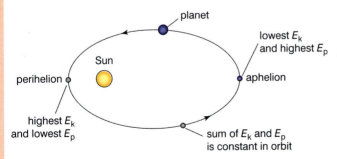

Δ Fig. 6.12 The total energy of an object, such as a comet, moving in an elliptical orbit around the Sun remains constant, but its kinetic energy $E_k$ and gravitational potential energy $E_p$ change.

## QUESTIONS

1. **SUPPLEMENT** State why the planets orbit the Sun.

2. **SUPPLEMENT** State how gravitational field strength changes as the distance from an object increases.

3. **SUPPLEMENT** Name the fastest moving planet.

4. **SUPPLEMENT** Explain why the speed of a comet changes as it gets closer to the Sun.

### TIME TAKEN BY LIGHT TO TRAVEL ACROSS THE SOLAR SYSTEM

The speed of light is immense at 300 million metres per second. Even at this speed, because of the vast distances involved, it can take many hours for the light to travel the length of the Solar System.

The Moon is our closest neighbour. The light from it takes about 1 second to reach us. The Sun is further away, and it takes several minutes for the light to reach us. If a solar flare erupts now on the Sun's surface, then we will see this event much later. The distant events we see have already happened – we are glimpsing into the past.

The distance $d$ travelled by light in a space in a time $t$ is given by the equation $d = c \times t$, where $c$ is the speed of light in a vacuum ($3.0 \times 10^8$ m/s).

### Worked example

The Sun is 150 million km away from the Earth.

Calculate the time, in minutes, it takes light to travel from the Sun to us.

Convert the distance into metres.

$d = 150$ million km $= 150 \times 10^6 \times 10^3 = 1.5 \times 10^{11}$ m

Substitute into the equation and rearrange.

$d = c \times t$

$1.5 \times 10^{11} = 3.0 \times 10^8 \times t$

$t = \dfrac{1.5 \times 10^{11}}{3.0 \times 10^8} = 500\,\text{s}$

Convert the time into minutes; 1 minute = 60 s.

$t = \dfrac{500}{60} = 8.3$ minutes

The light from the Sun takes about 8.3 minutes to reach the Earth.

## QUESTIONS

1. The light from the Moon takes 1.28 s to reach the Earth. Calculate how far the Moon is from the Earth.

2. The most distant planet Neptune is about $4.4 \times 10^{12}$ m from the Earth. Calculate the time, in hours, it takes light to travel from it to us.

# End of topic checklist

## Key terms

accretion disc, asteroid, comet, dwarf planet, interstellar gas and dust, minor planet, moons, phases (of the Moon), planet, seasons, Solar System, Sun

**SUPPLEMENT** average orbital speed, elliptical orbit, gravitational field strength gravity, orbital duration

## During your study of this topic you should have learned:

○ The Earth rotates on its axis once in approximately 24 hours (1 day).

○ Periodic cycle of day and night is because of the Earth rotating on its axis.

○ The Earth orbits the Sun once in approximately 365 days (1 year).

○ Seasons are the result of the Earth's tilted axis and its motion around the Sun.

○ The Moon orbits the Earth in approximately 1 month.

○ The phases of the Moon are the results of observing its half-lit face at different positions in its orbit around the Earth.

○ **SUPPLEMENT** The average orbital speed is defined by the equation $v = \dfrac{2\pi r}{T}$, where $r$ is the average radius of the orbit and $T$ is the orbital period.

○ The Solar System has one star (the Sun) and all the objects (planets, minor planets, asteroids and comets) that orbit it.

○ Some planets have moons orbiting them.

○ The accretion model of the Solar System explains the formation of the Solar System from a collapsing cloud of interstellar gas and dust.

○ Gravitational field strength at the surface of a planet depends on its mass.

○ Gravitational field strength around a planet decreases as the distance from the planet increases.

○ Most of the mass of the Solar System is contained by the Sun – this is why planets orbit the Sun.

○ Gravitational attraction from the Sun keeps the planets moving around the Sun in their orbits.

○ **SUPPLEMENT** Planets, minor planets and comets have elliptical orbits around the Sun.

○ **SUPPLEMENT** An object in an elliptical orbit travels faster when closer to the Sun.

○ **SUPPLEMENT** The gravitational field strength from the Sun decreases with increasing distance from it.

○ **SUPPLEMENT** The orbital speed of a planet decreases as its distance from the Sun increases.

# End of topic questions

*Note: the marks in brackets give an indication of the level of detail you should include in your answers.*

**1. a)** Name the force that keeps the Earth moving in its orbit around the Sun. (1 mark)

**b)** The diagram below shows some observations made by a student on the phases of the Moon.

| Date | 2 Feb | 4 Feb | 7 Feb | 16 Feb | 19 Feb | 22 Feb |
|------|-------|-------|-------|--------|--------|--------|
| Phase of the Moon | | | | | | |

   **i)** Use the observations to estimate the orbital duration (period) of the Moon. (2 marks)

   **ii)** State how you can improve the observations to get a better value of the orbital period. (1 mark)

**2. SUPPLEMENT** Some data on the three innermost planets in the Solar System is shown below.

| Planet | Mass/$10^{24}$ kg | Mean orbital distance from Sun/$10^6$ km | Closest distance to Sun/$10^6$ km | Furthest distance from the Sun/$10^6$ km | Density/ kg/m$^3$ | Surface gravitational field strength/N/kg |
|--------|------|------|------|------|------|------|
| Mercury | 0.33 | 57.9 | 46.0 | 69.8 | 5427 | 3.7 |
| Venus | 4.87 | 108.2 | 107.5 | 108.9 | 5243 | 8.9 |
| Earth | 5.97 | 149.6 | 147.1 | 152.1 | 5514 | 9.8 |

**a)** Explain why these planets have the same density according to the accretion model for the formation of the Solar System. (2 marks)

**b)** Suggest how the density of Jupiter may differ from the densities of these innermost planets. (1 mark)

**c)** State one reason why the surface gravitational field strength is not the same for each of the planets. (1 mark)

**d) SUPPLEMENT** Name the planet with the most elliptical orbit. (1 mark)

**3. a)** Which of the following objects does **not** orbit around the Sun? (1 mark)

   A Jupiter    B Comet    C Moon    D Asteroid

**b)** Name a dwarf planet. (1 mark)

**c)** A graph of gravitational field strength of Mars against distance $d$ from its centre is shown below.

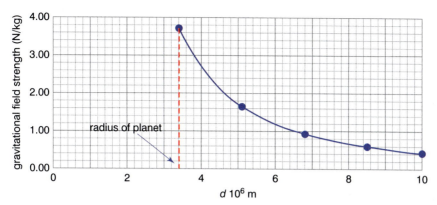

**i)** Describe the variation of gravitational field strength with $d$.        (1 mark)

**ii)** Suggest how the graph will change for a minor planet of the same radius but different mass.        (2 marks)

**iii)** A student suggests that the gravitational field strength is inversely proportional to $d$. Use the graph to deduce whether or not this suggestion is correct.        (2 marks)

**4.** Halley's comet orbits around the Sun in an elliptical orbit. Its average distance from the Sun is $2.7 \times 10^{12}$ m and its orbital duration (period) is 75 years.

**a) SUPPLEMENT** State when the comet will be fastest in its orbit.        (1 mark)

**b) SUPPLEMENT** Calculate the mean orbital speed in m/s of the comet. Assume 1 year = $3.15 \times 10^7$ s.        (3 marks)

**c) SUPPLEMENT** We will next see Halley's comet in the night sky in 2061. Its distance from the Earth will then be about $2.3 \times 10^{11}$ m.

Calculate the time light will take to travel a distance of $2.3 \times 10^{11}$ m.        (2 marks)

Δ Fig. 6.13 The bright patches of light are not stars, but thousands of distant galaxies imaged by the Hubble Space Telescope.

# Stars and the Universe

## INTRODUCTION

A galaxy is a collection of billions of stars held together in space by their own gravity. Our Sun belongs to a galaxy we call the Milky Way. Astronomers believe that there could be as many as a hundred billion galaxies in the space around us. Some are so far away that light from them has yet to reach us on the Earth. Our nearest galaxy is Andromeda Galaxy. The gravitational force between our Milky Way and Andromeda Galaxy will one day make them collide into each other. We do not need to worry about this, because it will happen many billions of years from now.

### KNOWLEDGE CHECK

✓ Microwaves, infrared, visible and ultraviolet are regions of the electromagnetic spectrum.
✓ **SUPPLEMENT** Nuclear fusion is the joining of nuclei.
✓ Like charges repel and unlike charges attract.
✓ **SUPPLEMENT** Speed of light is $3.0 \times 10^8$ m/s in a vacuum.

### LEARNING OBJECTIVES

✓ Know that the Sun is a star of medium size, consisting mostly of hydrogen and helium, and that it radiates most of its energy in the infrared, visible and ultraviolet regions of the electromagnetic spectrum.
✓ **SUPPLEMENT** Know that stars are powered by nuclear reactions that release energy and that in stable stars the nuclear reactions involve the fusion of hydrogen into helium.
✓ State that: galaxies are made up of many billions of stars; the Sun is a star in the galaxy known as the Milky Way; other stars that make up the Milky Way are much further away from the Earth than the Sun is from the Earth; astronomical distances can be measured in light-years, where one light-year is the distance travelled in (the vacuum of) space by light in one year.
✓ **SUPPLEMENT** Know that one light-year is equal to $9.5 \times 10^{15}$ m.
✓ **SUPPLEMENT** Describe the life cycle of a star: a star is formed from interstellar clouds of gas and dust that contain hydrogen; a protostar is an interstellar cloud collapsing and increasing in temperature as a result of its internal gravitational attraction; a protostar becomes a stable star when the inward force of gravitational attraction is balanced by an outward force due to the high temperature in the centre of the star; all stars eventually run out of hydrogen as fuel for the nuclear reaction;

most stars expand to form red giants and more massive stars expand to form red supergiants when most of the hydrogen in the centre of the star has been converted to helium; a red giant from a less massive star forms a planetary nebula with a white dwarf star at its centre; a red supergiant explodes as a supernova, forming a nebula containing hydrogen and new heavier elements, leaving behind a neutron star or a black hole at its centre; the nebula from a supernova may form new stars with orbiting planets.

✓ Know that the Milky Way is one of many billions of galaxies making up the Universe and that the diameter of the Milky Way is approximately 100 000 light-years.

✓ Describe redshift as an increase in the observed wavelength of electromagnetic radiation emitted from receding stars and galaxies.

✓ Know that the light emitted from distant galaxies appears redshifted in comparison with light emitted on the Earth.

✓ Know that redshift in the light from distant galaxies is evidence that the Universe is expanding and supports the Big Bang Theory.

✓ **SUPPLEMENT** Know that microwave radiation of a specific frequency is observed at all points in space around us and is known as cosmic microwave background radiation (CMBR).

✓ **SUPPLEMENT** Explain that the CMBR was produced shortly after the Universe was formed and that this radiation has been expanded into the microwave region of the electromagnetic spectrum as the Universe expanded.

✓ **SUPPLEMENT** Know that the speed $v$ at which a galaxy is moving away from the Earth can be found from the change in wavelength of the galaxy's starlight due to redshift.

✓ **SUPPLEMENT** Know that the distance of a far galaxy $d$ can be determined using the brightness of a supernova in that galaxy.

✓ **SUPPLEMENT** Define the Hubble constant $H_0$ as the ratio of the speed at which the galaxy is moving away from the Earth to its distance from the Earth; recall and use the equation $H_0 = \dfrac{v}{d}$.

✓ **SUPPLEMENT** Know that the current estimate for $H_0$ is $2.2 \times 10^{-18}$ per second.

✓ **SUPPLEMENT** Know that the equation $\dfrac{d}{v} = \dfrac{1}{H_0}$ represents an estimate for the age of the Universe and that this is evidence for the idea that all the matter in the Universe was present at a single point.

## THE SUN AS A STAR

If you look up at the sky at night you will see stars with a range of colours and brightness. The colour of a star is linked to its surface temperature – blue stars are hotter than red stars. Most of the yellow-coloured stars are just like our Sun.

Our Sun is a medium-size star consisting mostly of hydrogen and helium. It radiates its energy in the form of electromagnetic radiation mostly in the infrared, visible and ultraviolet regions of the electromagnetic spectrum.

△ Fig. 6.14 Our Sun is just a medium-size star.

Some stars are astonishingly huge. VY Canis Majoris is a cooler red star that is about 1400 times bigger than the Sun. By contrast, some stars are tiny. The star awkwardly named EBLM J0555-57Ab, discovered in 2017, is only the size of Saturn.

## NUCLEAR FUSION

How does the Sun produce its energy? The Sun produces energy by nuclear fusion reactions. In these reactions, enormous energy is released when hydrogen nuclei join, or fuse, together to form helium nuclei, see Fig. 6.15.

Fusion reactions take place deep within the core of the Sun where the pressures are immense and the temperature high at around 15 million °C. The positively charged hydrogen nuclei would normally stay away from each other because like charges repel. However, at these high temperatures, the hydrogen nuclei are travelling fast enough to get close enough to fuse with each other, and produce helium and lots of energy.

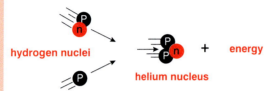

hydrogen nuclei

helium nucleus

+ energy

Δ Fig. 6.15 In a single fusion reaction, two hydrogen nuclei fuse together to produce a helium nucleus and lots of energy.

## QUESTIONS

1. Other than visible light, name two other electromagnetic waves radiated from the Sun.

2. **SUPPLEMENT** State what is released when hydrogen nuclei fuse together.

3. **SUPPLEMENT** Suggest why high temperatures help with fusion reactions.

## STARS

Our Sun, with its Solar System, is part of a galaxy known as the Milky Way. Far away from the bright city lights, the Milky Way can be seen in the night sky, see Fig. 6.16.

A galaxy consists of a large number of stars and dust held together by gravity. There could be as many as 100 billion stars in a galaxy. Our Milky Way is spiral in shape, very much like galaxy NGC 628 shown in Fig. 6.17. Our Sun is close to the edge of the Milky Way and is in one of the spiralling arms of the Milky Way, much like the spiralling arms of the NGC 628 galaxy.

All the stars we see in the night sky are in our own galaxy. They are all much further away from us than our Sun. It is not easy to appreciate the enormous astronomical distances in metres, so astronomers use light-years instead. One light-year is the distance travelled, in the vacuum of space, by light in one year. The nearest star to our Sun is 4.2 light-years or 630 billion metres. Our Milky Way has diameter 100 000 light-years or $9.5 \times 10^{20}$ m.

Δ Fig. 6.16 The Milky Way as seen in Namibia.

Δ Fig. 6.17 The NGC 628 spiral galaxy is similar to our Milky Way.

SUPPLEMENT

### LIGHT-YEAR

We know that the speed of light in a vacuum is $3.0 \times 10^8$ metres per second. This can be used to determine light-year in metres, as shown below.

light-year = speed of light in metres per second × I year in seconds

light-year = $3.0 \times 10^8 \times (365 \times 24 \times 3600)$

light-year = $9.5 \times 10^{15}$ m

To convert distance from:
- light-years to metres, you multiply by $9.5 \times 10^{15}$
- metres to light-years, you divide by $9.5 \times 10^{15}$.

1. What is the Milky Way?

2. State how many stars there are in a galaxy.

3. **SUPPLEMENT** A star is a distance of 7.2 light-years from us. State how many years it would take for the light from this star to reach us.

4. **SUPPLEMENT** The star VY Canis Majoris is $3.6 \times 10^{19}$ m from the Sun. Calculate this distance in light-years.

5. **SUPPLEMENT** The centre of the Milky Way is about 25 000 light-years from us. Calculate this distance in metres.

**SUPPLEMENT**

## LIFE CYCLE OF A STAR

A star is formed from interstellar clouds of gas and dust. The ultimate mass of the star depends on the original mass of the interstellar gas and dust cloud. Larger clouds will produce massive stars.

### Birth of a star

The gas is mainly hydrogen, with tiny amounts of helium. The internal gravitational attraction of the gas and dust particles collapses the cloud and makes it spin, and also increases its temperature. The gas cloud eventually spins faster, heats up and becomes a protostar.

The temperature within the core of a protostar can be about 15 million °C and fusion reactions between hydrogen nuclei occur to make helium nuclei. Fusion reactions release enormous energy, which further increases the temperature of the protostar. The protostar glows brightly. It becomes a stable star when the inward force of gravitational attraction is balanced by the outward force due to the high temperature in the centre of the star. The star will keep shining for millions to billions of years. This is the stage of our Sun right now.

### Fate of the star

The final fate of the star depends on its mass.

When a star with a similar mass to our Sun starts to run out of hydrogen in the core, it can no longer generate energy by fusion reactions to form helium. The core of the star becomes unstable and starts to contract. The outer layer of the star, which is mostly hydrogen, starts to expand. As it swells up, it cools and glows red in colour. The star has now become a red giant. Within the core of a red giant, helium starts to fuse into carbon. When the helium runs out, the core collapses again. The outer layers of the star are pushed away forming a planetary nebula (see Fig. 6.18) and the core collapses to become a white dwarf.

When a star more massive than the Sun runs low on hydrogen (the fuel for nuclear reactions) it starts to fuse helium into carbon. The star gets hotter and hotter and expands. It becomes a supergiant. Eventually this massive star explodes as a supernova. The explosion ejects into space a nebula containing hydrogen, and new heavier elements such as iron, gold and uranium are formed during this explosion. The remaining core of the star contracts and may form an extremely dense neutron star or, if the original star was extremely massive, a black hole. Black holes are even denser than neutron stars. Their gravitational pull is so huge that even light cannot escape from it.

The nebula from a supernova may, over billions of years, form new stars with orbiting planets, like our Solar System.

Fig. 6.19 shows that the life cycle of a star depends on its original mass.

△ Fig. 6.18 A planetary nebula in the constellation Aquarius.

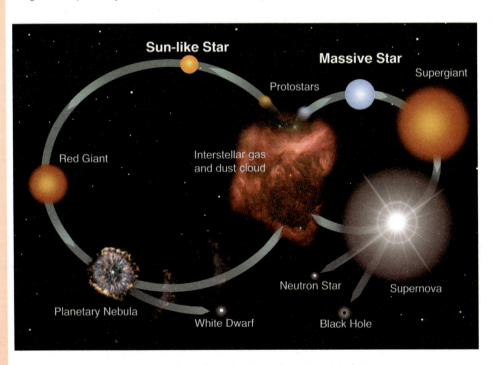

△ Fig. 6.19 Life cycle of stars. The fate of the star depends on its original mass.

1. **SUPPLEMENT** State why a star starts to expand into a red giant.

2. **SUPPLEMENT** Name two objects created at the end of the life cycle of a star that is much more massive than our Sun.

3. **SUPPLEMENT** Explain the conditions required for a stable star.

**SCIENCE IN CONTEXT**

# WHITE DWARFS

To the naked eye, one of the brightest stars in the night sky is Sirius. Powerful telescopes however show that Sirius is not one but two stars orbiting around each other. The main star, Sirius A, is large and bright, and its smaller companion, Sirius B, is a dim white dwarf.

The surface of Sirius B has a temperature of about 25 000 °C. It is much hotter than our Sun. What makes it dim in the night sky is its physical size. It has a diameter the same as our Earth, yet its mass is almost that of our Sun. Sirius B, like many other white dwarfs, is extremely dense.

Here are some amazing facts about white dwarfs like Sirius B.

△ Fig. 6.20 Subrahmanyan Chandrasekhar was awarded the 1983 Nobel Prize in Physics for working out the maximum mass of a white dwarf.

- The material of a white dwarf can be 200 000 times denser than water.

- The surface gravitational field strength can be 3500 000 N/kg. As a comparison, the surface field strength of the Sun is 290 N/kg and for the Earth it is only 10 N/kg.

- The mass of a white dwarf cannot exceed 1.44 times the mass of the Sun. This limit is known as Chandrasekhar limit, after Subrahmanyan Chandrasekhar, the Indian-born physicist.

- A white dwarf does not generate any energy from fusion reactions. It steadily cools down by radiating energy from its surface for a couple of billion years.

- A white dwarf can steal material from a neighbouring star and eventually become a supernova, releasing about $10^{44}$ J of energy in a short period of time.

**Challenge Question:** The majority of the stars in our Milky Way will evolve into white dwarfs. Why is it that we do not see the night skies full of these mysterious white dwarfs?

## THE UNIVERSE

The Universe is everything we can see and detect around us. Our Sun is part of the Milky Way. The Milky Way is about 100 000 light-years in diameter. The Milky Way is one of about 100 billion galaxies that make up the Universe. Some galaxies, like the Andromeda galaxy, are close to us, but some are so far away that light from them has yet to reach us. The space between galaxies is mostly vacuum. The Universe is huge – it could have a diameter of about 90 billion light-years.

### Big Bang Theory

The Big Bang Theory is a model used to explain how the Universe came into existence, and also its subsequent evolution. The Universe began from a single point, then for some unknown reason it began to expand from a hot explosion. This event, known as the Big Bang, was the birth of the Universe. Before the birth of the Universe, there was no space, no matter, and no time.

Space has been expanding and stretching ever since the Big Bang. Stars and galaxies created soon after the Big Bang have been carried away by the stretching of space. From the Earth, we see all the galaxies rushing away from us – this is evidence for the Big Bang and the expansion of the Universe.

How do astronomers know that the Big Bang took place some 14 billion years ago? The evidence comes from the redshift of light.

### Redshift

The spectrum from the Sun, observed from Earth, shows dark lines set against a continuous spectrum of colours. These dark lines are caused by the Sun's atmosphere absorbing specific colours of light emitted from the Sun. All the galaxies in the Universe are receding from us. The spectrum of light from the stars of a distant receding galaxy is almost identical to that of the Sun, but there is one major difference. All the dark lines observed in the spectrum are shifted towards the longer wavelengths. This is called redshift because the lines are shifted towards the red end of the visible spectrum, see Fig. 6.21. The redshift in the light from distant galaxies is evidence that the Universe is expanding and supports the Big Bang Theory.

There is an equivalent of redshift of light with sound waves. Imagine a police car moving away from us with its siren on. We would hear a lower-pitch sound, or detect sound of longer wavelength than if the police car was stationary.

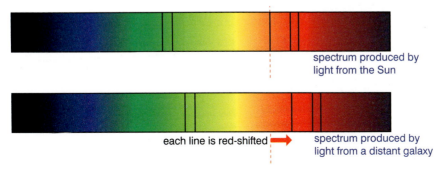

spectrum produced by light from the Sun

each line is red-shifted

spectrum produced by light from a distant galaxy

△ Fig. 6.21 The whole pattern of lines from a distant galaxy has been red-shifted compared with light from the Sun.

## COSMIC MICROWAVE BACKGROUND RADIATION (CMBR)

The Universe began from an extremely hot explosion. At the start of this creation, there was no matter in the Universe but it was full of short-wavelength electromagnetic radiation. As the Universe expanded, the fabric of space itself stretched, and this also stretched out these short-wavelength waves. We now observe these waves in the microwave region of the electromagnetic spectrum. Most of them have a wavelength of about 1 mm. The whole of the Universe is currently filled up with these microwaves. We can detect these microwaves, known as cosmic background radiation (CMBR), coming from all directions of space around us.

△ Fig. 6.22 Wilson and Penzias with their radio telescope.

The expansion of the Universe led to the cooling of its overall temperature. Its temperature now is about −270 °C.

The first-ever detection of CMBR was a pure accident. Two astrophysicists, Arno Penzias and Robert Wilson, were using a large radio telescope to communicate with orbiting satellites, but had problems because they could not get rid of 'static' noise coming from all directions of space. They even cleaned the bird droppings on their telescope to get rid of this unwanted signal. It was only through a chance conversation with other physicists that they realised that the telescope was picking up CMBR. For their pioneering work, both physicists were awarded the Nobel Prize in Physics in 1978.

## AGE OF THE UNIVERSE

The receding speed $v$ of a galaxy from the Earth can be determined from the change in the wavelength of starlight due to redshift. The greater the change in the wavelength, the greater the speed $v$. Some supernovas are unique – they release the same amount of energy when they explode. The brightness of a supernova in a particular galaxy can be used to determine the distance $d$ of the galaxy.

Fig. 6.23 shows a graph of $v$ against $d$. Although there is considerable scatter of the data, it is clear that $v$ is directly proportional to $d$. The further the galaxy is from us, the faster it is moving away from us. The gradient of the straight line is equal to the Hubble constant $H_0$. We can define the Hubble constant as the ratio of the speed at which the galaxy is moving away from the Earth to its distance from the Earth, therefore:

$$H_0 = \frac{v}{d}$$

The current estimate for $H_0$ is about $2.2 \times 10^{-18}$ per second.

The Universe is expanding – the galaxies are receding from each other because the space itself is expanding. If we could run time backwards, the Universe would be much smaller, denser, and hotter, and would eventually reach a single point just before its birth.

The age of the Universe in seconds can be estimated from the equation:

$$\text{age of Universe} = \frac{d}{v} = \frac{1}{H_0}$$

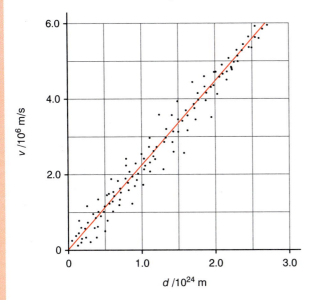

△ Fig. 6.23 Graph of receding speed $v$ against distance $d$ for galaxies in the Universe.

### WORKED EXAMPLE

The Hubble constant is about $2.2 \times 10^{-18}$ per second. Estimate the age of the Universe in years.

First, determine the age in seconds.

$$\text{age of Universe} = \frac{1}{H_0}$$

$$\text{age of Universe} = \frac{1}{2.2 \times 10^{-18}} = 4.45 \times 10^{17} \text{ seconds}$$

Now convert the age into years.

$$1 \text{ year} = 365 \times 24 \times 60 \times 60 = 3.15 \times 10^7 \text{ s}$$

$$\text{age of Universe} = \frac{4.45 \times 10^{17}}{3.15 \times 10^7} = 1.4 \times 10^{10} \text{ years}$$

1 billion years = $10^9$ years, therefore the age of the Universe is about 14 billion years.

1. State what happened to the Universe after the Big Bang.

2. State the significance of redshift in the starlight from a distant galaxy.

3. **SUPPLEMENT** Where would you detect cosmic background radiation (CMBR)?

4. **SUPPLEMENT** State how the distance of a galaxy is determined.

5. **SUPPLEMENT** Describe how spectrum of starlight can be used to determine the speed of a galaxy.

6. **SUPPLEMENT** State the relationship between receding speed $v$ of a galaxy and its distance $d$ from us.

7. **SUPPLEMENT** Estimate the Hubble constant given $v = 11\,000$ km/s and $d = 5.0 \times 10^{24}$ m.

# End of topic checklist

## Key terms

Big Bang Theory, galaxy, Milky Way, redshift

**SUPPLEMENT** black hole, cosmic microwave background radiation (CMBR), fusion, Hubble constant $H_0$, red giant, neutron star, planetary nebula, protostar, supergiant, supernova, white dwarf

## During your study of this topic you should have learned:

○ The Sun is a star of medium size, consisting mostly of hydrogen and helium.

○ The Sun radiates most of its energy in the infrared, visible and ultraviolet regions of the electromagnetic spectrum.

○ **SUPPLEMENT** Stars are powered by nuclear reactions that release energy.

○ A galaxy is made up of many billions of stars.

○ The Sun is a star in the galaxy known as the Milky Way.

○ Stars that make up the Milky Way are much further away from the Earth than the Sun is from the Earth.

○ Astronomical distances can be measured in light-years.

○ **SUPPLEMENT** One light-year is the distance travelled in (the vacuum of) space by light in one year.

○ **SUPPLEMENT** 1 light-year = $9.5 \times 10^{15}$ m.

○ **SUPPLEMENT** In stable stars the nuclear reactions involve the fusion of hydrogen into helium.

○ **SUPPLEMENT** A star is formed from interstellar clouds of gas and dust that contain hydrogen.

○ **SUPPLEMENT** A protostar is an interstellar cloud collapsing and increasing in temperature as a result of its internal gravitational attraction.

○ **SUPPLEMENT** A protostar becomes a stable star when the inward force of gravitational attraction is balanced by an outward force due to the high temperature in the centre of the star.

○ **SUPPLEMENT** All stars will eventually run out of hydrogen as fuel for the nuclear reaction.

○ **SUPPLEMENT** Most stars expand to form red giants.

○ **SUPPLEMENT** More massive stars expand to form red supergiants when most of the hydrogen in the centre of the star has been converted to helium.

○ **SUPPLEMENT** A red giant from a less massive star forms a planetary nebula with a white dwarf star at its centre.

○ **SUPPLEMENT** A red supergiant explodes as a supernova, forming a nebula containing hydrogen and new heavier elements, leaving behind a neutron star or a black hole at its centre.

○ **SUPPLEMENT** The nebula from a supernova may form new stars with orbiting planets.

○ The Milky Way is one of many billions of galaxies making up the Universe.

○ The diameter of the Milky Way is approximately 100 000 light-years.

○ Redshift is an increase in the observed wavelength of electromagnetic radiation emitted from receding stars and galaxies.

○ The light emitted from distant galaxies appears redshifted in comparison with light emitted on the Earth.

○ Redshift in the light from distant galaxies is evidence that the Universe is expanding, and supports the Big Bang Theory.

○ **SUPPLEMENT** Cosmic microwave background radiation (CMBR) is the microwave radiation of a specific frequency and is observed at all points in space around us.

○ **SUPPLEMENT** CMBR was produced shortly after the Universe was formed and has been expanded into the microwave region of the electromagnetic spectrum as the Universe expanded.

○ **SUPPLEMENT** The speed $v$ at which a galaxy is moving away from the Earth can be found from the change in wavelength of the galaxy's starlight due to redshift.

○ **SUPPLEMENT** The distance of a far galaxy $d$ can be determined using the brightness of a supernova in that galaxy.

○ **SUPPLEMENT** Hubble constant $H_0$ is defined as the ratio of the speed $v$ at which the galaxy is moving away from the Earth to its distance $d$ from the Earth; $H_0 = \dfrac{v}{d}$.

○ **SUPPLEMENT** The current estimate for $H_0$ is $2.2 \times 10^{-18}$ per second.

○ **SUPPLEMENT** Age of the Universe $= \dfrac{d}{v}$ and age of the Universe $= \dfrac{1}{H_0}$.

○ **SUPPLEMENT** The age of the universe is evidence for the idea that all the matter in the Universe was present at a single point.

# End of topic questions

*Note: the marks in brackets give an indication of the level of detail you should include in your answers.*

1. **a)** What is the name of the galaxy that contains the Earth and our Sun?

    **A** Andromeda

    **B** Milky Way

    **C** Canis Major

    **D** Virgo                                                                 (1 mark)

    **b)** State the diameter of our galaxy in light-years.                     (1 mark)

    **c)** There are about 100 000 000 000 stars in a galaxy.

    The mass of a typical star is $2.0 \times 10^{30}$ kg. Estimate the total mass of our galaxy.                                                           (2 marks)

2. The star Tau Ceti is similar to our Sun. It is about 12 light-years from us.

    **a)** State three types of electromagnetic radiation emitted by this star.   (3 marks)

    **b)** Explain why Tau Ceti must be in our Milky Way.                         (2 marks)

    **c)** Define the light-year.                                                 (1 mark)

    **d)** **SUPPLEMENT** Calculate the distance of Tau Ceti in metres.          (2 marks)

    **e)** **SUPPLEMENT** Explain how hydrogen within its core produces energy.   (2 marks)

3. **SUPPLEMENT a)** An astronomer keeps detecting microwave radiation coming from all directions of space.

    **i)** State what the astronomer is detecting.                              (1 mark)

    **ii)** Explain the significance of these microwaves.                        (3 marks)

    **b)** Explain the significance of redshift of starlight from a distant galaxy.   (1 mark)

**c)** The velocity $v$ against distance $d$ is shown for galaxies in the Universe.

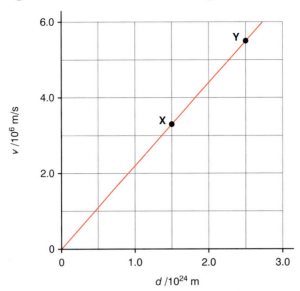

Two galaxies X and Y are marked on the graph.

**i)** State and explain which galaxy will show greater redshift. (2 marks)

**ii)** For galaxy Y, $v = 5.5 \times 10^6$ m/s and $d = 2.5 \times 10^{24}$ m.

Use this information to determine the age of the Universe in seconds. (3 marks)

## COMMENTS

**1. a)** The key technical term 'phases' of the Moon has been correctly stated.

**b)** The idea of gravitational attraction is correctly given. Objects, such as planets, orbit the Sun because of its gravitational pull.

To improve the answer, this needed to be expanded to include the idea that the Sun is far more massive than objects orbiting around it. The term 'big' is not equivalent to 'having greater mass'. The Sun being 'hot' has nothing to do with the question.

**c)** This answer is the inverse of the correct answer – so the rearranging was incorrect. The correct answer is:

$$\text{time} = \frac{5.0 \times 10^{12}}{3.0 \times 10^{8}} = 16\,700 \text{ s}$$

(4.6 hours)

# Exam-style questions

*Note: exam-style questions, sample answers and comments have been written by the authors. The marks awarded for these questions indicate the level of detail required in the answers. In examinations, the way marks are awarded may be different. References to assessment and/or assessment preparation are the publisher's interpretation of the syllabus requirements and may not fully reflect the approach of Cambridge Assessment International Education.*

## Example answer

## Question 1

**a)** State the evidence that the Moon orbits around the Earth. (1)

*The Moon shows phases - it must therefore be orbiting the Earth.* ✓

**b)** Explain why the objects in the Solar System orbit around the Sun. (2)

*Objects such as planets orbit the Sun because of its gravitational pull.* ✓

*Planets orbit the Sun because it is big and hot.* ✗

**c)** The dwarf planet Pluto is $5.0 \times 10^{12}$ m from the Earth.

The speed of light in vacuum is $3.0 \times 10^8$ m/s.

Calculate the time it takes for light from Pluto to reach the Earth. (3)

*distance = speed × time* ✓

*$5.0 \times 10^{12} = 3.0 \times 10^8 \times time$* ✓

*time = 0.00006 s* ✗

(Total 6 marks)

## Question 2

**a)** Describe the Milky Way and state its approximate diameter. (2)

**b)** Explain redshift of light from distant galaxies and its significance to the Universe. (3)

(Total 5 marks)

## Question 3 SUPPLEMENT

**a)  i)** Explain how astronomers determine the distance $d$ and speed $v$ of a distant galaxy. (2)

   **ii)** The figure below shows the Triangulum Galaxy.

For this galaxy, $d = 8.2 \times 10^{22}$ m and $v = 180\,000$ m/s.

Use this information to calculate the age of the Universe in   seconds. (3)

**b)** Explain how the cosmic microwave background radiation (CMBR) provides evidence for the Big Bang Theory. (3)

(Total 8 marks)

# Developing experimental skills

## INTRODUCTION

As part of your Cambridge IGCSE Physics course, you will develop practical skills and have to carry out investigative work in science.

This section provides guidance on carrying out an investigation.

The experimental and investigative skills are divided as follows:

**1.** Using and organising techniques, apparatus and materials
**2.** Planning experiments and investigations
**3.** Observing, measuring and recording
**4.** Interpreting observations and data
**5.** Evaluating methods

## 1. USING AND ORGANISING TECHNIQUES, APPARATUS AND MATERIALS

**Skill**: demonstrate knowledge of how to select and safely use techniques, apparatus and materials (including following a sequence of instructions where appropriate)

**Questions to ask**:

**How shall I use the equipment safely to minimise the risks – what are my safety precautions?**

✓ When writing a Risk Assessment, investigators need to be careful to check that they've matched the hazard with the technique used.

✓ You should be able to describe the precautions taken when carrying out an investigation.

**How much detail should I give in my description?**

✓ You need to give enough detail so that someone else who has not done the experiment would be able to carry it out to reproduce your results.

✓ You may need to draw, complete or label diagrams of apparatus and should be able to identify apparatus from diagrams and descriptions.

**How should I use the equipment to give me the precision I need?**

✓ You should know how to read the scales on the measuring equipment you are using.

✓ You need to show that you are aware of the precision needed.

EXAMPLE 1

◁ Fig. 7.1 The volume of liquid in a measuring cylinder must be read to the bottom of the meniscus. The volume in this measuring cylinder is 202 cm³ (ml), not 204 cm³.

## EXAMPLE 2

This is an extract from a student's notebook. It describes the precautions they took when investigating loading a spring.

### Precautions taken to improve reliability

*It's important to take precautions in order to make the readings as reliable as possible. I will view the scale at right angles in order to prevent a parallax error.*

### Safety measures

*Potential risk: The spring may break or the masses may fall off. The spring may flick and could damage face/eyes.*

*Safety measure: I will wear eye protection to protect my eyes in case the spring flicks up.*

### COMMENT

The student has identified a risk and described the precautions to be taken when carrying out the investigation.

## EXAMPLE 3

This is an extract from a student's notebook. It describes how they investigated terminal velocity.

### Experimental detail

The student's method is given below.

1  *The tube was marked every 10 cm using tape.*

2  *The ball was released carefully from the surface of the oil.*

3  *At the same time, a stopclock was started.*

4  *As the ball passed each mark, the time was noted.*

5  *Since the marks are 10 cm apart, the speed of the ball in each section of the tube can be calculated.*

## Precision and accuracy

An example from the notebook is:

*The speed measured to the nearest 0.1 cm/s.*

**COMMENT**

The method is well written and detailed. Point 1 could have been improved if the student had noted the width of the tape used.
The student has appreciated the accuracy that can be achieved using this method.

## 2. PLANNING EXPERIMENTS AND INVESTIGATIONS

**Skill**: to devise and plan investigations, drawing on physics knowledge and understanding in selecting appropriate techniques.

**Questions to ask:**

**What do I already know about the area of physics I am investigating and how can I use this knowledge and understanding to help me with my plan?**

✓ Think about what you have already learned and any investigations you have already done that are relevant to this investigation.

✓ List the factors that might affect the process you are investigating.

**What is the best method or technique to use?**

✓ Think about whether you can use or adapt a method that you have already used.

✓ A method, and the measuring instruments, must be able to produce **valid** measurements. A measurement is valid if it measures what it is supposed to be measuring.

You will make a decision as to which technique to use based on:

✓ the accuracy and precision of the results required; investigators might require results that are as accurate and precise as possible but if you are doing a quick comparison, or a preliminary test to check a range over which results should be collected, a high level of accuracy and precision may not be required

✓ the simplicity or difficulty of the techniques available, or the cost of the equipment required.

✓ the scale, for example using standard laboratory equipment or on a micro-scale, which may give results in a shorter time period

✓ the time available to do the investigation

✓ health and safety considerations.

**What am I going to measure?**

✓ The factor you are investigating is called the **independent variable**. A **dependent variable** is affected or changed by the independent variable that you select.

✓ You need to choose a range of measurements that will be enough to allow you to plot a graph of your results and so find out the pattern in your results.

✓ You should be able to explain why you have chosen your range rather than a lower or higher range.

**How am I going to control the other variables?**

✓ These are **control variables**. Some of these may be difficult to control.

✓ You must decide how you are going to control any other variables in the investigation and so ensure that you are using a fair test and that any conclusions you draw are valid.

**What equipment is suitable and will give me the accuracy and precision I need?**

✓ The **accuracy** of a measurement is how close it is to its true value.

✓ **Precision** is related to the smallest scale division on the measuring instrument that you are using; for example, when measuring a distance, a rule marked in millimetres will give greater precision than one divided into centimetres only.

✓ A set of precise measurements also refers to measurements that have very little spread about the mean value.

✓ You need to be sensible about selecting your devices and make a judgement about the degree of precision. Think about what is the least precise variable you are measuring and choose suitable measuring devices. There is no point having instruments that are much more precise than the precision you can measure the variable to.

**What are the potential hazards of the equipment and technique I will be using and how can I reduce the risks associated with these hazards?**

✓ Be prepared to suggest safety precautions when presented with details of a physics investigation.

**EXAMPLE 4**

You have been asked to design and plan an investigation to explore the motion of a trolley down a ramp. In a previous investigation you have investigated such motion using ticker tape so you are familiar with what happens and the measurements you need to take.

## What do I already know?

Previously you have investigated the motion of a trolley down a ramp. You know that you can use ticker tape to measure the distance the trolley travels in a given time.

## What is the best method or technique to use?

The technique you used in your previous investigation can be re-used. You set up the apparatus as shown in the diagram.

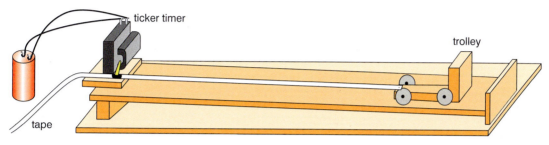

△ Fig. 7.2 Trolley and ramp apparatus for the investigation.

## What am I going to measure?

You are investigating the motion of a trolley down a ramp. You will measure the length of each 5-dot strip of ticket tape with a ruler.

## How am I going to control the other variables?

It is important that you decide on the angle at which to set the ramp at the start. As you have carried out this investigation before, you can look back and see what angle you used previously and decide whether you will use the same angle, or increase or decrease it.

## What equipment is suitable and will it give me the accuracy and precision I need?

You now know what you will need to measure and so can decide on your measuring devices.

| Measurement | Quantity | Device |
| --- | --- | --- |
| Length of ticker tape | 5-dot strips | Ruler so can measure to nearest mm |

△ Table 7.1 Suitable equipment for experiment.

Choosing a ruler marked in mm is just right for the measurement of the length.

## What are the potential hazards and how can I reduce the risks?

The hazards are as follows:

✔ trolley and ramp.

In terms of the equipment and technique, the major hazard will be the trolley rolling off the end of the ramp. You can limit this hazard by putting a buffer at the end of the ramp as shown in Fig. 7.2.

# 3. OBSERVING, MEASURING AND RECORDING

**Skill**: Make and record observations, measurements and estimates.

**Questions to ask**:

## How many different measurements or observations do I need to take?

✓ Sufficient readings have been taken to ensure that the data are consistent.

✓ It is usual to repeat an experiment to get more than one measurement. If an investigator takes just one measurement, this may not be typical of what would normally happen when the experiment was carried out.

✓ When repeat readings are consistent they are said to be **repeatable**.

## Do I need to repeat any measurements or observations that are anomalous?

✓ An **anomalous result** or **outlier** is a result that is not consistent with other results.

✓ You want to be sure a single result is accurate (as in Example 5). So you will need to repeat the experiment until you get close agreement in the results you obtain.

✓ If an investigator has made repeat measurements, they would normally use these to calculate the arithmetical mean (or just mean or average) of these data to give a more accurate result. You calculate the mean by adding together all the measurements, and dividing by the number of measurements. Be careful, though: anomalous results should not be included when taking averages.

✓ Anomalous results might be the consequence of an error made in measurement. But sometimes outliers are genuine results. If you think an outlier has been introduced by careless practical work, you should omit it when calculating the mean. But you should examine possible reasons carefully before just leaving it out.

✓ You are taking a number of readings in order to see a changing pattern. For example, measuring the speed every 10 cm for 60 cm (so six different readings). It is likely that you will plot your results onto a graph and then draw a **line of best fit**.

✓ You can often pick an anomalous reading out from a results table (or a graph if all the data points have been plotted), as well as the mean, to show the range of data. It may be a good idea to repeat this part of the practical again, but it's not necessary if the results show good consistency.

✓ If you are confident that you can draw a line of best fit through most of the points, it is not necessary to repeat any measurements that are obviously inaccurate. If, however, the pattern is not clear enough to draw a graph then readings will need to be repeated.

# How should I record my measurements or observations – is a table the best way? What headings and units should I use?

✓ A table is often the best way to record results.

✓ Headings should be clear.

✓ If a table contains numerical data, do not forget to include units; data are meaningless without them.

✓ The units should be the same as those that are on the measuring equipment you are using.

✓ Sometimes you are recording observations that are not quantities. Putting observations in a table with headings is a good way of presenting this information.

## EXAMPLE 5

The student from Example 3 has recorded the results in a table as shown below.

| Distance fallen through oil (cm) | Speed 1st experiment (cm/s) | Speed 2nd experiment (cm/s) | Speed 3rd experiment (cm/s) |
|---|---|---|---|
| 0 | 0.0 | 0.1 | 0.1 |
| 10 | 2.4 | 2.4 | 2.3 |
| 20 | 4.4 | 4.3 | 4.4 |
| 30 | 5.6 | 5.6 | 5.7 |
| 40 | 6.0 | 5.9 | 5.9 |
| 50 | 6.4 | 6.4 | 6.3 |
| 60 | 6.4 | 6.3 | 6.4 |

△ Table 7.2 Readings from investigation.

## EXAMPLE 6

In an experiment to investigate the efficiency of a small motor the student has sensibly recorded her results in a table. Notice each column has a heading *and* units.

| Mass lifted/ kg | Distance lifted/m | Useful work done/J | Voltage of motor/V | Current in motor/A | Time to lift the mass/s | Electrical energy supplied/J |
|---|---|---|---|---|---|---|
| 0.01 | 1.0 | | 2.4 | 0.20 | 22.0 | |
| 0.03 | 1.0 | | 2.4 | 0.22 | 24.4 | |
| 0.05 | 1.0 | | 2.4 | 0.25 | 26.5 | |
| 0.07 | 1.0 | | 2.3 | 0.28 | 27.6 | |
| 0.09 | 1.0 | | 2.3 | 0.29 | 28.7 | |

△ Table 7.3 Table of results.

EXAMPLE 7

In another experiment the student has recorded his results obtained in an experiment to investigate the strength of an electromagnet as the current in the coil varies.

variable resistor

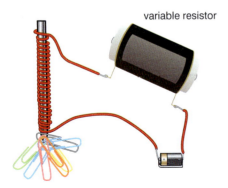

△ Fig. 7.3 Apparatus for experiment.

| Current/A | Number of paper clips held |
|-----------|----------------------------|
| 0 | 0 |
| 0.3 | 2 |
| 0.5 | 5 |
| 0.7 | 6 |
| 0.9 | 9 |
| 1.0 | 9 |

△ Table 7.4 Results of experiment.

**COMMENT**

In this table of results:

the description of each measurement is clear.

the units are given in each case.

# 4. INTERPRETING OBSERVATIONS AND DATA

**Skill**: Interpret and evaluate experimental observations and data.

**Questions to ask**:

## What is the best way to show the pattern in my results? Should I use a bar chart, line graph or scatter graph?

✓ Graphs are usually the best way of demonstrating trends in data.

✓ A bar chart or bar graph is used when one of the variables is a **categoric variable**; for example, when the melting points of the oxides of the group 2 elements are shown for each oxide, the names are categoric and not continuous variables.

✓ A line graph is used when both variables are continuous, for example time and temperature, time and volume.

✓ Scatter graphs can be used to show the intensity of a relationship, or degree of *correlation*, between two variables.

✓ Sometimes a line of best fit is added to a scatter graph, but usually the points are left without a line.

When drawing bar charts or line graphs:

✓ Choose scales that take up most of the graph paper

✓ Make sure the axes are linear and allow points to be plotted accurately. Each square on an axis should represent the same quantity. For example, one big square = 5 or 10 units; not 3 units

✓ Label the axes with the variables (ideally with the independent variable on the *x*-axis)

✓ Make sure the axes have units

✓ If more than one set of data is plotted use a key to distinguish the different data sets.

## If I use a line graph should I join the points with a straight line or a smooth curve?

✓ When you draw a line, do not just join the dots!

✓ Remember there may be some points that don't fall on the curve – these may be incorrect or anomalous results.

✓ A graph will often make it obvious which results are anomalous and so it would not be necessary to repeat the experiment (see Example 4).

## Do I have to calculate anything from my results?

✓ It will be usual to calculate means from the data.

✓ Sometimes it is helpful to make other calculations, before plotting a graph; for example, you might calculate $\dfrac{1}{time}$ for a rate of reaction experiment.

✓ Sometimes you will have to make some calculations before you can draw any conclusions.

**Can I draw a conclusion from my analysis of the results, and what physics knowledge and understanding can be used to explain the conclusion?**

✓ You need to use your physics knowledge and understanding to explain your conclusion.

✓ It is important to be able to add some explanation which refers to relevant scientific ideas in order to justify your conclusion.

**What is the best way to show the pattern in my results?**

✓ If the experiment involves **continuous variables,** a line graph is needed.

**Straight line or a smooth curve?**

✓ The results obtained will either require a smooth curve or a straight line of best fit. The shape of the results should show you which is needed. In physics experiments you will often need to draw a line of best fit.

**Do I have to calculate anything from my results?**

✓ If you have to calculate a quantity you will often be able to do this by looking at the change in steepness/gradient of the curve.

**Can I draw a conclusion from my analysis of the results?**

✓ You need to write a sentence summarising what you have learned from your investigation.

✓ Make sure that you write a clear statement. You might refer, for example, to 'the gradient of the line' at points 1, 2 and 3 to make your conclusion even more precise.

**What physics knowledge and understanding can be used to explain the conclusion?**

✓ You need to be able to explain your results using your knowledge of the physics of the situation.

### COMMENT

A good conclusion will make direct links to scientific knowledge in relation to the topic.

## 5 EVALUATING METHODS

**Skill**: Evaluate methods and suggest possible improvements

**Questions to ask**:

### Do any of my results stand out as being inaccurate or anomalous?

✓ You need to look for any anomalous results or outliers that do not fit the pattern.

✓ You can often pick this out from a results table (or a graph if all the data points have been plotted), as well as the mean, to show the range of data.

### What reasons can I give for any inaccurate results?

✓ When answering questions like this it is important to be specific. Answers such as 'experimental error' are too vague.

✓ It is often possible to look at the practical technique and suggest explanations for anomalous results.

✓ When you carry out the experiment you will have a better idea of which possible sources of error are more likely.

✓ Try to give a specific source of error and avoid statements such as 'the measurements must have been wrong'.

Your conclusion will be based on your findings, but must take into consideration any uncertainty in these introduced by any possible sources of error. You should discuss where these have come from in your evaluation.

**Error** is a difference between a measurement you make, and its true value.

The two types of errors are:

✓ random error

✓ systematic error.

With **random error**, measurements vary in an unpredictable way. This can occur when the instrument you're using to measure lacks sufficient precision to indicate differences in readings. It can also occur when it is difficult to make a measurement.

With **systematic error**, readings vary in a controlled way. They are either consistently too high or too low. One reason could be down to the way you are making a reading, e.g. taking a burette reading at the wrong point on the meniscus, or not being directly in front of an instrument when reading from it.

What an investigator *should not* discuss in an evaluation are problems introduced by using faulty equipment, or by using the equipment inappropriately. These errors can, or could have been, eliminated, by:

✓ checking equipment

✓ practising techniques before the investigation, and taking care and patience when carrying out the practical.

## Overall was the method or technique I used precise enough?

✓ If your results were good enough to provide a confident answer to the problem you were investigating, the method probably was good enough.

✓ If you realise your results are not precise when you compare your conclusion with the actual answer, it may be that you have a **systematic error** (an error that has been made in obtaining all the results). A systematic error would indicate an overall problem with the experimental method.

✓ If your results do not show a convincing pattern then it is fair to assume that your method or technique was not precise enough and there may have been a **random error** (i.e. measurements vary in an unpredictable way).

## If I were to do the investigation again what would I change or improve upon?

✓ Having identified possible errors it is important to say how these could be overcome. Again you should try and be absolutely precise.

✓ When suggesting improvements, do not just say 'do it more accurately next time' or 'measure the volumes more accurately next time'.

✓ For example, if you were measuring small lengths, you could improve the method by using a vernier scale to measure the lengths rather than a ruler.

### EXAMPLE 8

A student was measuring how current varies with voltage. He used the circuit shown in Fig. 7.4.

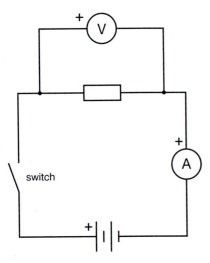

△ Fig. 7.4 Circuit used to measure how current varies with voltage.

## Do any of my results stand out as being inaccurate or anomalous?

The student plotted his results on a graph, as shown in Fig. 7.5. An inaccurate result stands out from the rest, as shown by the circle on the graph. Given the pattern obtained with the other results there is no real need to repeat the result – you could be very confident that the result should have followed the pattern set by the others. A result like this is referred to as an anomalous result. It was an error but not a systematic error.

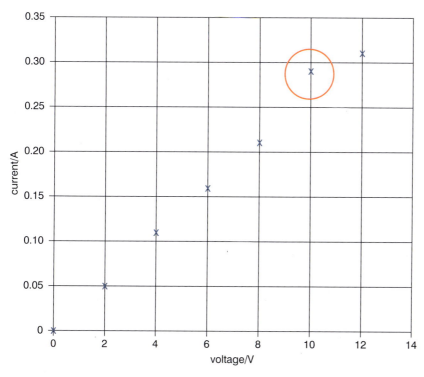

△ Fig. 7.5 Graph of results.

## What reasons can I give for any inaccurate results?

The possible source of the error is that one of the variables was noted incorrectly.

## Was the method or technique I used precise enough?

You can be reasonably confident that using digital meters for the current and voltage readings will give you precise measurements.

## How can I improve the investigation?

For example, you could take readings after the component has heated up so that the steady state resistance is noted.

# Preparing for your examinations

## INTRODUCTION

Examinations will test how good your understanding of scientific ideas is, how well you can apply your understanding to new situations and how well you can analyse and interpret information you have been given. The assessments are opportunities to show how well you can do these.

To prepare for your exams you need to:

✓ have a good knowledge and understanding of science
✓ be able to apply this knowledge and understanding to familiar and new situations
✓ be able to interpret and evaluate evidence that you have just been given.

You need to be able to do these things under exam conditions.

## EXAMINATION TECHNIQUES

To help you to work to your best abilities in exams, there are a few simple steps to follow.

### Check your understanding of the question

✓ **Read the introduction to each question carefully before moving on to the questions themselves**.
✓ Look in detail at any **diagrams, graphs** or **tables**.
✓ Underline or circle the **key words** in the question.
✓ **Make sure you answer the question that is being asked** rather than the one you wish had been asked!
✓ Make sure that you understand the meaning of the '**command words**' in the questions.

### REMEMBER
Any information you are given is there to help you to answer the question.

✓ **Calculate:** work out from given facts, figures or information

✓ **Comment:** give an informed opinion

✓ **Compare:** identify/comment on similarities and/or differences

✓ **Deduce:** conclude from available information

✓ **Define:** give precise meaning

✓ **Describe:** state the points of a topic / give characteristics and main features

✓ **Determine:** establish an answer using the information available

✓ **Explain:** set out purposes or reasons / make the relationships between things evident / provide why and/or how and support with relevant evidence

✓ **Give:** produce an answer from a given source or recall/memory

✓ **Identify:** name/select/recognise

✓ **Justify:** support a case with evidence/argument

✓ **Predict:** suggest what may happen based on available information

✓ **Sketch:** make a simple freehand drawing showing the key features, taking care over proportions

✓ **State:** express in clear terms

✓ **Suggest:** apply knowledge and understanding to situations where there are a range of valid responses in order to make proposals / put forward considerations

*The information in this section is taken from the Cambridge International syllabus for examination from 2023. You should always refer to the appropriate syllabus document for the year of your examination to confirm the details and for more information. The syllabus document is available on the Cambridge International website at www. cambridgeinternational.org.*

## Check the number of marks for each question

✓ Look at the **number of marks** allocated to each question.

✓ Look at the **space provided** to guide you as to the length of your answer.

✓ Make sure you include at least as many points in your answer as there are marks.

✓ Do not use any more space than the space that has been provided in the examination paper.

Beware of continually writing too much because it probably means you are not really answering the questions.

## Use your time effectively

✓ Don't spend so long on some questions that you don't have time to finish the paper.

✓ If you are really stuck on a question, leave it, finish the rest of the paper and come back to it at the end.

✓ Even if you eventually have to guess at an answer, this gives you a better chance of getting it right than if you leave it blank.

## ANSWERING QUESTIONS

✓ In short-answer questions, **don't write more than you are asked for**.

✓ Present the information in a logical sequence.

✓ Don't be afraid to also use **labelled diagrams** or **flow charts** if it helps you to show your answer more clearly.

✓ **In calculations always show your working**. Even if your final answer is incorrect, part of your attempt may be correct.

✓ Write down your answers to as many **significant figures** as are used in the numbers in the question (and no more). If the question doesn't state how many significant figures, then a good general rule is to quote 3 significant figures.

✓ Don't round off too early in calculations with many steps – it's always better to give too many significant figures than too few.

✓ Use the correct **units**. In some questions the units will be mentioned, for example, 'Calculate the mass in grams'. The units may also be given on the answer line.

✓ When you've finished your exam, check through your paper to make sure you've answered all the questions.

✓ Check that you haven't missed any questions at the end of the paper or turned over two pages at once and missed questions.

✓ Cover over your answers and read through the questions again and check that your answers are as good as you can make them.

**REMEMBER**

It is important that you understand the methods used by scientists when carrying out investigative work and are able to answer questions on them.

# Glossary

**acceleration** A change in speed divided by the time taken to change.

**air resistance** The drag caused by something moving through air.

**alpha particle** A particle emitted from the nuclei of radioactive atoms, consisting of two protons and two neutrons.

**alternating current (a.c.)** Electrical current that repeatedly reverses its direction, like mains electricity.

**ammeter** An instrument that measures electrical current in amperes.

**ampere** A unit of current measuring the electric charge that flows during one second.

**amplitude** The maximum change of the medium from normal in a wave. For example, the height of a water wave above the level of calm water.

**analogue** Describes a quantity that can change smoothly, like the position of a pointer over a dial (the opposite of digital).

**angle of reflection** The angle between the reflected light ray and the normal to the surface of the material.

**angle of refraction** The angle between the refracted light ray and the normal to the surface inside the material.

**atomic number** The number of protons found in the nucleus of an atom.

**average speed** The distance an object has moved, divided by the time taken.

**background radiation** The level of radiation found due to natural processes in the environment.

**becquerel** The unit for the radioactivity of a substance. One becquerel is one decay per second.

**beta particle** A type of nuclear radiation emitted as an electron by a radioactive nucleus.

**biofuels** Energy resource derived from plants.

**boiling point** The temperature at which a substance changes state from a liquid to a gas.

**Brownian motion** The random motion of pollen grains on the surface of water (also the random motion of smoke particles in air).

**centripetal force** The force that acts towards a centre. A centripetal force is needed to move in a circle.

**charge** A fundamental property of matter that produces all electrical effects. It is equal to current × time.

**chemical energy** Energy stored in molecules. Batteries and fuels contain stored chemical energy.

**circuit breaker** A device that breaks a circuit when there is an increase in current.

**commutator** The part of an electric motor that allows the coils to be connected to the opposite terminals each time the motor rotates through 180°.

**condensation** The change of state from a gas to a liquid.

**conduction** The transfer of heat energy through a material.

**conductors, electricity** Substances that conduct electricity well.

**conductors, thermal** Substances that conduct heat very well.

**convection** Heat transfer in a liquid or gas – when particles in a warmer region gain energy and move into cooler regions carrying this energy with them.

**conventional current** Movement of positive charge that is imagined to move from the positive terminal to the negative terminal of a battery. Equivalent in effect to the real flow of negative charge in the opposite direction.

**coulomb** The unit of electric charge.

**crest** The highest part of a wave.

**critical angle** The angle of incidence within a material which gives an angle of refraction of 90.

**current, electric** A flowing electric charge caused by the flow of electrons.

**density** The mass, in kilograms, of a one metre cube of a substance: mass divided by volume.

**diffraction** Waves spreading into the shadow when they pass an edge.

**digital** Describes quantities that can only be displayed as numbers (the opposite of analogue).

**diode** A device that lets electricity flow through it one way only.

**direct current (d.c.)** Current that always flows in the same direction.

**dispersion** Splitting white light into the colours that it is made of.

**distance–time graph** A visual representation of how distance travelled varies with time.

**double-insulated** When a device has a casing that is made of an insulator and does not need an earth wire.

**earth wire** A wire connecting the case of an electrical appliance, through the earth pin on a three-pin plug, to earth.

**efficiency** Useful energy output divided by total energy output.

**elastic** Describes materials that go back to their original shape and size after you stretch them.

**electric current** Flowing electric charge.

**electric field** A region in which any electrical charges will feel a force.

**electromagnetic induction** A changing magnetic force can induce electric current in a wire.

**electromagnetic spectrum** The 'family' of electromagnetic radiations (from longest to shortest wavelength): radio, microwave, infra-red, visible light, ultraviolet, X-rays, gamma rays. In order of frequency, the order is reversed. They all travel at the same speed in a vacuum.

**electromagnetic wave** A wave that transfers energy – it can travel through a vacuum and travel at the speed of light.

**electromagnets** Magnets made from a coil of wire. The magnetic force is made when electric current flows in the coil. The magnetic force is stronger when the coil is wrapped around a piece of iron.

**electron** Negatively charged particles with almost no mass that form the outer portion of all atoms.

**evaporation** The change of state from a liquid to a gas.

**extension** The increase in length when something is stretched.

**fluid** Any liquid or gas.

**focal length** The distance between the centre of a lens and the principal focus.

**force** Change in momentum divided by time taken.

**fossil fuel** Non-renewable energy resource such as coal, oil or natural gas.

**free fall** Movement under the effect of the force of gravity alone.

**frequency** The number of vibrations per second or number of peaks or troughs that pass a point each second, measured in hertz (Hz). It is equal to 1/time period.

**friction** The force that resists when you try to move something. It can cause insulators to become charged.

**fuse** A special wire that protects an electric circuit. If the current gets too large, the fuse melts and stops the current.

**gamma ray** Ionising electromagnetic radiation – radioactive and dangerous to human health.

**gradient** The slope of a curve.

**gravitational field strength** The force of gravity on a mass of one kilogram. The unit is the newton per kilogram, and it is different on different planets.

**gravitational potential energy** A form of stored energy given by mass $\times g \times$ height.

**gravity** A force that causes objects in the Solar System to travel in repeating cycles of motion called orbits.

**half-life** The time it takes for half of the radioactive nuclei in a sample to decay.

**Hooke's law** The extension of a spring is in direct proportion to the force applied to it, as long as the force is smaller than the material's elastic limit.

**induction** When something is affected without touching it. An electric force can induce charge in a conductor. A changing magnetic force can induce electric current in a wire.

**infrared** The part of the electromagnetic spectrum that has a slightly longer wavelength than the visible spectrum.

**insulators (of electricity)** Substances that do not conduct electricity.

**insulators (of heat)** Substances that do not conduct heat very well.

**interference** When waves combine with each other as they collide.

**internal energy** The energy inside an object.

**inversely proportional** The relationship between two quantities if one doubles when the other halves.

**ion** An atom (or group of atoms) with a positive or negative charge, caused by losing or gaining electrons.

**ionising radiation** Charged particles or high-energy light rays that ionise the material they travel through.

**isotope** Atoms of the same element that contain different numbers of neutrons. Isotopes have the same atomic number but different mass numbers.

**joule** The unit of energy. One joule is the energy needed to push an object through one metre with a one newton force.

**kinetic energy** The energy of moving objects, equal to $\frac{1}{2} \times$ mass $\times$ (speed)$^2$.

**kinetic particle model** The theory describing the movement of particles in solids, liquid and gases.

**latent heat (or energy)** The energy required for a substance to change state.

**light-dependent resistor** A resistor with a resistance that decreases when light is shone on it.

**longitudinal wave** A wave in which the change of the medium is parallel to the direction of the wave. Sound is an example.

**loudspeaker** A device that produces sound when connected to an alternating supply.

**magnetic field** The region in which magnetic materials feel a force.

**magnetic field lines** The lines that show the path a free North pole would follow.

**magnetic materials** Materials that are attracted to magnets and can be made into magnets. Iron, cobalt and nickel are magnetic materials.

**magnetic softness** When materials lose their magnetism.

**magnifying glass** A converging lens used to provide an enlarged virtual image of an object.

**mass** The amount of material in an object, measured in kilograms.

**mass number** The number of protons and neutrons in the nucleus of an atom.

**melting** The change of state from a solid to a liquid.

**moment** Force × perpendicular distance from the pivot.

**momentum** Mass × velocity.

**nucleon number** The total number of protons and neutrons within a nucleus.

**neutron** A particle in the nucleus of atoms that has mass but no charge.

**non-renewable (resources)** An energy resource that will run out, such as oil or natural gas.

**nuclear fission** The process where a large nucleus absorbs a neutron and then splits into two large fragments, releasing energy and further neutrons.

**nuclear fusion** The process where the nuclei of small atoms such as hydrogen join together to form a larger nucleus, releasing energy.

**nucleus, atomic** The tiny centre of an atom, made up of protons and neutrons.

**nuclide** A nucleus that contains a particular number of protons and neutrons.

**orbital speed** How fast one object orbits another. It is calculated from orbital speed = (2 × π × orbital radius)/time.

**parallel** Describes a circuit in which the current splits up into more than one path.

**pitch** Whether a note sounds high or low to your ear.

**potential difference (p.d.)** The energy transferred from one coulomb of charge between two points. Measured in volts. Often called the 'voltage'.

**potential energy** A form of stored energy.

**power** The amount of energy transferred every second, equal to work done/time taken. Power can be transferred from somewhere (e.g. a power station) or to somewhere (e.g. electric kettle).

**pressure** The effect of a force spread out over an area. Pressure is equal to force/area.

**pressure difference (in a fluid)** Equal to density × $g$ × height difference.

**primary coil** The input coil of a transformer. You connect it to the voltage you want to change.

**principal focus** A point where the parallel light rays arriving along the principal axis of the lens all cross over.

**principle of conservation of energy** Energy cannot be created or destroyed.

**principle of conservation of momentum** The total initial momentum of colliding objects is equal to the total momentum of the objects after the collision.

**principle of moments** The sum of clockwise moments about a point is equal to the sum of the anticlockwise moments about the same point.

**proton** Positively charged, massive particles found in the nucleus of an atom.

**proton number** The number of protons within a nucleus (also known as the atomic number).

**radiation** Energy, such as electromagnetic rays, that travels in straight lines.

**radio wave** The part of the electromagnetic spectrum that has a long wavelength and is used for communications.

**radioactive** Describes a substance that has nuclei that are not stable.

**radioactive decay** Natural and random change of a nucleus.

**radioactivity** The emission of particles or energy from an unstable nucleus.

**random** A decay of a nucleus that cannot be predicted and is not affected by other nuclei.

**reflection** When waves bounce off a mirror. The angle of incidence is the same size as the angle of reflection.

**refraction** When waves change direction because they have gone into a different medium. They change direction because their speed changes.

**refractive index** Indicates how strongly a particular material changes the direction of light, where $n = \sin i / \sin r$ and $n = 1/\sin c$.

**renewable (resource)** An energy resource that is constantly available or can be replaced as it is used, such as solar power or wind power.

**resistance** The property of an electrical conductor that limits how easily an electric current flows through it. Measured in ohms.

**semiconductor** A material that does not conduct electricity as well as metal, for example, but conducts electricity better than an insulator, such as plastic.

**series** Describes a circuit in which the current travels along one path through every component.

**solidification** The change of state from a liquid to a solid.

**spectrum** The 'rainbow' of colours that make up white light: red, orange, yellow, green, blue, indigo and violet.

**speed** A measure of how far something moves every second. Average speed = distance travelled/time taken.

**speed–time graph** A graph of how speed varies with time.

**spontaneous** The decay of a nucleus cannot be affected by external factors such as temperature.

**thermistor** A resistor made from semiconductor material: its resistance decreases as temperature increases.

**transformer** A machine that changes the voltage of a.c. electricity. The ratio of the number of turns in the coils is the same as the ratio of the voltages produced. A step-up transformer increases the voltage. A step-down transformer decreases the voltage.

**transverse wave** A wave in which the change of the medium is at 90 degrees to the direction of the wave. Light is an example.

**trough** The lowest part of a wave.

**turbine** A machine that rotates. It is pushed by the movement of a fluid such as air or water.

**ultraviolet** The part of the electromagnetic spectrum that has a slightly longer wavelength than the visible spectrum.

**variable resistor** A component with a resistance that can be manually altered.

**velocity** The speed and direction of an object.

**virtual image** An image that cannot be projected onto a screen.

**volt** A unit of voltage. The energy carried by one coulomb of electric charge.

**voltage** A measure of the energy carried by an electric current.

**watt** A unit of power. One watt is one joule transferred every second.

**wavefront** The moving line that joins all the points on the crest of a wave.

**wavelength** The distance between the same points of successive waves, for example, the distance from one crest to the next.

**wave speed** Equal to frequency × wavelength.

**weight** The force of gravity on a mass, equal to mass × gravitational field strength. The unit of weight is the newton.

**work** The energy transferred when a job is done, equal to force × distance moved in the direction of the force.

# Answers

*All answers, including answers to exam-style questions, have been written by the authors. In examinations, the way marks are awarded may be different. These are the answers to the questions in each topic. Answers to end of topic and exam-style questions are in the Teacher's Guide.*

## SECTION 1: MOTION, FORCES AND ENERGY

### Motion

#### Page 20

1. **a)** The cars move along the road in the same direction, a constant distance apart.

   **b)** If they are moving towards each other, they will collide head on. If they are moving apart, they will continue to do so.

   **c)** The cars will move along the road, a constant distance apart in the opposite direction to **a**).

2. average speed = $\dfrac{10\,000}{15} \times 60 = 11.1\,\text{m/s}$

3. distance = speed × time = 1.5 × 15 = 22.5 m

4. time taken = $\dfrac{1500}{0.50}$ = 3000 s or 50 mins

#### Page 22

1. A straight line with a constant positive gradient.

2. **a)** Constant speed between $t = 0$ and $t = 4.0\,\text{s}$ and stationary after $t = 4.0\,\text{s}$.

   **b)** speed = $\dfrac{20}{4.0} = 5.0\,\text{m/s}$

   **c)** average speed = $\dfrac{20}{8.0} = 2.5\,\text{m/s}$

#### Page 25

1. Distance.

2. **a)** The object has a constant deceleration.

   **b)** distance = area under graph = $\dfrac{1}{2} \times 10 \times 4.0 = 20\,\text{m}$

   **c)** average speed = $\dfrac{20}{4.0} = 5.0\,\text{m/s}$

   **d)** acceleration = gradient = $-\dfrac{10}{4.0} = -2.5\,\text{m/s}^2$; deceleration = 2.5 m/s²

3. $a = \dfrac{19.6}{2.0} = 9.8\,\text{m/s}^2$

4. $a = \dfrac{(0 - 45)}{3.0} = -15\,\text{m/s}^2$ The minus sign implies deceleration (slowing down).

5. change in speed = 0.5 × 4.0 = 2.0 m/s final speed = 2.0 + change in speed = 4.0 m/s

#### Page 29

1. 9.8 m/s²

2. speed = 0 + 9.8 × 2.0 = 19.6 m/s, estimate ≈ 20 m/s

3. Terminal velocity is the constant velocity an object falls through the air, when the weight of the object is equal to the air resistance. The resultant force on the object is zero and object has zero acceleration.

4. **a)** D

   **b)** distance = 50 × 30 = 1500 m

### Mass and weight

#### Page 34

1. Mass is the amount of matter in an object that is at rest relative to the observer (person) doing the measurement. Weight is the gravitational force on an object that has mass.

**2.** weight = $60 \times 9.8 = 588\,\text{N}$

**3.** mass = $\dfrac{500}{9.8} = 51.0\,\text{kg}$

## Density

### Page 43

**1. a)** volume = $2.0 \times 4.0 \times 5.0 = 40\,\text{cm}^3$

   **b)** density = $\dfrac{\text{mass}}{\text{volume}} = \dfrac{312}{40} = 7.8\,\text{g/cm}^3$

**2.** The bread contains more air spaces, making the overall density less.

**3.** Wood is less dense than sea water.

### Page 45

**1.** Any one from: baby oil, vegetable oil, water or milk

**2.** The density of liquid C is less than the density of liquid A; and the density of liquid A is less than the density of liquid B.

## Forces

### Page 50 (top)

**1.** A force can change
   - the speed of an object
   - the shape of an object
   - the direction the object is moving in.

**2.** Examples:
   - The braking force on a car can change the speed of a car.
   - Compression forces from the hand can change the shape of a soft-ball.
   - Hitting a tennis ball coming towards you with a racket can change the direction of the ball.

### Page 50 (bottom)

**1.** Walking – if there is no friction, you would skid.

**2.** Pushing something (crate) along the ground – friction makes it hard work.

### Page 53

**1.** The object travels in a straight line at constant speed (or velocity) or remain stationary.

**2.** The speed or direction of motion of the object will change; it will either accelerate or decelerate.

**3.** The weight of the gymnast.

### Page 58

**1.** force = $kx = 0.20 \times 0.05 = 0.01\,\text{N}$

**2.** force = $0.100 \times 9.8 = 0.98\,\text{N}$; $k = \dfrac{0.98}{0.05} = 19.6\,\text{N/m}$ (or $0.196\,\text{N/cm}$)

**3.** $x = \dfrac{600}{30} = 20\,\text{cm}$

### Page 60

**1.** (resultant) force = mass × acceleration ($F = ma$)

**2.** force = $60 \times 10 = 600\,\text{N}$

**3.** $a = \dfrac{F}{m} = \dfrac{2560}{3.2} = 800\,\text{m/s}^2$

### Page 62

**1.** The Moon would move in a straight line in the direction it was travelling when gravity ceased.

**2.** The car would slide and carry on in a straight line.

**3.** The person would move in a straight line in the direction the person was travelling when gravity ceased.

### Page 65

**1.** The size of the force and the perpendicular distance between the force and the pivot (turning point).

**2.** moment = $4.0 \times 0.50 = 2.0\,\text{N m}$

**3.** moment = $5.0 \times 0.25 = 1.25\,\text{N m}$

**4.** $x = \dfrac{\text{moment}}{\text{force}} = \dfrac{1.6}{4.0} = 0.40\,\text{m}$

**5.** $400x = 300 \times 2.0$; $x = 1.5\,\text{m}$

**Page 67**

1. The point at which the weight of an object appears to act.

2. The heavy base means that the centre of mass is lower; the wide base means it has to tip further before the centre of gravity falls outside the pivot, which would cause the vase to tip over.

## Momentum

**Page 73**

1. momentum = $0.058 \times 40 =$ $2.32\,\text{kg}\,\text{m/s}$

2. momentum = $2000 \times 25 =$ $50\,000\,\text{kg}\,\text{m/s}$

3. mass = $\dfrac{\text{momentum}}{\text{velocity}} = \dfrac{20\,000}{20} =$ $1000\,\text{kg}$

4. velocity = $\dfrac{\text{momentum}}{\text{mass}} = \dfrac{37\,500}{1500} =$ $25\,\text{m/s}$

**Page 77**

1. momentum = mass × velocity. Momentum is a vector quantity – it has both magnitude and direction.

2. For a particular change in momentum, the longer the change takes, the smaller the force will be. So, if a parachutist bends their knees when they land, the landing takes a longer time and so the force is reduced.

3. $1.0 \times 5.0 = 2.0v$; $v = 2.5\,\text{m/s}$

4. $60 \times 6.0 = 90v$; $v = 4.0\,\text{m/s}$

5. a) momentum = $4000 \times 25 =$ $100\,000\,\text{kg}\,\text{m/s}$

   b) $100\,000\,\text{kg}\,\text{m/s}$ (same, since momentum is conserved)

   c) $100\,000 = 1000v$; $v = 100\,\text{m/s}$

## Energy, work and power

**Page 84**

1. Any four from: kinetic, gravitational potential, chemical, elastic (strain), nuclear, electrostatic and internal (thermal)

2. For a given mass, a faster moving object will have greater kinetic energy. So, the runner with the greater speed will have the greater kinetic energy.

3. The force on the apple, which is its weight.

4. 60%

**Page 85**

1. $E_\text{p} = 5.0 \times 9.8 \times 2.0 = 98\,\text{J}$

2. $E_\text{k} = \dfrac{1}{2} \times 2.0 \times 2.0^2 = 4.0\,\text{J}$

**Page 94**

1. light → electrical

2. D

3. Fuel is burned and steam is produced in a boiler. The steam turns a turbine. The turbine drives a generator. The generator produces electricity. The electricity is supplied to homes, industry, etc.

4. Internal (thermal)

**Page 96**

1. work done = $50 \times 5.0 = 250\,\text{J}$

2. force = $\dfrac{4000}{8.0} = 500\,\text{N}$

3. work done = $40 \times 2.0 = 80\,\text{J}$

4. distance = $\dfrac{300}{6.0} = 50\,\text{m}$

5. force = $\dfrac{800}{2.0} = 400\,\text{N}$

6. work done = $(1.2 \times 9.8) \times 0.90 =$ $10.6\,\text{J}$

7. $E_\text{k} = \dfrac{1}{2} \times 900 \times 8.0^2 = 28\,800\,\text{J}$;

   force = $\dfrac{28\,800}{100} = 288\,\text{N}$

## Page 98

1. The man has twice the weight, so the force is double, but the time is the same.
2. The machine transfers energy at a great rate.
3. watt (W)
4. power $= \dfrac{1200}{5.0} = 240\,\text{W}$
5. a) work done $= (60 \times 9.8) \times 5.0 = 2940\,\text{J}$

   b) power $= \dfrac{2940}{60} = 49\,\text{W}$

## Pressure

### Page 107

1. For the pin, the force is concentrated over a smaller area – there is a greater pressure.
2. pressure $= \dfrac{\text{force}}{\text{area}} = \dfrac{100}{0.20} = 500\,\text{Pa}$
3. force $= \text{pressure} \times \text{area} = 40 \times 2.0 = 80\,\text{N}$
4. area $= \dfrac{\text{force}}{\text{pressure}} = \dfrac{500}{640} = 0.78\,\text{m}^2$

### Page 112

1. Depth and density of the fluid.
2. $\Delta p = 1000 \times 9.8 \times 8.0 = 78\,400\,\text{Pa}$ (78.4 kPa)
3. $\Delta p = 1030 \times 9.8 \times 100 = 1\,009\,400\,\text{Pa}$ (1009.4 kPa)
4. total pressure $= 100\,000 + (1030 \times 9.8 \times 30) = 402.8\,\text{kPa}$.
5. total pressure $= 100\,000 + (13\,600 \times 9.8 \times 0.15) = 120\,\text{kPa}$

## SECTION 2: THERMAL PHYSICS

### Kinetic particle model of matter

### Page 129

1. It increases – either as faster and larger vibration in solids, or as faster translational and vibrational motion in liquids and faster translational motion in gases.

2. Compressing a gas pushes the particles closer together; in a liquid they are already close to each other and will repel if pushed closer.
3. a) The particles are closely packed together in a regular arrangement in a solid.
   b) The particles are closely packed together in an irregular (random) arrangement in a liquid.
   c) The particles are widely spaced apart and randomly arranged.
4. A

### Page 131

1. The molecules are always moving about with random speeds and directions; they spread out throughout the container.
2. $-273\,°\text{C}$ (absolute zero)
3. The particles stop moving; they have zero kinetic energy at absolute zero.

### Page 133

1. This is the random motion of microscopic particles (smoke particles, dust particles, pollen grains) in a fluid (gas or liquid).
2. The microscopic particles are being constantly bombarded by molecules of the fluid. The molecules themselves must have random motion.
3. Molecules collide with the walls. There is a change in momentum, hence force is exerted on the wall. Since pressure is force per unit area, there is pressure exerted by the colliding molecules on the walls.

### Page 134

1. a) 273 K
   b) 373 K
   c) 673 K
2. a) 327 °C
   b) −173 °C
   c) −270 °C

1. As pressure increases, the volume decreases.
2. Pressure increases as temperature increases.
3. $pV$ = constant; $350 \times 150 = 100 \times V$; $V = 525\,cm^3$

## Thermal properties and temperature

### Page 142

1. Metals expand as their temperatures rise. So, if strips of two metals are bound closely together, and are warmed, they bend and buckle.
2. volume = $1.04 \times 200 = 416\,cm^3$
3. The particles vibrate more as the temperature goes up. The particles vibrate more and move slightly further apart. Therefore, the solid expands in all directions.
4. The particles move around faster around each other as the temperature goes up. The particles move slightly further apart. Therefore, the liquid expands in all directions.

### Page 145

1. J/kg °C
2. Pure water would be difficult to heat up, because it has the largest specific heat capacity.
3. total energy = $(2.0 \times 910 \times 80) +$ $(3.0 \times 4200 \times 80) = 1.15 \times 10^6\,J$
4. energy = $50 \times 480 = 24\,000\,J$; $c =$ $24\,000/(0.300 \times 53) = 1500\,J/kg\,°C$

### Page 146

1. The temperature reduces.
2. Greater temperature and greater surface area will both increase the rate of evaporation.
3. The surface area of the hot water increases. Therefore, fast-moving molecules can escape at a greater rate from the surface.

### Page 147

1. Boiling occurs at a specific temperature for the substance. The energy absorbed by the substance is used to change state from liquid to gas.
2. Fast-moving molecules escape the liquid. The molecules go from being close together (liquid state) to being further apart (gas state).
3. Fast-moving molecules escape the surface of the liquid. As a result, the liquid will cool down.

## Transfer of thermal energy

### Page 153

1. A
2. Any two, e.g. copper, aluminium, steel.
3. Vibrations passed from atoms at the hot end to atoms at the cooler end. Also, kinetic energy of free electrons is transferred to the atoms at the cooler end.
4. Wood has fewer free electrons (per unit volume) compared with metals.
5. Liquids are poor conductors because of weaker chemical bonds between atoms and also fewer free electrons (per unit volume) than conductors.

### Page 154

1. The particles (atoms and molecules) are free to move.
2. Warm air expands, which makes it less dense. Less dense air floats up above denser (cooler) air.
3. Warm air above the lamp rises, which makes the windmill spin.
4. Fibres in the insulation create air pockets. This restricts the movement of the air and so convection currents cannot form.

### Page 157

1. In convection, particles (atoms and molecules) move from hot to cooler ends; this does not happen in conduction.

**2.** Object at the higher temperature of 300 K.

**3.** Surface temperature and surface area of the object.

**4.** The dull black disc is a good emitter of (infrared) radiation – so it will cool faster than the shiny white disc.

**5.** White coloured houses are poor absorbers of (infrared) radiation. So, houses do not get too hot.

### Page 160

**1.** Convection

**2. a)** Vacuum – there are no particles for conduction.

  **b)** Vacuum – has no particles to form convection currents.

  **c)** Silver surfaces – reflect the (infrared) radiation, and also poor emitter and absorber.

**3. a)** A car radiator does not lose energy by radiation. Instead, it transfers thermal energy from the hot water away by blowing air over its surface.

  **b)** Radiation

### SECTION 3: WAVES

### General properties of waves

### Page 173

**1. a)** The vibrations are parallel to the direction in which the wave travels.

  **b)** The vibrations are at right angles to the direction travel (propagation).

**2. a)** The distance between two adjacent peaks (or troughs).

  **b)** The number of complete waves that go past a point per unit time.

  **c)** he maximum particle displacement of the wave from the undisturbed position.

**3.** distance = 5.0 × 3.0 = 15 m

**4.** A

### Page 176

**1.** Both waves are oscillations that carry energy from one place to another. Example of transverse wave: water waves (S-wave and electromagnetic waves). Example of longitudinal wave: sound (P-wave).

**2.** Reflect, refract and diffract.

**3. a)** $v = \dfrac{f}{\lambda} = 10 \times 2.0 = 20\,\text{cm/s}$

  **b)** About 2.0 cm (the same as the wavelength)

### Light

### Page 184

**1.** The light from the bottom of the pond is refracted away from the normal as it leaves the pond, so this makes the pool look shallower than it really is.

**2.** The sound waves will refract *away* the normal because the speed of sound increases as it travels from air into helium.

### Page 186

**1.** $\dfrac{\sin 50°}{\sin r} = 1.5;\ r = 33.3°$

**2.** $\dfrac{\sin i}{\sin 25°} = 1.4;\ i = 36.3°$

**3.** $\dfrac{\sin 55°}{\sin 35°} = n;\ n = 1.43$

**4. a)** The refractive index of water is greater than 1 (the refractive index of vacuum), therefore light travels slower in water.

  **b)** The material with the largest refractive index, therefore the material is diamond.

  **c)** water: speed = $\dfrac{3.0 \times 10^8}{1.33} = 2.26 \times 10^8\,\text{m/s}$

  glass: speed = $\dfrac{3.0 \times 10^8}{1.52} = 1.97 \times 10^8\,\text{m/s}$

diamond: speed $= \dfrac{3.0 \times 10^8}{2.42} =$
$1.24 \times 10^8 \, \text{m/s}$
(The prediction in **b** was correct)

## Page 190

1. The angle of incidence in glass when the angle of refraction is 90° is called the critical angle.
2. For total internal reflection to occur, the light must travel from glass to air; into a material with *lower* refractive index.
3. **a)** $1.71 = \dfrac{1}{\sin c}$; $c = 35.8°$
   **b)** $1.49 = \dfrac{1}{\sin c}$; $c = 42.2°$
   **c)** $1.31 = \dfrac{1}{\sin c}$; $c = 49.8°$

## Page 195

1. The point on the principal axis where all the parallel rays incident on the lens converge .
2. **a)**

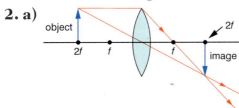

   **b)** The image is *real*, *inverted* and *same size* as the object.
3. For a converging lens the beam will produce a bright point-image on a screen. No image can be formed on a screen with a diverging lens.
4. Short-sightedness is a condition where distant objects can be seen clearly, but not close objects. A close object forms an image in front of the retina. Vision is corrected by using a diverging lens.

## Page 196

1. Violet
2. The frequency decreases from violet to red.
3. It has a unique wavelength and colour.

## Electromagnetic spectrum

## Page 203

1. They have the same speed.
2. C
3. Gamma rays have shorter wavelength (or higher frequency).
4. Gamma rays, ultraviolet, visible light, infrared and microwaves
5. **a)** $3.0 \times 10^8 \, \text{m/s}$
   **b)** distance $= 2.0 \times 3.0 \times 10^8 = 6.0 \times 10^8 \, \text{m}$

## Page 207

1. Communications (radio and television), radio-astronomy and RFID security.
2. Any three from: infrared, microwaves, ultraviolet, X-rays and gamma rays. (Allow: intense light).
3. A
4. Ultraviolet, X-rays and gamma rays.
5. It would be the same as cooking food; the microwaves will cause heating.

## Page 209

1. Low-Earth orbit and geostationary.
2. Radio waves.
3. Microwaves can penetrate through walls.
4. Digital signals are easier to process, and transmit at high speed over long distances. The signals can also be regenerated, so information is not affected by 'noise'.

## Sound

### Page 214

**1.** High-pressure regions.

**2. a)** 20 cm
**b)** 10 cm (this is half a wavelength)

**3.** The lowest frequency of sound we can hear is 20 Hz. This is below 20 Hz, so no we cannot hear sound of frequency 15 Hz.

**4.** Liquid of some sort, and definitely not a gas.

### Page 219

**1.** Frequency is greater than 20 kHz, so it is ultrasound.

**2.** Loudness depends on the amplitude of the wave.

**3.** Pitch depends on the frequency of sound.

**4.** distance = 4000 × 0.00015 = 0.60 m;

depth = $\dfrac{0.60}{2}$ = 0.30 m (30 cm)

## SECTION 4: ELECTRICITY AND MAGNETISM

## Simple phenomena of magnetism

### Page 229

**1.** The marked-north pole will repel the north pole, or attract the south pole, of the other magnet.

**2.** The Earth's north must be a magnetic south pole.

### Page 230

**1.** Pure iron.

**2.** Steel.

**3.** A magnetic material is one that can be magnetised, either temporary or permanently. A nonmagnetic material cannot be magnetised.

### Page 231

**1. a)** The permanent magnet will not attract a non-magnetic material.

**b)** Soft iron will always be attracted to the permanent magnet.

**2.** The end of the soft iron will become a temporary south pole; so there will always be an attraction.

### Page 233

**1.** A region of space where a magnetic pole will experience a force.

**2.** From north to south (or towards south, or away from north pole).

**3.** Iron filings or (plotting) compass.

**4.** The field is strongest close to the poles as indicated by the closely-packed magnetic field lines.

## Electrical quantities

### Page 242

**1.** A

**2.** Negative because it has more electrons than protons.

**3.** number of electrons = $\dfrac{0.16 \times 10^{-6}}{1.6 \times 10^{-19}}$

= $1.0 \times 10^{12}$

**4.** The storm clouds rub against each other, and so electrons are transferred between them. As a result, the clouds become charged.

### Page 248

**1. a)** $Q = It = 3.0 \times 5.0 = 15$ C
**b)** $Q = 2.0 \times 10 = 20$ C
**c)** $Q = 4.0 \times 23 = 92$ C
**d)** $Q = 1.5 \times 30 = 45$ C

**2.** $I = \dfrac{Q}{t} = \dfrac{120}{(4.0 \times 60)} = 0.50$ A

**3.** $t = \dfrac{Q}{I} = \dfrac{60}{0.5} = 120$ s

### Page 251

**1.** $V = IR = 2.0 \times 5.0 = 10\,\Omega$

**2. a)** $R = \dfrac{V}{I} = \dfrac{3.0}{0.50} = 6.0\,\Omega$

**b)** $Q = It = 0.50 \times 10 = 5.0$ C

**c)** $R = \dfrac{V}{I} = \dfrac{6.0}{0.80} = 7.5\,\Omega$

The resistance of the lamp has increased.

## Page 256

1. Length and cross-sectional area of the wire.
2. Its resistance will increase because it becomes longer and thinner.
3. Resistance is directly proportional to the length of the wire.

   Therefore, resistance = $\dfrac{10}{30} \times 6.0 = 2.0\,\Omega$
4. Resistance is inversely proportional to the cross-sectional area of the wire.

   Therefore, resistance = $\dfrac{1}{2} \times 12 = 6.0\,\Omega$

## Page 258

1. $P = VI = 110 \times 2.0 = 220\,\text{W}$
2. $V = \dfrac{P}{I} = \dfrac{20}{2.0} = 10\,\text{V}$
3. $E = IVt = 3.0 \times 12 \times 60 = 2160\,\text{J}$
4. $I = \dfrac{E}{Vt} = \dfrac{4800}{(12 \times 120)} = 3.33\,\text{A}$
5. $V = \dfrac{E}{It} = \dfrac{24}{(2.0 \times 1.0)} = 12\,\text{V}$

## Page 260

1. energy = $0.20 \times 0.50 = 0.10\,\text{kWh}$; cost = $0.10 \times 18 = 1.8\,\text{p}$
2. energy = $1.5 \times 4.0 = 6.0\,\text{kWh}$; cost = $6.0 \times 18 = 108\,\text{p}$
3. lamp: energy = $0.020 \times 24 = 0.48\,\text{kWh}$

   heater: energy = $1.92 \times \dfrac{1}{4} = 0.48\,\text{kWh}$
   Same cost for both.

## Electric circuits

## Page 270

1. a) $R_c = 330 + 330 = 660\,\Omega$
   b) $R_c = 500 + 120 = 620\,\Omega$
2. a) $R_c = 100 + 200 = 300\,\Omega$
   b) $I = \dfrac{V}{R} = \dfrac{3.0}{300} = 0.010\,\text{A}$

3. a) p.d. across lamp = $5.0 - 3.0 = 2.0\,\text{V}$
   b) $R = \dfrac{V}{I} = \dfrac{2.0}{0.10} = 20\,\Omega$

## Page 273

1. When one lamp stops working, the other lamps are not affected.
2. a) $R_c = \dfrac{100 \times 100}{100 + 100} = 50\,\Omega$

   b) $R_c = \dfrac{10 \times 20}{10 + 20} = 6.67\,\Omega$
3. a) $1.5\,\text{A}$
   b) $3.5\,\text{A}$
   c) $25\,\text{mA}$
4. $R = \dfrac{6.0}{0.10} = 60\,\Omega$ and $R = \dfrac{6.0}{0.20} = 30\,\Omega$

   combined resistance = $\dfrac{6.0}{0.30} = 20\,\Omega$

   (or $R_c = \dfrac{60 \times 30}{60 + 30} = 20\,\Omega$)

## Electrical safety

## Page 287

1. Brown wire: live, connected to fuse. Blue wire: neutral wire. Green and yellow wire: earth wire.
2. It melts if the current gets too high, and hence 'breaks' the circuit.
3. The student should not choose the 'nearest' fuse, but the 'nearest above'. If the appliance requires 6.0 A, the 5.0 A fuse will melt when the appliance is used.
4. The earth connection needs to be a low resistance path. This means that, in the event of a fault occurring, a high current can pass through this wire to the ground.
5. The casing cannot become live because plastic is not an electrical conductor.

## Electromagnetic effects

### Page 294

1. An e.m.f. is induced in a wire when it moves through a magnetic field, or when the magnetic field moves around it, or when the strength of the magnetic field around it changes.

2. No e.m.f. is induced because there is no relative motion between the wire and the magnetic field.

3. The strength of the magnetic field and the speed of the conductor in the magnetic field.

4. Direction of current is as shown:

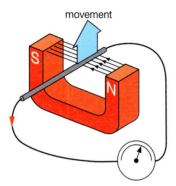

### Page 297

1. There is relative motion between the coil and the magnetic field, and this produces an e.m.f.

2. Induced current can be increased by using stronger magnetic field.

### Page 300

1. For both, the magnetic field lines come out of the north pole and curve round towards the south pole. Both have north and south poles with field lines close together at these poles.

2. The magnetic field lines are parallel within the core of the solenoid – this is where the magnetic field is uniform.

3. a) A coil is wrapped around a soft iron core. The coil is connected to a battery (or power supply). A current passing through the coil makes the iron core magnetic.
   b) Circuit similar to Fig. 4.76 with a thermistor in place of the LDR, and a fan instead of the motor.

### Page 305

1. Increase the number of turns, or the current or the strength of the magnetic field.

2. The current-carrying wires close to the south and north poles of the magnet experience opposite forces. These opposite forces acting on the coil makes it rotate.

3. Without the split-ring commutator the coil will not rotate.

4. The direction of rotation will remain the same when both current and field are reversed because the directions of the forces on the wires are unchanged.

### Page 307

1. When the secondary coil has more turns than the primary coil, the voltage increases in the same proportion. This is a step-up transformer. A transformer with fewer turns on the secondary coil than on the primary coil is a step-down transformer and produces a smaller voltage in the secondary coil.

2. $\dfrac{V_P}{V_s} = \dfrac{N_P}{N_s}$; $\dfrac{2.0}{V_s} = \dfrac{20}{100}$; output voltage $= 20\,V$

3. $\dfrac{V_P}{V_s} = \dfrac{N_P}{N_s}$; $\dfrac{1.5}{V_s} = \dfrac{60}{240}$; output voltage $= 6.0\,V$

4. a) $\dfrac{V_P}{V_s} = \dfrac{N_P}{N_s}$; $2.24\,V_s = \dfrac{50}{600}$; output voltage $= 24\,V$

**b)** $I = \dfrac{24}{12} = 2.0\,\text{A}$

**c)** $24 \times 2.0 = 2.0 \times I_p$; current = 24 A

### Page 309

1. High voltage transmission reduces power loss in the cables.
2. The voltage is stepped-up at the power station for high voltage transmission then stepped down again before use.
3. **a)** power lost $= I^2 R = 80^2 \times 4.0 = 25\,600\,\text{W}$
   **b)** percentage $= \dfrac{25\,600}{4\,000\,000} \times 100 = 0.64\%$

## SECTION 5: NUCLEAR PHYSICS

### The nuclear model of the atom

### Page 323

1. By removing electron (or electrons) from the atom.
2. **a)** Thin metal (gold) sheets or foils.
   **b)** Most of the atom is empty space (vacuum).
   **c)** Very small, dense (has most of the mass of the atom) and positively charged.

### Page 325

1. It is positive because of the positively charged protons.
2. **a)** 92
   **b)** 235
   **c)** 143
3. The two helium (He) nuclides are the isotopes because each has 2 protons.
4. hydrogen: relative charge = 1 and relative mass = 3
   uranium: relative charge = 92 and relative mass = 235

### Page 326

1. Nuclear power station.
2. Two smaller nuclei join together to make a single larger nucleus.

3. There is a small reduction in the total mass of the particles before and after the reaction; this reduction in mass means that energy is released in both fission and fusion reactions.

### Radioactivity

### Page 332

1. Radioactivity in the air (radon gas).
2. Counts per second, or counts per minute.
3. The activity of the Brazil nuts is quite small for the amount we can eat. The count rate is only slightly higher than the background count.)
4. count rate $= \dfrac{4000}{100} = 40\,\text{counts/s}$

### Page 334

1. Alpha radiation.
2. Beta radiation.
3. The range of alpha particles is about 5 cm in air, so standing 1 m away from the source is safe.
4. Alpha and beta particles are charged particles. They will therefore experience electric and magnetic forces.

### Page 337

1. Two protons and two neutrons are emitted. The proton number is reduced by 2 and the nucleon number is reduced by 4.
2. A neutron changes into a proton. The proton number increases by 1 and there is no change to the nucleon number.
3. $^{235}_{92}\text{U} \rightarrow\ ^{231}_{90}\text{Th} +\ ^{4}_{2}\alpha$
4. The nucleus left behind (the daughter nucleus) has one extra proton. The number of protons within the nucleus determines the element, therefore the daughter nucleus belongs to a different element. The element change is from polonium (Po) to astatine (At).

1. The half-life of a particular isotope is the time it takes for half of the nuclei of that isotope in any sample to decay.

2. The count rate has decreased by a factor of 8. This is equivalent to 3 half-lives.
   Therefore, time = 3 × 8.0 = 24.0 hours.

3. **a)** The graph levels off at 10 counts per min.
   **b)** At time = 0, the corrected count rate = 80 counts per min. After 10 minutes, the corrected count rate = 40 counts per min. The corrected count rate is halved after 10 minutes, so half-life = 10 mins.

## Page 344

1. Alpha particles cannot travel through the casing of the detector, so people are safe around it.

2. C

3. Sterilising water (or food or medical equipment), radiotherapy, medical tracer and diagnosing cracks in solids.

4. Kills or mutates living cells. Too much exposure can lead to cancer.

5. Use shielding (lead-aprons) and reduce exposure times. Also, best to keep your distance from the gamma sources.

## SECTION 6: SPACE PHYSICS

### Earth and the Solar System

### Page 357

1. Summer

2. time = $\frac{1}{4}$ orbital period

   time = $\frac{30}{4}$ = 7.5 days

3. The Earth rotates on its axis towards the east.

### Page 358

1. Neptune
2. Mercury and Venus
3. Comet is a small object made of ice and rock orbiting the Sun.
4. Asteroids are mainly found between the orbits of Mars and Jupiter.

### Page 360

1. D
2. A circle.
3. Comets

### Page 361

1. Gravitational force / gravity
2. Mercury, Venus, Earth and Mars.
3. Methane / water / ammonia / carbon monoxide / nitrogen
4. It starts to rotate and the collapsing also leads to the cloud becoming hotter.
5. Gases have low melting points.

### Page 363

**1a)** Temperature decreases as distance increases (apart from Venus).
 **b)** Orbital period increases as the distance increases.
**2.** Mercury and Venus.
**3.** Mercury
**4.** orbital period = $\frac{59800}{365.2}$
   orbital period = 164 years
**5a)** $\frac{1900}{5.97}$ = 320
 **b)** 2668.81 × 10²⁴ kg
 **c)** $\frac{2668.81 \times 10^{24}}{2.0 \times 10^{30}}$ = 0.0013

The total mass of the planets is 0.13% of the mass of the Sun (or the total mass of the Solar System).

**6.** $v = \dfrac{2\pi r}{T}$

$r = 227.0 \times 10^6 \times 10^3$ m and
$T = 687.0 \times 24 \times 3600$ s

$v = \dfrac{2\pi \times 227.0 \times 10^6 \times 10^3}{687.0 \times 24 \times 3600 \text{ s}}$

$v = 24000$ m/s

### Page 365 (top)

**1.** Planets experience a gravitational force from the Sun.

**2.** Gravitational field strength decreases (as the distance from the planet increases).

**3.** Mercury

**4.** The kinetic energy of the comet increases as it gets closer to the Sun
because its gravitational potential energy decreases.

### Page 365 (bottom)

**1.** distance $= c \times t = 3.0 \times 10^8 \times 1.28$

distance $= 3.84 \times 10^8$ m

**2.** $\dfrac{4.4 \times 10^{12}}{3.0 \times 10^8}$ or 14667 s

$t = \dfrac{14667}{3600}$

$t = 4.1$ hours

## Stars and the Universe

### Page 372

**1.** Infrared

Ultraviolet

**2.** Helium nuclei.

**3.** The positively charged hydrogen nuclei repel each other.

At high temperature, the hydrogen nuclei move fast enough to get close enough to each other and fuse.

### Page 374

**1.** It is our galaxy.

**2.** 100 billion stars.

**3.** 7.2 years

**4.** distance $= \dfrac{3.6 \times 10^{19}}{9.5 \times 10^{15}}$

distance $= 3800$ light-years

**5.** distance $= 25\,000 \times 9.5 \times 10^{15}$

distance $= 2.4 \times 10^{20}$ m

### Page 376

**1.** The star expands because it has run out of hydrogen.

**2.** Neutron star or black hole.

**3.** The inward force of gravitational attraction is balanced by the outward force due to the high temperature in the centre of the star.

### Page 380

**1.** It started to expand.

**2.** Redshift implies the galaxy is moving away from us.

**3.** All directions of space.

**4.** From the brightness of a supernova in that galaxy.

**5.** The speed can be determined from the change in the wavelength of light from the galaxy due to redshift.

**6.** As $d$ increases, $v$ increases **or** $v$ is directly proportional to $d$.

**7.** $H_0 = \dfrac{v}{d}$

$H_0 = \dfrac{11\,000 \times 1000}{5.0 \times 10^{24}}$

$H_0 = 2.2 \times 10^{-18}$ per second

# Index